Beauty Pop

1

Story & Art by
Kiyoko Arai

Beauty Pop

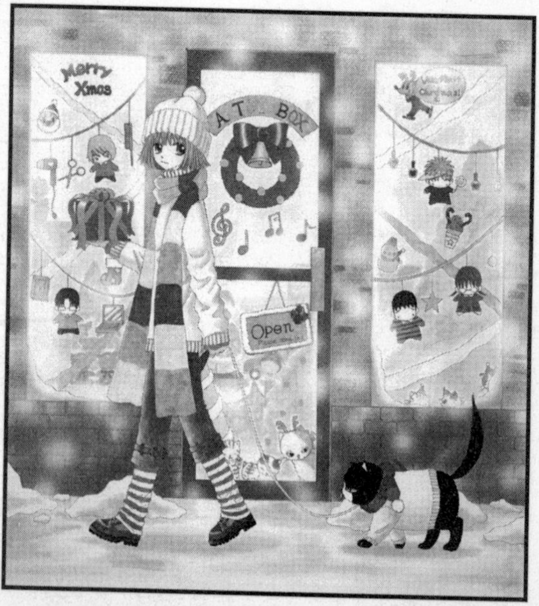

Merry Xmas
Open

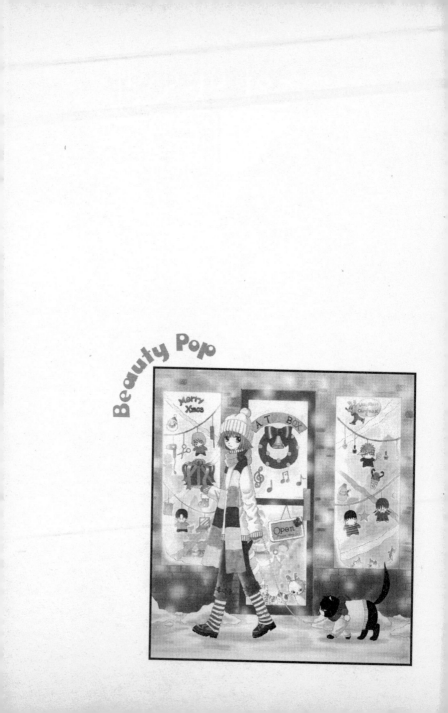

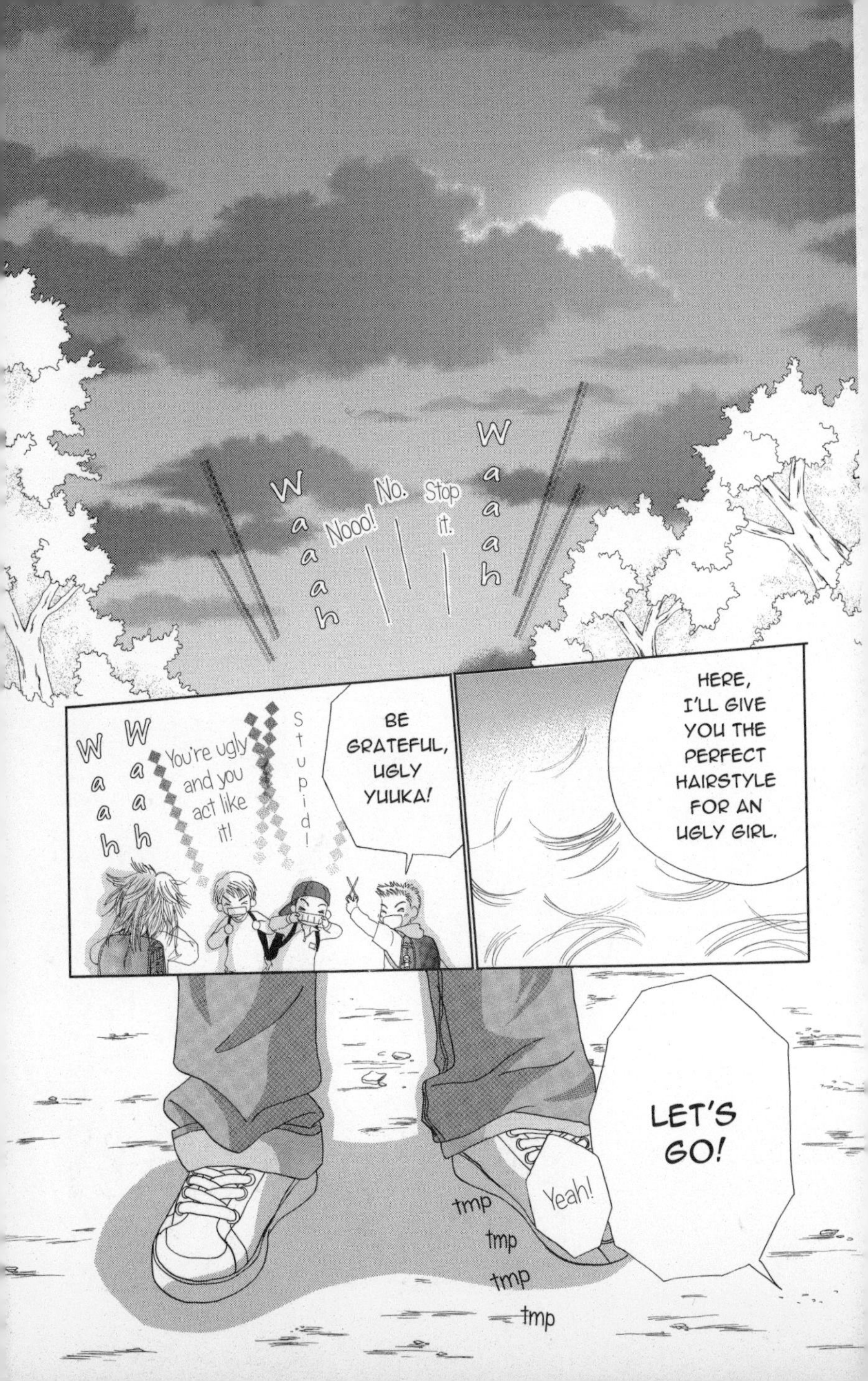
Waaah
Stop it.
No.
Nooo!
Waaah
HERE, I'LL GIVE YOU THE PERFECT HAIRSTYLE FOR AN UGLY GIRL.
BE GRATEFUL, UGLY YUUKA!
Stupid!
You're ugly and you act like it!
Waaah
Waaah
LET'S GO!
Yeah!
tmp
tmp
tmp
tmp

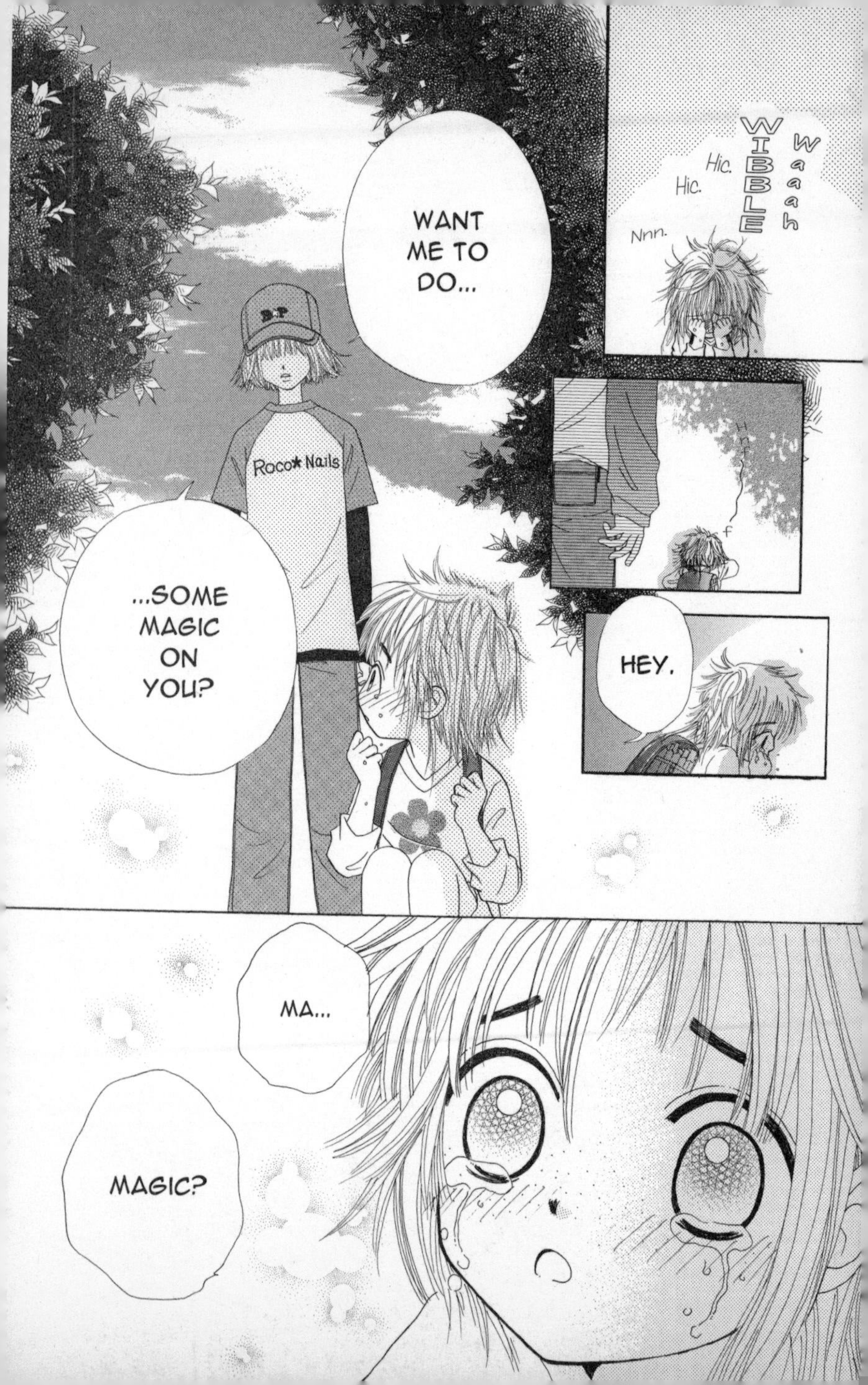
Waaah
WIBBLE
Hic.
Hic.
Nnn.
Hnf~ f
HEY.
WANT ME TO DO...
...SOME MAGIC ON YOU?
Roco★Nails
MA...
MAGIC?

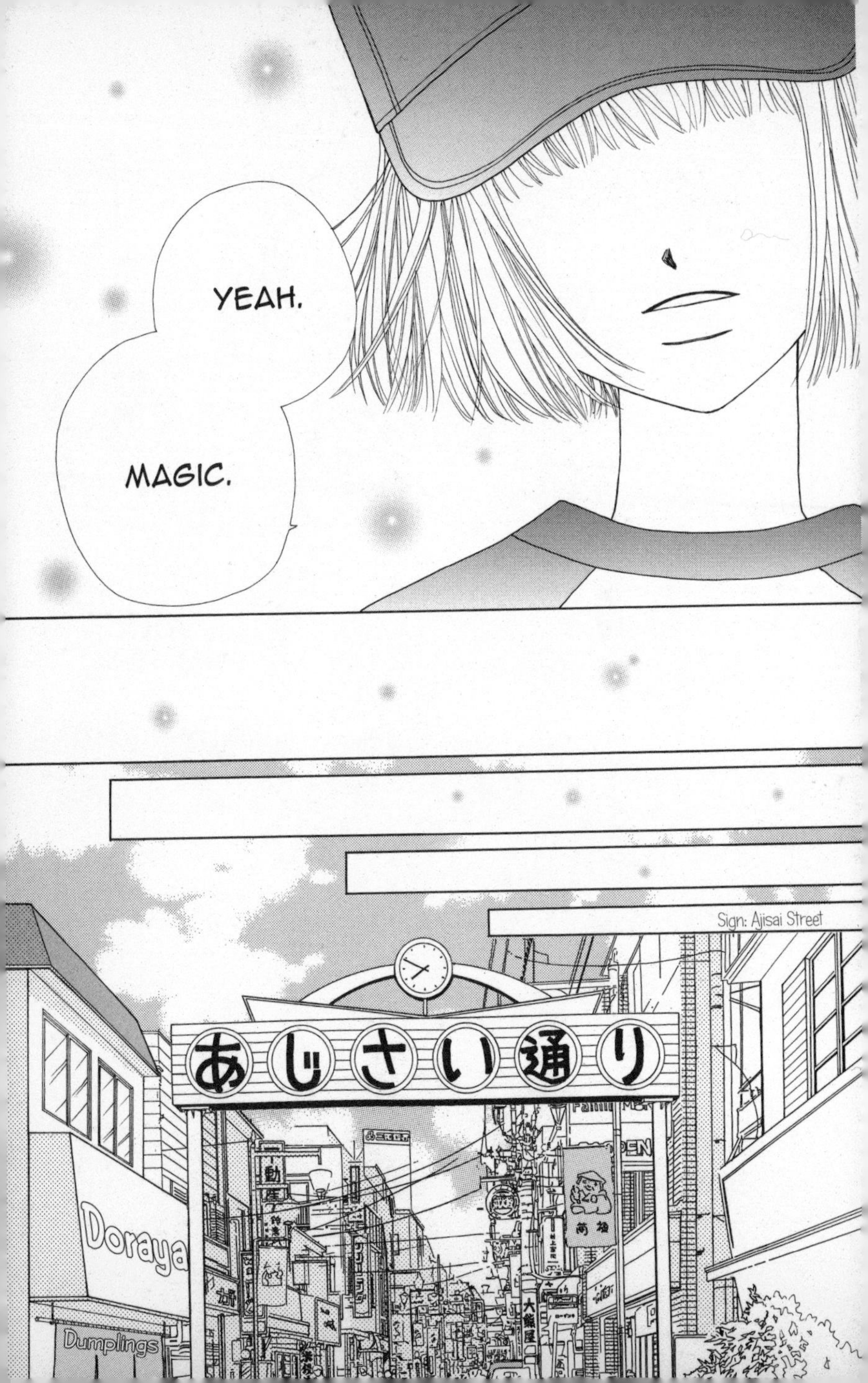
YEAH.
MAGIC.
Sign: Ajisai Street
あじさい通り
Doraya
Dumplings

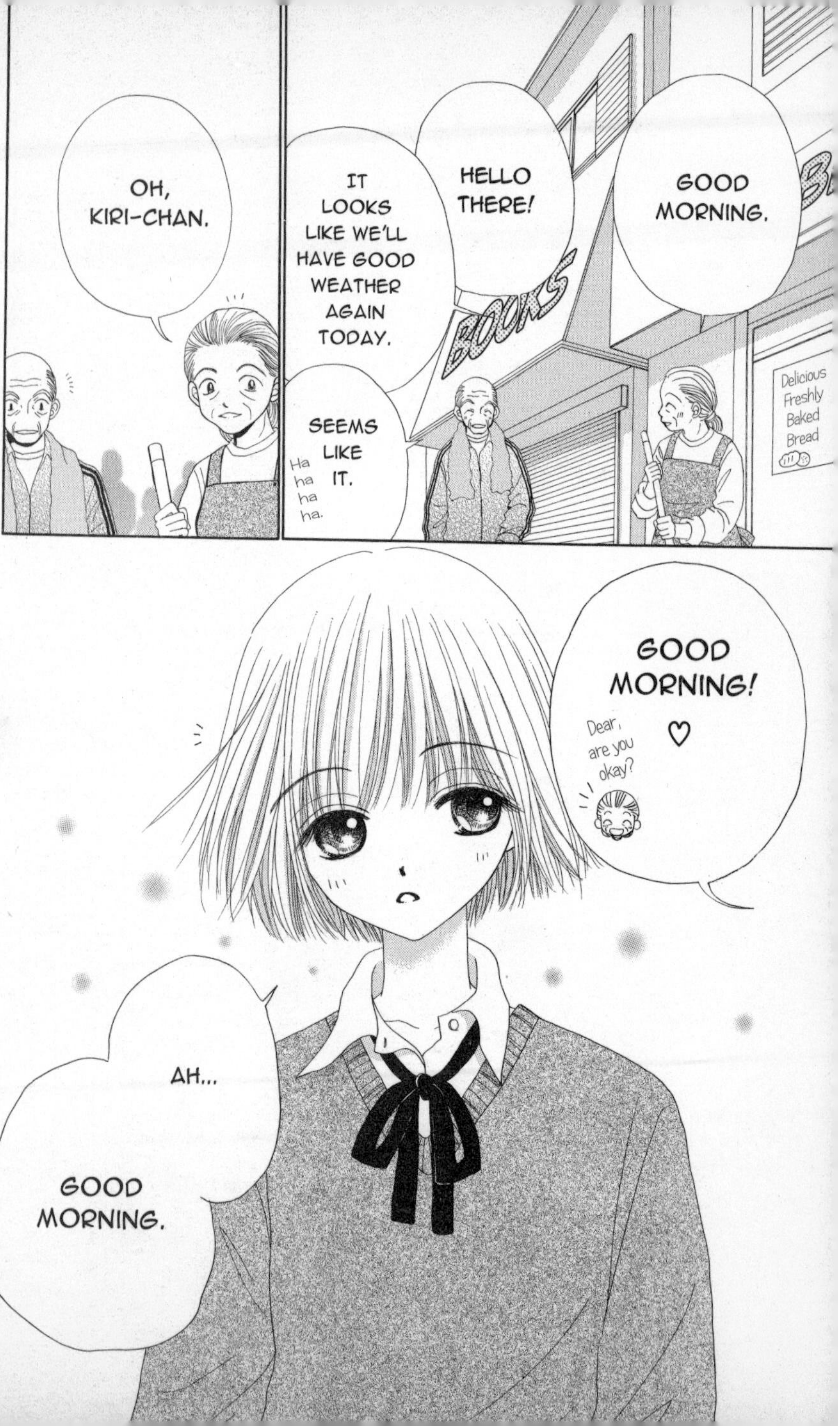
GOOD MORNING.
Delicious Freshly Baked Bread
HELLO THERE!
BOOKS
IT LOOKS LIKE WE'LL HAVE GOOD WEATHER AGAIN TODAY.
SEEMS LIKE IT.
Ha ha ha ha.
OH, KIRI-CHAN.
GOOD MORNING! ♡
Dear, are you okay?
AH... GOOD MORNING.

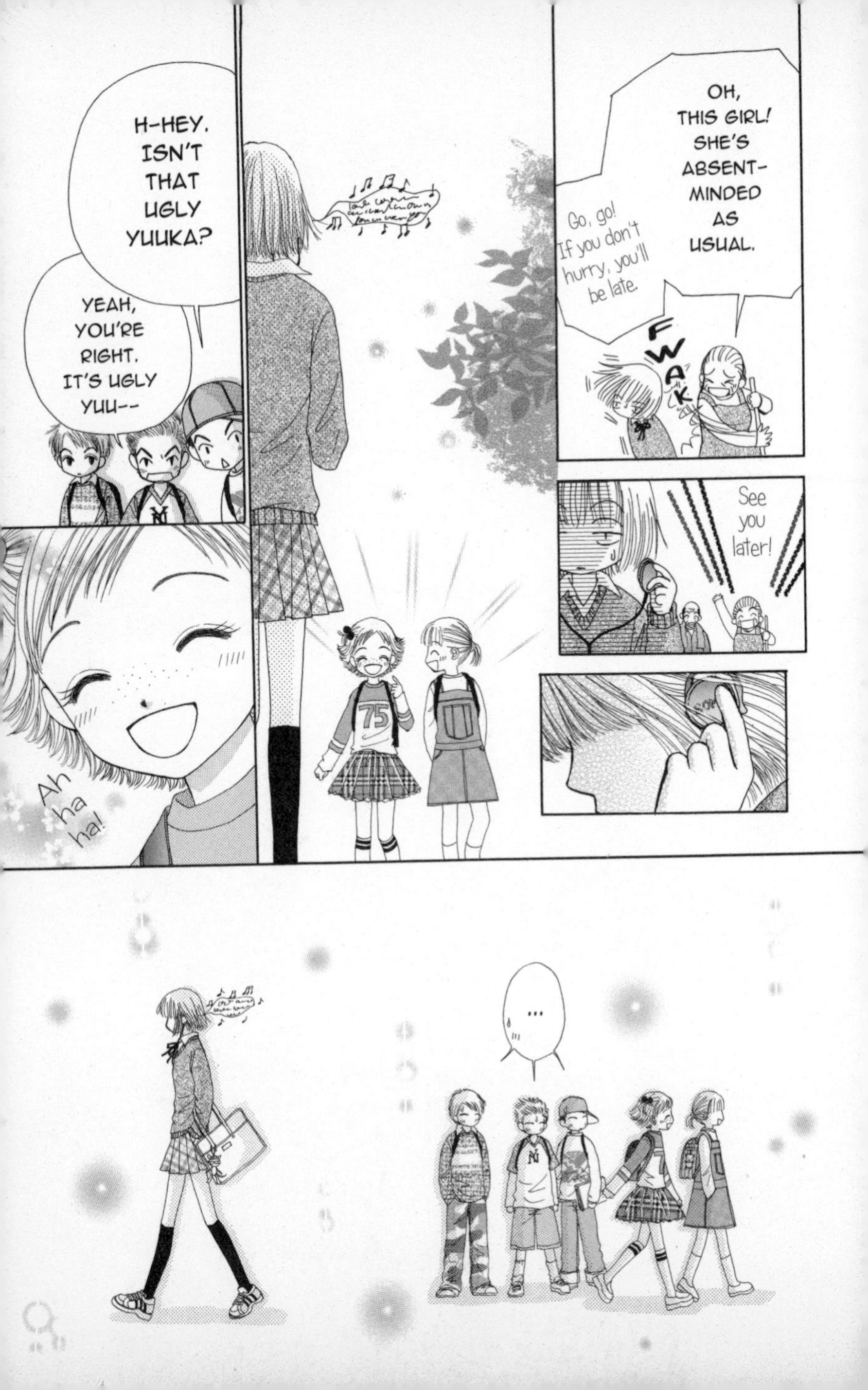
OH, THIS GIRL! SHE'S ABSENT-MINDED AS USUAL.
Go, go! If you don't hurry, you'll be late.
FWAK
See you later!
H-HEY. ISN'T THAT UGLY YUUKA?
YEAH, YOU'RE RIGHT. IT'S UGLY YUU--
Ah ha ha!
...

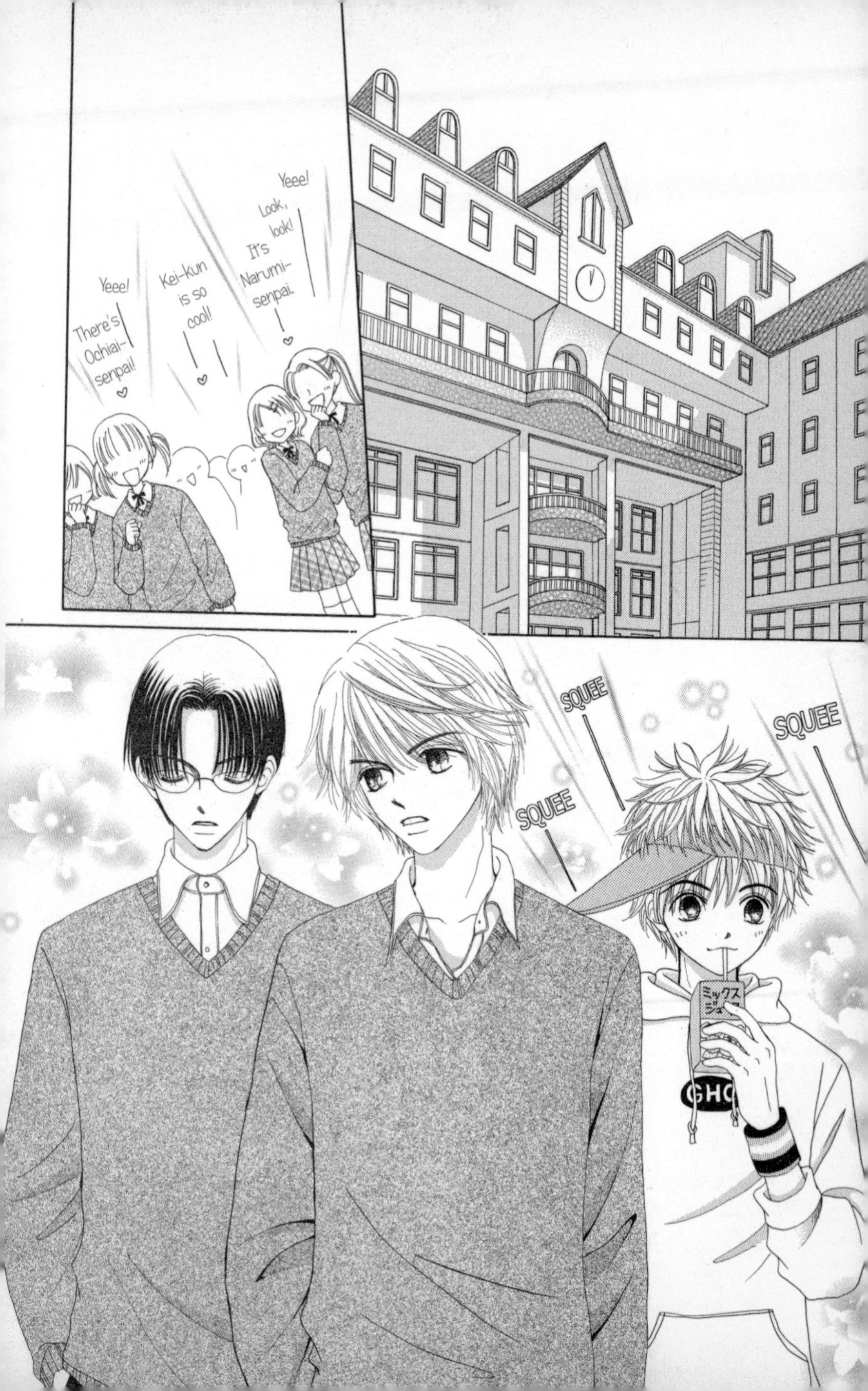
Yeee! Look, look! It's Narumi-senpai!
Kei-kun is so cool!
Yeee! There's Ochiai-senpai!
SQUEE
SQUEE
SQUEE

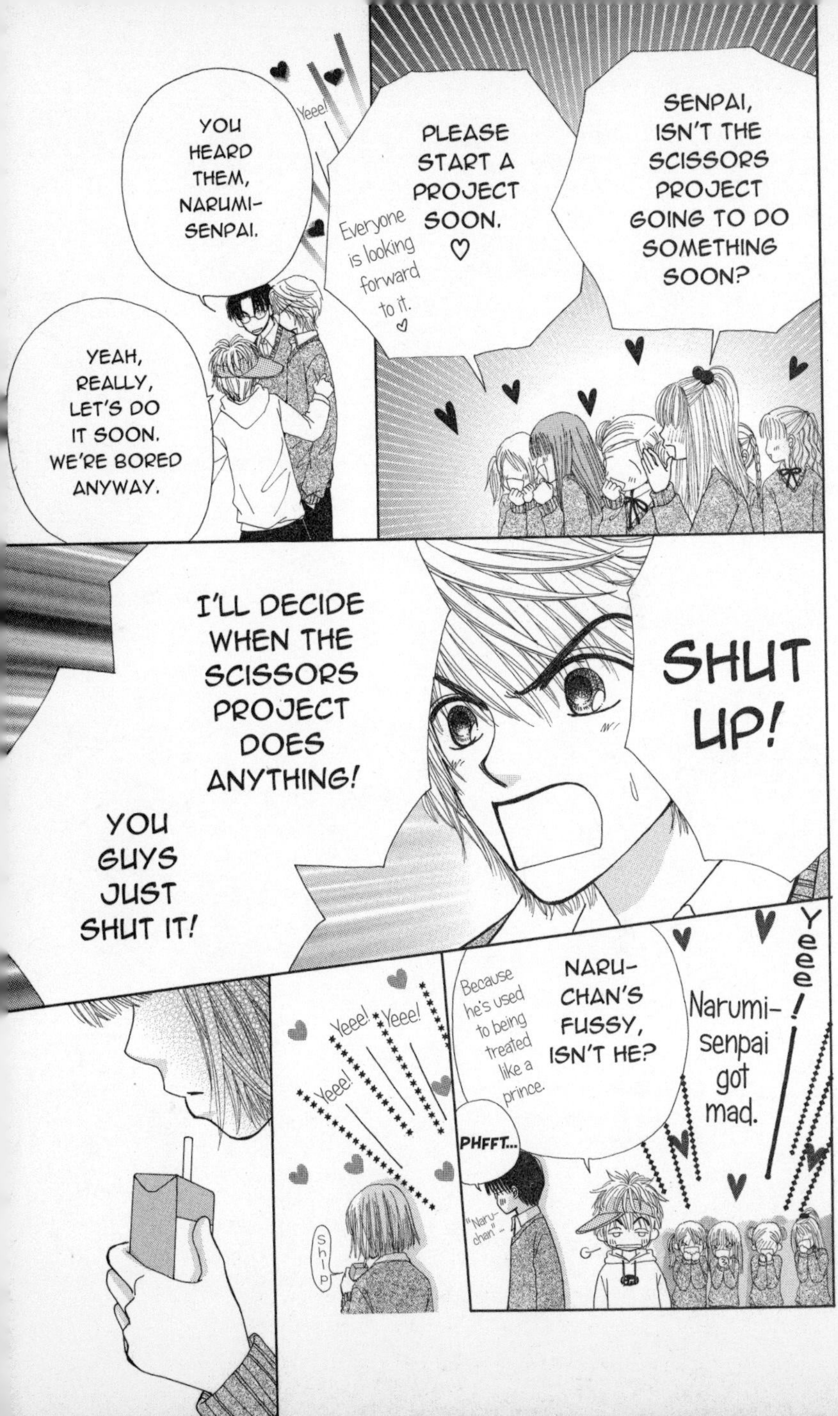
SENPAI, ISN'T THE SCISSORS PROJECT GOING TO DO SOMETHING SOON?
PLEASE START A PROJECT SOON. ♡
Everyone is looking forward to it. ♡
Yeee!
YOU HEARD THEM, NARUMI-SENPAI.
YEAH, REALLY, LET'S DO IT SOON. WE'RE BORED ANYWAY.
SHUT UP!
I'LL DECIDE WHEN THE SCISSORS PROJECT DOES ANYTHING!
YOU GUYS JUST SHUT IT!
Yeee!
Narumi-senpai got mad.
NARU-CHAN'S FUSSY, ISN'T HE?
Because he's used to being treated like a prince.
PHFFT...
"Naru-chan"...
Yeee!
Yeee!
Yeee!
Shlp

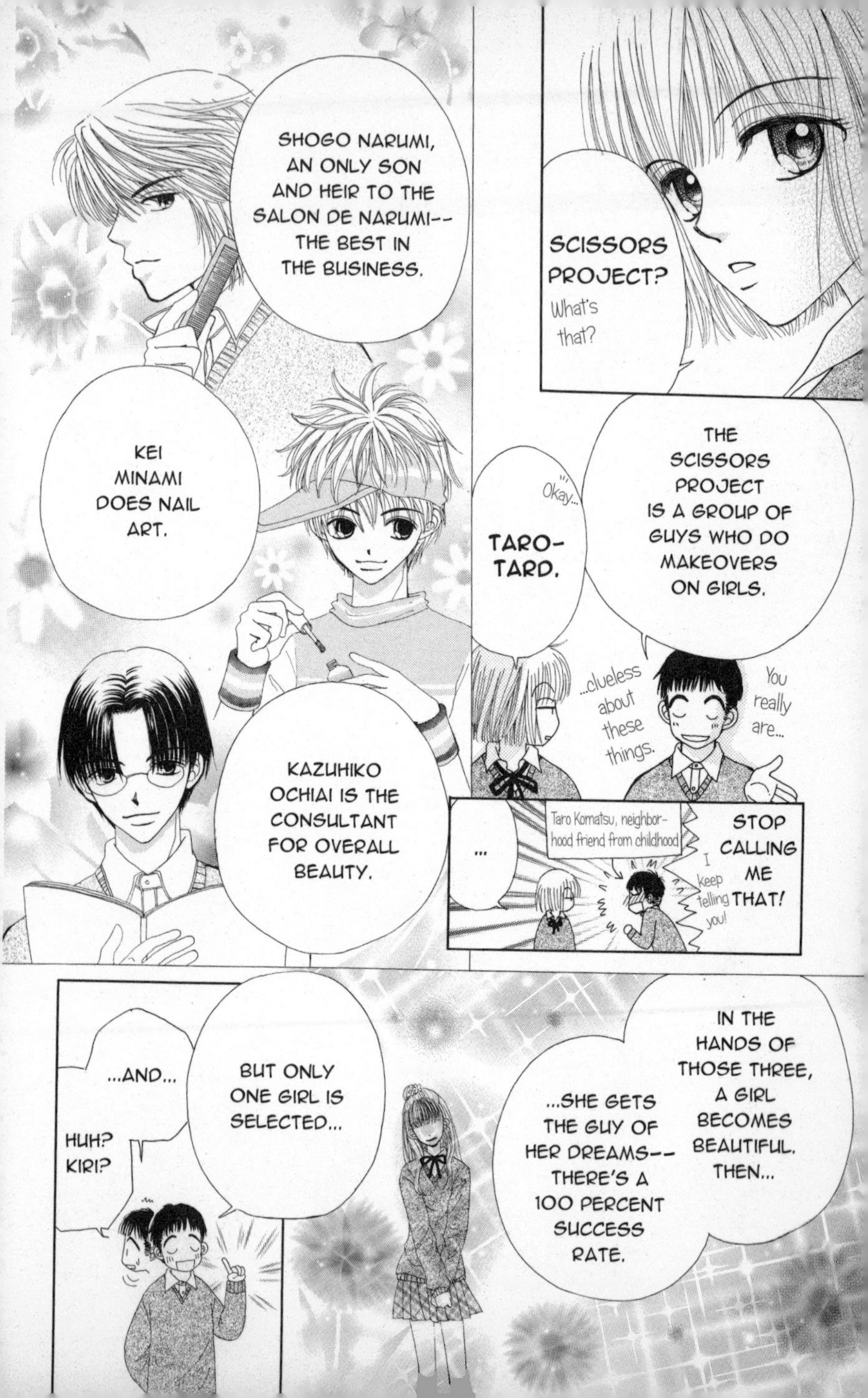
SCISSORS PROJECT?
What's that?
THE SCISSORS PROJECT IS A GROUP OF GUYS WHO DO MAKEOVERS ON GIRLS.
You really are...
...clueless about these things.
Okay...
TARO-TARD.
STOP CALLING ME THAT!
I keep telling you!
Taro Komatsu, neighborhood friend from childhood
...
SHOGO NARUMI, AN ONLY SON AND HEIR TO THE SALON DE NARUMI--THE BEST IN THE BUSINESS.
KEI MINAMI DOES NAIL ART.
KAZUHIKO OCHIAI IS THE CONSULTANT FOR OVERALL BEAUTY.
IN THE HANDS OF THOSE THREE, A GIRL BECOMES BEAUTIFUL. THEN...
...SHE GETS THE GUY OF HER DREAMS--THERE'S A 100 PERCENT SUCCESS RATE.
BUT ONLY ONE GIRL IS SELECTED...
...AND...
HUH? KIRI?

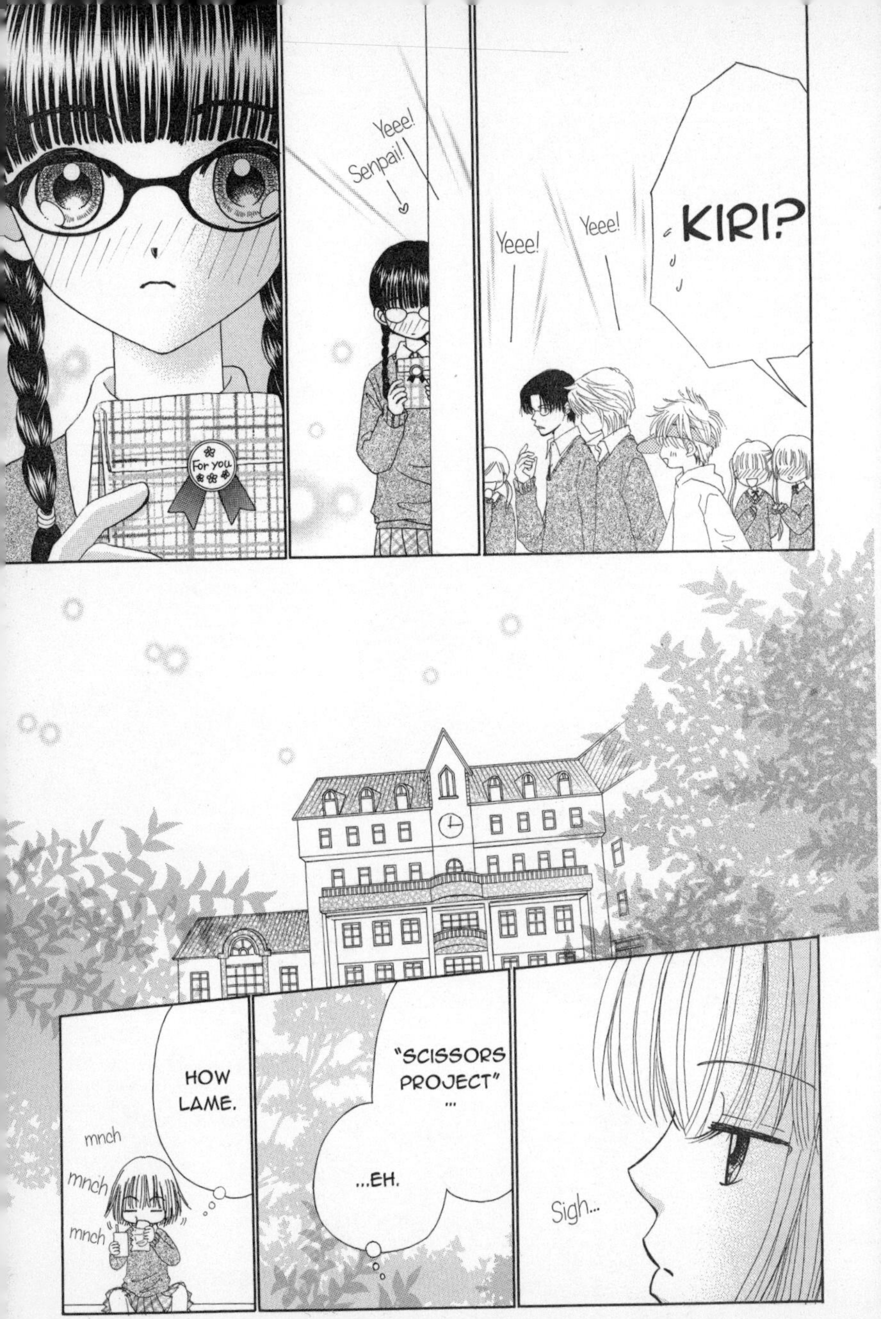
KIRI?
Yeee!
Yeee!
Yeee!
Senpai!
For you
Sigh...
"SCISSORS PROJECT" ...
...EH.
HOW LAME.
mnch
mnch
mnch

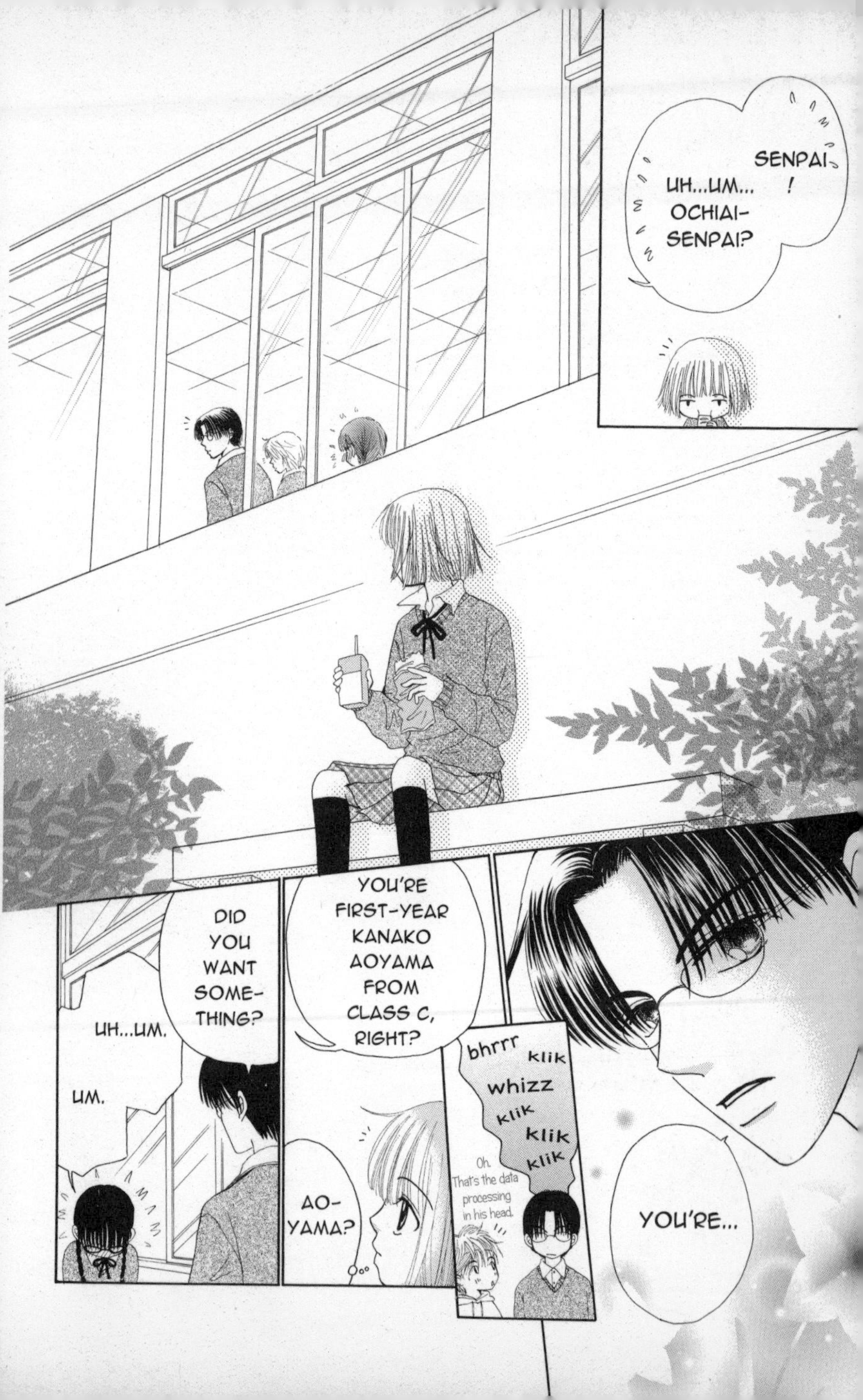

UH...UM... OCHIAI-SENPAI?
SENPAI!
YOU'RE...
bhrrr
klik
whizz
klik
klik
klik
Oh. That's the data processing in his head.
YOU'RE FIRST-YEAR KANAKO AOYAMA FROM CLASS C, RIGHT?
AO-YAMA?
DID YOU WANT SOME-THING?
UH...UM.
UM.

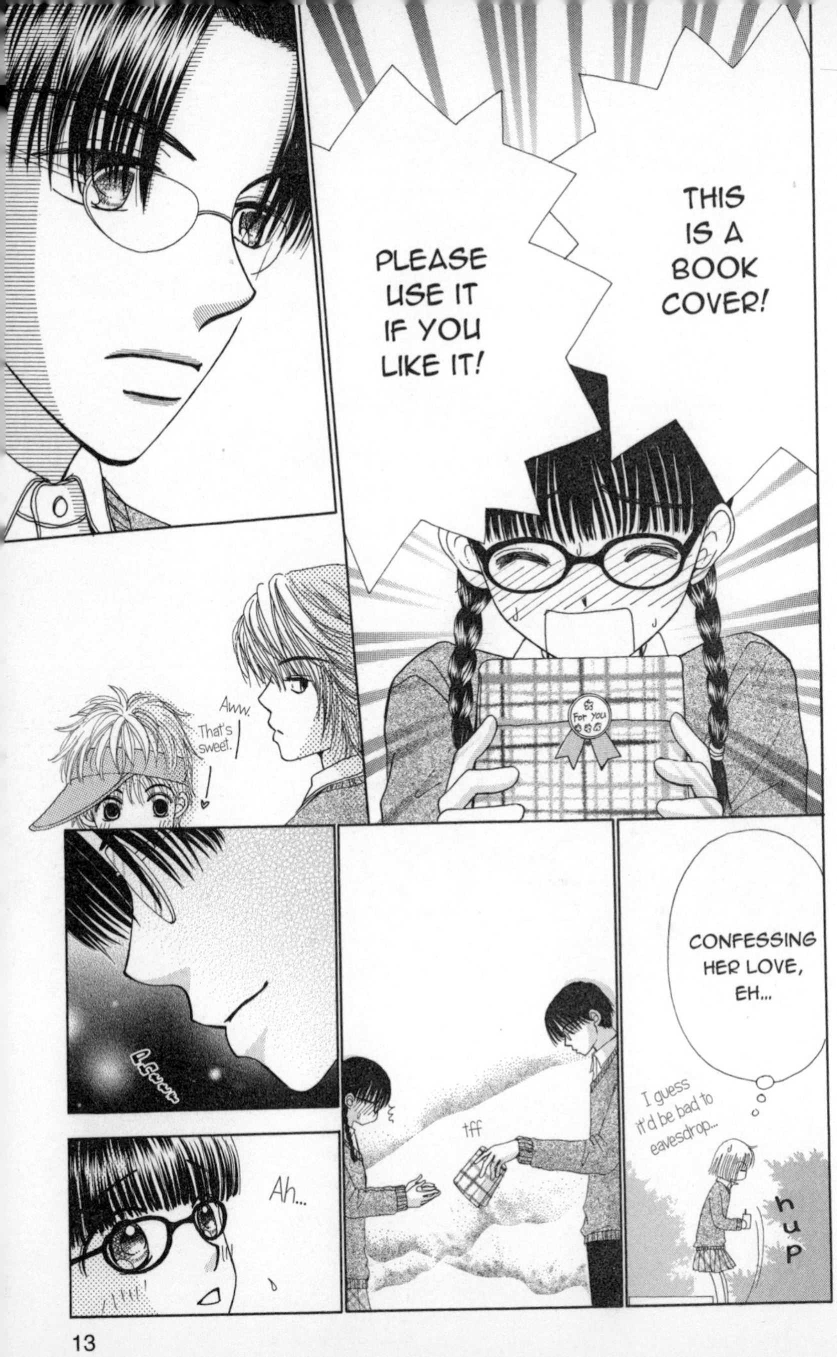
THIS IS A BOOK COVER!
PLEASE USE IT IF YOU LIKE IT!
For you
Aww. That's sweet.
CONFESSING HER LOVE, EH...
I guess it'd be bad to eavesdrop...
hup
tff
Ah...

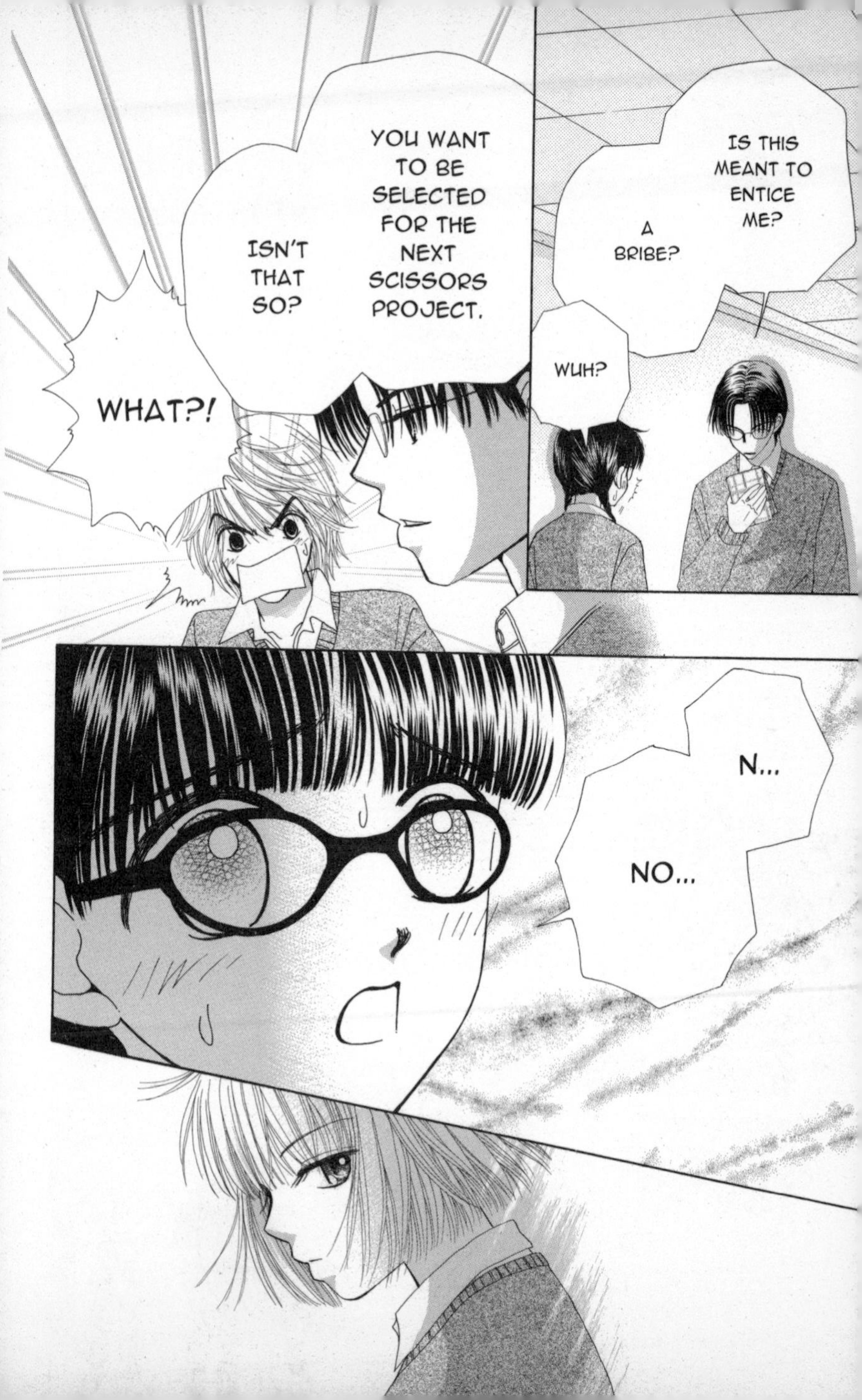
IS THIS MEANT TO ENTICE ME?
A BRIBE?
WUH?
YOU WANT TO BE SELECTED FOR THE NEXT SCISSORS PROJECT.
ISN'T THAT SO?
WHAT?!
N...
NO...

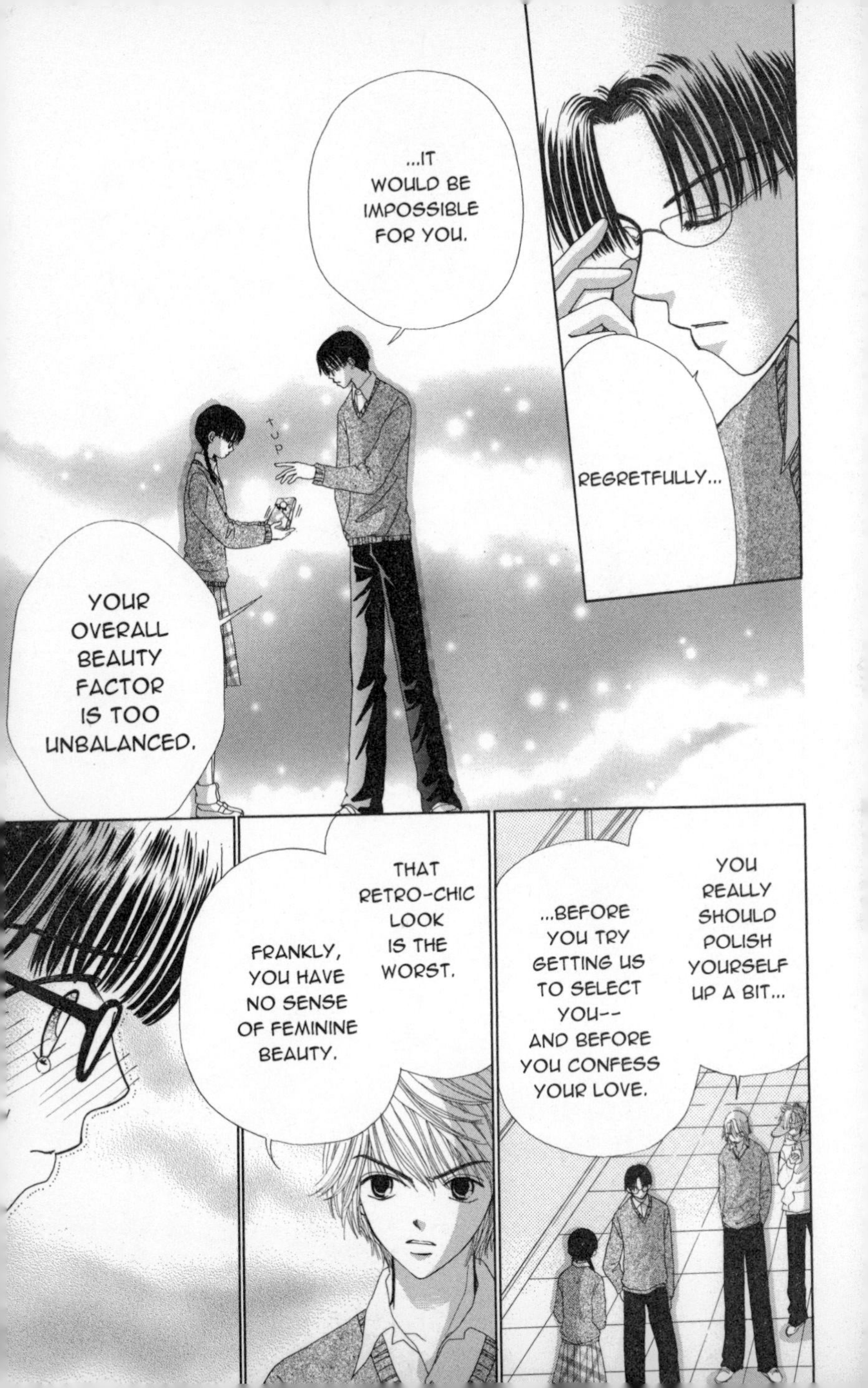
REGRETFULLY...
...IT WOULD BE IMPOSSIBLE FOR YOU.
TUP
YOUR OVERALL BEAUTY FACTOR IS TOO UNBALANCED.
YOU REALLY SHOULD POLISH YOURSELF UP A BIT...
...BEFORE YOU TRY GETTING US TO SELECT YOU-- AND BEFORE YOU CONFESS YOUR LOVE.
THAT RETRO-CHIC LOOK IS THE WORST.
FRANKLY, YOU HAVE NO SENSE OF FEMININE BEAUTY.

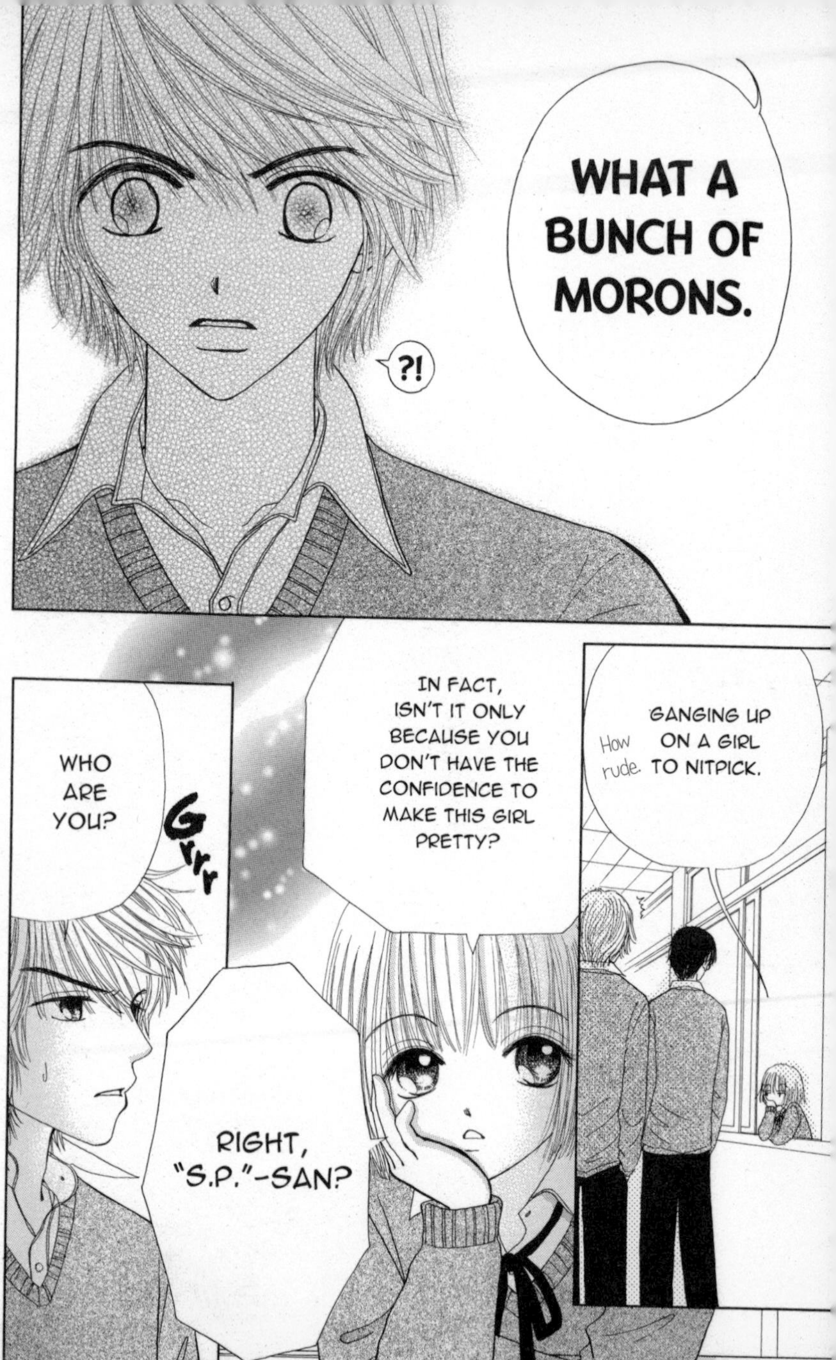
WHAT A BUNCH OF MORONS.
?!
GANGING UP ON A GIRL TO NITPICK.
How rude.
IN FACT, ISN'T IT ONLY BECAUSE YOU DON'T HAVE THE CONFIDENCE TO MAKE THIS GIRL PRETTY?
RIGHT, "S.P."-SAN?
WHO ARE YOU?
Grrr

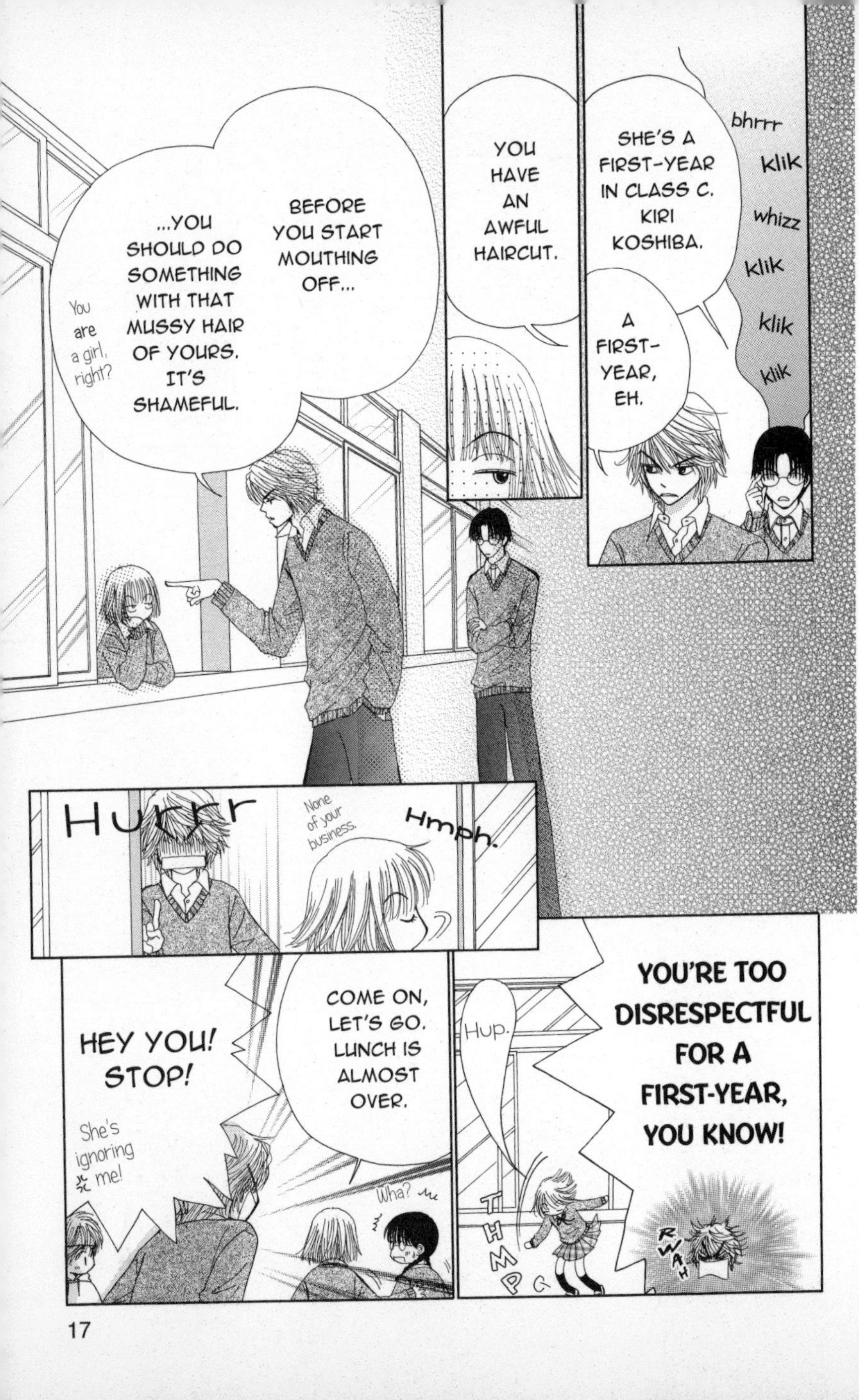
bhrrr
klik
whizz
klik
klik
klik
SHE'S A FIRST-YEAR IN CLASS C. KIRI KOSHIBA.
A FIRST-YEAR, EH.
YOU HAVE AN AWFUL HAIRCUT.
BEFORE YOU START MOUTHING OFF...
...YOU SHOULD DO SOMETHING WITH THAT MUSSY HAIR OF YOURS. IT'S SHAMEFUL.
You are a girl, right?
Hmph.
None of your business.
Hurrr
YOU'RE TOO DISRESPECTFUL FOR A FIRST-YEAR, YOU KNOW!
Hup.
THMP
RWAH
COME ON, LET'S GO. LUNCH IS ALMOST OVER.
HEY YOU! STOP!
She's ignoring me!
Wha?

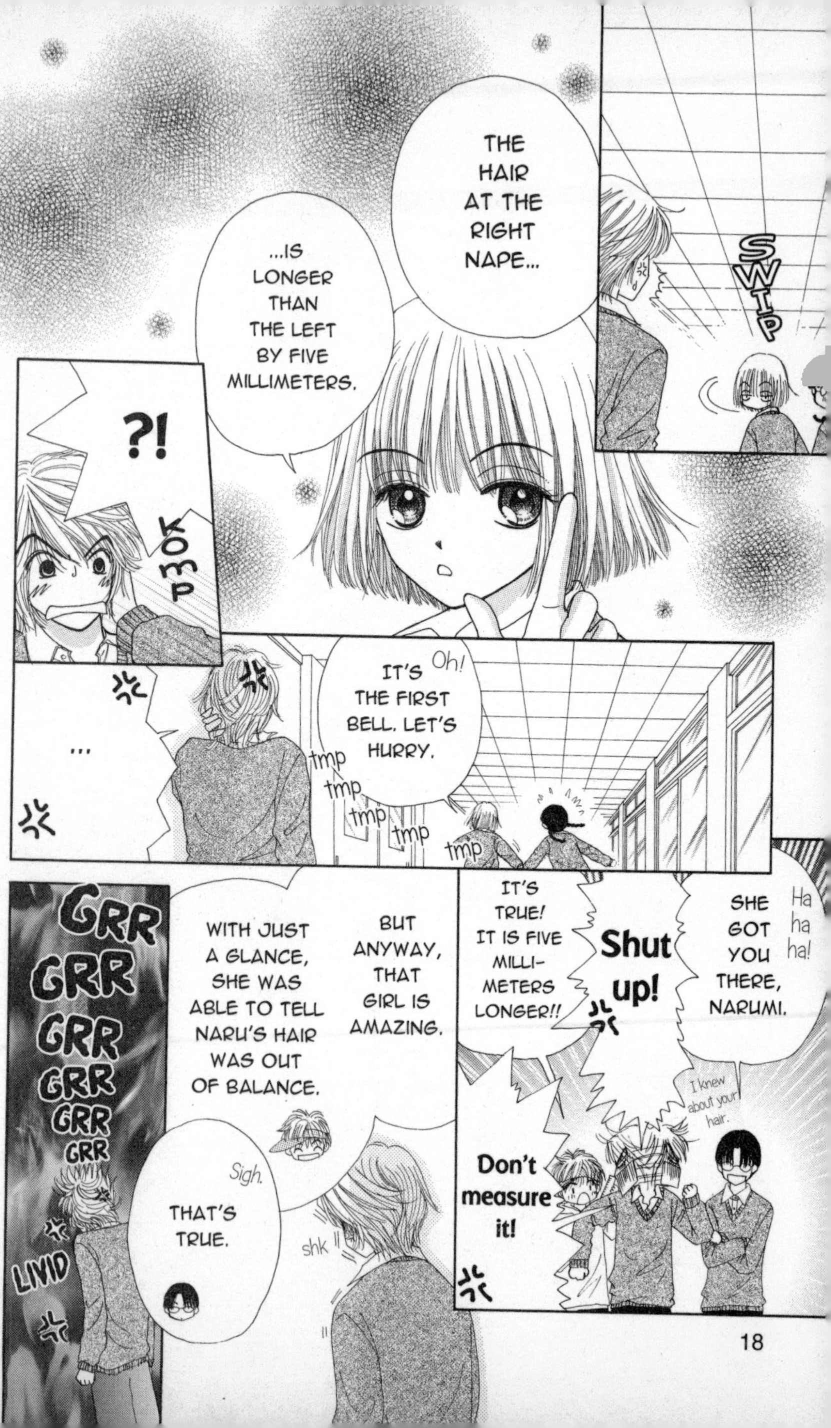
SWIP
THE HAIR AT THE RIGHT NAPE...
...IS LONGER THAN THE LEFT BY FIVE MILLIMETERS.
?!
KOMP
Oh!
IT'S THE FIRST BELL. LET'S HURRY.
tmp tmp tmp tmp tmp
...
SHE GOT YOU THERE, NARUMI.
Ha ha ha!
I knew about your hair.
Shut up!
IT'S TRUE! IT IS FIVE MILLI-METERS LONGER!!
Don't measure it!
BUT ANYWAY, THAT GIRL IS AMAZING.
WITH JUST A GLANCE, SHE WAS ABLE TO TELL NARU'S HAIR WAS OUT OF BALANCE.
Sigh.
THAT'S TRUE.
shk
GRR GRR GRR GRR GRR GRR
LIVID

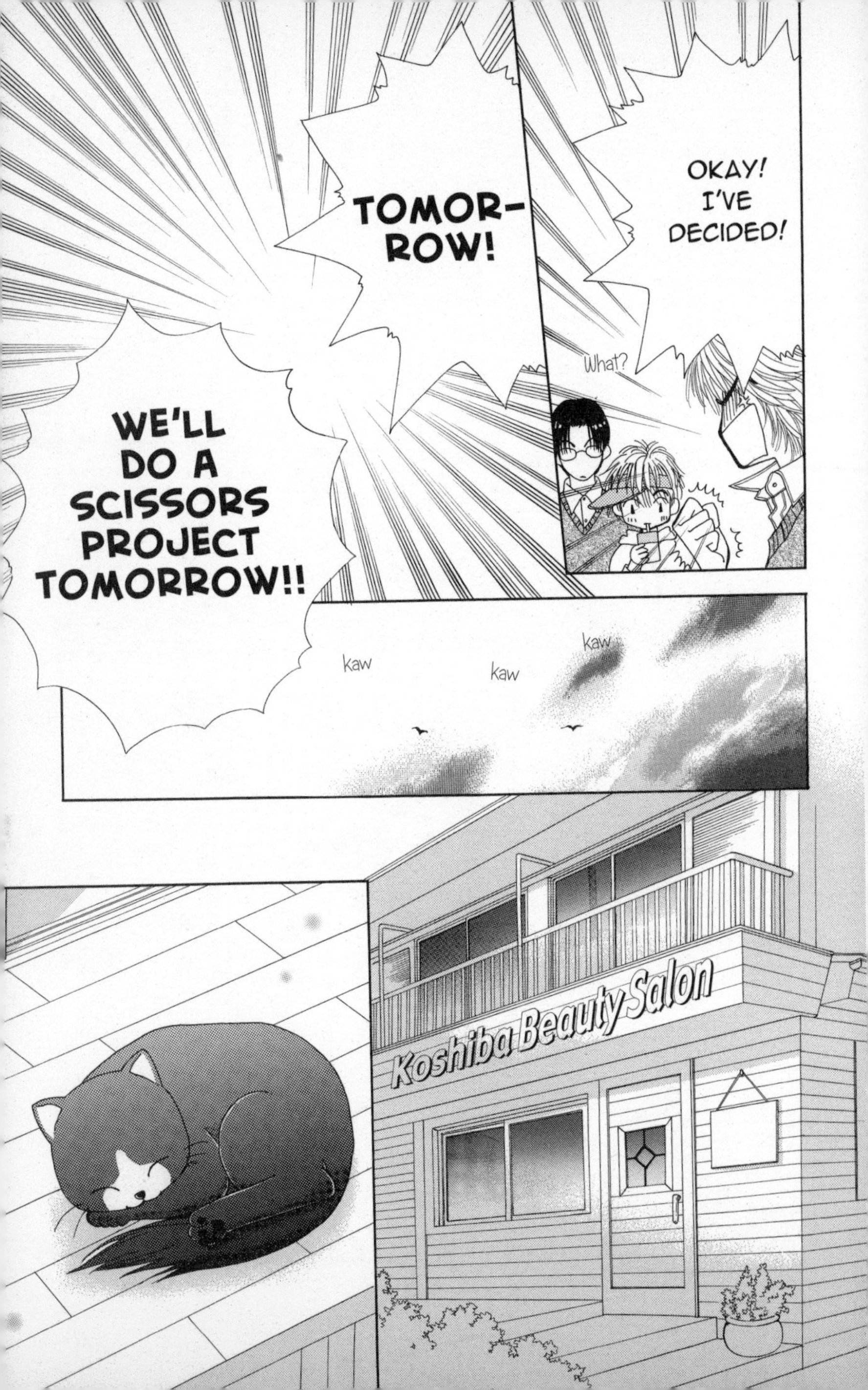

OKAY! I'VE DECIDED!
What?
TOMOR-ROW!
WE'LL DO A SCISSORS PROJECT TOMORROW!!
kaw
kaw
kaw
Koshiba Beauty Salon

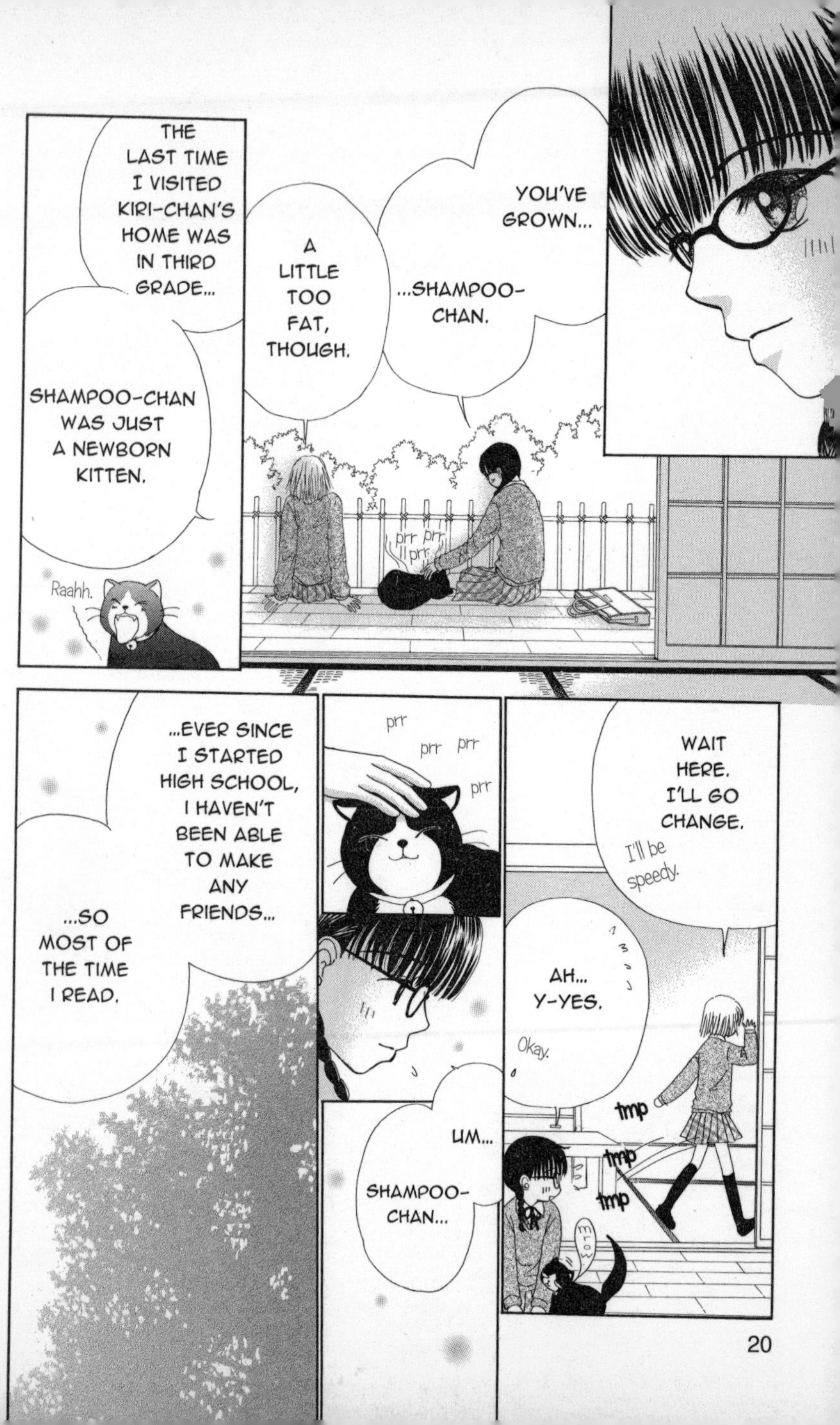
YOU'VE GROWN...
...SHAMPOO-CHAN.
prr prr prr
A LITTLE TOO FAT, THOUGH.
THE LAST TIME I VISITED KIRI-CHAN'S HOME WAS IN THIRD GRADE...
SHAMPOO-CHAN WAS JUST A NEWBORN KITTEN.
Raahh.
WAIT HERE. I'LL GO CHANGE.
I'll be speedy.
AH... Y-YES.
Okay.
tmp
tmp
tmp
prr
prr prr
prr
UM...
SHAMPOO-CHAN...
...EVER SINCE I STARTED HIGH SCHOOL, I HAVEN'T BEEN ABLE TO MAKE ANY FRIENDS...
...SO MOST OF THE TIME I READ.

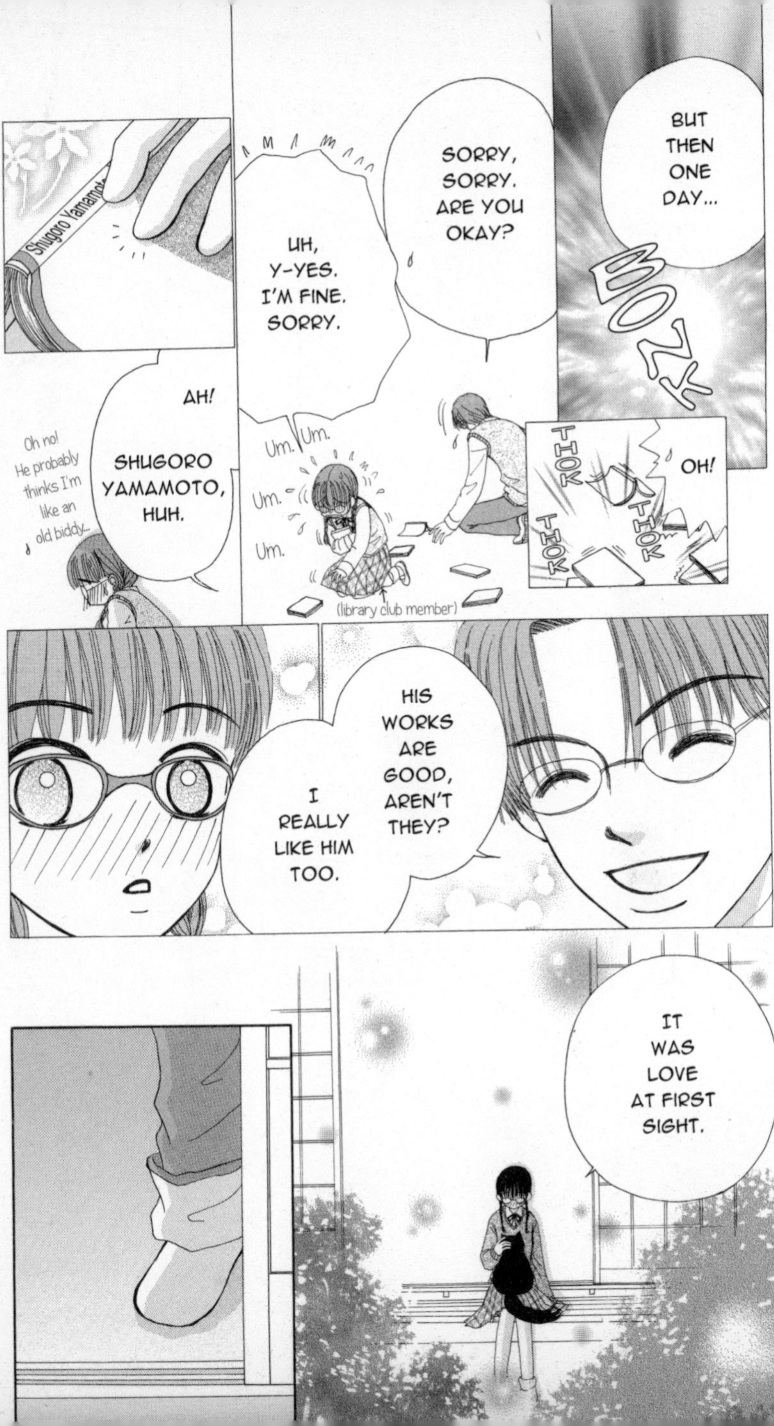
BUT THEN ONE DAY...
BONK
THOK
THOK
THOK
OH!
SORRY, SORRY. ARE YOU OKAY?
UH, Y-YES. I'M FINE. SORRY.
Um. Um.
Um.
Um.
(library club member)
Shugoro Yamamoto
AH!
SHUGORO YAMAMOTO, HUH.
Oh no! He probably thinks I'm like an old biddy...
HIS WORKS ARE GOOD, AREN'T THEY?
I REALLY LIKE HIM TOO.
IT WAS LOVE AT FIRST SIGHT.

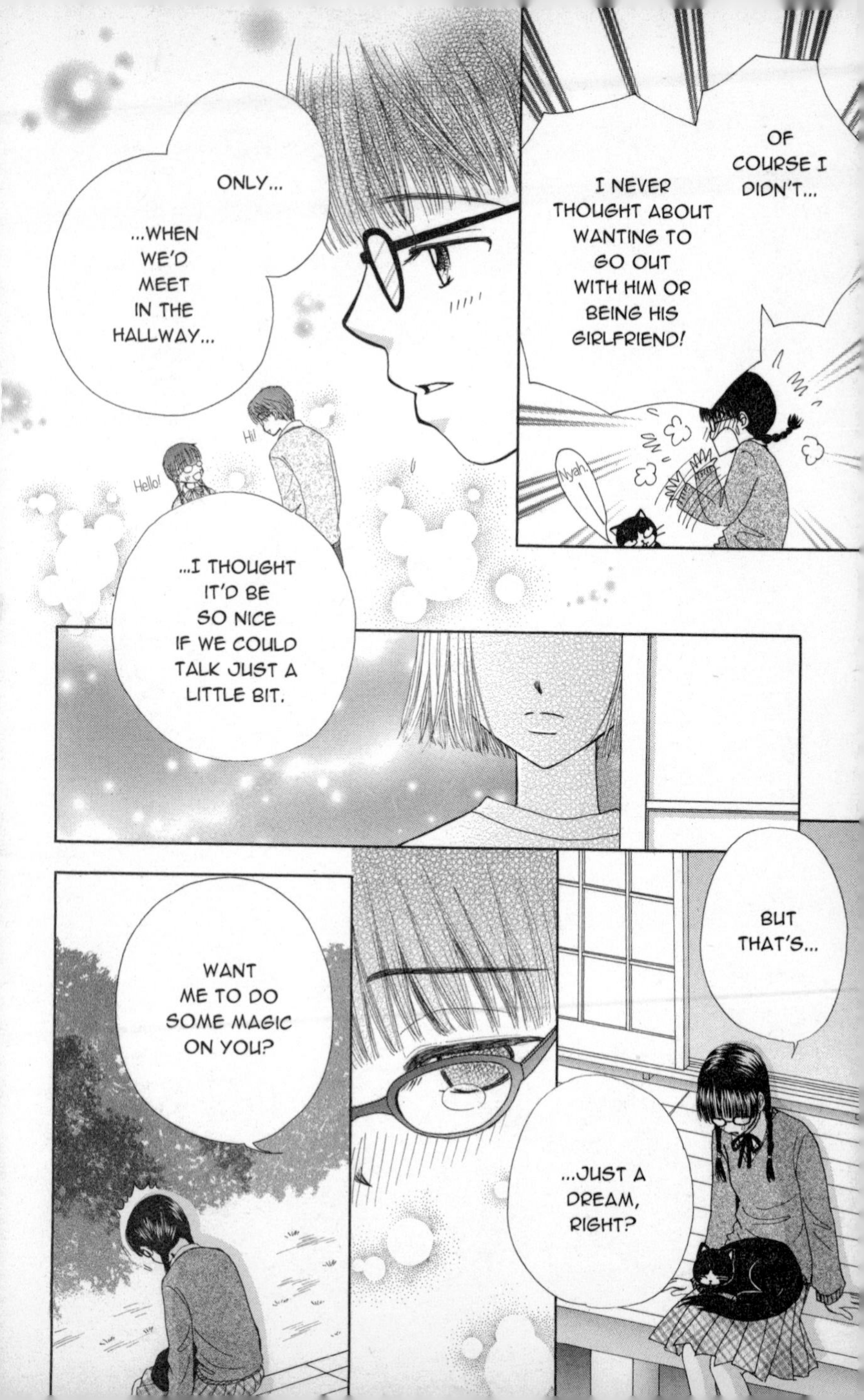
OF COURSE I DIDN'T...
I NEVER THOUGHT ABOUT WANTING TO GO OUT WITH HIM OR BEING HIS GIRLFRIEND!
Nyah.
ONLY...
...WHEN WE'D MEET IN THE HALLWAY...
Hi!
Hello!
...I THOUGHT IT'D BE SO NICE IF WE COULD TALK JUST A LITTLE BIT.
BUT THAT'S...
...JUST A DREAM, RIGHT?
WANT ME TO DO SOME MAGIC ON YOU?

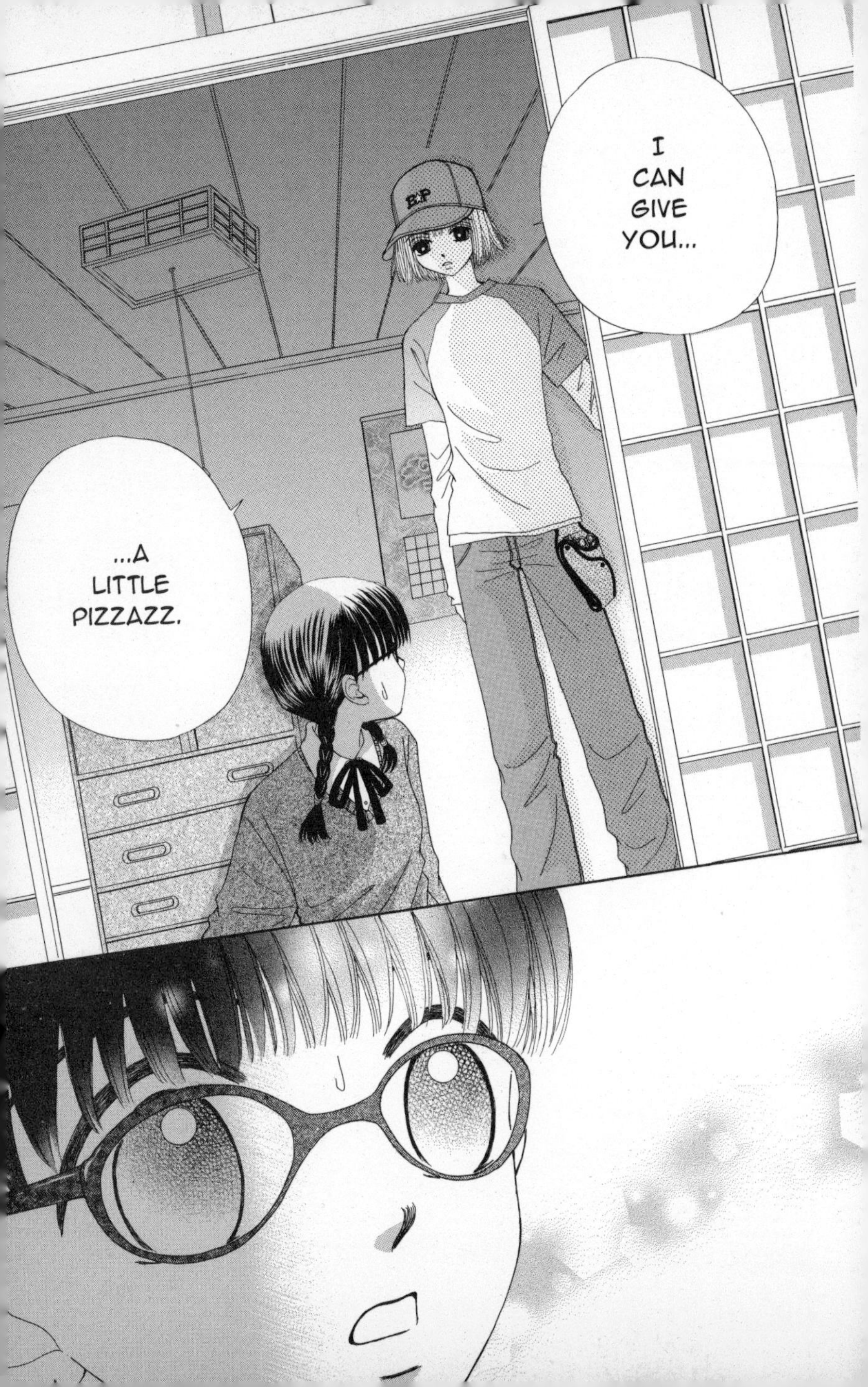
I CAN GIVE YOU...
...A LITTLE PIZZAZZ.

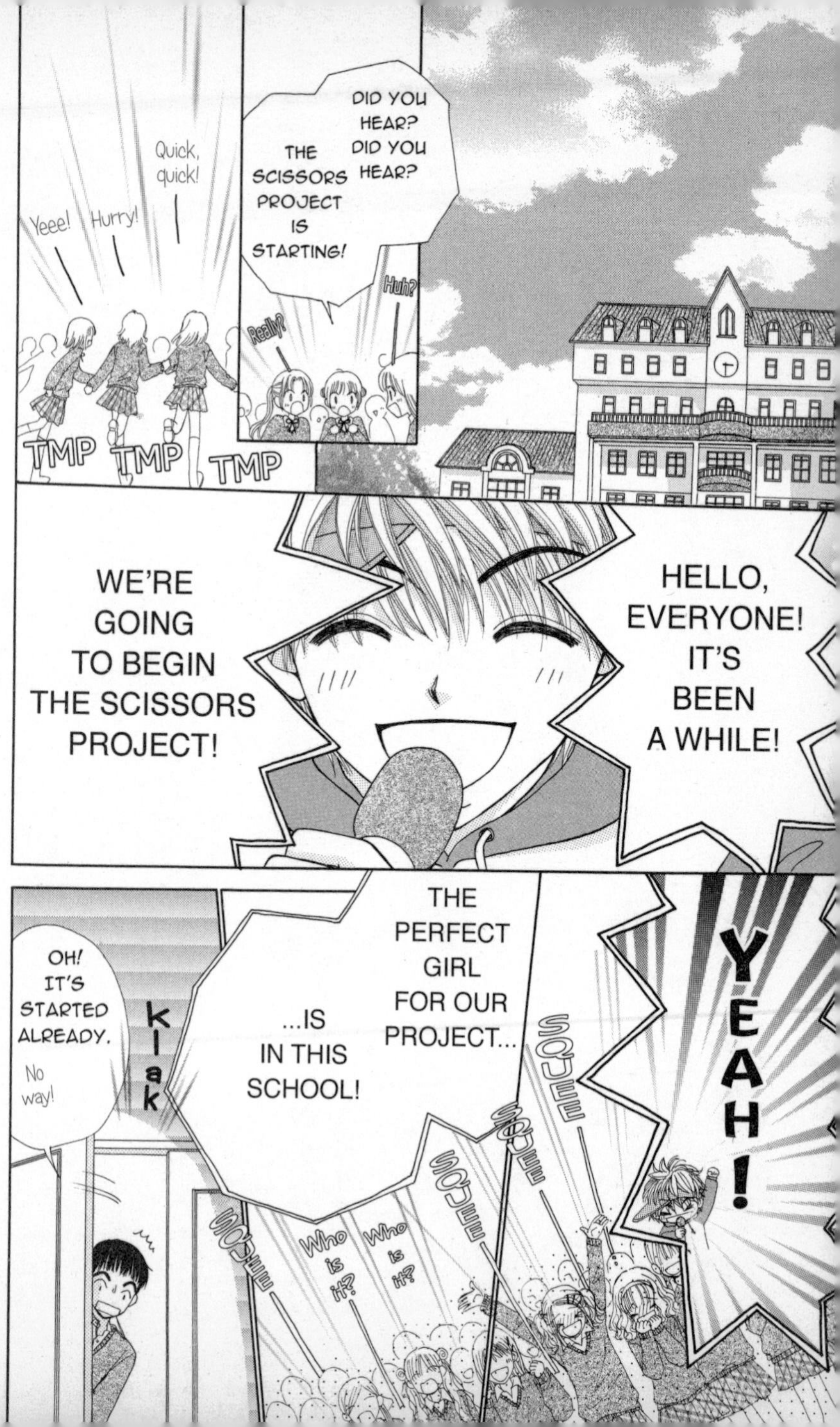
DID YOU HEAR? DID YOU HEAR?
THE SCISSORS PROJECT IS STARTING!
Huh?
Really?
Quick, quick!
Hurry!
Yeee!
TMP
TMP
TMP
HELLO, EVERYONE! IT'S BEEN A WHILE!
WE'RE GOING TO BEGIN THE SCISSORS PROJECT!
YEAH!
THE PERFECT GIRL FOR OUR PROJECT...
...IS IN THIS SCHOOL!
SQUEE
SQUEE
SQUEE
SQUEE
Who is it?
Who is it?
OH! IT'S STARTED ALREADY.
No way!
klak

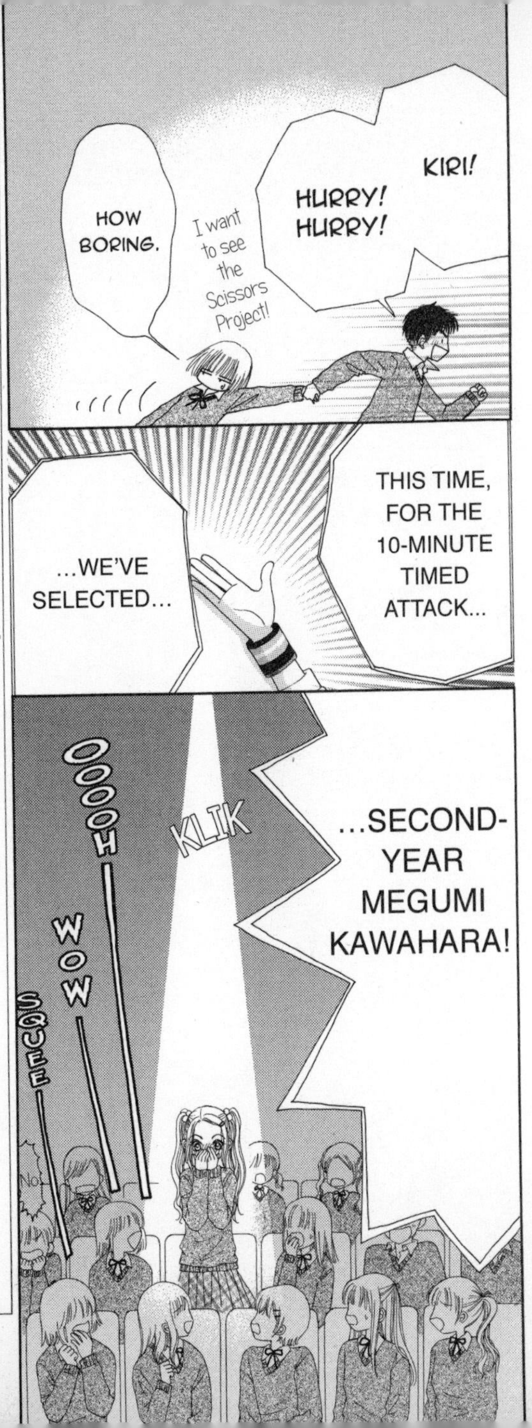
KIRI!
HURRY! HURRY!
I want to see the Scissors Project!
HOW BORING.
THIS TIME, FOR THE 10-MINUTE TIMED ATTACK...
...WE'VE SELECTED...
...SECOND-YEAR MEGUMI KAWAHARA!
KLIK
OOOOOH
WOW
SQUEE

K's Club Talk

Everyone, it's been a while. (For those new to my manga, welcome!) This work has turned out to be totally different from my previous work, *Dr. Rin*, but I'm really enjoying writing it! The main charcter, Kiri, has a personality type that I've wanted to use for quite a long time. In *Ciao*, niko-pachi* characters are the norm, so everyone around me was worried whether Kiri would be accepted. However, she was well received--beyond my expectations--by the readers, and Kiri is probably the most popular character in B.P. right now. I'm relieved. If there's an opportunity, I want to hold a vote to rank the popularity of all the characters.~

● ★ ●

By the way, did you all know that beauticians hold their scissors with the thumb and the third finger when cutting hair? A beautician I know says that they hold ordinary scissors with their thumb and third finger even when they're cutting paper, cloth, and everything else! How fascinating~~! Amazing~!

*niko-pachi: eager, smiling sweetly

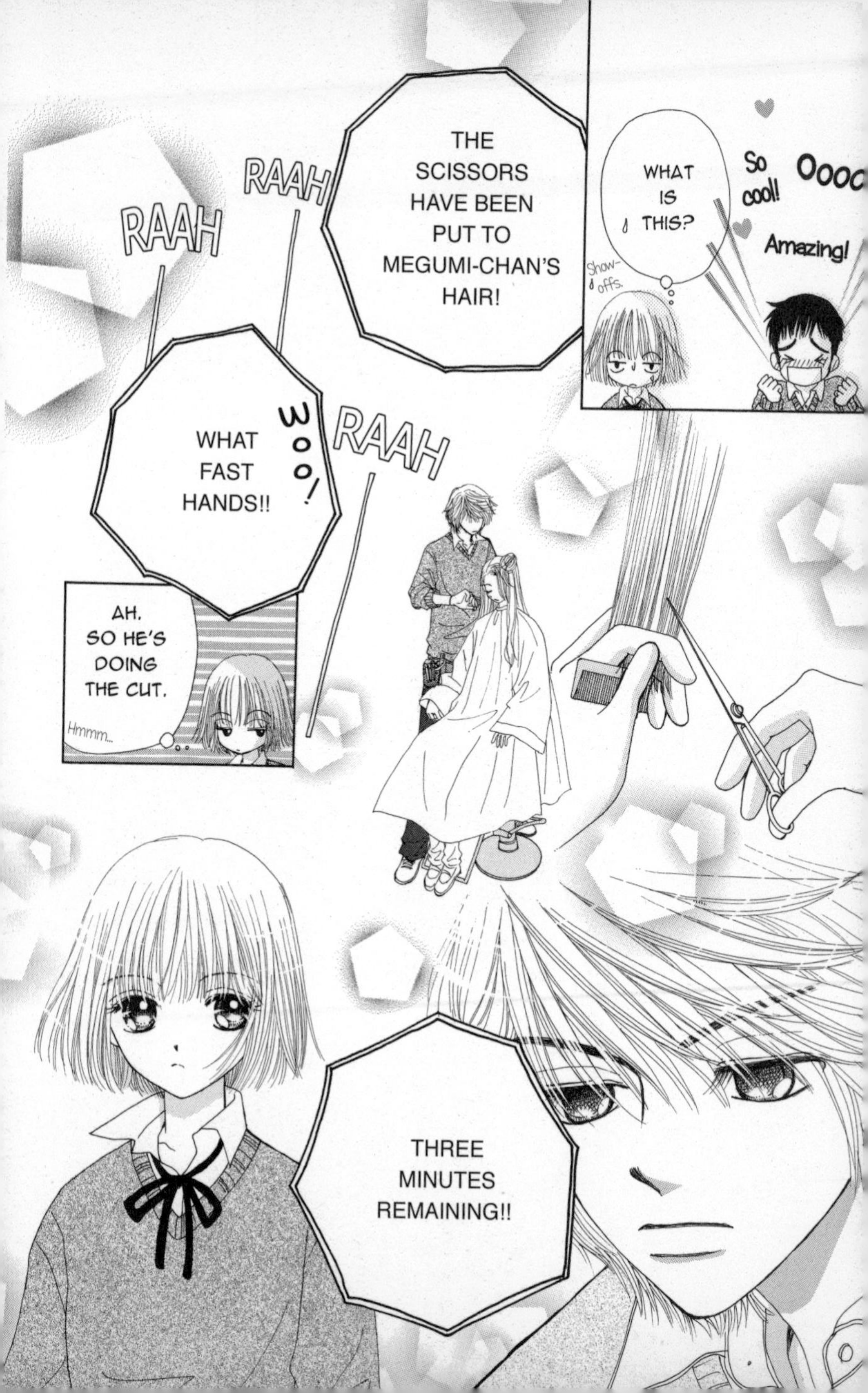
So cool!
Oooo
Amazing!
WHAT IS THIS?
Show-offs.
THE SCISSORS HAVE BEEN PUT TO MEGUMI-CHAN'S HAIR!
RAAH
RAAH
RAAH
Wooo!
WHAT FAST HANDS!!
AH. SO HE'S DOING THE CUT.
Hmmm...
THREE MINUTES REMAINING!!

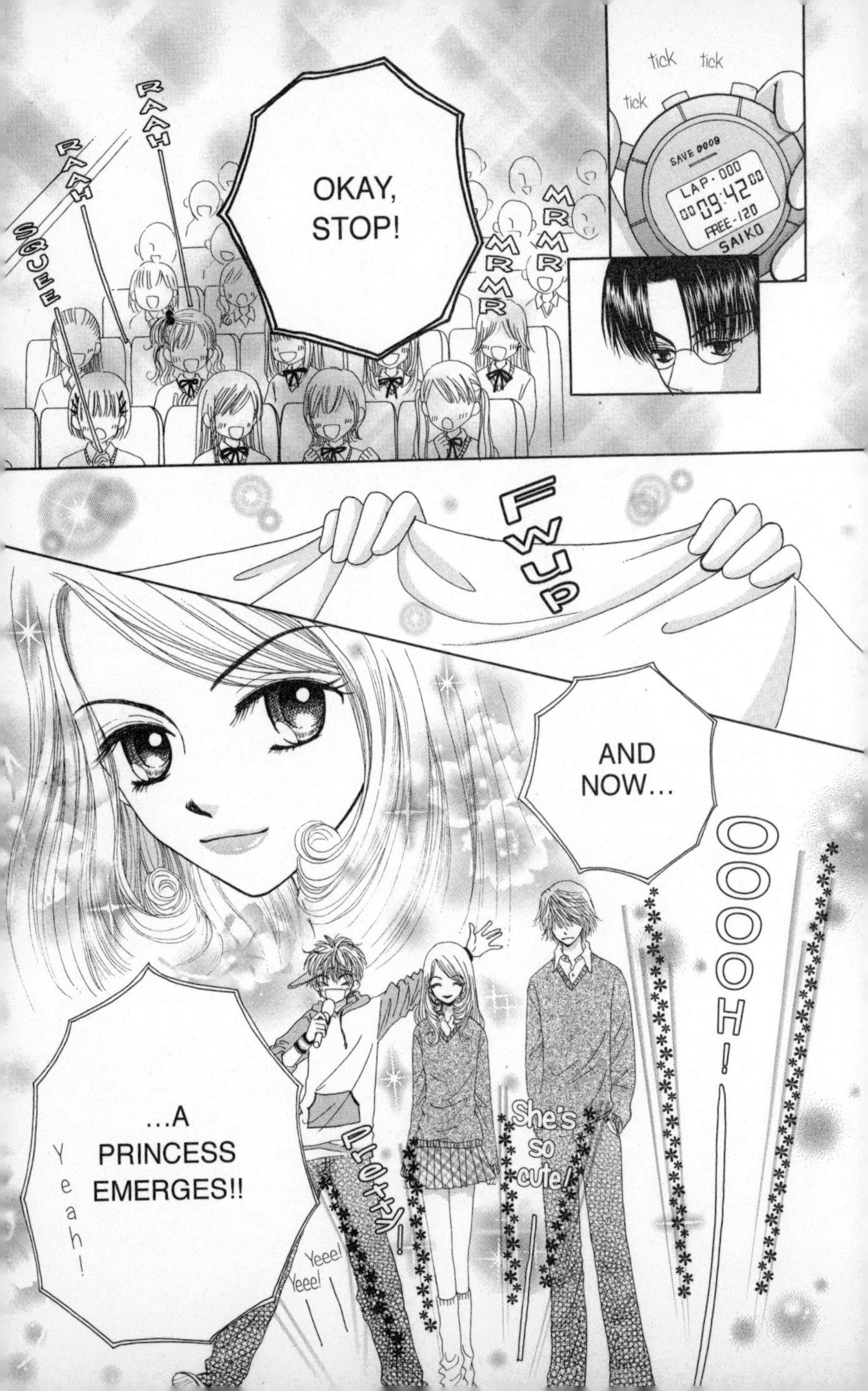
tick
tick
tick
SAVE 0009
LAP 000
09:42
FREE-120
SAIKO
OKAY, STOP!
MRMR
MRMR
RAAH
RAAH
SQUEE
FWUP
AND NOW…
OOOOOH!
She's so cute!
Pretty!
…A PRINCESS EMERGES!!
Yeah!
Yeee!
Yeee!

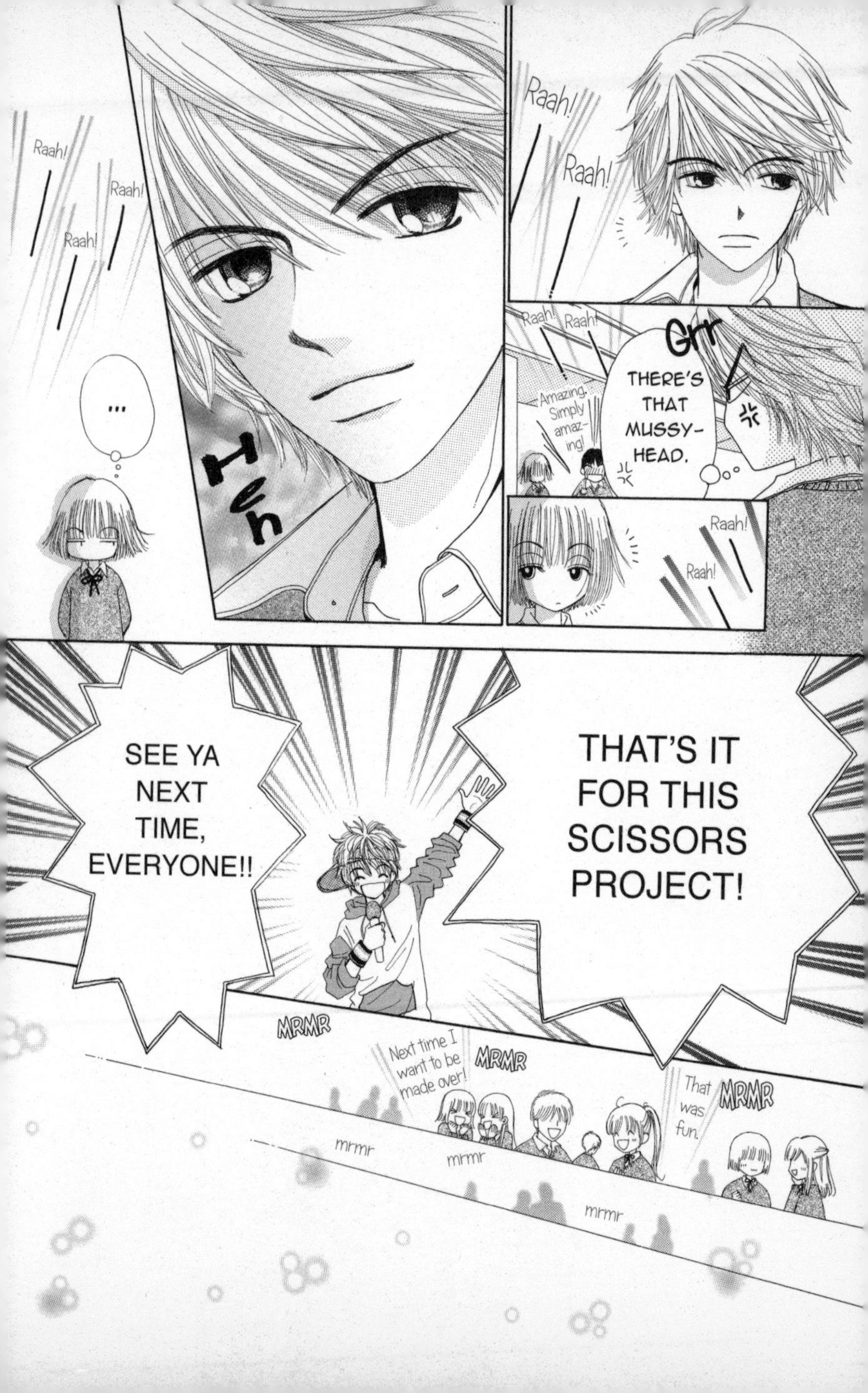
Raah!
Raah!
Raah! Raah!
Grr
THERE'S THAT MUSSY-HEAD.
Amazing. Simply amazing!
Raah!
Raah!
Heh
Raah!
Raah!
Raah!
...
THAT'S IT FOR THIS SCISSORS PROJECT!
SEE YA NEXT TIME, EVERYONE!!
MRMR
That was fun.
MRMR
Next time I want to be made over!
MRMR
mrmr
mrmr
mrmr

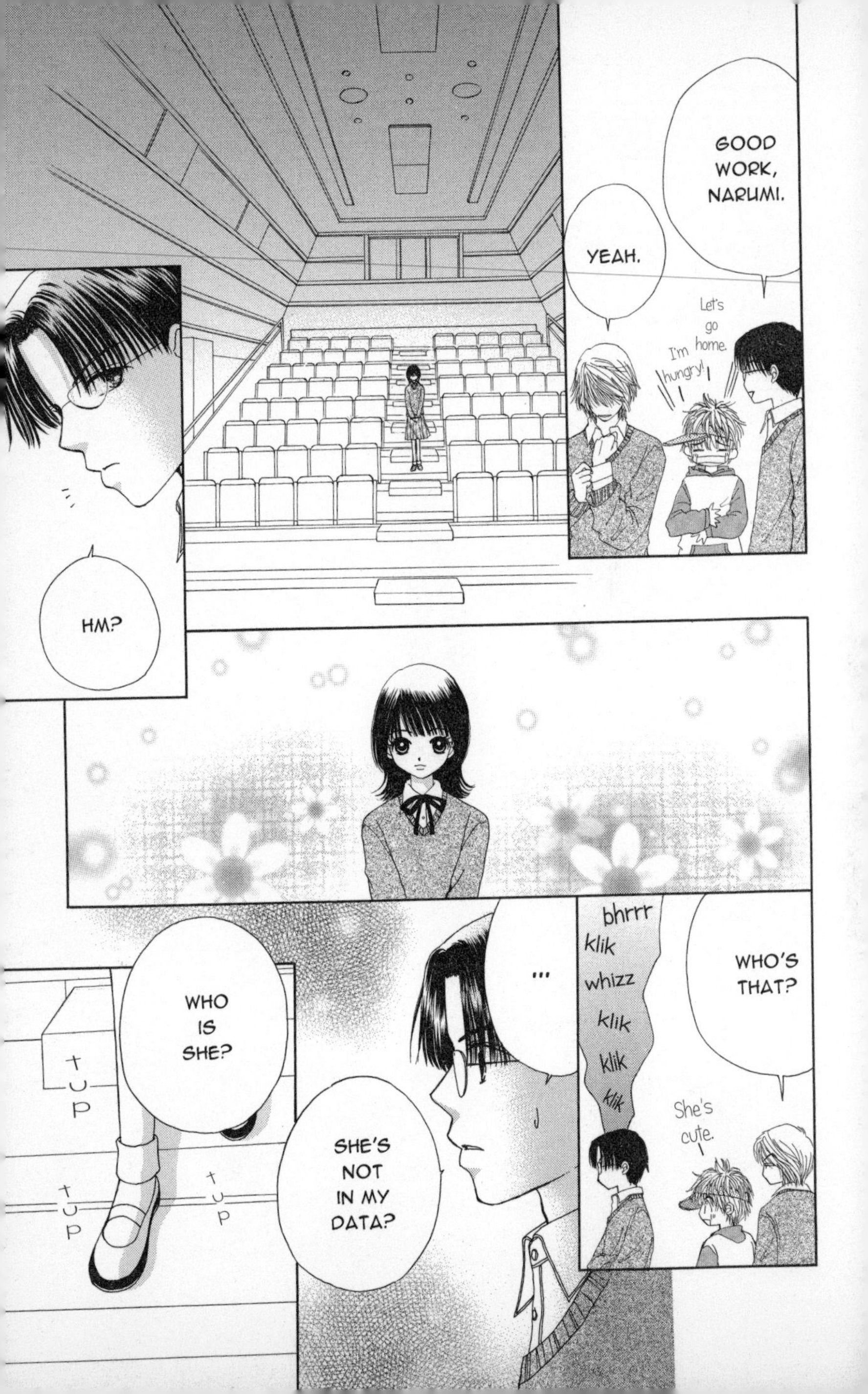
GOOD WORK, NARUMI.
YEAH.
Let's go home.
I'm hungry!
HM?
WHO'S THAT?
She's cute.
bhrrr
klik
whizz
klik
klik
klik
...
SHE'S NOT IN MY DATA?
WHO IS SHE?
TUP
TUP
TUP

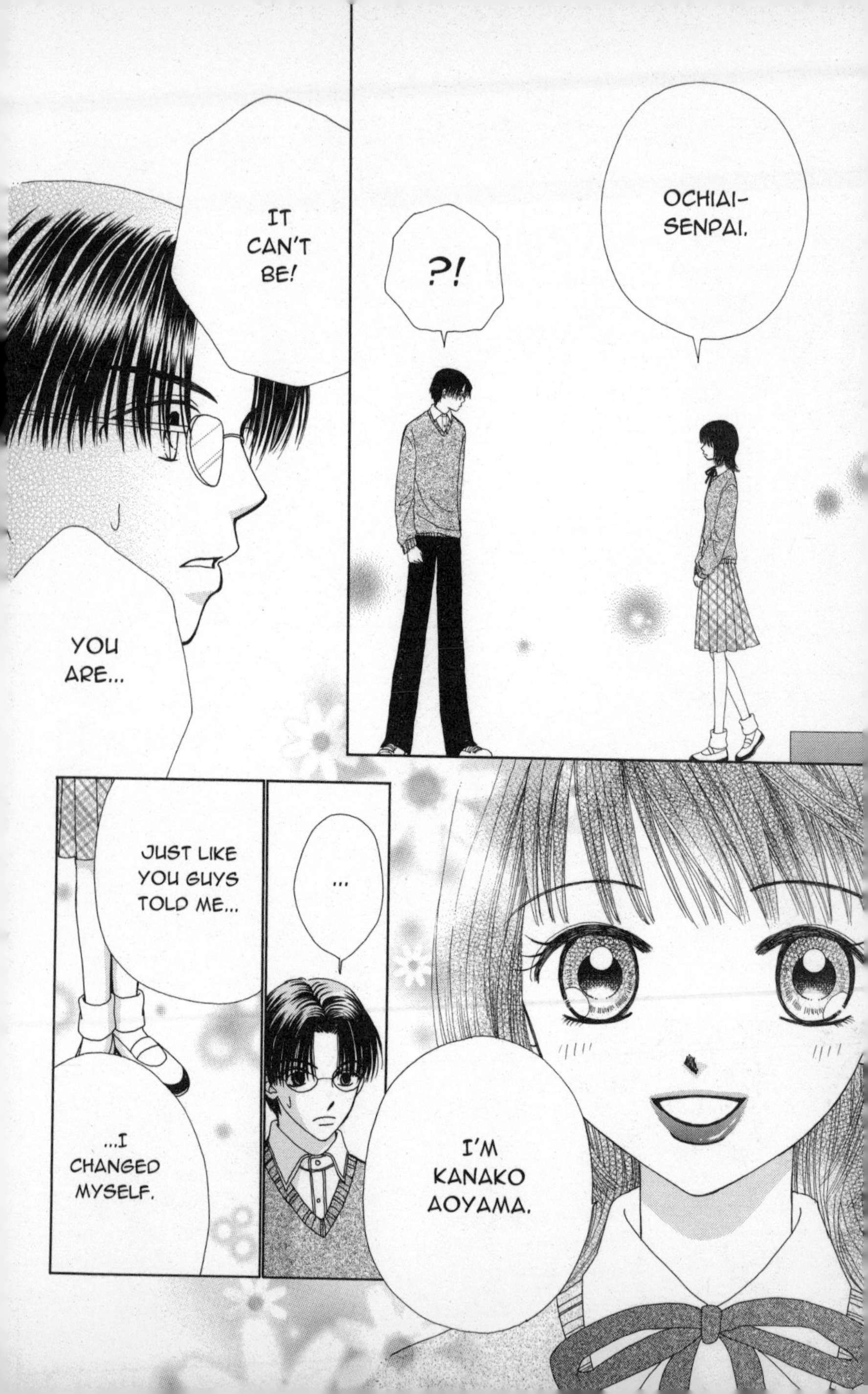
OCHIAI-SENPAI.
?!
IT CAN'T BE!
YOU ARE...
I'M KANAKO AOYAMA.
...
JUST LIKE YOU GUYS TOLD ME...
...I CHANGED MYSELF.

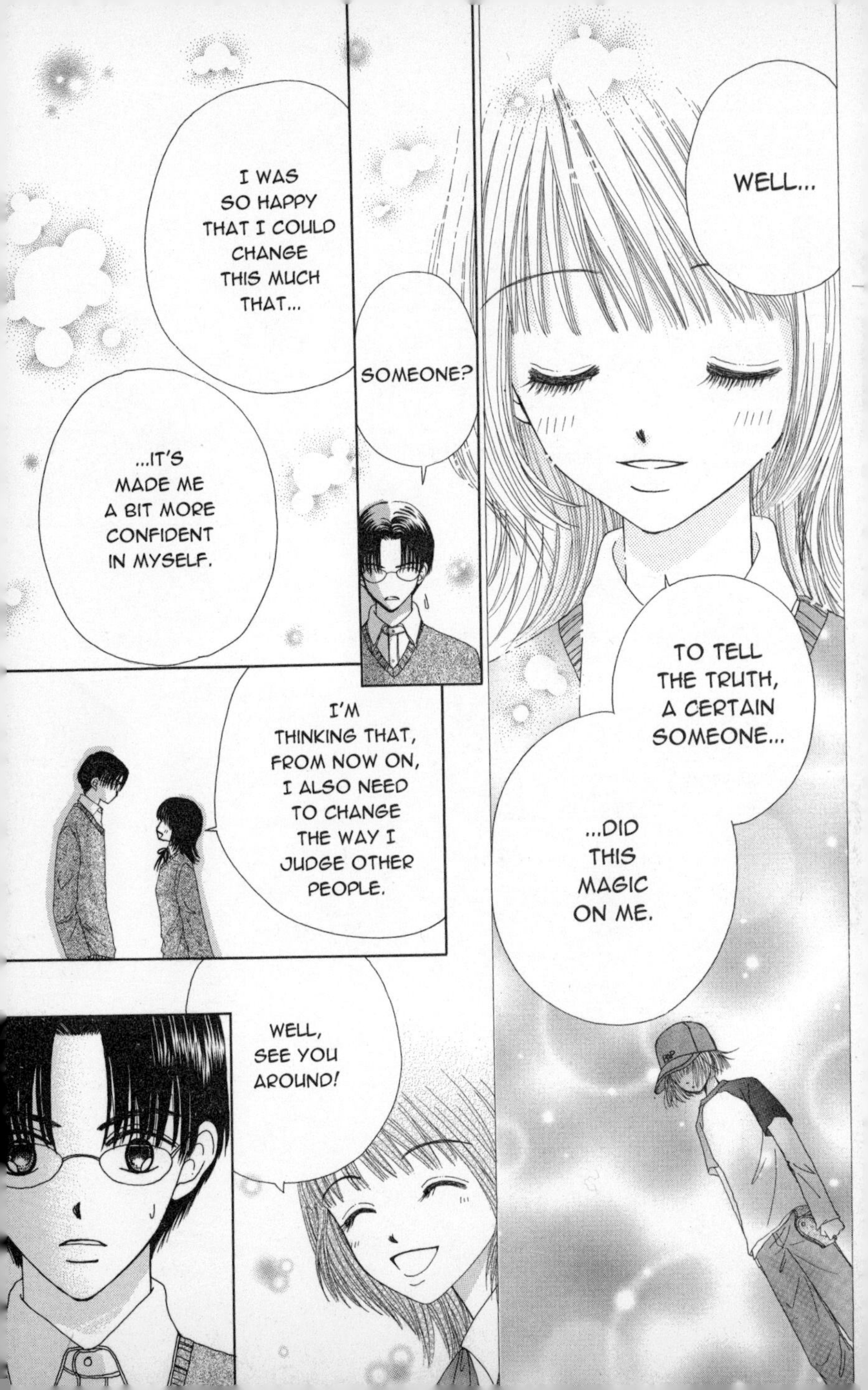
WELL...
TO TELL THE TRUTH, A CERTAIN SOMEONE...
...DID THIS MAGIC ON ME.
SOMEONE?
I WAS SO HAPPY THAT I COULD CHANGE THIS MUCH THAT...
...IT'S MADE ME A BIT MORE CONFIDENT IN MYSELF.
I'M THINKING THAT, FROM NOW ON, I ALSO NEED TO CHANGE THE WAY I JUDGE OTHER PEOPLE.
WELL, SEE YOU AROUND!

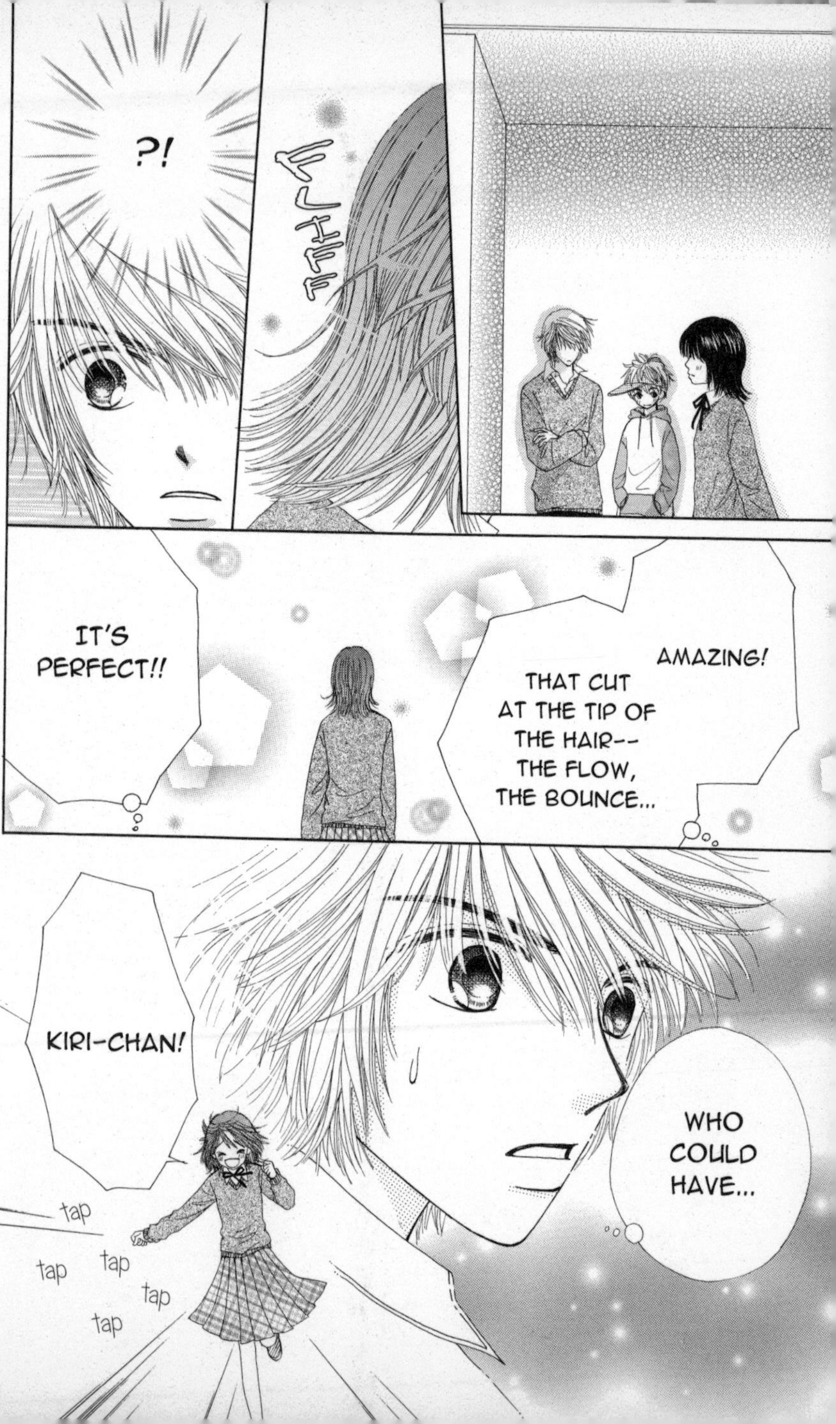
FLIFF
?!
AMAZING!
THAT CUT AT THE TIP OF THE HAIR-- THE FLOW, THE BOUNCE...
IT'S PERFECT!!
WHO COULD HAVE...
KIRI-CHAN!
tap
tap
tap
tap
tap

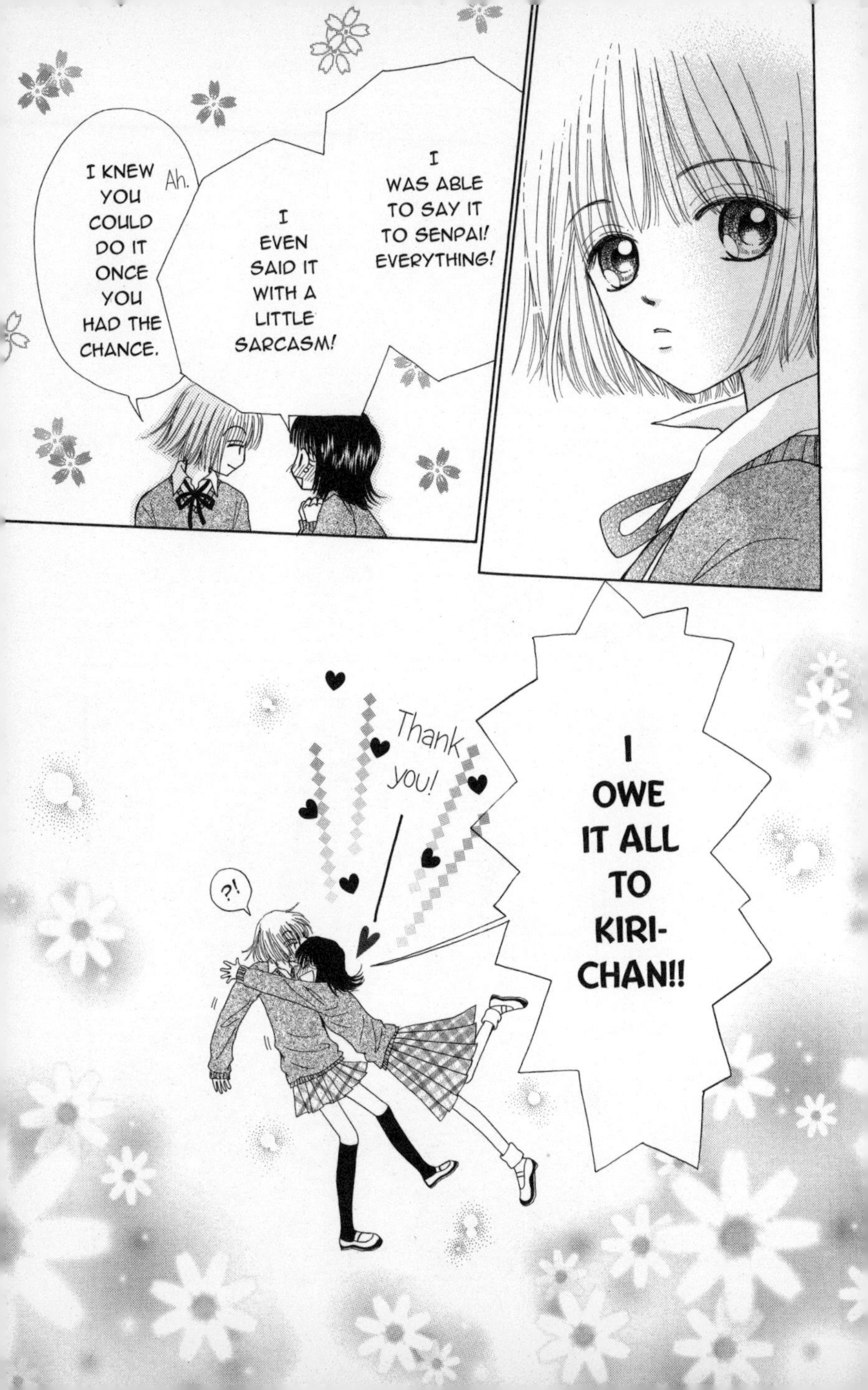
I WAS ABLE TO SAY IT TO SENPAI! EVERYTHING!
I EVEN SAID IT WITH A LITTLE SARCASM!
Ah.
I KNEW YOU COULD DO IT ONCE YOU HAD THE CHANCE.
I OWE IT ALL TO KIRI-CHAN!!
Thank you!
?!

Beauty Pop

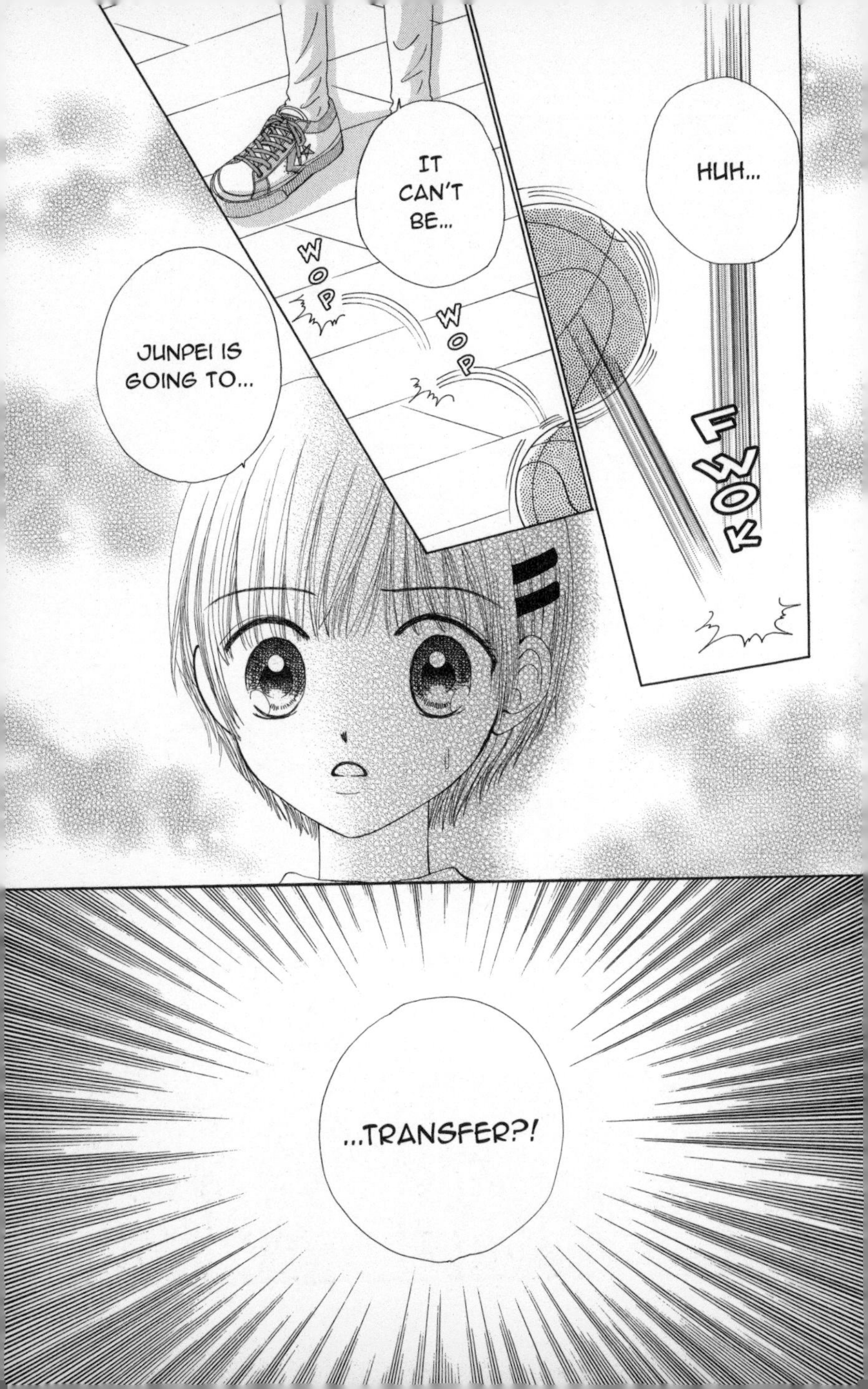
HUH...
FWOK
IT CAN'T BE...
WOP
WOP
JUNPEI IS GOING TO...
...TRANSFER?!

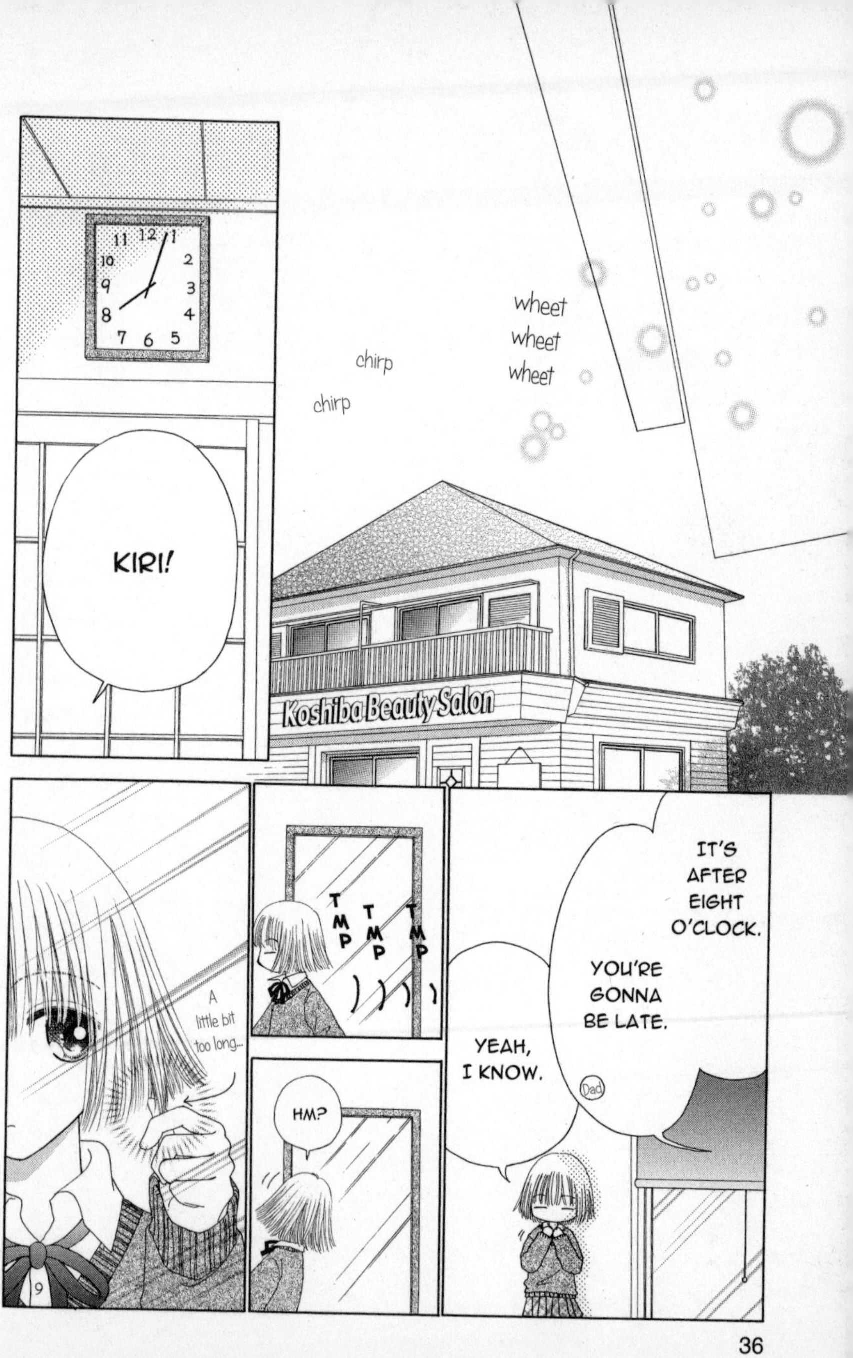
wheet
wheet
wheet
chirp
chirp
Koshiba Beauty Salon
KIRI!
IT'S AFTER EIGHT O'CLOCK.
YOU'RE GONNA BE LATE.
Dad
YEAH, I KNOW.
TMP TMP TMP
HM?
A little bit too long...

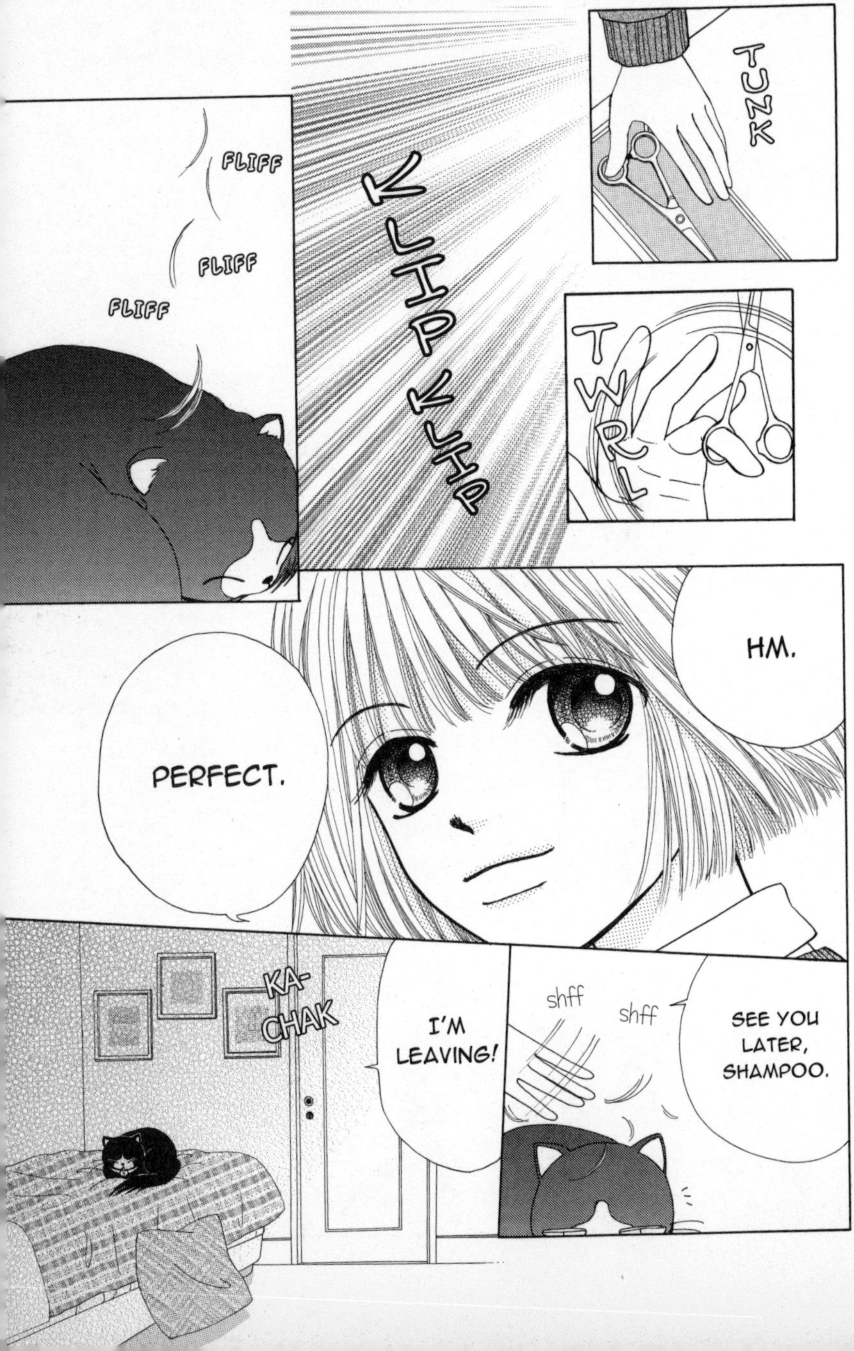
TUNK
TWRL
KLIP KLIP
FLIFF
FLIFF
FLIFF
HM.
PERFECT.
SEE YOU LATER, SHAMPOO.
shff
shff
I'M LEAVING!
KA-CHAK

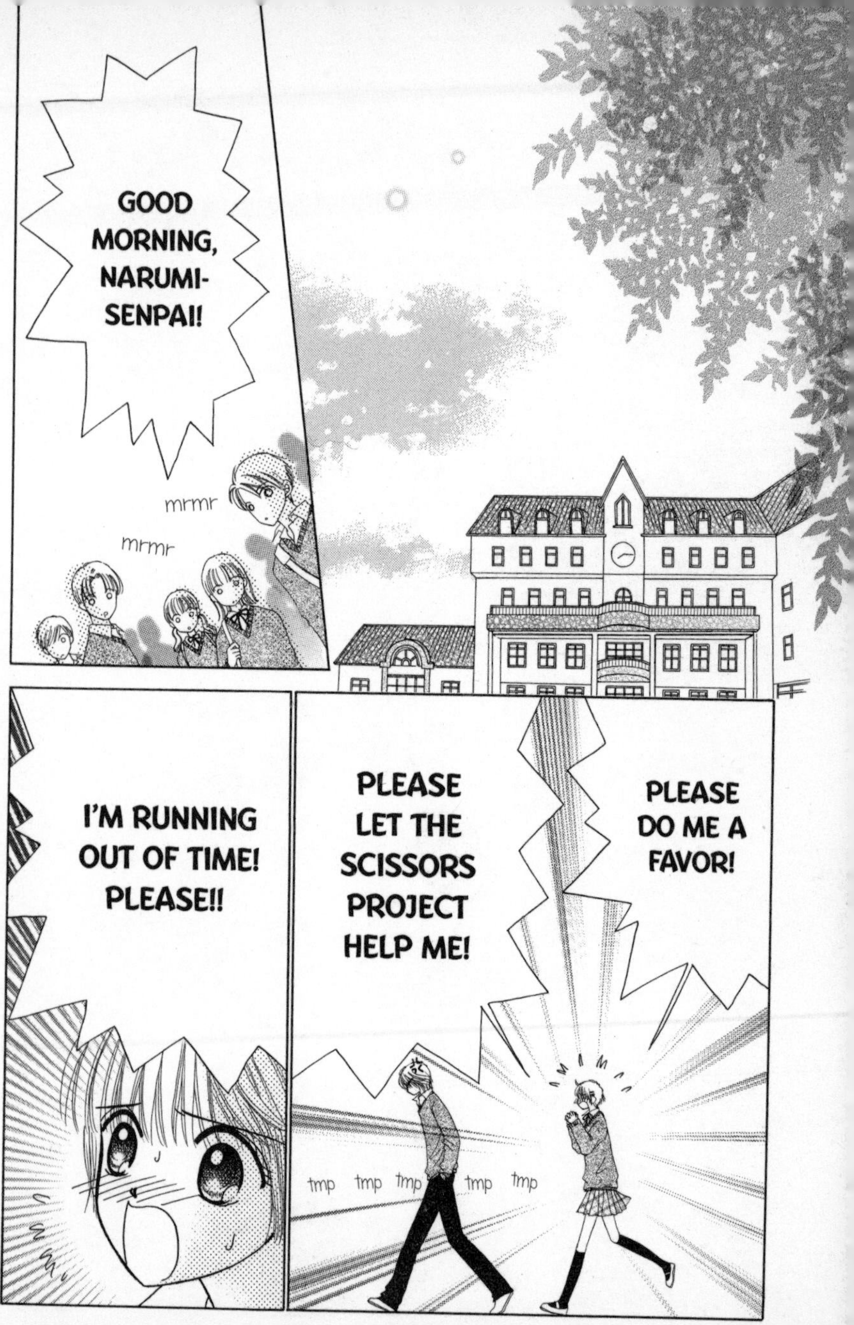
GOOD MORNING, NARUMI-SENPAI!
mrmr
mrmr
PLEASE DO ME A FAVOR!
PLEASE LET THE SCISSORS PROJECT HELP ME!
tmp tmp tmp tmp tmp
I'M RUNNING OUT OF TIME! PLEASE!!

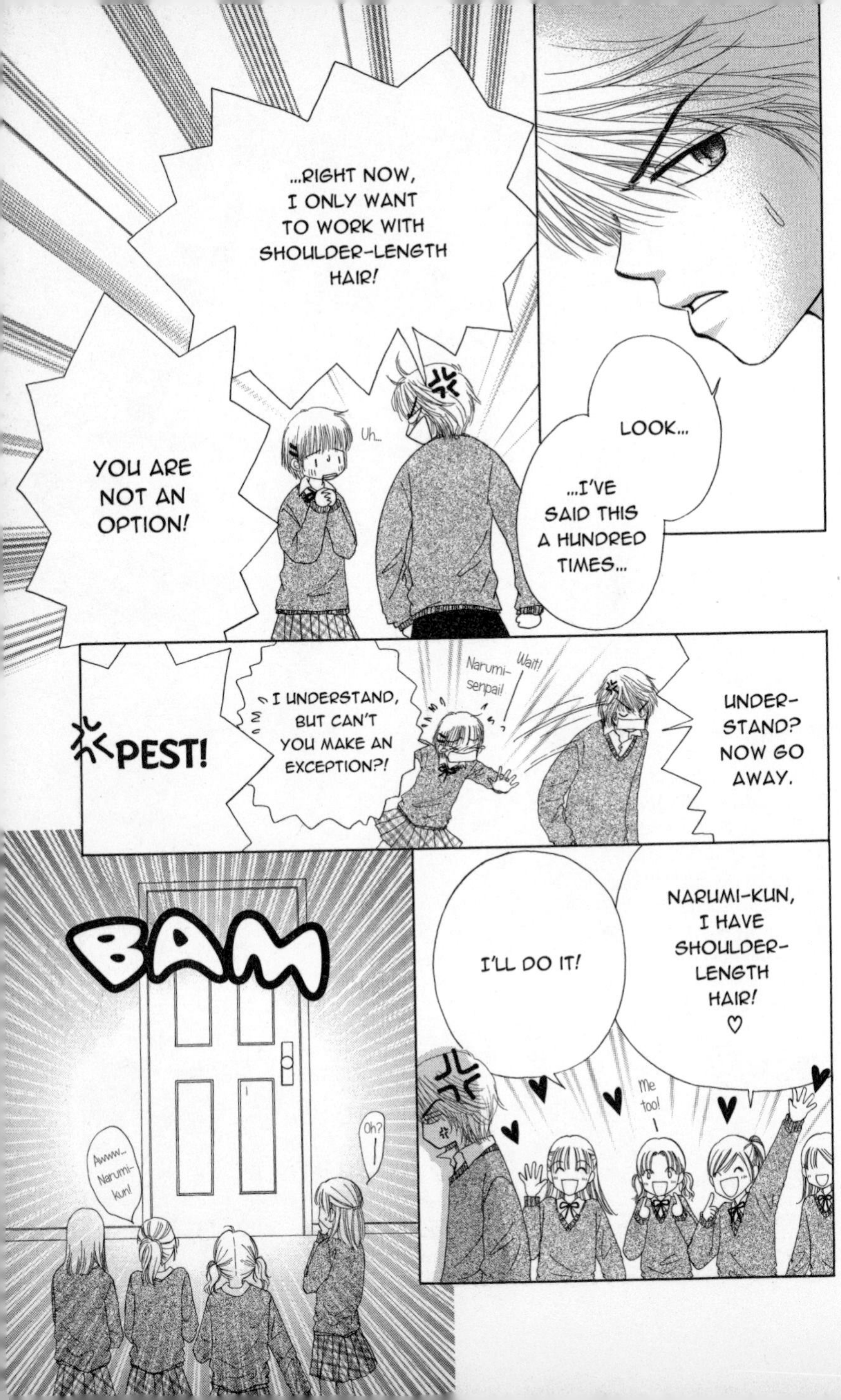

LOOK...
...I'VE SAID THIS A HUNDRED TIMES...
...RIGHT NOW, I ONLY WANT TO WORK WITH SHOULDER-LENGTH HAIR!
Uh...
YOU ARE NOT AN OPTION!
UNDER-STAND? NOW GO AWAY.
Wait!
Narumi-senpai!
I UNDERSTAND, BUT CAN'T YOU MAKE AN EXCEPTION?!
PEST!
NARUMI-KUN, I HAVE SHOULDER-LENGTH HAIR! ♡
I'LL DO IT!
Me too!
BAM
Oh?
Awww... Narumi-kun!

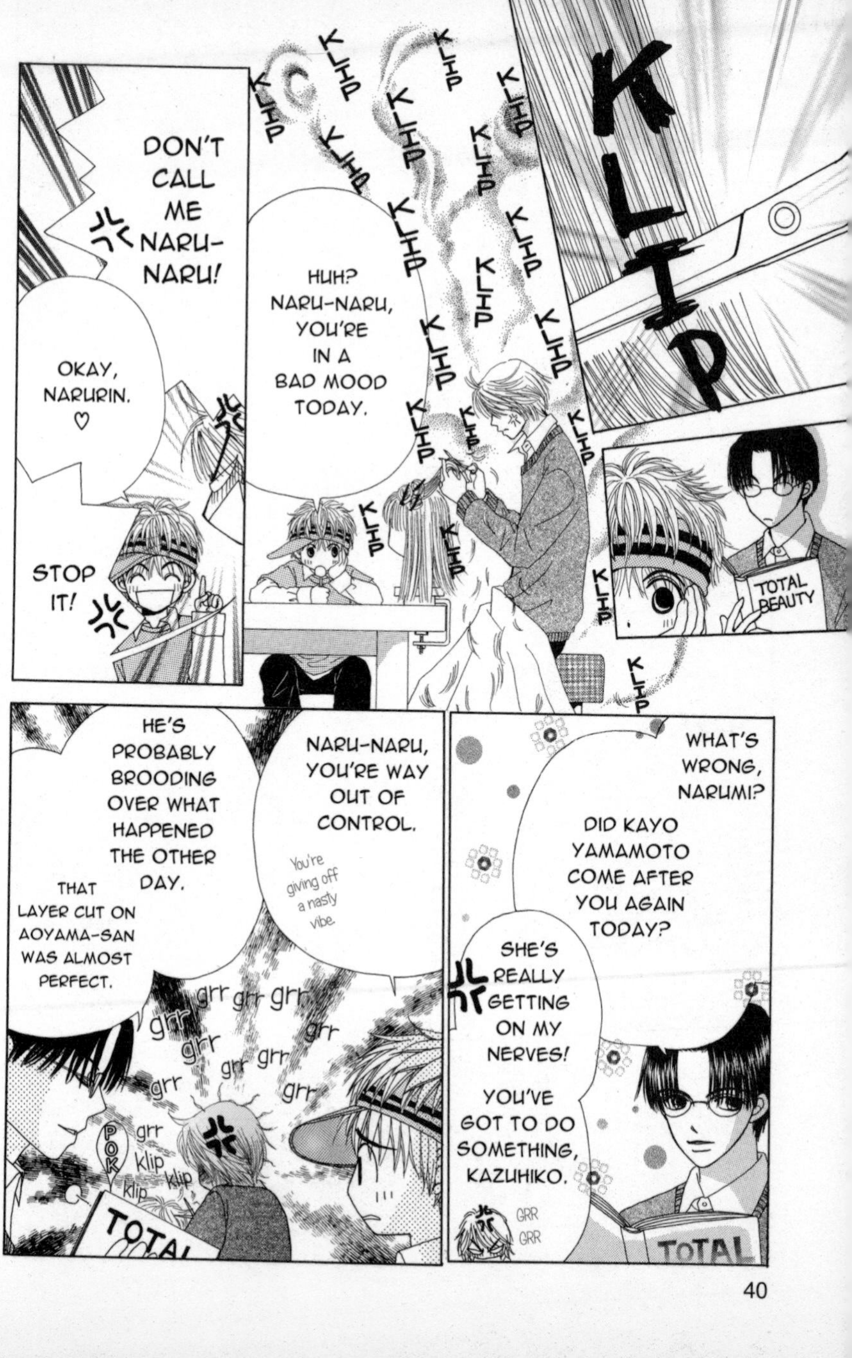
KLIP
TOTAL BEAUTY
KLIP KLIP KLIP KLIP KLIP KLIP KLIP KLIP KLIP KLIP KLIP KLIP KLIP KLIP KLIP KLIP
HUH? NARU-NARU, YOU'RE IN A BAD MOOD TODAY.
DON'T CALL ME NARU-NARU!
OKAY, NARURIN. ♡
STOP IT!
WHAT'S WRONG, NARUMI?
DID KAYO YAMAMOTO COME AFTER YOU AGAIN TODAY?
SHE'S REALLY GETTING ON MY NERVES!
YOU'VE GOT TO DO SOMETHING, KAZUHIKO.
GRR GRR
TOTAL
NARU-NARU, YOU'RE WAY OUT OF CONTROL.
You're giving off a nasty vibe.
HE'S PROBABLY BROODING OVER WHAT HAPPENED THE OTHER DAY.
THAT LAYER CUT ON AOYAMA-SAN WAS ALMOST PERFECT.
grr grr grr grr grr grr grr grr grr grr
POK
grr
klip klip klip
TOTAL

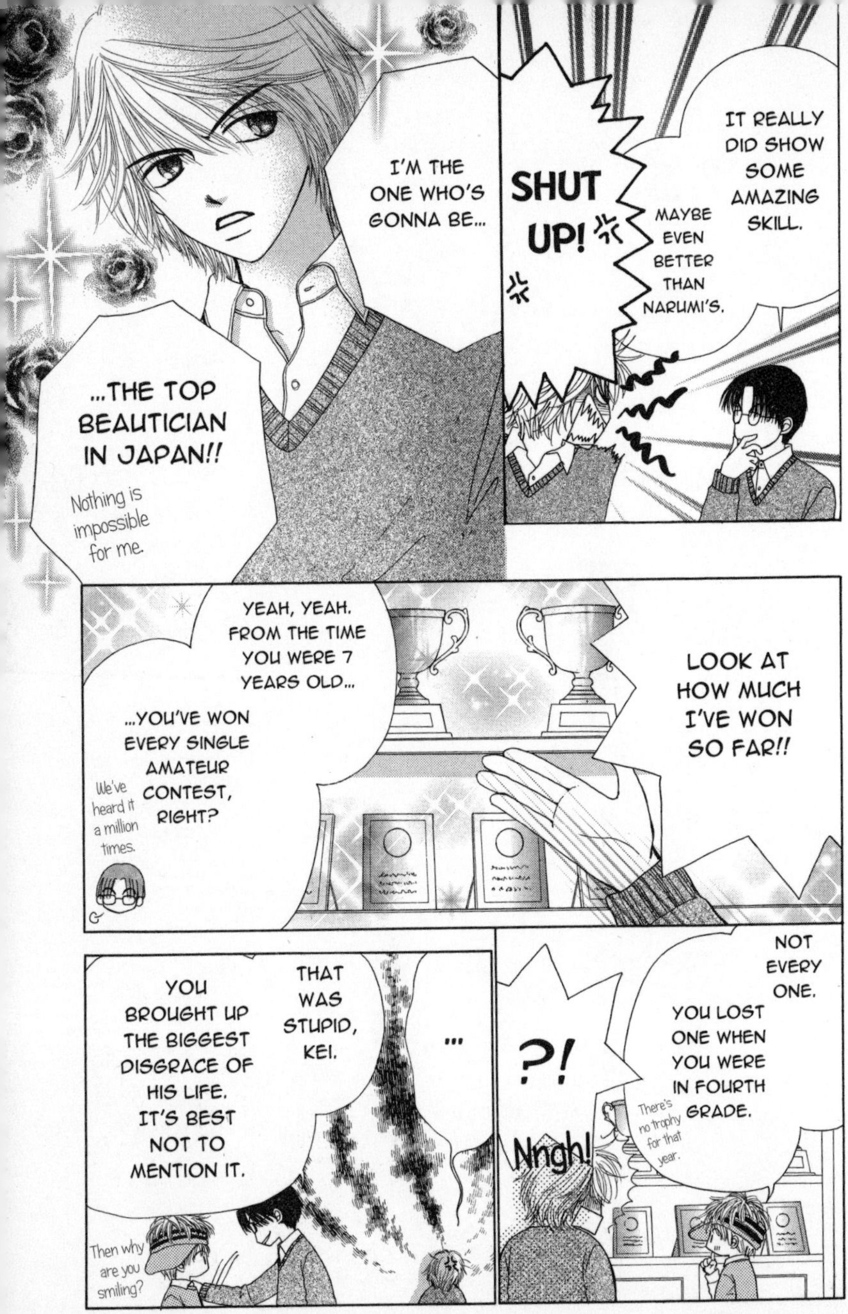
IT REALLY DID SHOW SOME AMAZING SKILL.
MAYBE EVEN BETTER THAN NARUMI'S.
SHUT UP!
I'M THE ONE WHO'S GONNA BE...
...THE TOP BEAUTICIAN IN JAPAN!!
Nothing is impossible for me.
LOOK AT HOW MUCH I'VE WON SO FAR!!
YEAH, YEAH. FROM THE TIME YOU WERE 7 YEARS OLD...
...YOU'VE WON EVERY SINGLE AMATEUR CONTEST, RIGHT?
We've heard it a million times.
NOT EVERY ONE.
YOU LOST ONE WHEN YOU WERE IN FOURTH GRADE.
There's no trophy for that year.
?!
Nngh!
...
THAT WAS STUPID, KEI.
YOU BROUGHT UP THE BIGGEST DISGRACE OF HIS LIFE. IT'S BEST NOT TO MENTION IT.
Then why are you smiling?

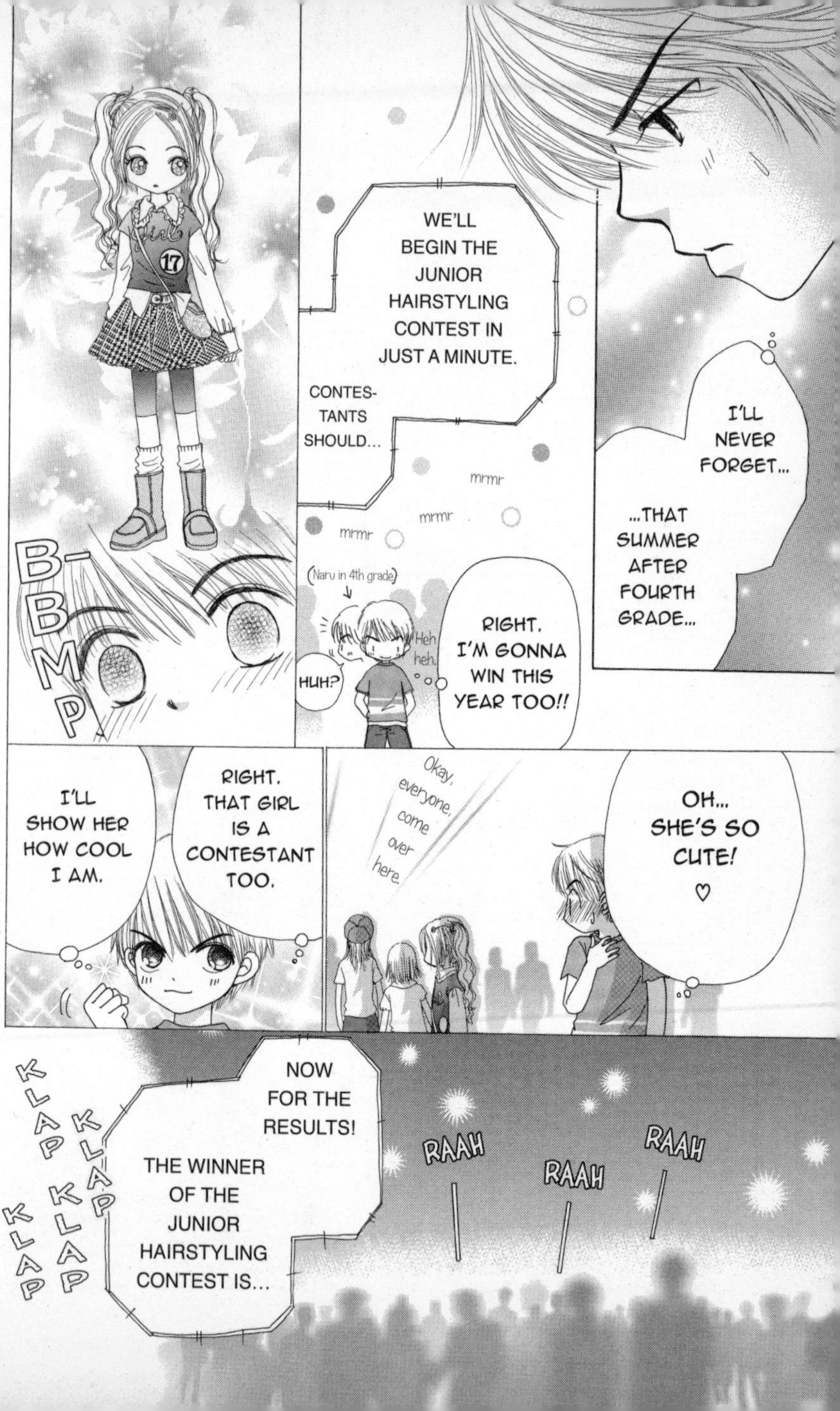
I'LL NEVER FORGET...
...THAT SUMMER AFTER FOURTH GRADE...
WE'LL BEGIN THE JUNIOR HAIRSTYLING CONTEST IN JUST A MINUTE.
CONTES- TANTS SHOULD...
mrmr
mrmr
mrmr
(Naru in 4th grade)
RIGHT. I'M GONNA WIN THIS YEAR TOO!!
Heh heh.
HUH?
B-BMP
OH... SHE'S SO CUTE! ♡
Okay, everyone, come over here.
RIGHT. THAT GIRL IS A CONTESTANT TOO.
I'LL SHOW HER HOW COOL I AM.
RAAH
RAAH
RAAH
NOW FOR THE RESULTS!
THE WINNER OF THE JUNIOR HAIRSTYLING CONTEST IS...
KLAP
KLAP
KLAP
KLAP

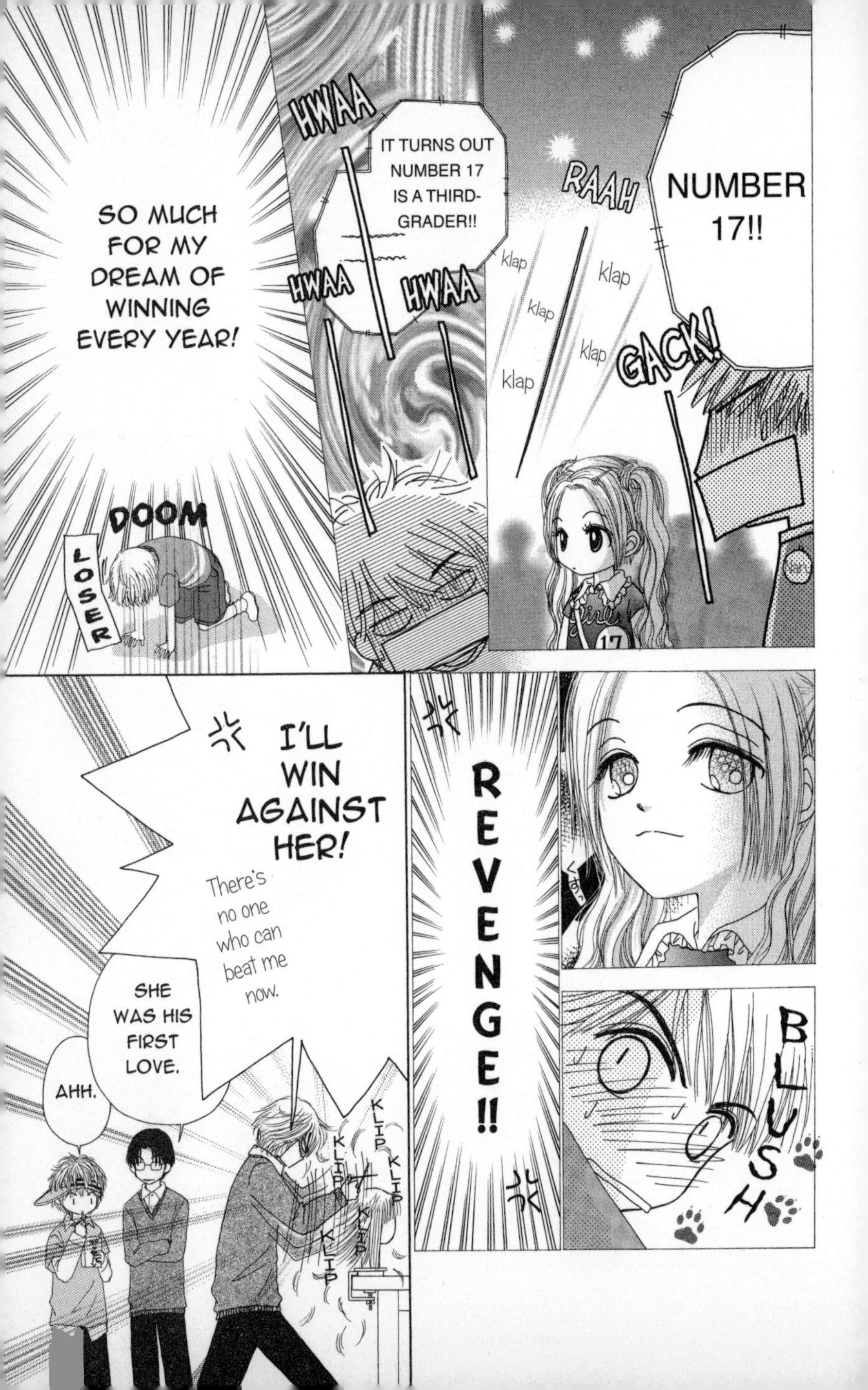
NUMBER 17!!
RAAH
klap
klap
klap
klap
klap
GACK!
HWAA
IT TURNS OUT NUMBER 17 IS A THIRD-GRADER!!
HWAA
HWAA
SO MUCH FOR MY DREAM OF WINNING EVERY YEAR!
DOOM
LOSER
BLUSH
REVENGE!!
I'LL WIN AGAINST HER!
There's no one who can beat me now.
SHE WAS HIS FIRST LOVE.
AHH.
KLIP
KLIP
KLIP
KLIP
KLIP

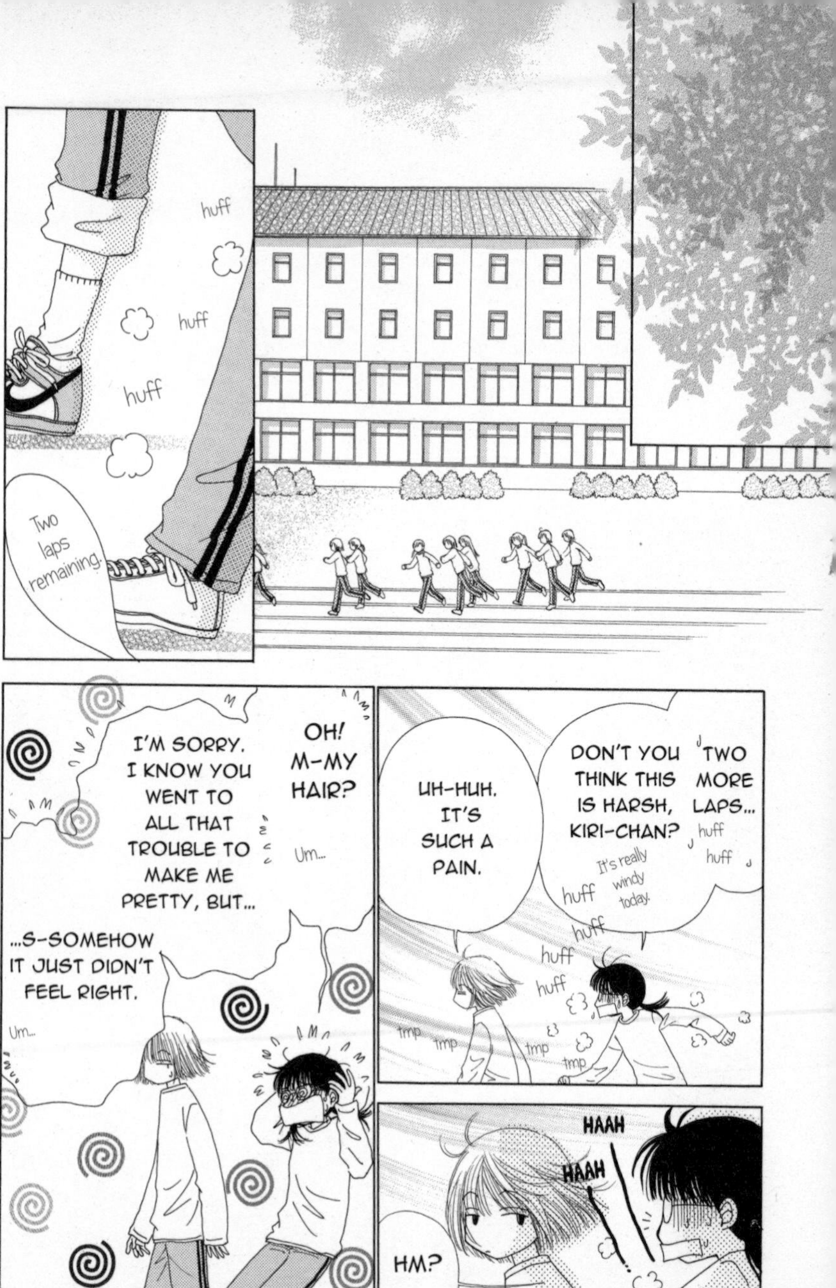
huff
huff
huff
Two laps remaining.
TWO MORE LAPS...
huff
huff
DON'T YOU THINK THIS IS HARSH, KIRI-CHAN?
It's really windy today.
UH-HUH. IT'S SUCH A PAIN.
huff
huff
huff
huff
tmp
tmp
tmp
tmp
HAAH
HAAH
HM?
OH! M-MY HAIR?
Um...
I'M SORRY. I KNOW YOU WENT TO ALL THAT TROUBLE TO MAKE ME PRETTY, BUT...
...S-SOMEHOW IT JUST DIDN'T FEEL RIGHT.
Um...

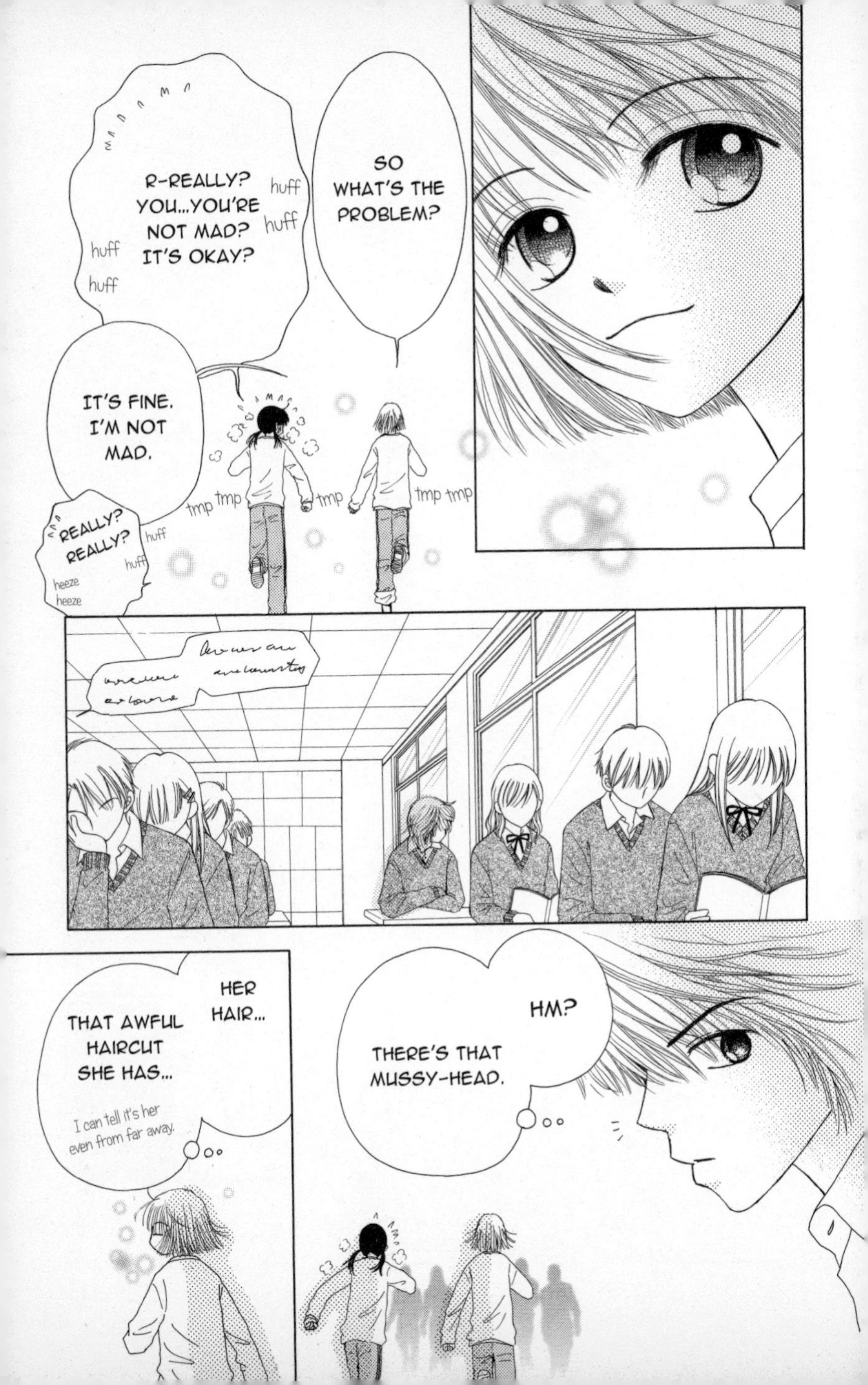
SO WHAT'S THE PROBLEM?
R-REALLY? YOU...YOU'RE NOT MAD? IT'S OKAY?
huff huff
huff huff
IT'S FINE. I'M NOT MAD.
REALLY? REALLY?
huff huff
heeze heeze
tmp tmp
tmp
tmp tmp
HM?
THERE'S THAT MUSSY-HEAD.
HER HAIR...
THAT AWFUL HAIRCUT SHE HAS...
I can tell it's her even from far away.

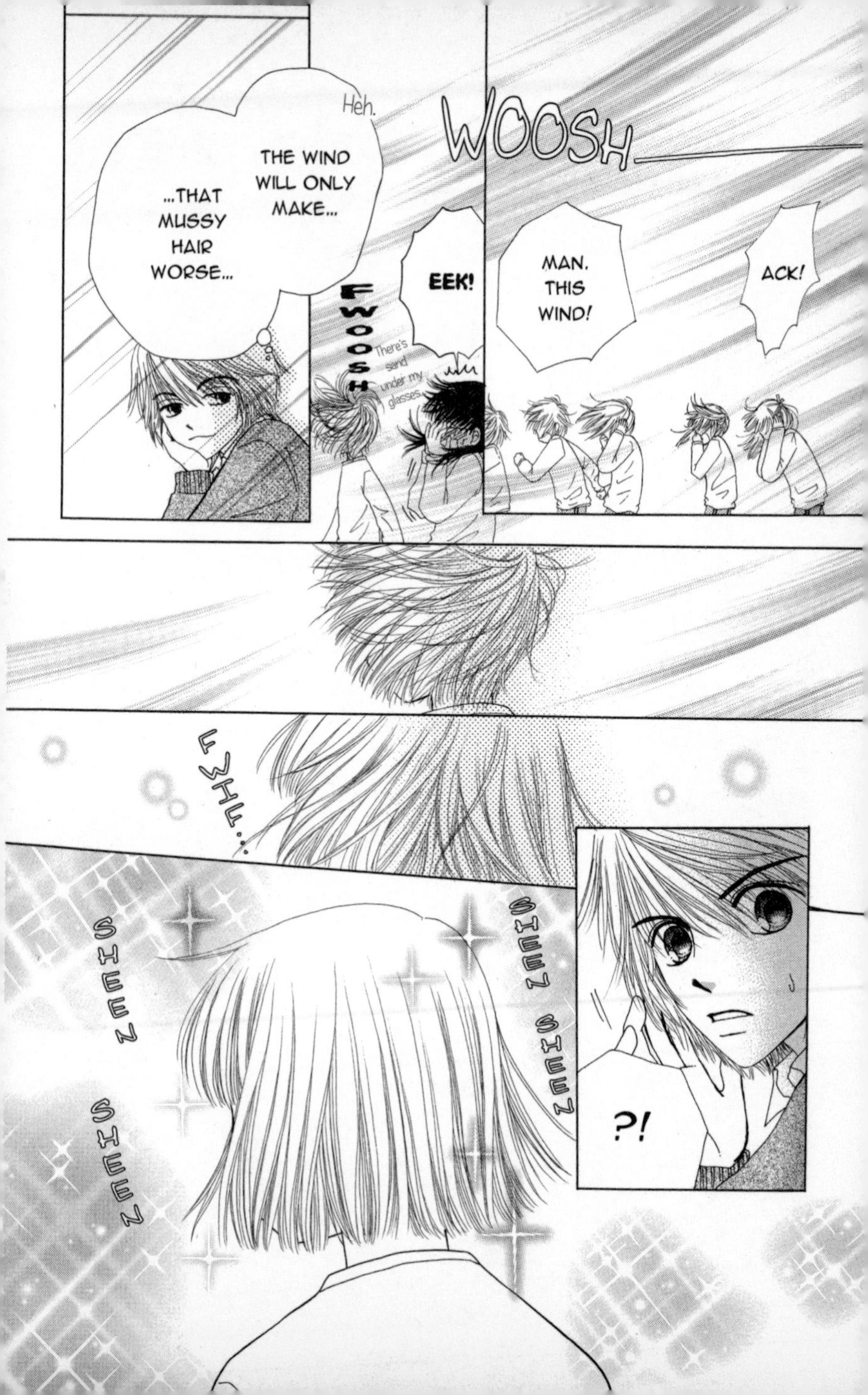
WOOSH
MAN. THIS WIND!
ACK!
EEK!
FWOOSH
There's sand under my glasses.
Heh.
THE WIND WILL ONLY MAKE... ...THAT MUSSY HAIR WORSE...
FWIF...
?!
SHEEN SHEEN SHEEN
SHEEN
SHEEN

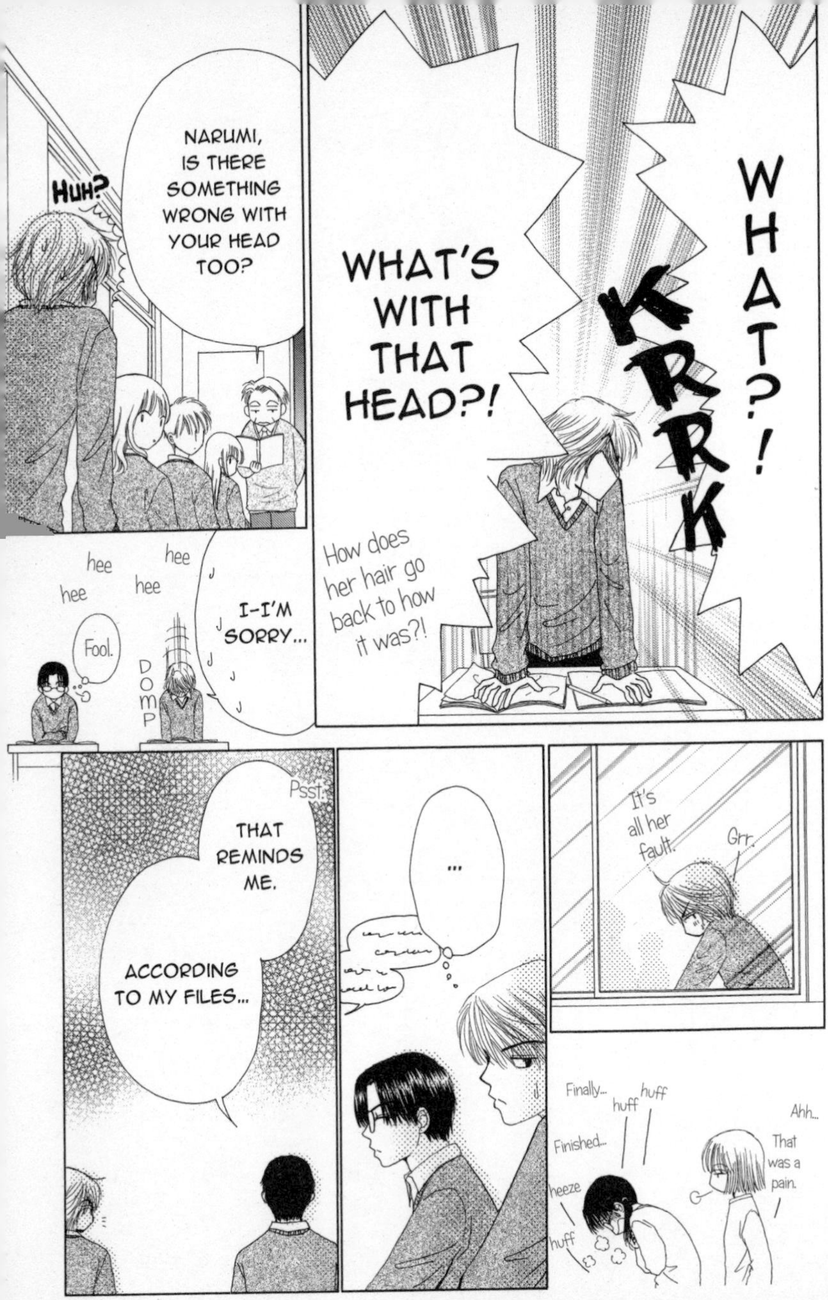
WHAT?!
KRRK
WHAT'S WITH THAT HEAD?!
How does her hair go back to how it was?!
HUH?
NARUMI, IS THERE SOMETHING WRONG WITH YOUR HEAD TOO?
I-I'M SORRY...
hee hee
hee hee
DOMP
Fool.
It's all her fault.
Grr.
...
Psst.
THAT REMINDS ME.
ACCORDING TO MY FILES...
Ahh... That was a pain.
Finally... huff huff
Finished...
heeze huff

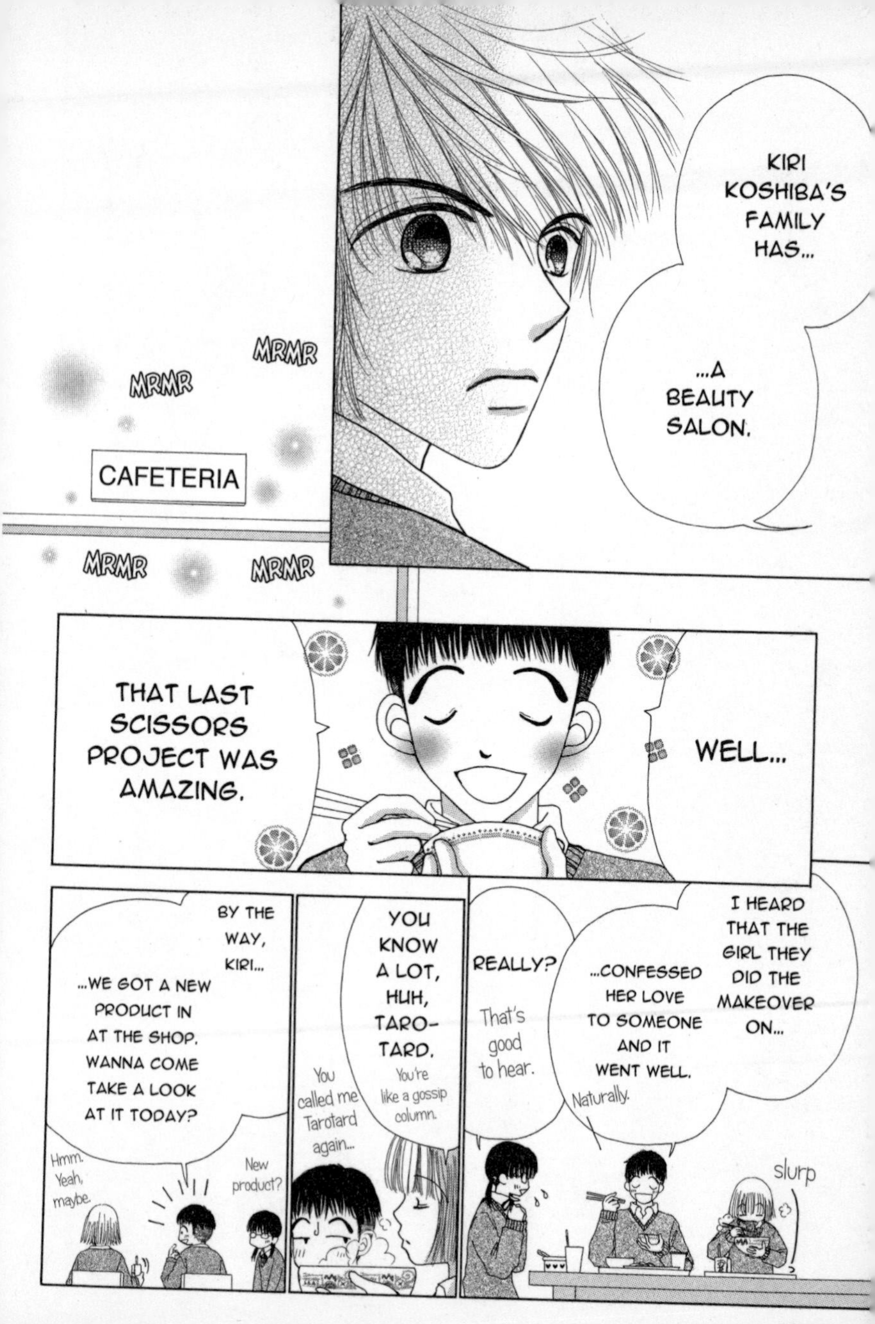
KIRI KOSHIBA'S FAMILY HAS...
...A BEAUTY SALON.
MRMR
MRMR
CAFETERIA
MRMR
MRMR
WELL...
THAT LAST SCISSORS PROJECT WAS AMAZING.
I HEARD THAT THE GIRL THEY DID THE MAKEOVER ON...
...CONFESSED HER LOVE TO SOMEONE AND IT WENT WELL.
Naturally.
REALLY?
That's good to hear.
slurp
YOU KNOW A LOT, HUH, TARO-TARD.
You're like a gossip column.
You called me Tarotard again...
BY THE WAY, KIRI...
...WE GOT A NEW PRODUCT IN AT THE SHOP. WANNA COME TAKE A LOOK AT IT TODAY?
New product?
Hmm. Yeah, maybe.

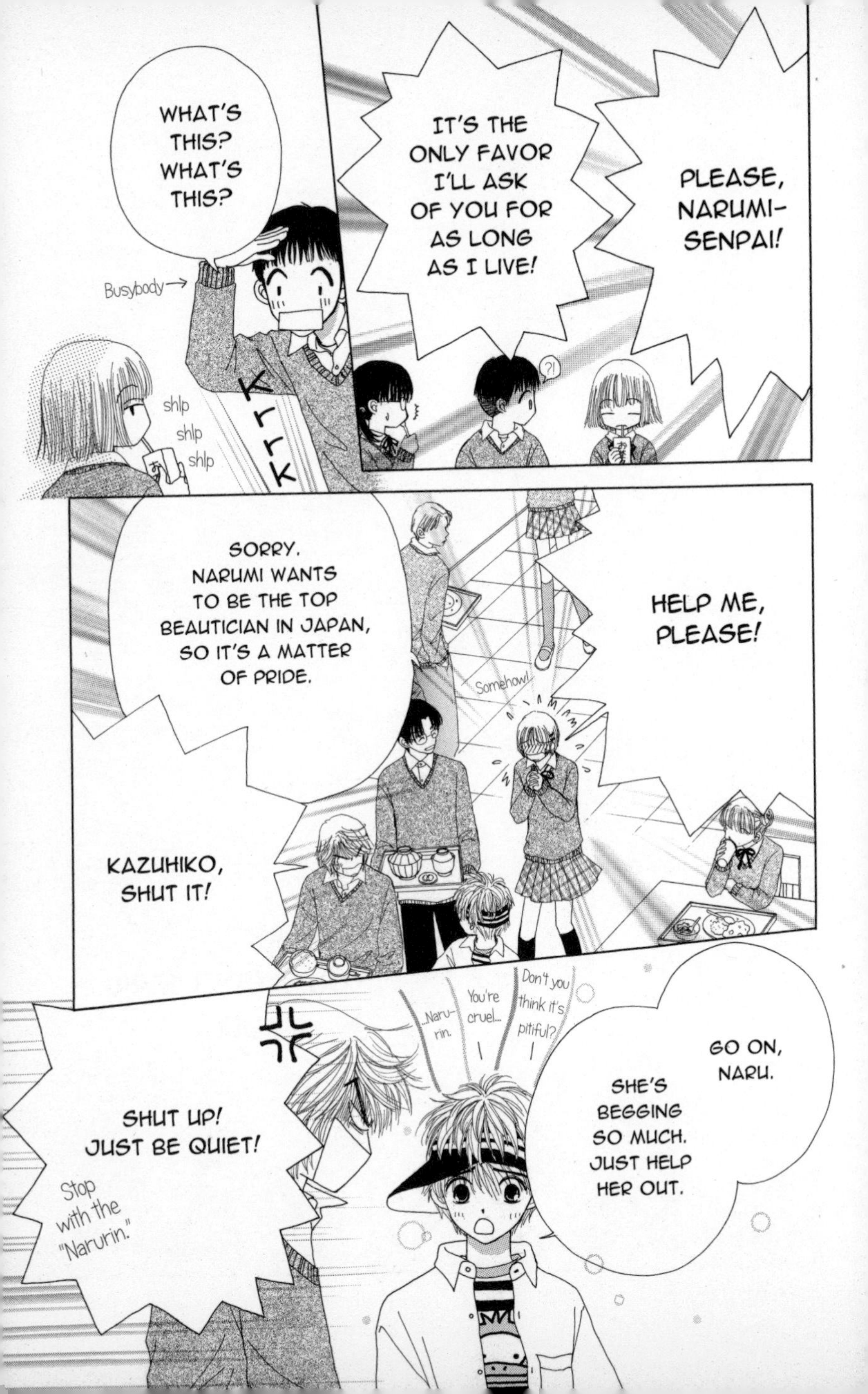
PLEASE, NARUMI-SENPAI!
IT'S THE ONLY FAVOR I'LL ASK OF YOU FOR AS LONG AS I LIVE!
?!
WHAT'S THIS? WHAT'S THIS?
Busybody→
Krrk
shlp shlp shlp
HELP ME, PLEASE!
Somehow!
SORRY. NARUMI WANTS TO BE THE TOP BEAUTICIAN IN JAPAN, SO IT'S A MATTER OF PRIDE.
KAZUHIKO, SHUT IT!
GO ON, NARU.
SHE'S BEGGING SO MUCH. JUST HELP HER OUT.
Don't you think it's pitiful?
You're cruel...
...Naru-rin.
SHUT UP! JUST BE QUIET!
Stop with the "Narurin."

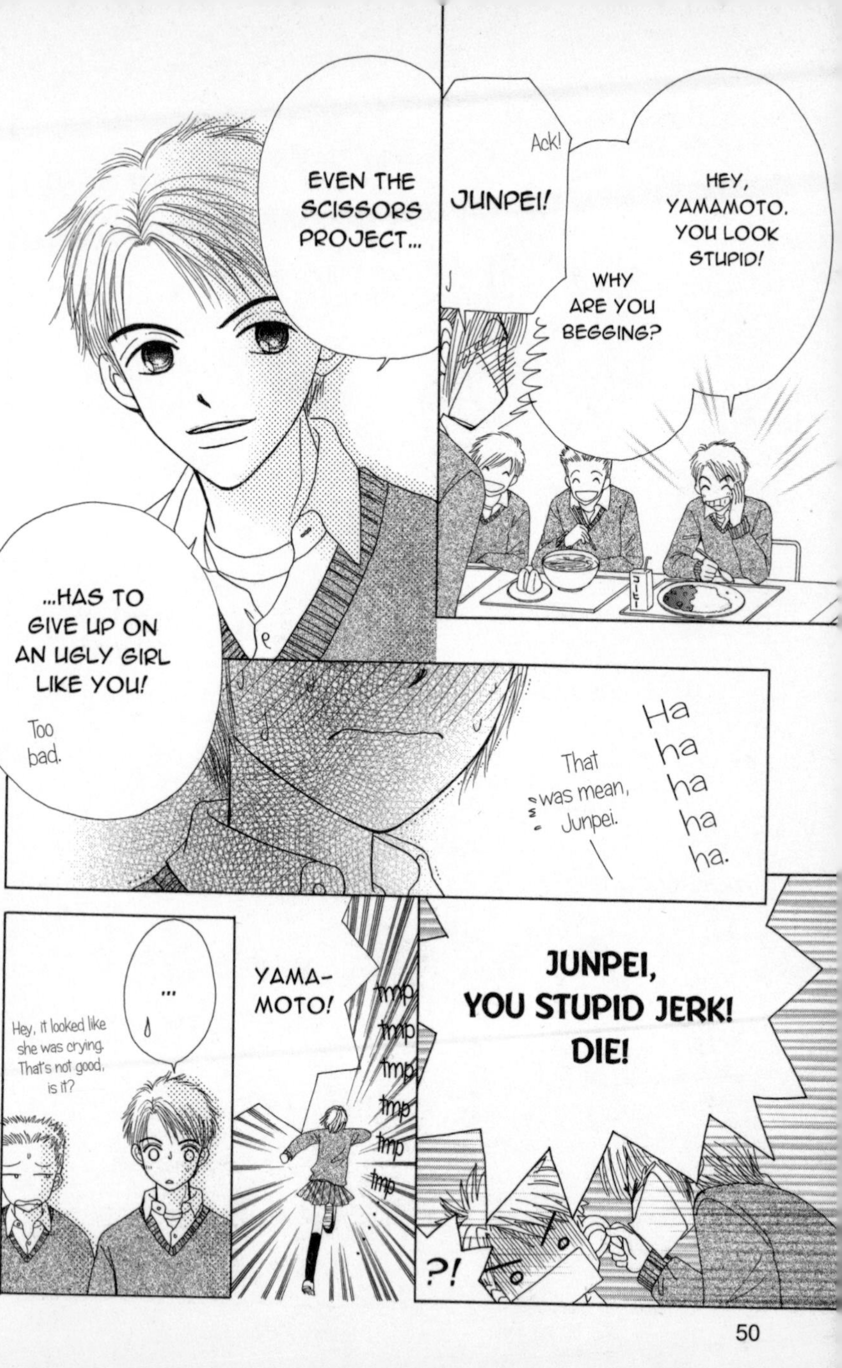
HEY, YAMAMOTO. YOU LOOK STUPID!
Ack!
JUNPEI!
WHY ARE YOU BEGGING?
EVEN THE SCISSORS PROJECT...
...HAS TO GIVE UP ON AN UGLY GIRL LIKE YOU!
Too bad.
Ha ha ha ha ha.
That was mean, Junpei.
JUNPEI, YOU STUPID JERK! DIE!
?!
YAMA-MOTO!
tmp tmp tmp tmp tmp tmp
...
Hey, it looked like she was crying. That's not good, is it?

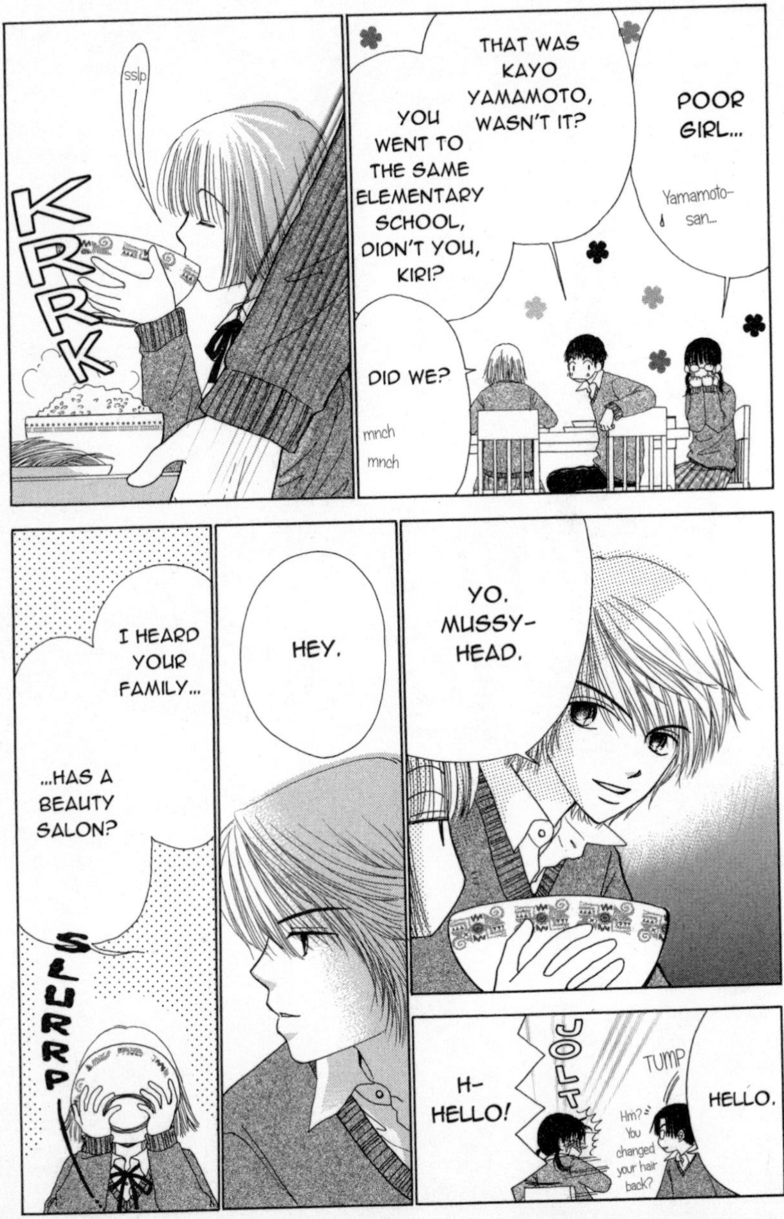
POOR GIRL...
Yamamoto-san...
THAT WAS KAYO YAMAMOTO, WASN'T IT?
YOU WENT TO THE SAME ELEMENTARY SCHOOL, DIDN'T YOU, KIRI?
DID WE?
mnch mnch
sslp
KRRK
YO. MUSSY-HEAD.
HELLO.
TUMP
Hm? You changed your hair back?
JOLT
H- HELLO!
HEY.
I HEARD YOUR FAMILY...
...HAS A BEAUTY SALON?
SLURRP

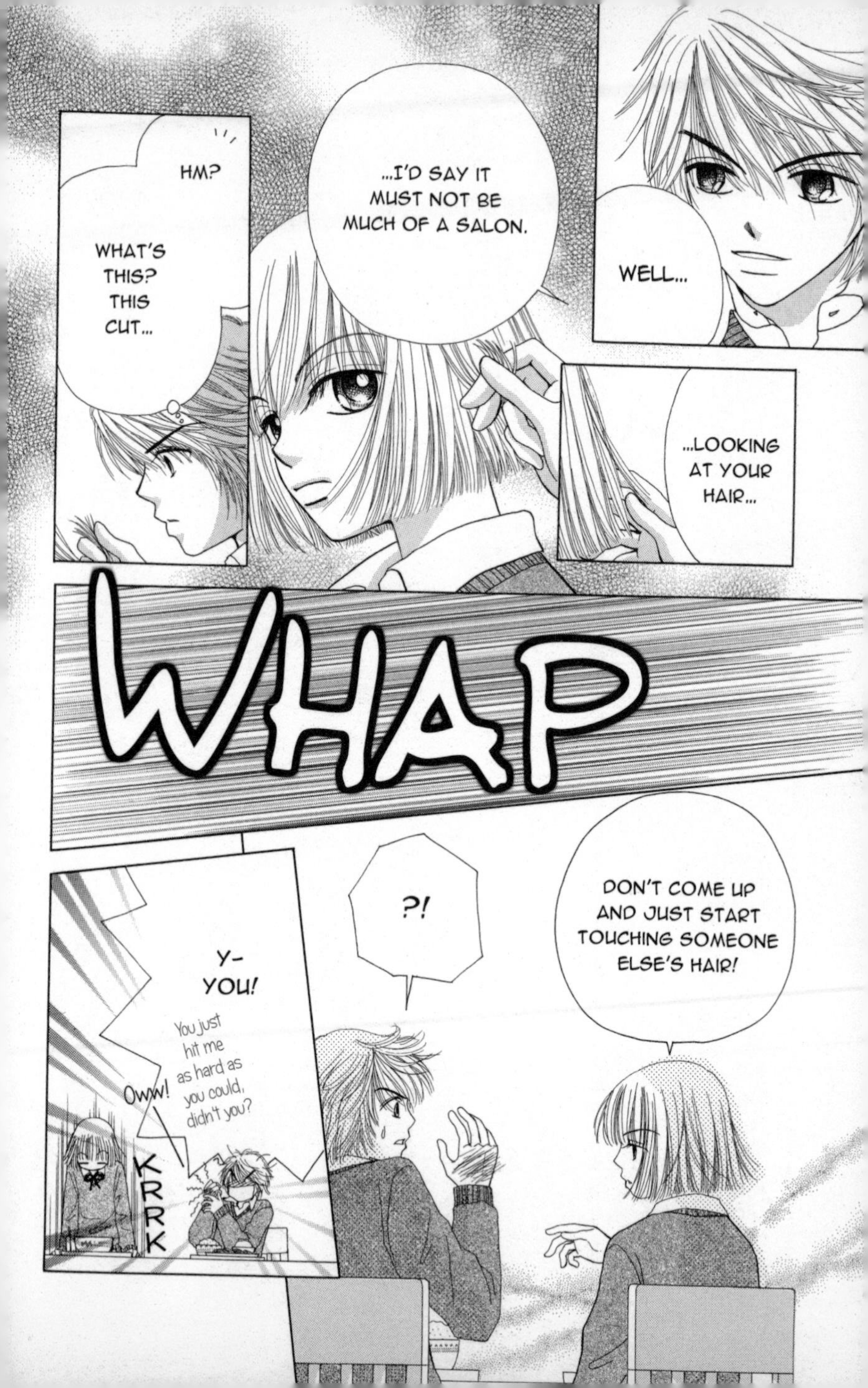
WELL...
...LOOKING AT YOUR HAIR...
...I'D SAY IT MUST NOT BE MUCH OF A SALON.
HM?
WHAT'S THIS? THIS CUT...
WHAP
DON'T COME UP AND JUST START TOUCHING SOMEONE ELSE'S HAIR!
?!
Y- YOU!
You just hit me as hard as you could, didn't you?
Oww!
KRRK

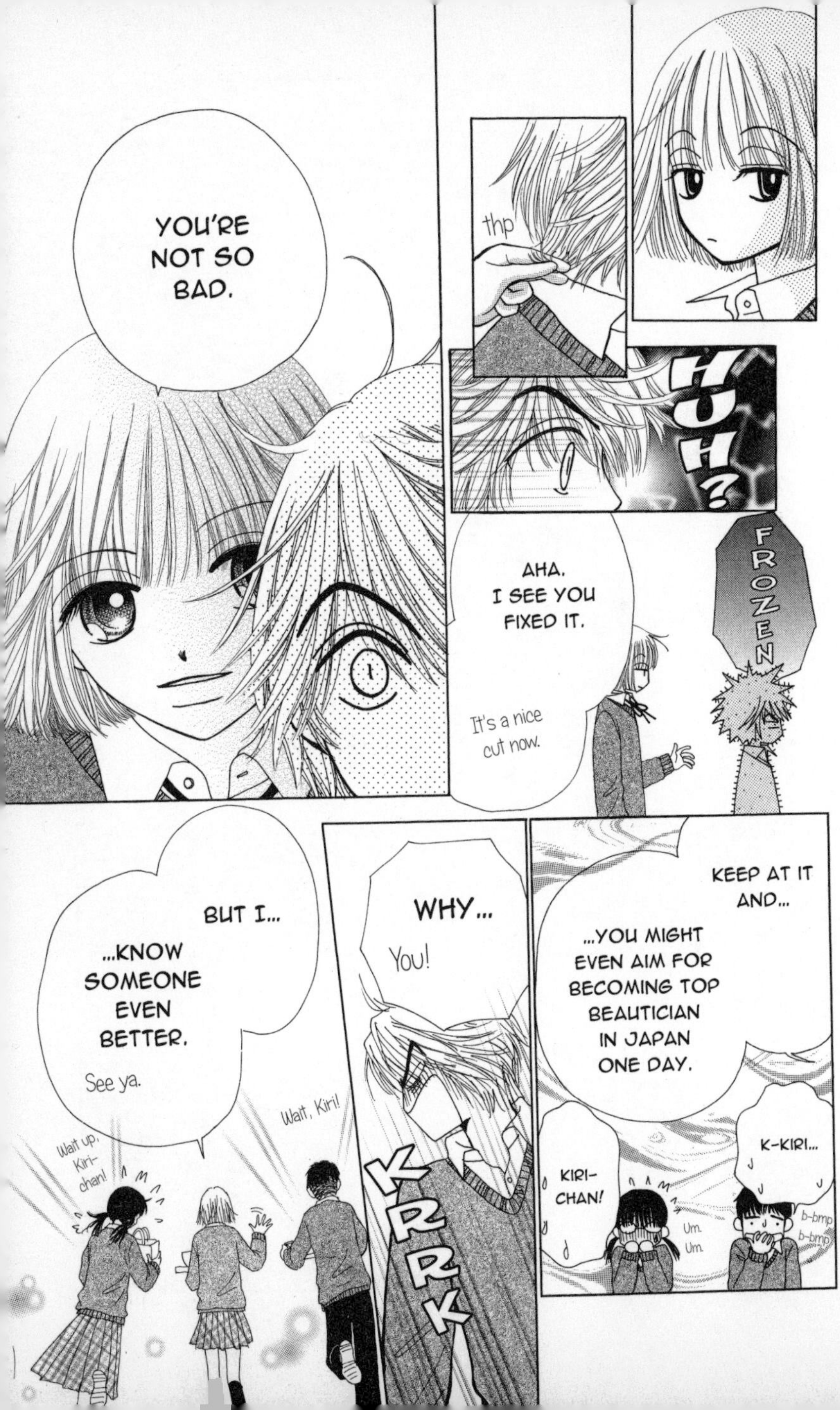
thp
HUH?
FROZEN
AHA. I SEE YOU FIXED IT.
It's a nice cut now.
YOU'RE NOT SO BAD.
KEEP AT IT AND...
...YOU MIGHT EVEN AIM FOR BECOMING TOP BEAUTICIAN IN JAPAN ONE DAY.
K-KIRI...
b-bmp b-bmp
KIRI-CHAN!
Um. Um.
WHY...
You!
KRRK
BUT I...
...KNOW SOMEONE EVEN BETTER.
See ya.
Wait, Kiri!
Wait up, Kiri-chan!

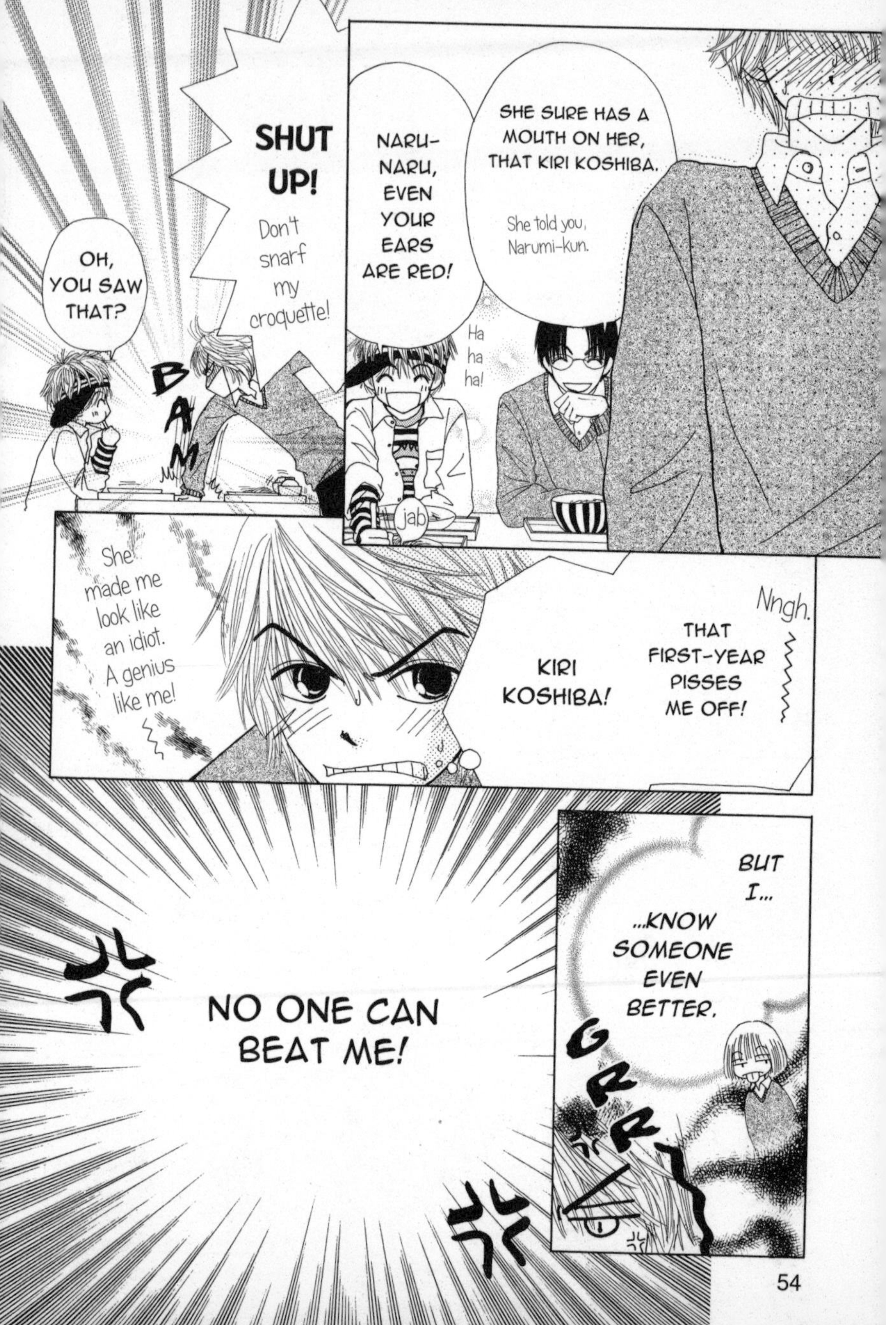
SHE SURE HAS A MOUTH ON HER, THAT KIRI KOSHIBA.
She told you, Narumi-kun.
NARU-NARU, EVEN YOUR EARS ARE RED!
Ha ha ha!
jab
SHUT UP!
Don't snarf my croquette!
BAM
OH, YOU SAW THAT?
Nngh.
THAT FIRST-YEAR PISSES ME OFF!
KIRI KOSHIBA!
She made me look like an idiot. A genius like me!
BUT I...
...KNOW SOMEONE EVEN BETTER.
GRR
NO ONE CAN BEAT ME!

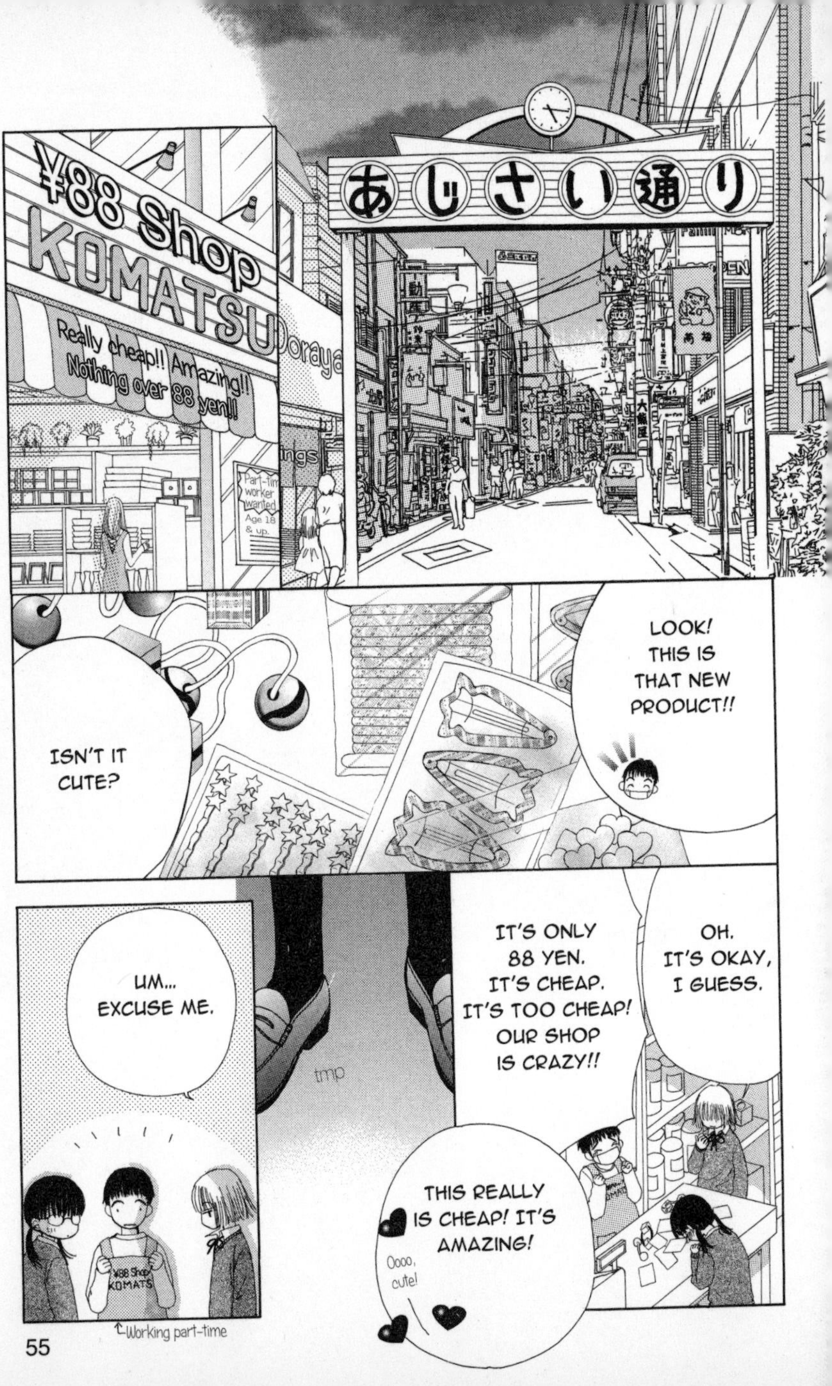
あじさい通り
¥88 Shop
KOMATSU
Really cheap!! Amazing!! Nothing over 88 yen!!
Part-time worker wanted
Age 18 & up.
LOOK! THIS IS THAT NEW PRODUCT!!
ISN'T IT CUTE?
OH. IT'S OKAY, I GUESS.
IT'S ONLY 88 YEN. IT'S CHEAP. IT'S TOO CHEAP! OUR SHOP IS CRAZY!!
THIS REALLY IS CHEAP! IT'S AMAZING!
Oooo, cute!
tmp
UM... EXCUSE ME.
¥88 Shop KOMATS
Working part-time

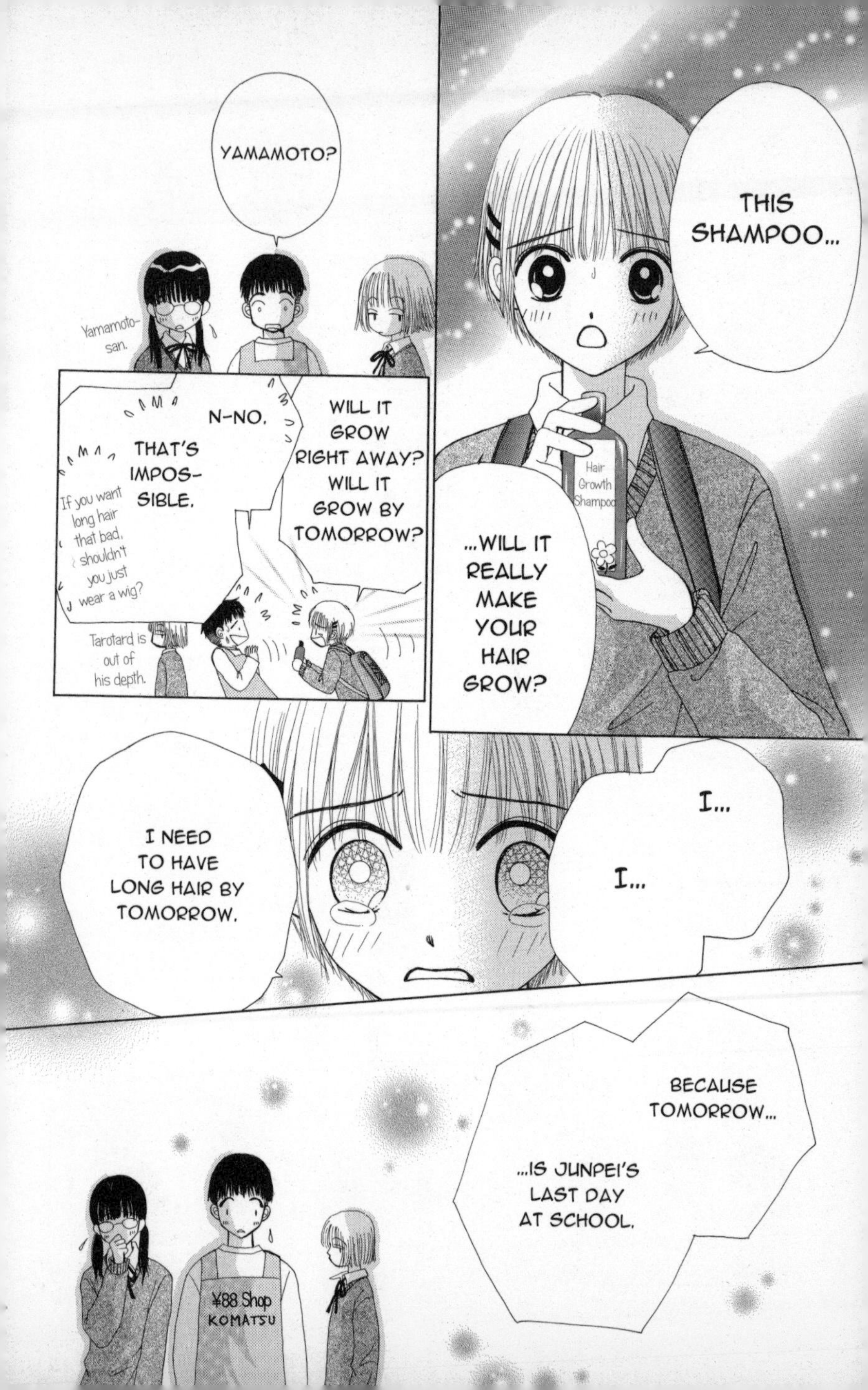
THIS SHAMPOO...
Hair Growth Shampoo
...WILL IT REALLY MAKE YOUR HAIR GROW?
YAMAMOTO?
Yamamoto-san.
WILL IT GROW RIGHT AWAY? WILL IT GROW BY TOMORROW?
N-NO. THAT'S IMPOS-SIBLE.
If you want long hair that bad, shouldn't you just wear a wig?
Tarotard is out of his depth.
I...
I...
I NEED TO HAVE LONG HAIR BY TOMORROW.
BECAUSE TOMORROW...
...IS JUNPEI'S LAST DAY AT SCHOOL.
¥88 Shop
KOMATSU

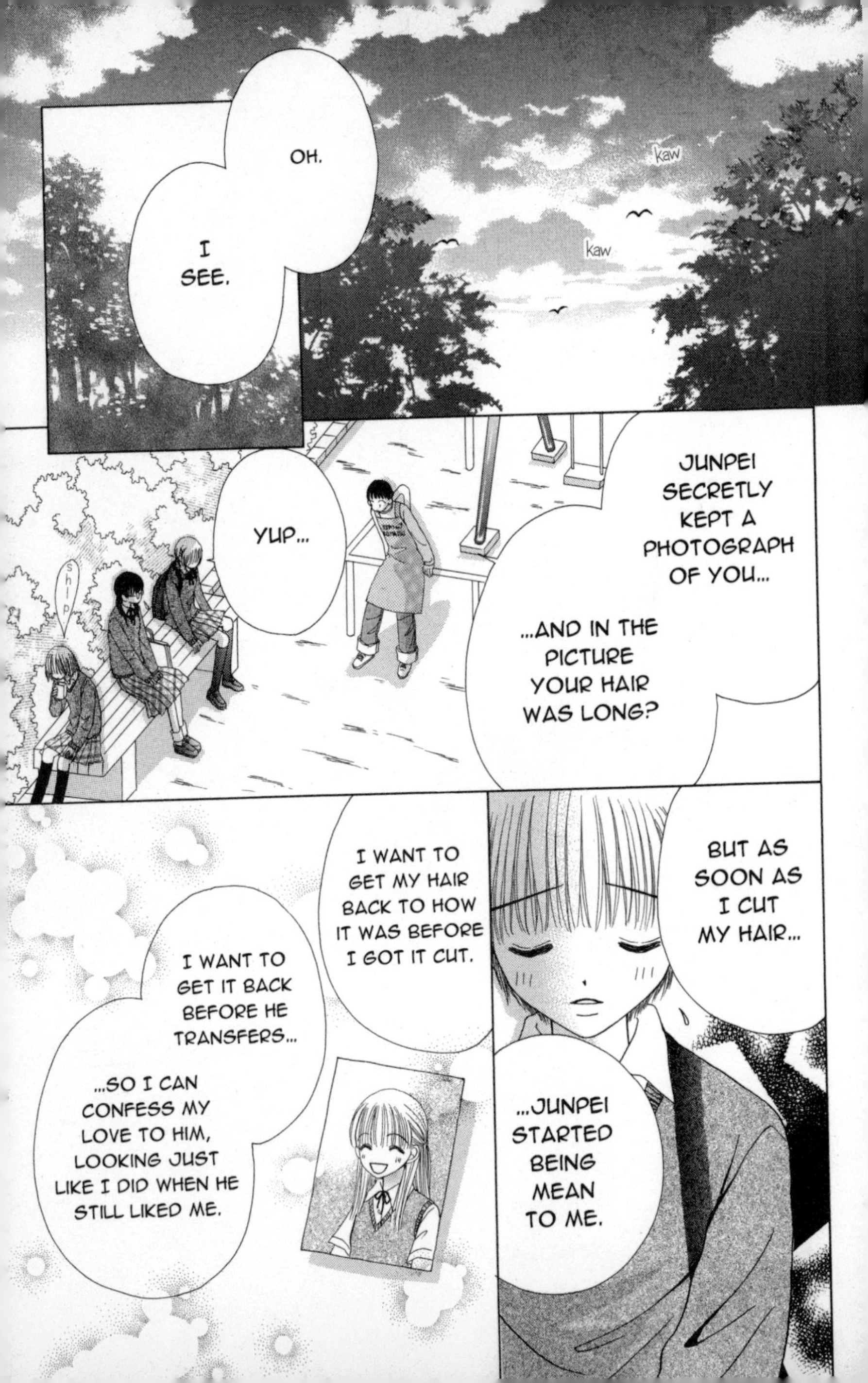
kaw
kaw
OH.
I SEE.
JUNPEI SECRETLY KEPT A PHOTOGRAPH OF YOU...
...AND IN THE PICTURE YOUR HAIR WAS LONG?
YUP...
shlp
BUT AS SOON AS I CUT MY HAIR...
...JUNPEI STARTED BEING MEAN TO ME.
I WANT TO GET MY HAIR BACK TO HOW IT WAS BEFORE I GOT IT CUT.
I WANT TO GET IT BACK BEFORE HE TRANSFERS...
...SO I CAN CONFESS MY LOVE TO HIM, LOOKING JUST LIKE I DID WHEN HE STILL LIKED ME.

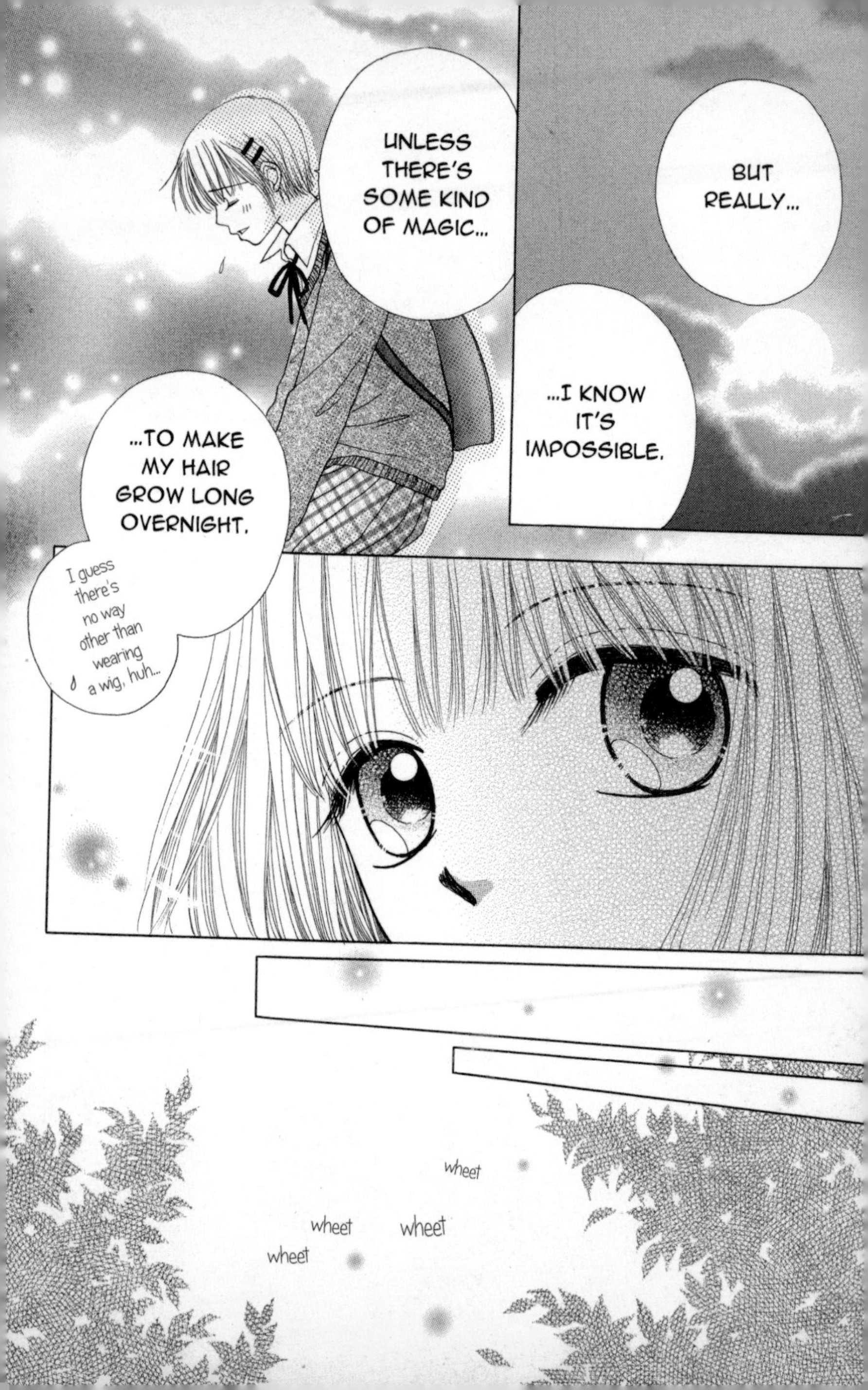
BUT REALLY...
...I KNOW IT'S IMPOSSIBLE.
UNLESS THERE'S SOME KIND OF MAGIC...
...TO MAKE MY HAIR GROW LONG OVERNIGHT.
I guess there's no way other than wearing a wig, huh...
wheet
wheet
wheet
wheet

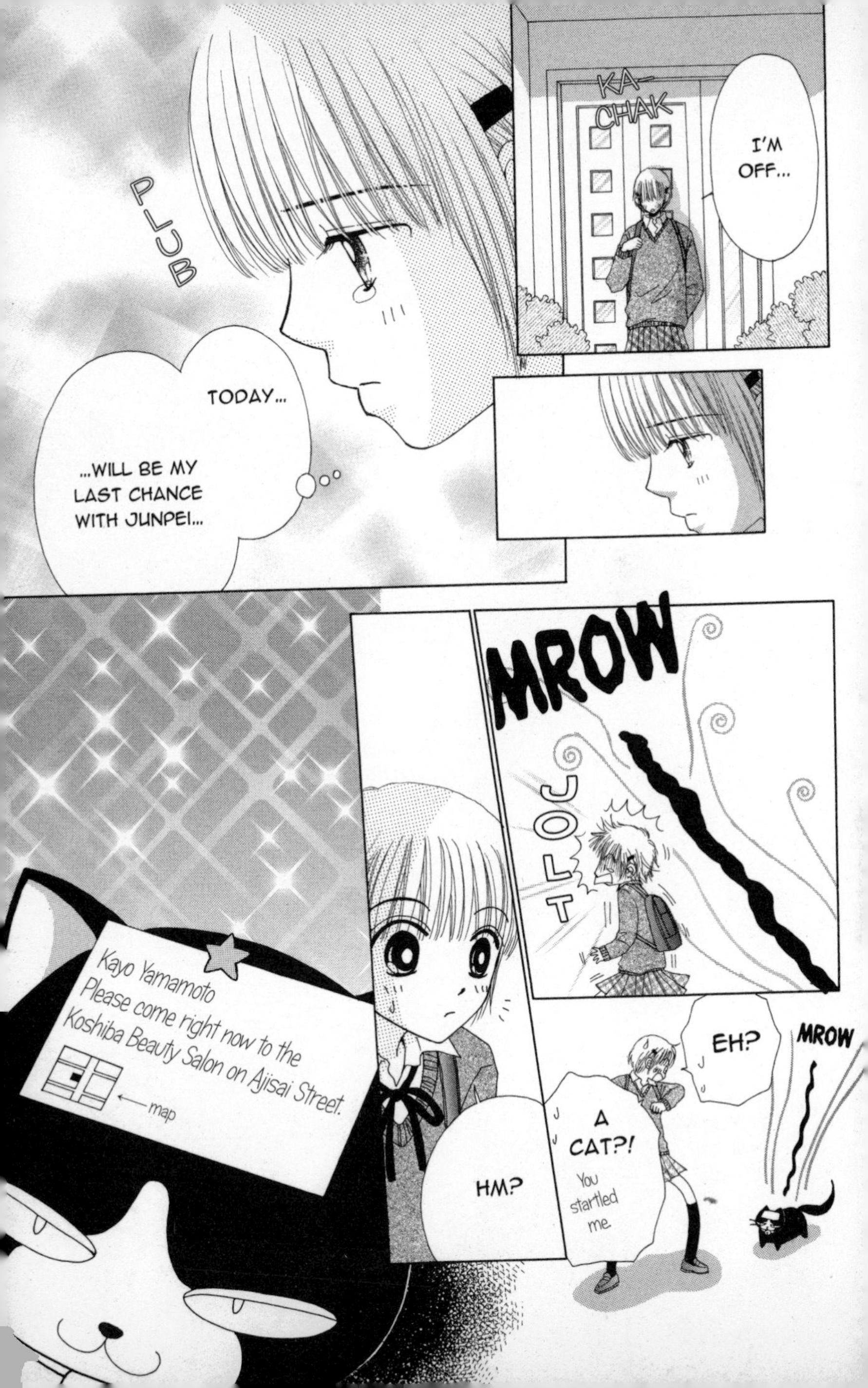
KA-CHAK
I'M OFF...
PLUB
TODAY...
...WILL BE MY LAST CHANCE WITH JUNPEI...
MROW
JOLT
Kayo Yamamoto
Please come right now to the Koshiba Beauty Salon on Ajisai Street.
map
EH?
MROW
A CAT?!
You startled me.
HM?

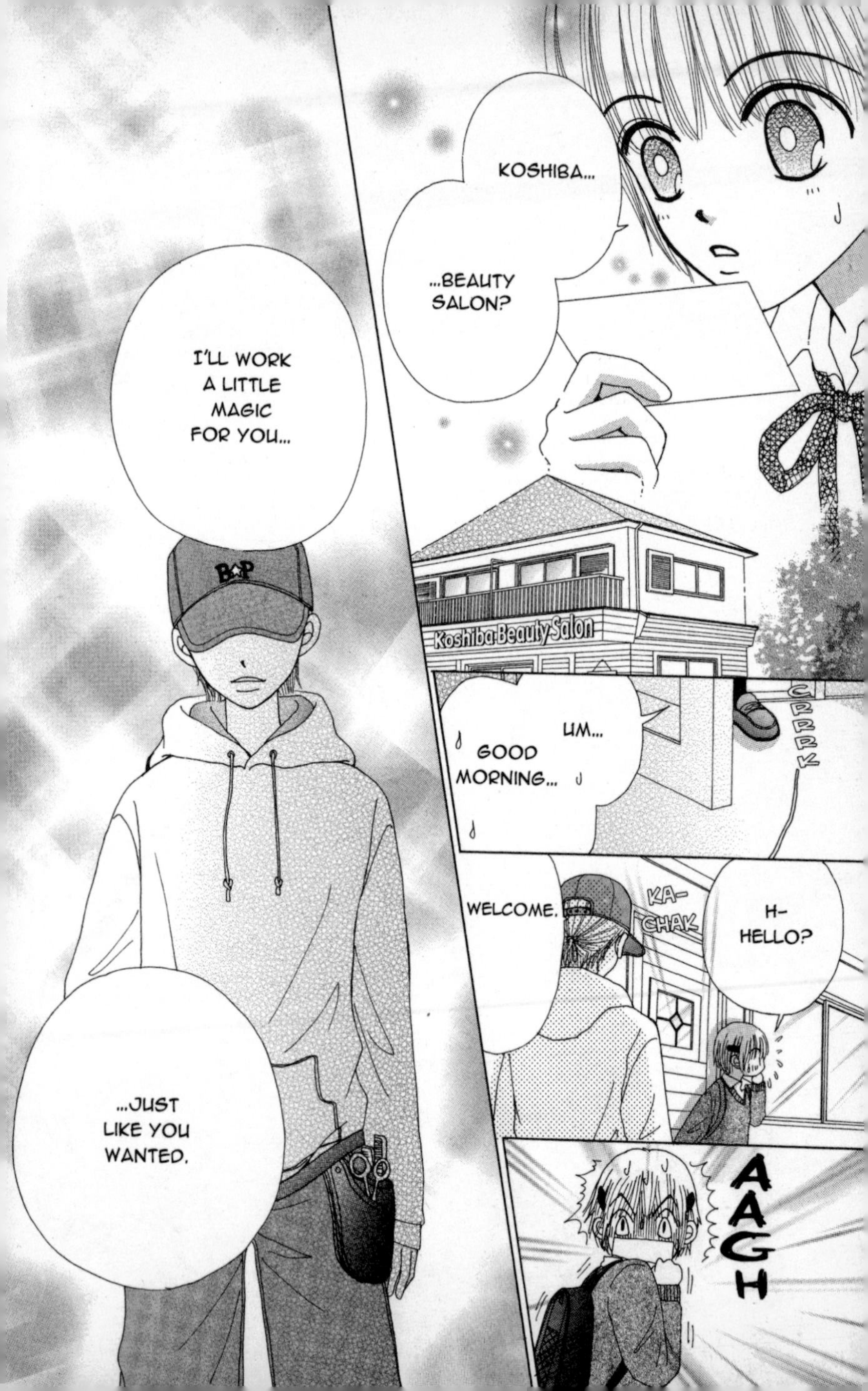
KOSHIBA...
...BEAUTY SALON?
Koshiba Beauty Salon
CRRRK
UM...
GOOD MORNING...
H-HELLO?
KA-CHAK
WELCOME.
AAGH
I'LL WORK A LITTLE MAGIC FOR YOU...
...JUST LIKE YOU WANTED.

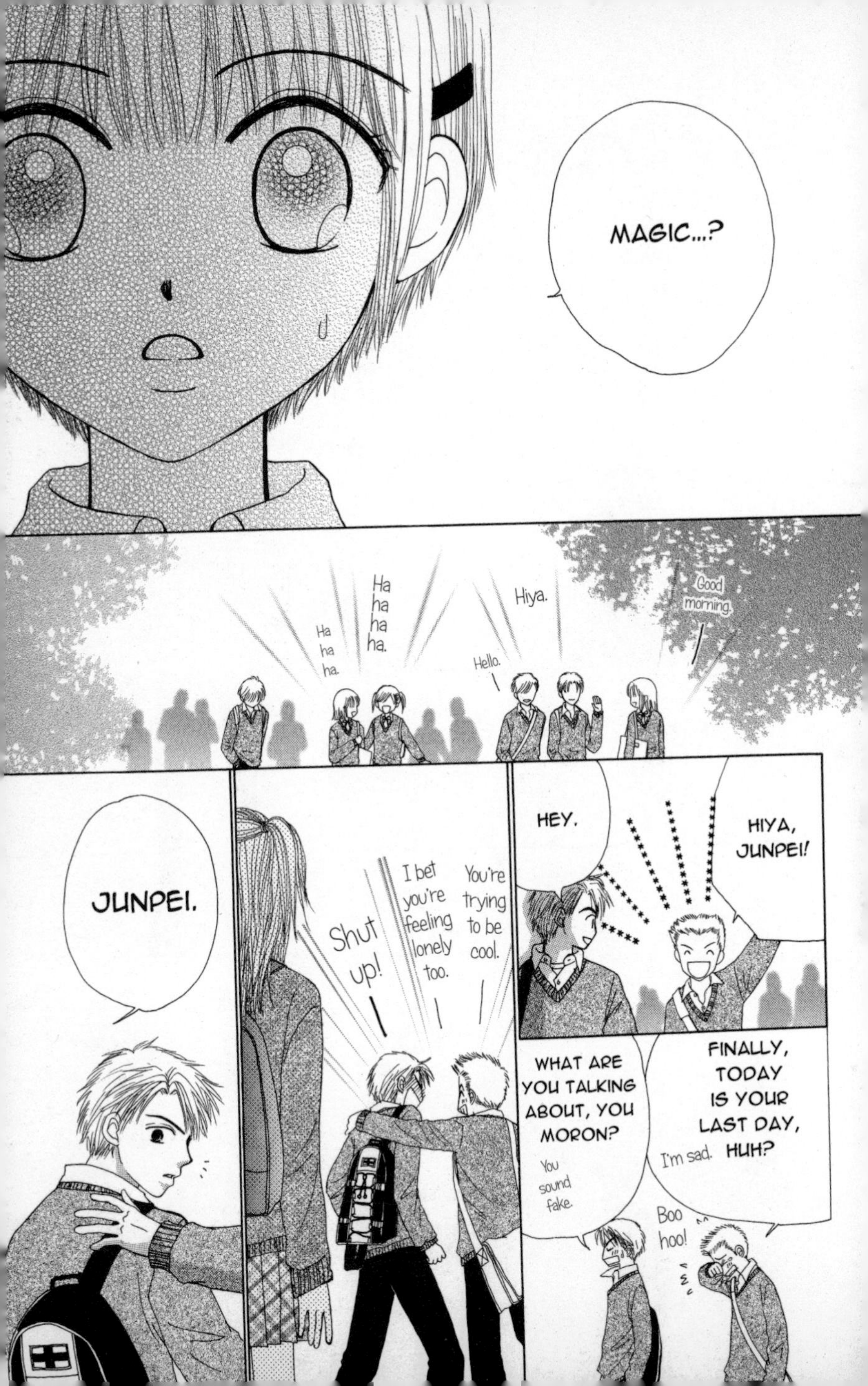
MAGIC...?
Good morning.
Hiya.
Hello.
Ha ha ha ha.
Ha ha ha.
HIYA, JUNPEI!
HEY.
FINALLY, TODAY IS YOUR LAST DAY, HUH?
I'm sad.
WHAT ARE YOU TALKING ABOUT, YOU MORON?
You sound fake.
Boo hoo!
You're trying to be cool.
I bet you're feeling lonely too.
Shut up!
JUNPEI.

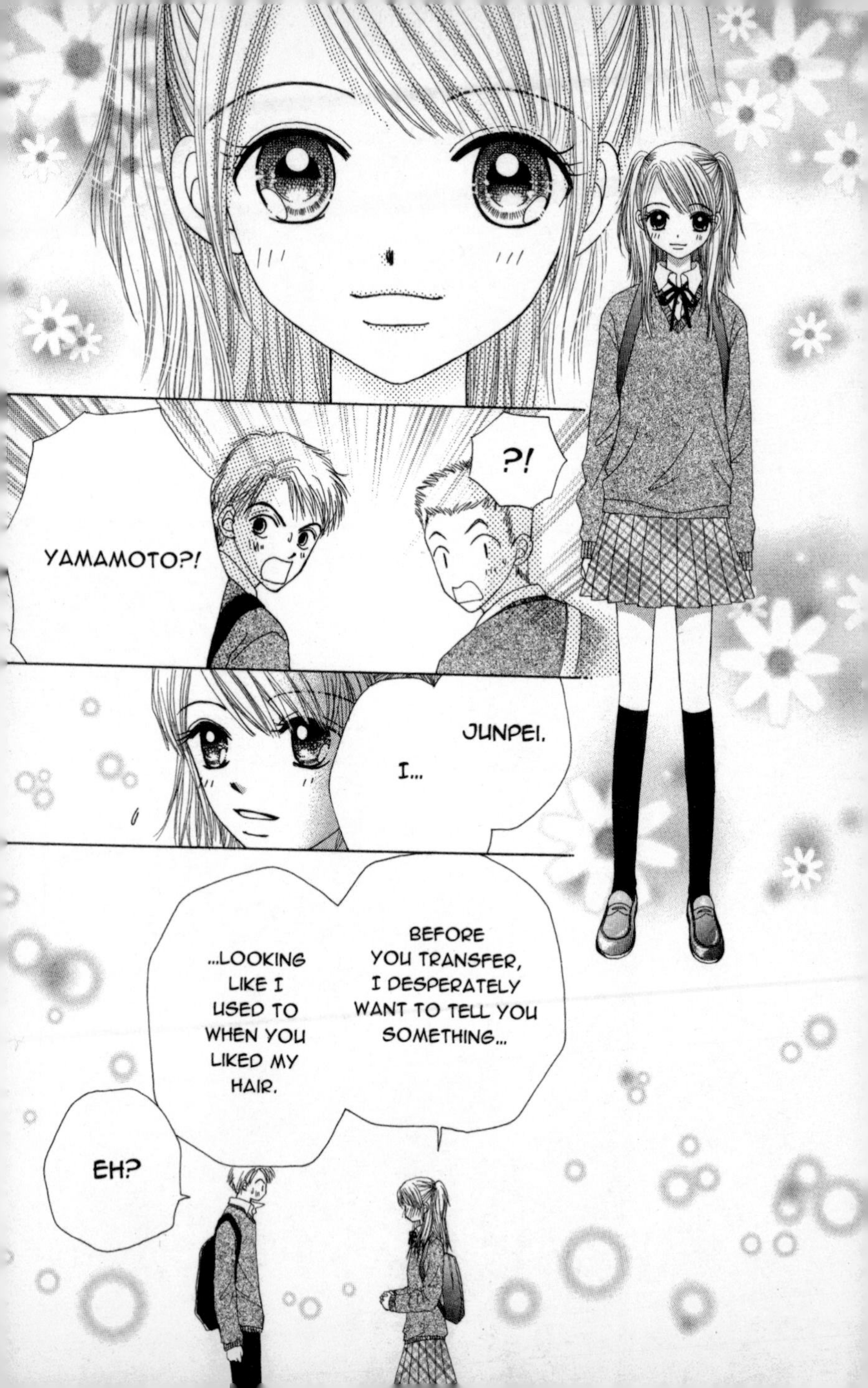
?!
YAMAMOTO?!
JUNPEI.
I...
BEFORE YOU TRANSFER, I DESPERATELY WANT TO TELL YOU SOMETHING...
...LOOKING LIKE I USED TO WHEN YOU LIKED MY HAIR.
EH?

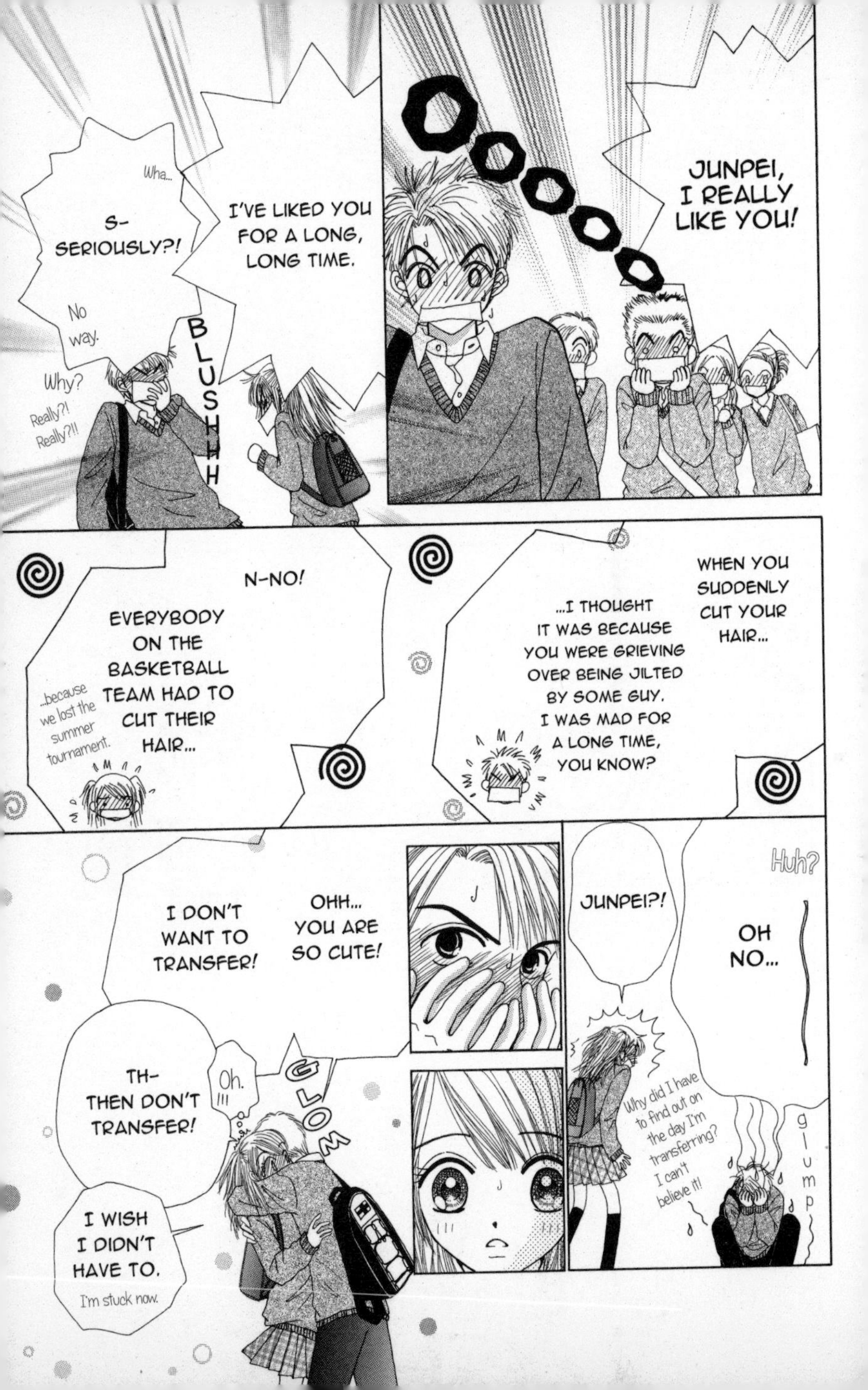
JUNPEI, I REALLY LIKE YOU!
I'VE LIKED YOU FOR A LONG, LONG TIME.
BLUSHHH
Wha...
S- SERIOUSLY?!
No way.
Why?
Really?! Really?!!
WHEN YOU SUDDENLY CUT YOUR HAIR...
...I THOUGHT IT WAS BECAUSE YOU WERE GRIEVING OVER BEING JILTED BY SOME GUY. I WAS MAD FOR A LONG TIME, YOU KNOW?
N-NO!
EVERYBODY ON THE BASKETBALL TEAM HAD TO CUT THEIR HAIR...
...because we lost the summer tournament.
Huh?
JUNPEI?!
OH NO...
Why did I have to find out on the day I'm transferring? I can't believe it!
glump
OHH... YOU ARE SO CUTE!
I DON'T WANT TO TRANSFER!
GLOM
Oh. !!!
TH- THEN DON'T TRANSFER!
I WISH I DIDN'T HAVE TO.
I'm stuck now.

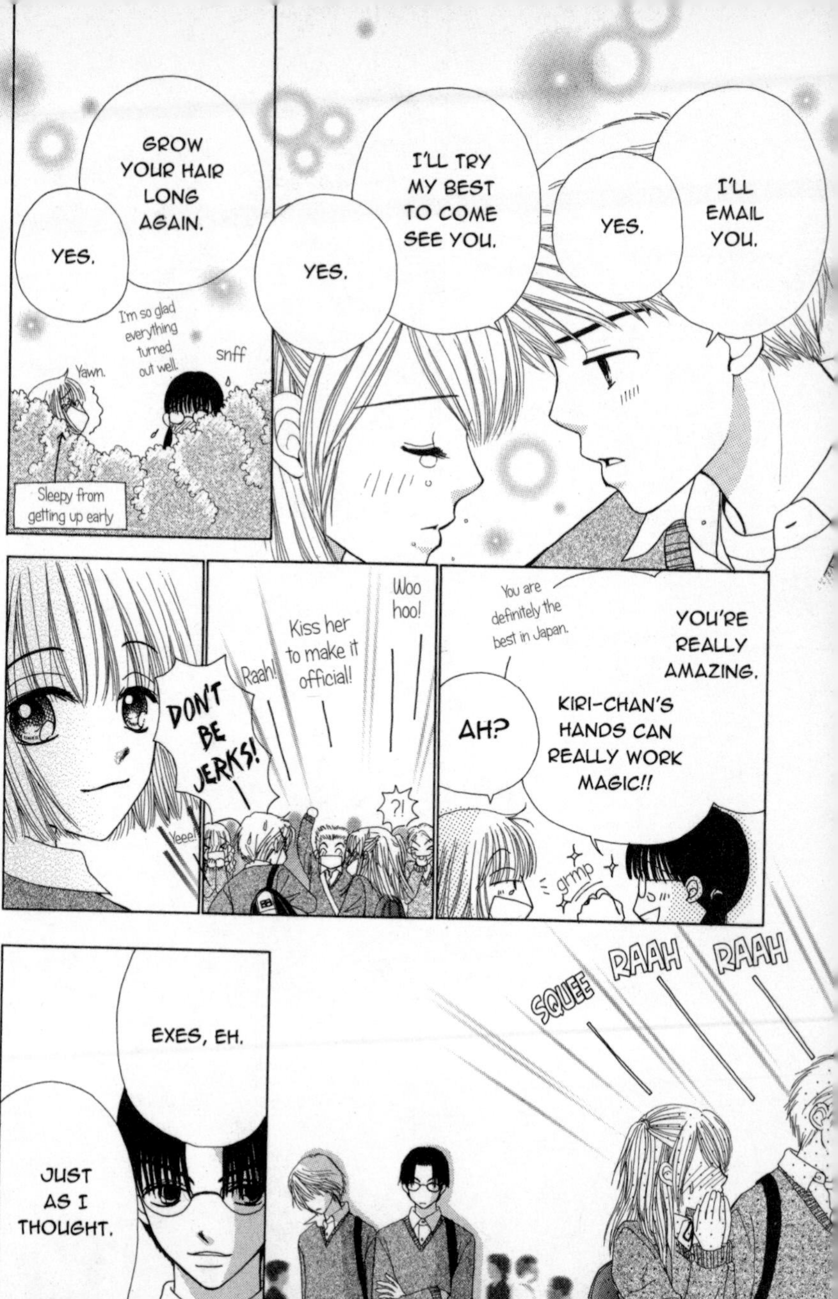
I'LL EMAIL YOU.
YES.
I'LL TRY MY BEST TO COME SEE YOU.
YES.
GROW YOUR HAIR LONG AGAIN.
YES.
I'm so glad everything turned out well.
snff
Yawn.
Sleepy from getting up early
You are definitely the best in Japan.
YOU'RE REALLY AMAZING.
AH?
KIRI-CHAN'S HANDS CAN REALLY WORK MAGIC!!
grmp
Woo hoo!
Kiss her to make it official!
Raah!
?!
DON'T BE JERKS!
Yeee!
RAAH
RAAH
SQUEE
EXES, EH.
JUST AS I THOUGHT.

※Exes=extensions

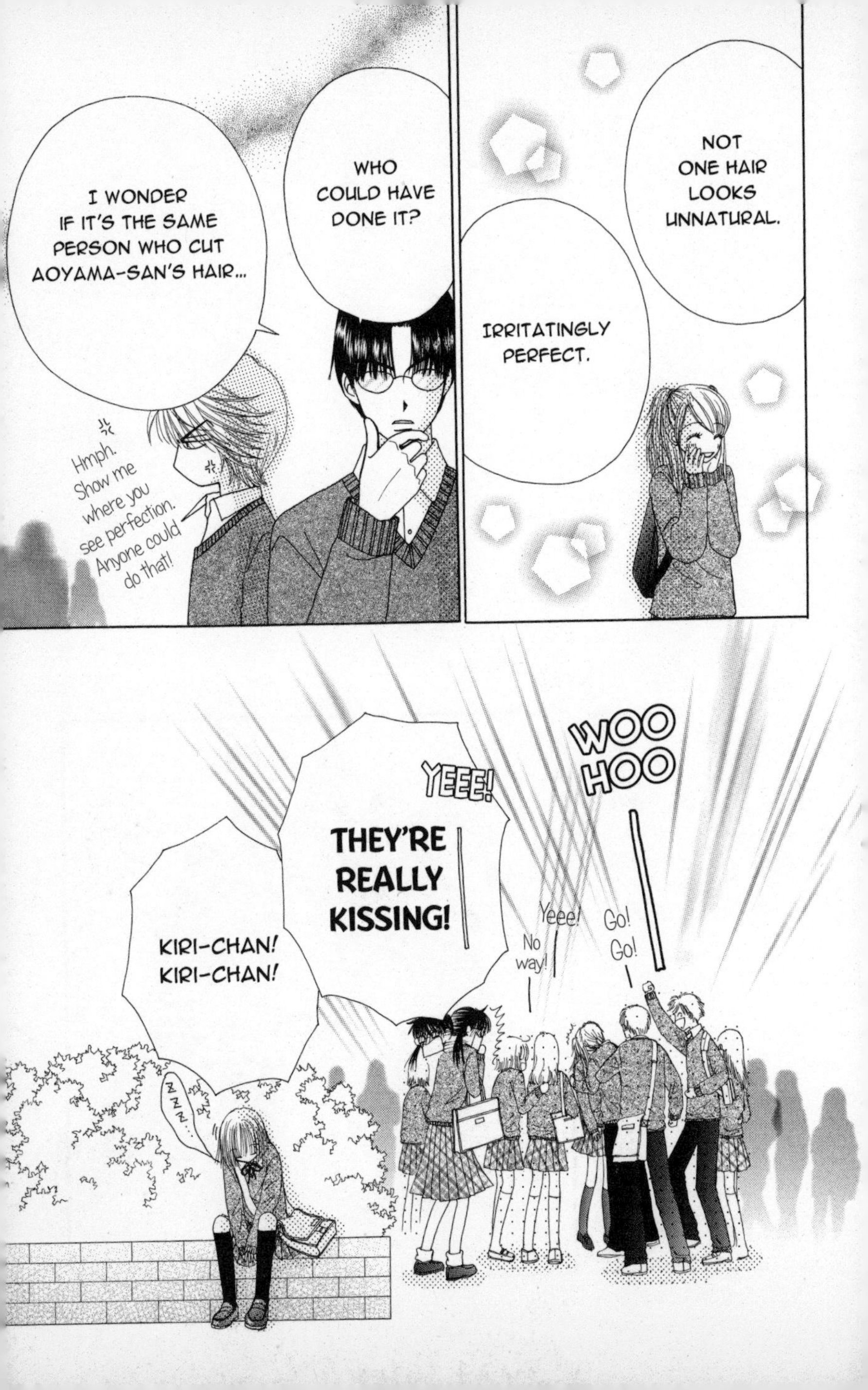
NOT ONE HAIR LOOKS UNNATURAL.
IRRITATINGLY PERFECT.
WHO COULD HAVE DONE IT?
I WONDER IF IT'S THE SAME PERSON WHO CUT AOYAMA-SAN'S HAIR...
Hmph. Show me where you see perfection. Anyone could do that!
WOO HOO
YEEE!
THEY'RE REALLY KISSING!
Go! Go!
Yeee!
No way!
KIRI-CHAN! KIRI-CHAN!

Beauty Pop

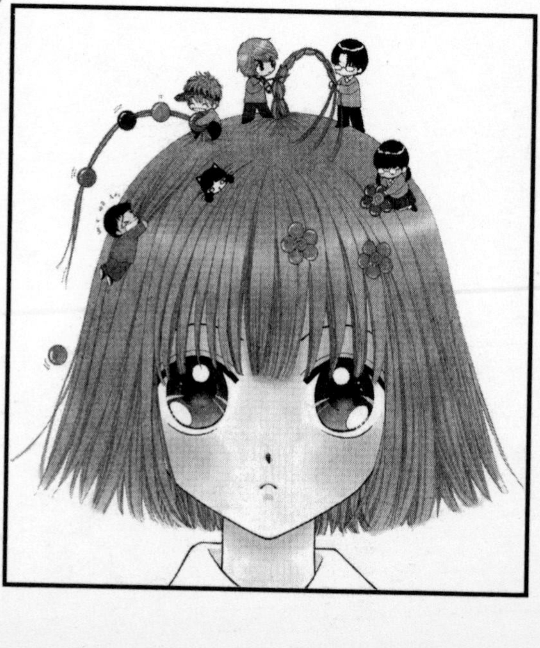

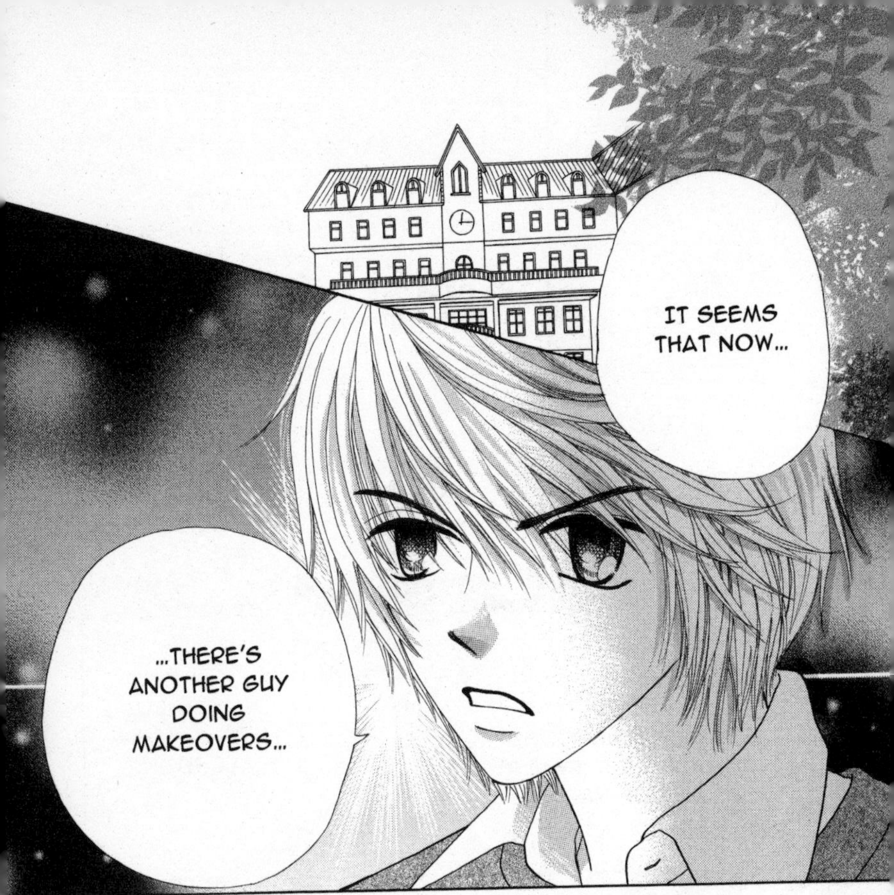
IT SEEMS THAT NOW...
...THERE'S ANOTHER GUY DOING MAKEOVERS...
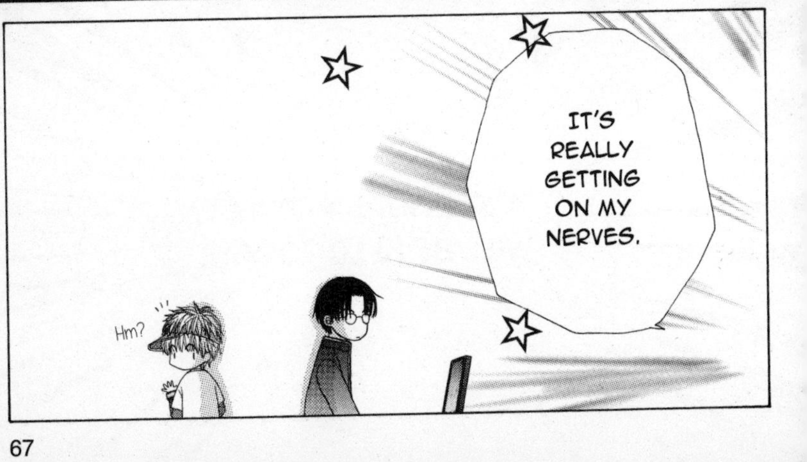
IT'S REALLY GETTING ON MY NERVES.
Hm?

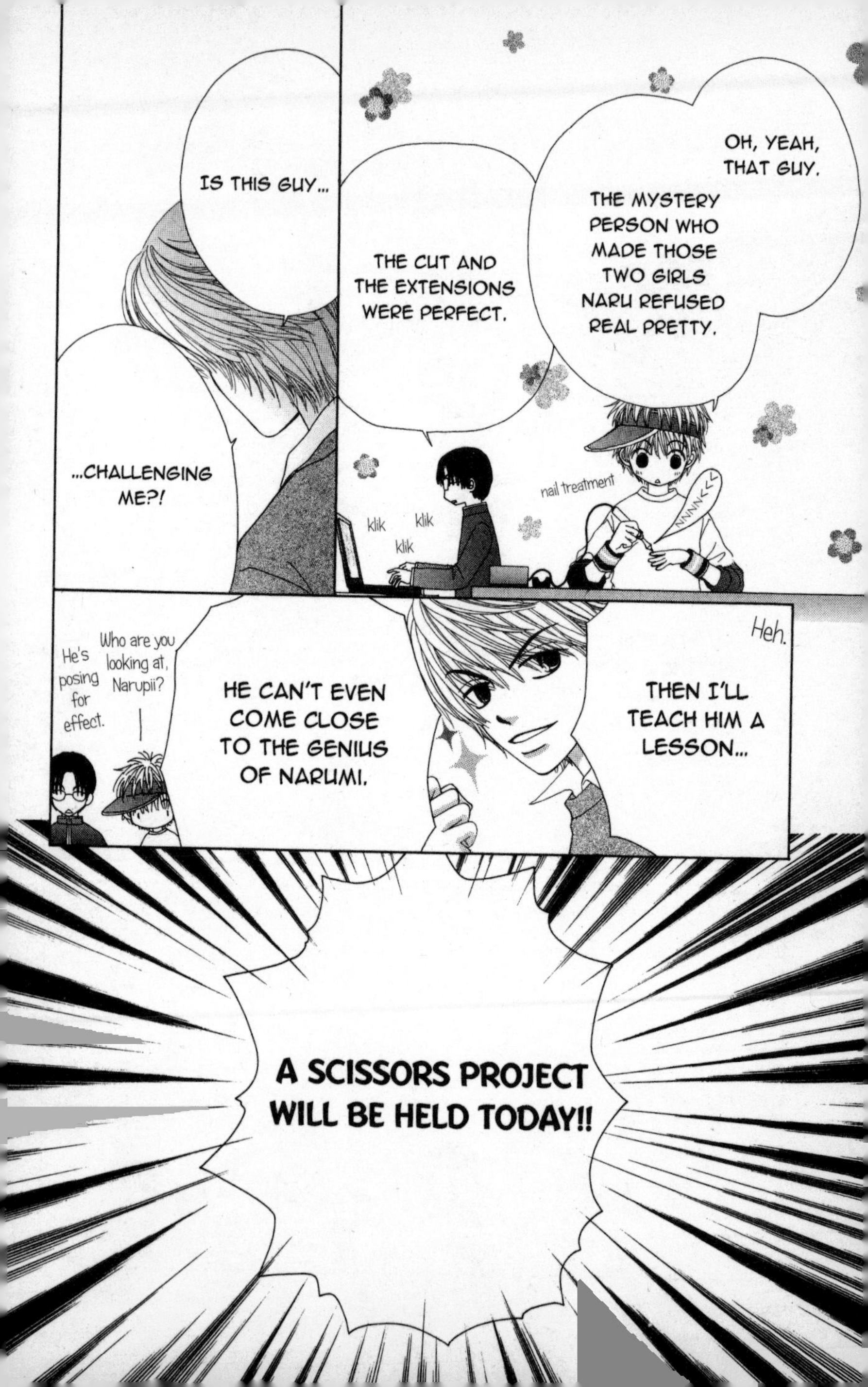
OH, YEAH, THAT GUY.
THE MYSTERY PERSON WHO MADE THOSE TWO GIRLS NARU REFUSED REAL PRETTY.
THE CUT AND THE EXTENSIONS WERE PERFECT.
nail treatment
klik klik klik
IS THIS GUY...
...CHALLENGING ME?!
Heh.
THEN I'LL TEACH HIM A LESSON...
HE CAN'T EVEN COME CLOSE TO THE GENIUS OF NARUMI.
Who are you looking at, Narupii?
He's posing for effect.
A SCISSORS PROJECT WILL BE HELD TODAY!!

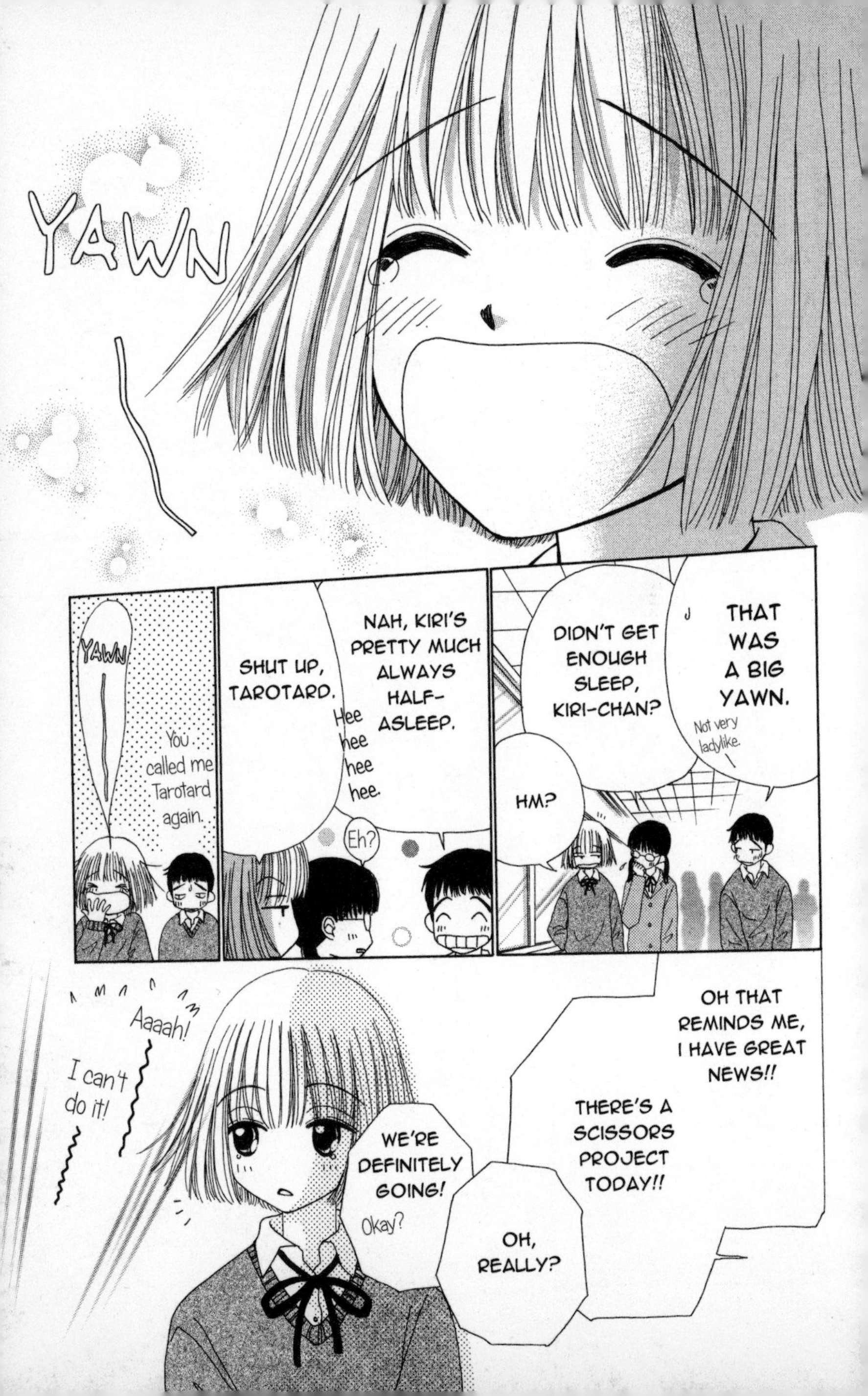
YAWN
THAT WAS A BIG YAWN.
Not very ladylike.
DIDN'T GET ENOUGH SLEEP, KIRI-CHAN?
HM?
NAH, KIRI'S PRETTY MUCH ALWAYS HALF-ASLEEP.
Hee hee hee hee.
SHUT UP, TAROTARD.
Eh?
YAWN
You called me Tarotard again.
OH THAT REMINDS ME, I HAVE GREAT NEWS!!
THERE'S A SCISSORS PROJECT TODAY!!
OH, REALLY?
WE'RE DEFINITELY GOING!
Okay?
Aaaah!
I can't do it!

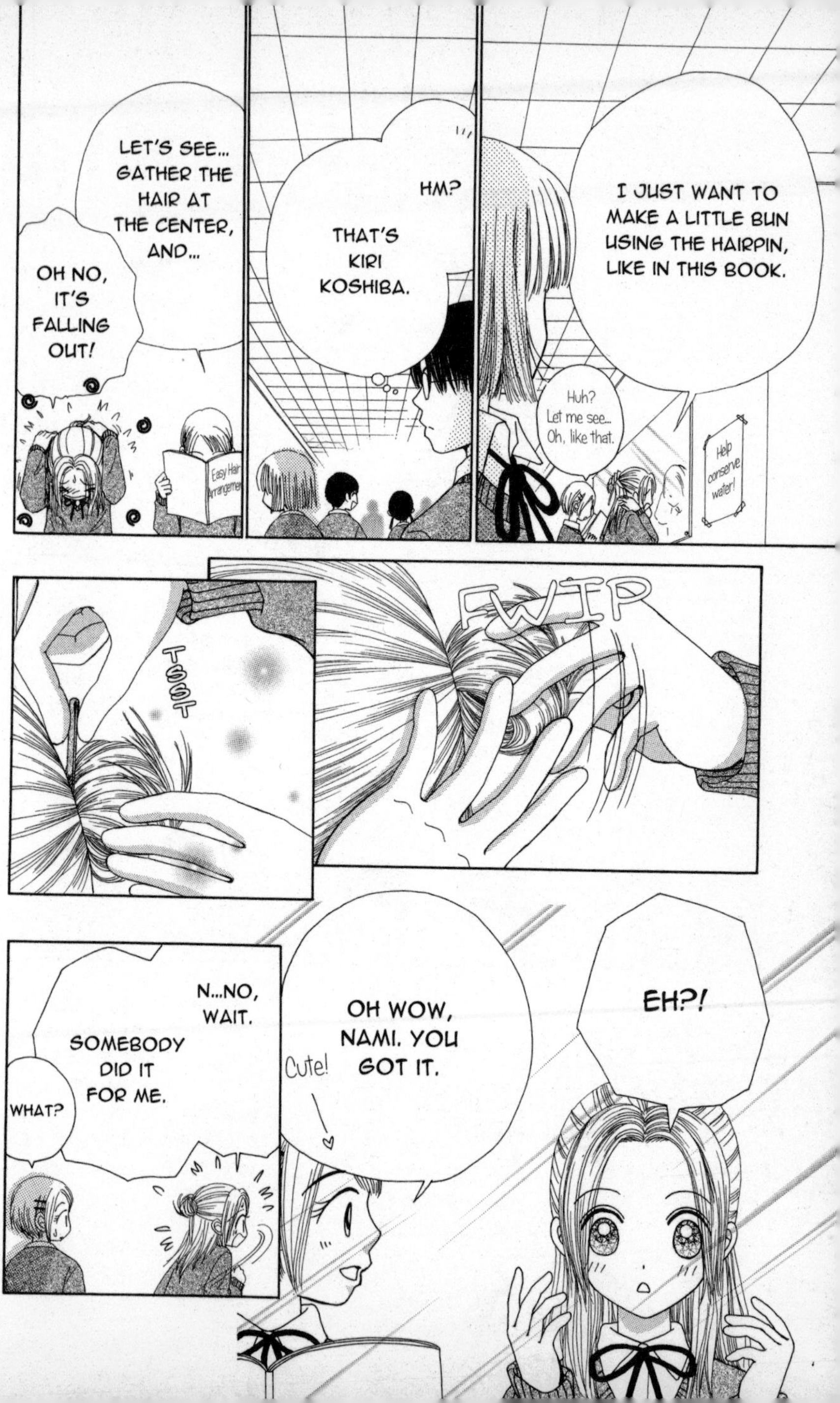
I JUST WANT TO MAKE A LITTLE BUN USING THE HAIRPIN, LIKE IN THIS BOOK.
Huh? Let me see... Oh, like that.
Help conserve water!
HM?
THAT'S KIRI KOSHIBA.
LET'S SEE... GATHER THE HAIR AT THE CENTER, AND...
OH NO, IT'S FALLING OUT!
Easy Hair Arrangem
FWIP
TSST
EH?!
OH WOW, NAMI. YOU GOT IT.
Cute!
N...NO, WAIT.
SOMEBODY DID IT FOR ME.
WHAT?

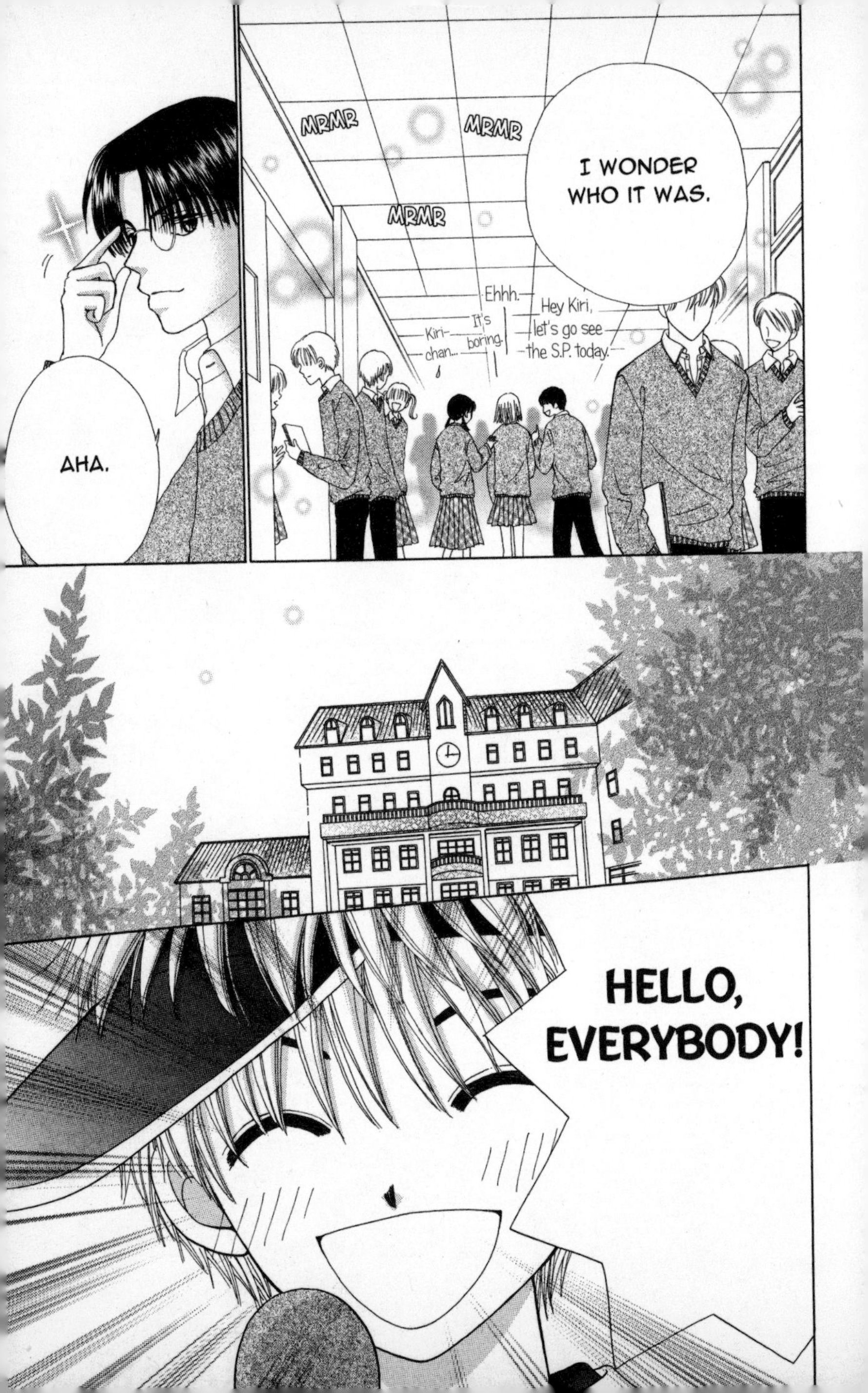
I WONDER WHO IT WAS.
MRMR
MRMR
MRMR
Hey Kiri, let's go see the S.P. today.
Ehhh.
It's boring.
Kiri-chan...
AHA.
HELLO, EVERYBODY!

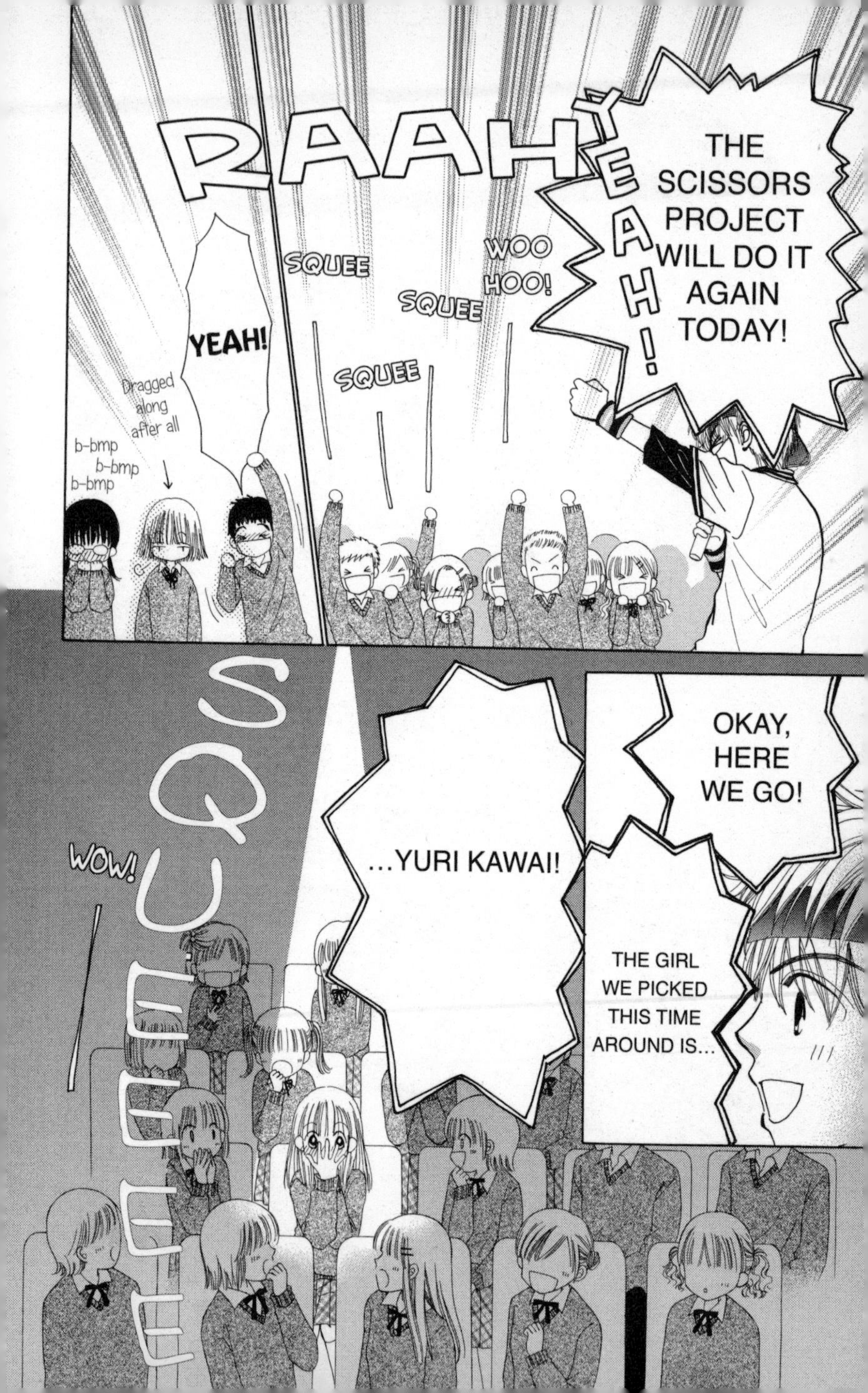
YEAH!
THE SCISSORS PROJECT WILL DO IT AGAIN TODAY!
RAAAH
WOO HOO!
SQUEE
SQUEE
SQUEE
YEAH!
Dragged along after all
b-bmp
b-bmp
b-bmp
OKAY, HERE WE GO!
THE GIRL WE PICKED THIS TIME AROUND IS...
...YURI KAWAI!
SQUEEEE
WOW!

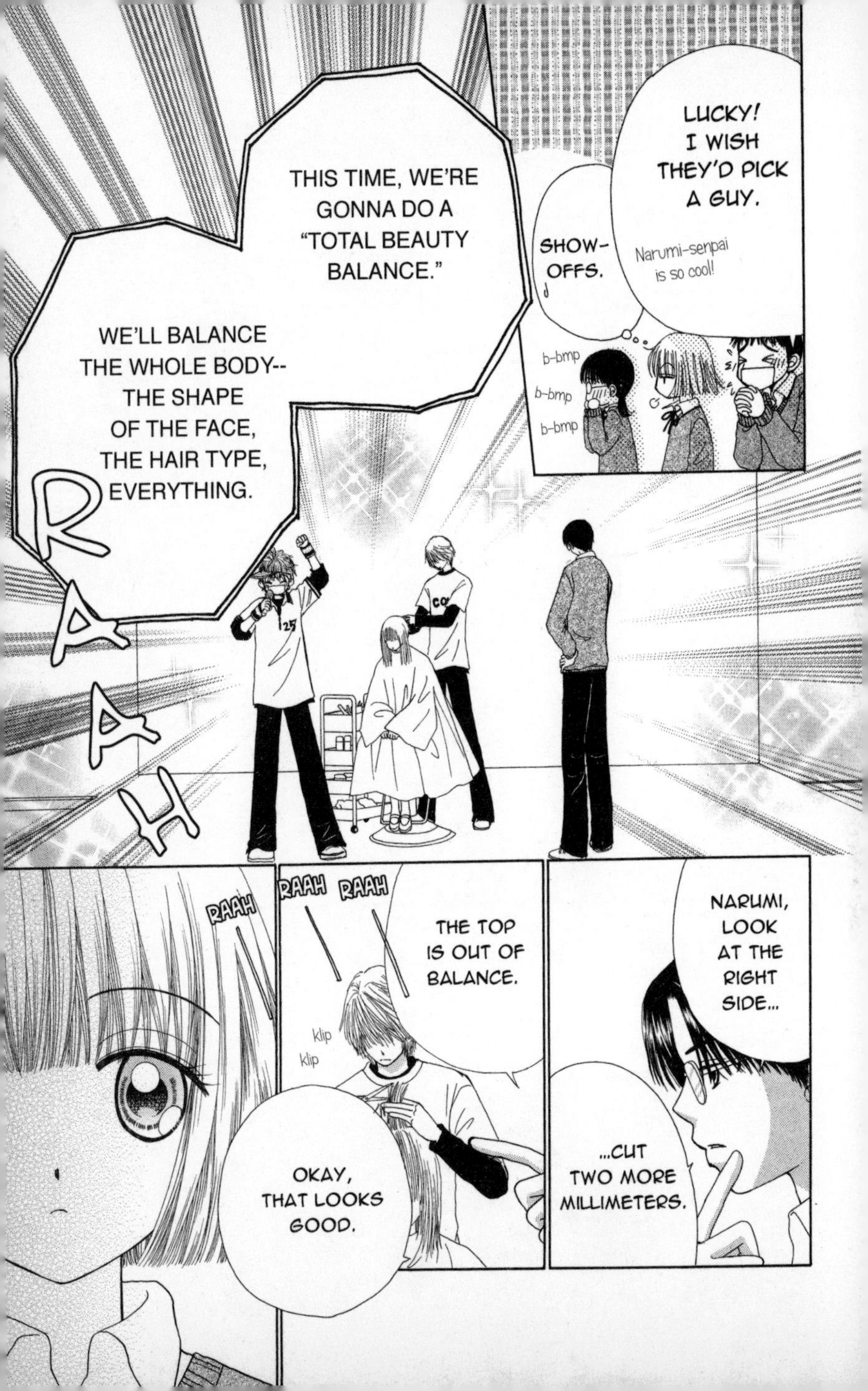
LUCKY! I WISH THEY'D PICK A GUY.
Narumi-senpai is so cool!
SHOW-OFFS.
b-bmp b-bmp b-bmp
THIS TIME, WE'RE GONNA DO A "TOTAL BEAUTY BALANCE."
WE'LL BALANCE THE WHOLE BODY-- THE SHAPE OF THE FACE, THE HAIR TYPE, EVERYTHING.
RAAH
NARUMI, LOOK AT THE RIGHT SIDE...
...CUT TWO MORE MILLIMETERS.
RAAH RAAH
THE TOP IS OUT OF BALANCE.
klip klip
OKAY, THAT LOOKS GOOD.
RAAH

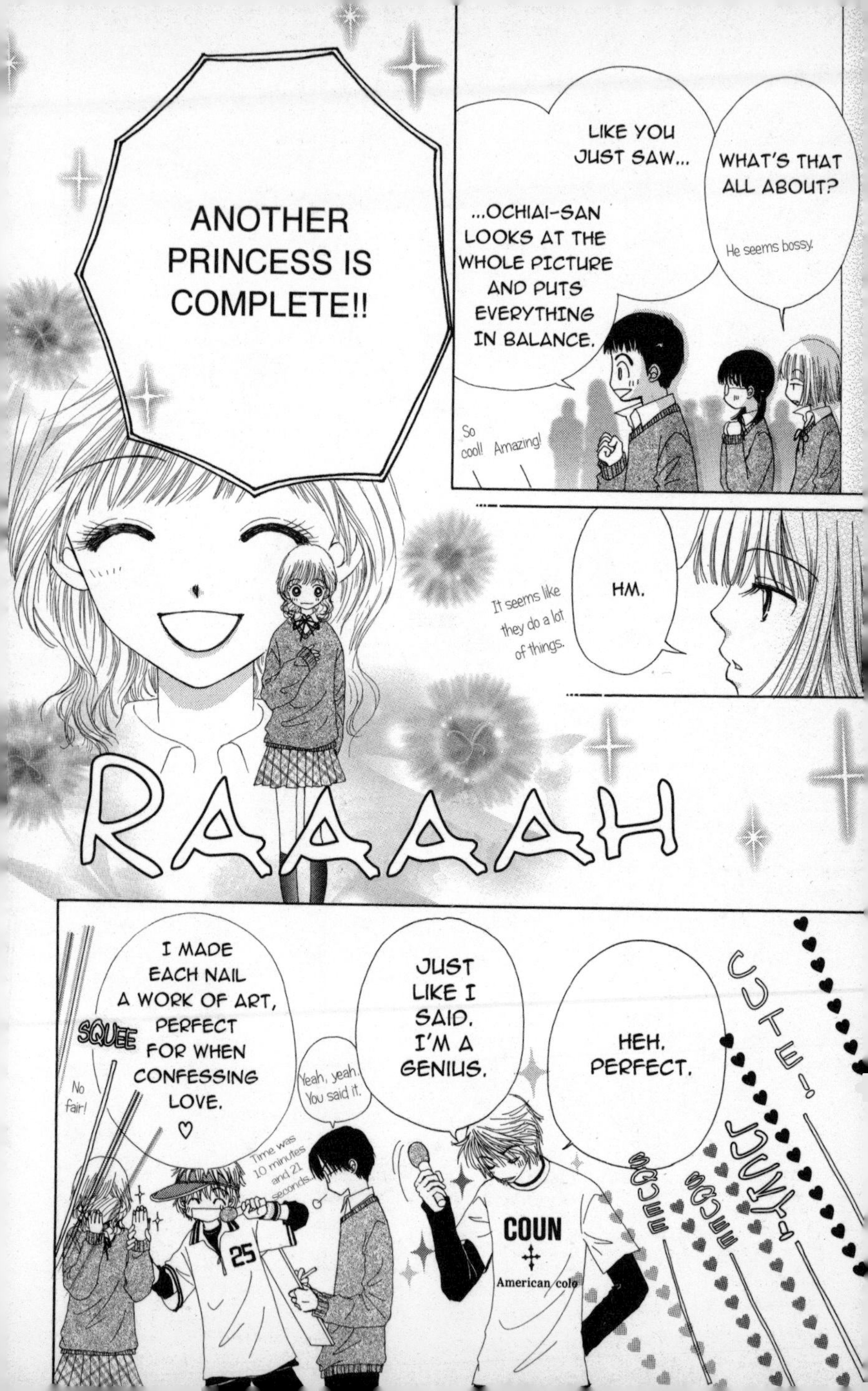

WHAT'S THAT ALL ABOUT?
He seems bossy.
LIKE YOU JUST SAW...
...OCHIAI-SAN LOOKS AT THE WHOLE PICTURE AND PUTS EVERYTHING IN BALANCE.
So cool! Amazing!
HM.
It seems like they do a lot of things.
ANOTHER PRINCESS IS COMPLETE!!
RAAAAH
CUTE! JUICY!
SQUEE SQUEE
HEH. PERFECT.
COUN
American colo
JUST LIKE I SAID. I'M A GENIUS.
Yeah, yeah. You said it.
Time was 10 minutes and 21 seconds...
25
I MADE EACH NAIL A WORK OF ART, PERFECT FOR WHEN CONFESSING LOVE. ♡
SQUEE
No fair!

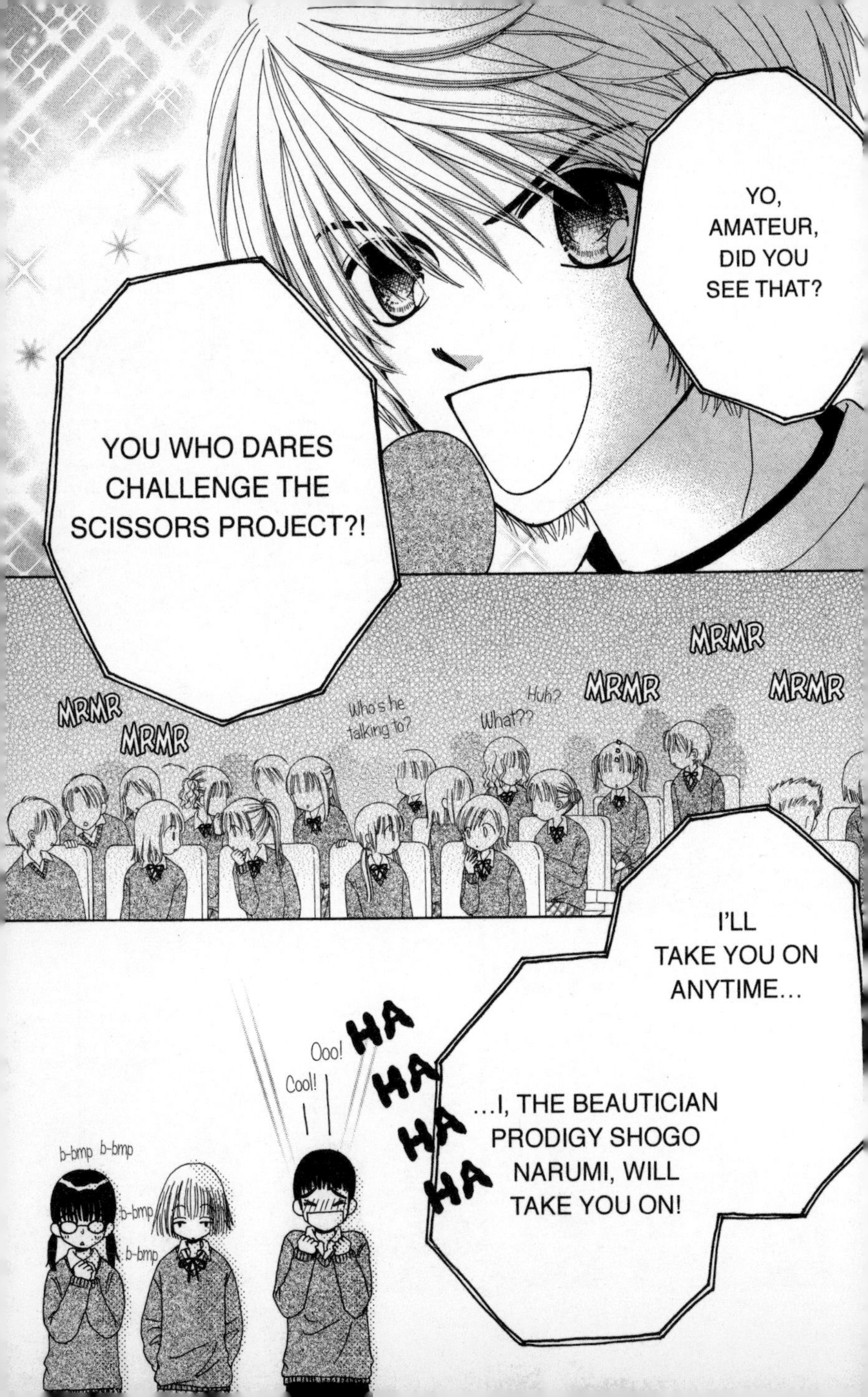
YO, AMATEUR, DID YOU SEE THAT?
YOU WHO DARES CHALLENGE THE SCISSORS PROJECT?!
MRMR
MRMR
MRMR
Huh?
What??
Who's he talking to?
MRMR
MRMR
I'LL TAKE YOU ON ANYTIME...
...I, THE BEAUTICIAN PRODIGY SHOGO NARUMI, WILL TAKE YOU ON!
HA HA HA HA
Ooo!
Cool!
b-bmp b-bmp
b-bmp
b-bmp

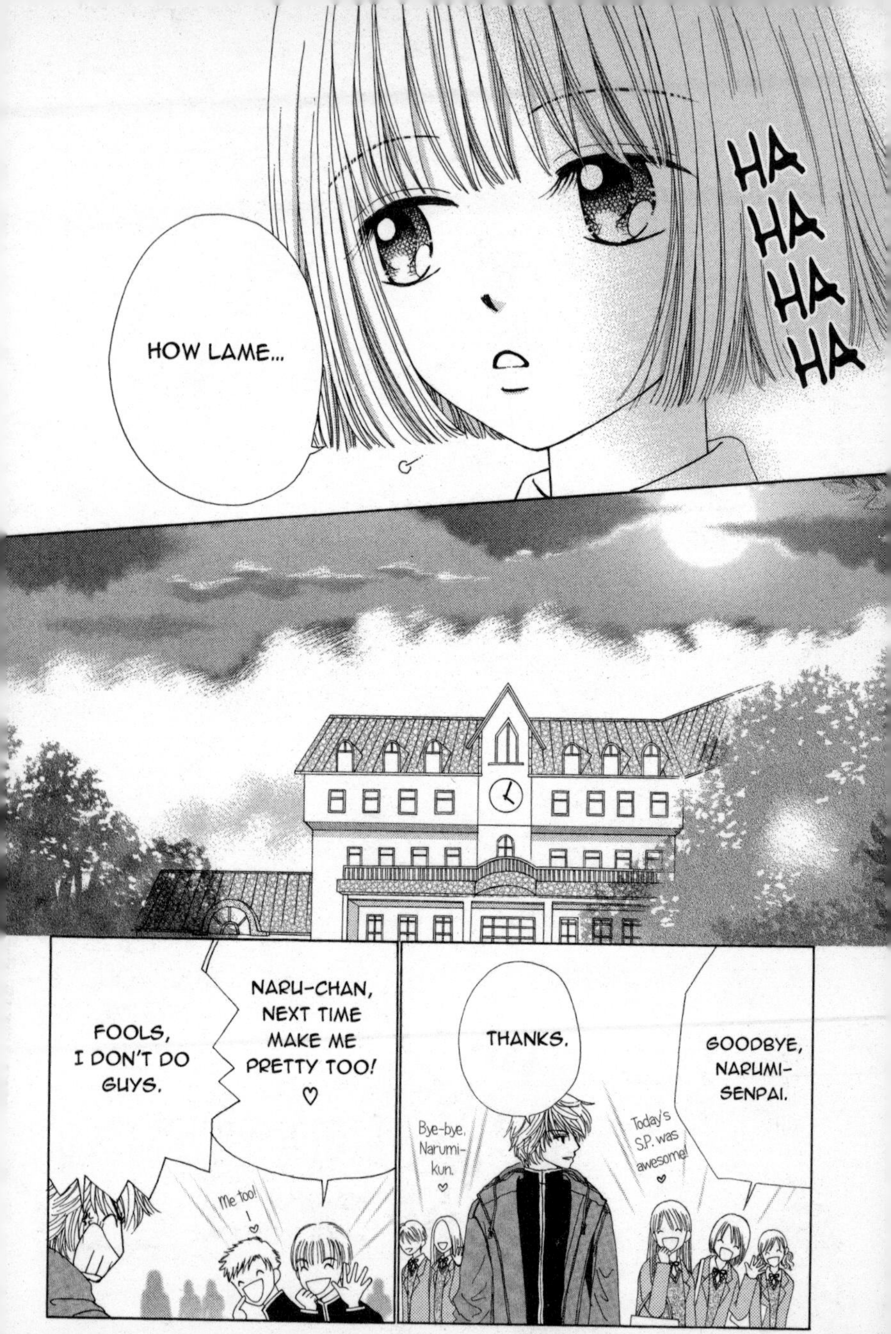
HA HA HA HA
HOW LAME...
GOODBYE, NARUMI-SENPAI.
Today's S.P. was awesome! ♡
THANKS.
Bye-bye, Narumi-kun. ♡
NARU-CHAN, NEXT TIME MAKE ME PRETTY TOO! ♡
Me too! ♡
FOOLS, I DON'T DO GUYS.

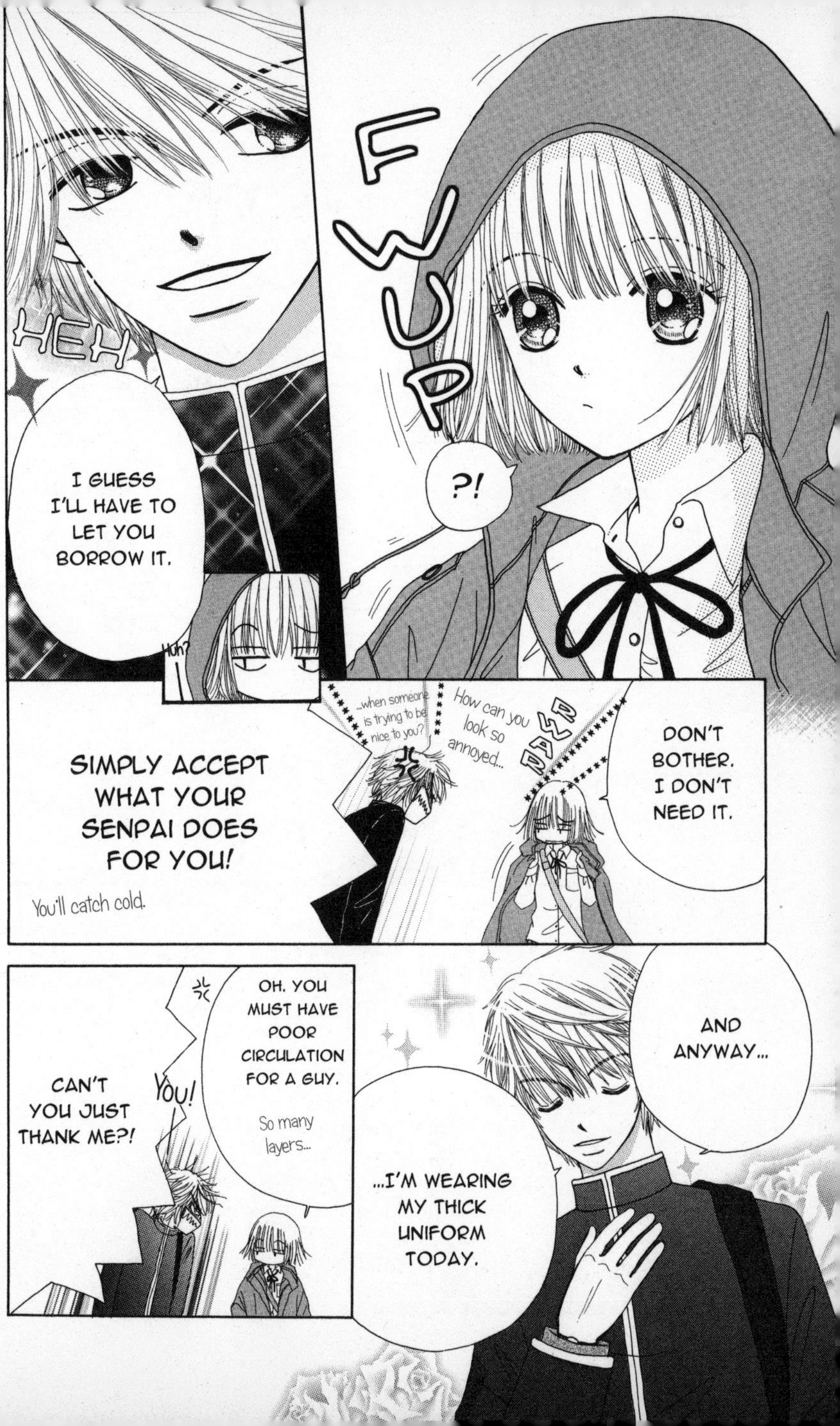
FWUP
?!
HEH
I GUESS I'LL HAVE TO LET YOU BORROW IT.
Huh?
DON'T BOTHER. I DON'T NEED IT.
PWAP
How can you look so annoyed...
...when someone is trying to be nice to you?
SIMPLY ACCEPT WHAT YOUR SENPAI DOES FOR YOU!
You'll catch cold.
AND ANYWAY...
...I'M WEARING MY THICK UNIFORM TODAY.
OH. YOU MUST HAVE POOR CIRCULATION FOR A GUY.
So many layers...
YOU!
CAN'T YOU JUST THANK ME?!

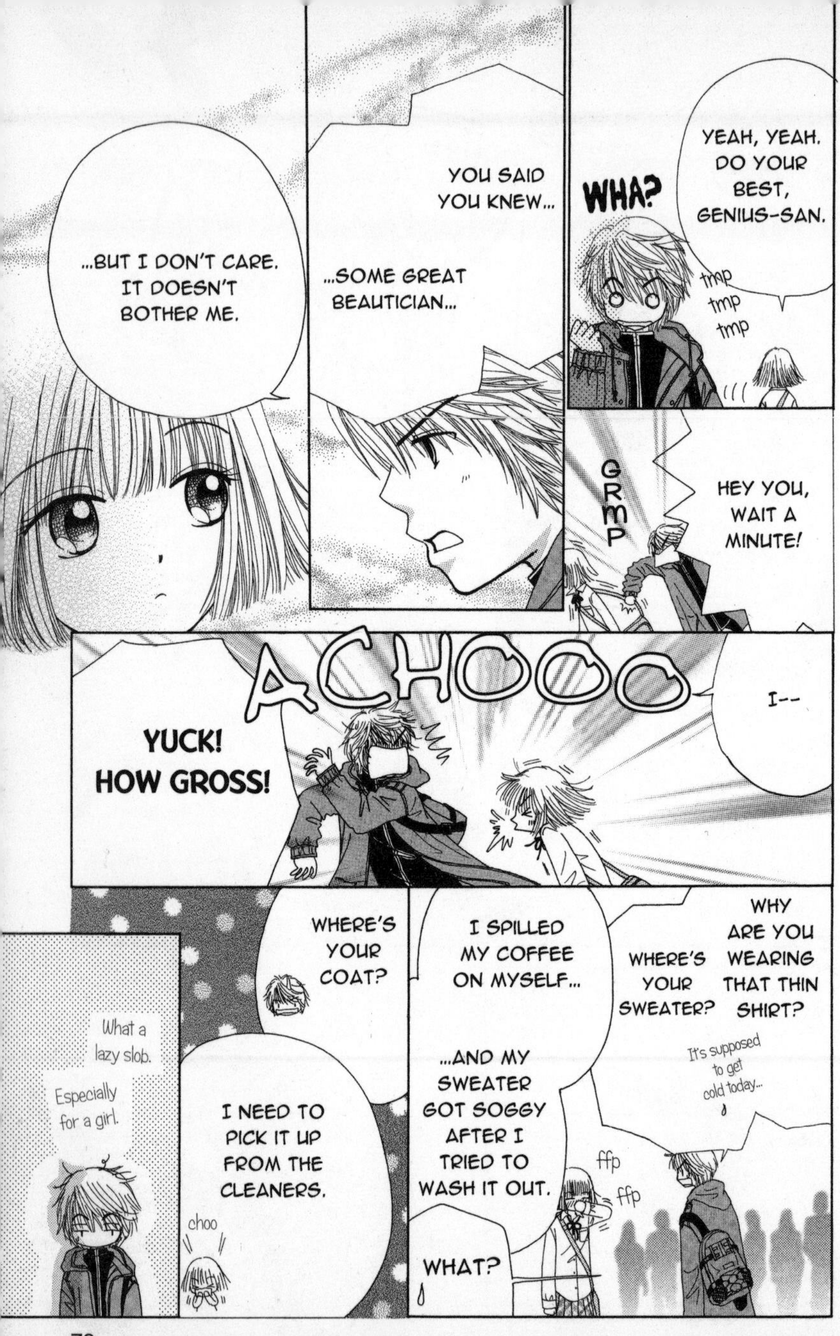
YEAH, YEAH. DO YOUR BEST, GENIUS-SAN.
WHA?
tmp tmp tmp
GRMP
HEY YOU, WAIT A MINUTE!
YOU SAID YOU KNEW...
...SOME GREAT BEAUTICIAN...
...BUT I DON'T CARE. IT DOESN'T BOTHER ME.
I--
ACHOOO
YUCK! HOW GROSS!
WHY ARE YOU WEARING THAT THIN SHIRT?
WHERE'S YOUR SWEATER?
It's supposed to get cold today...
I SPILLED MY COFFEE ON MYSELF...
...AND MY SWEATER GOT SOGGY AFTER I TRIED TO WASH IT OUT.
ffp
ffp
WHAT?
WHERE'S YOUR COAT?
I NEED TO PICK IT UP FROM THE CLEANERS.
choo
What a lazy slob.
Especially for a girl.

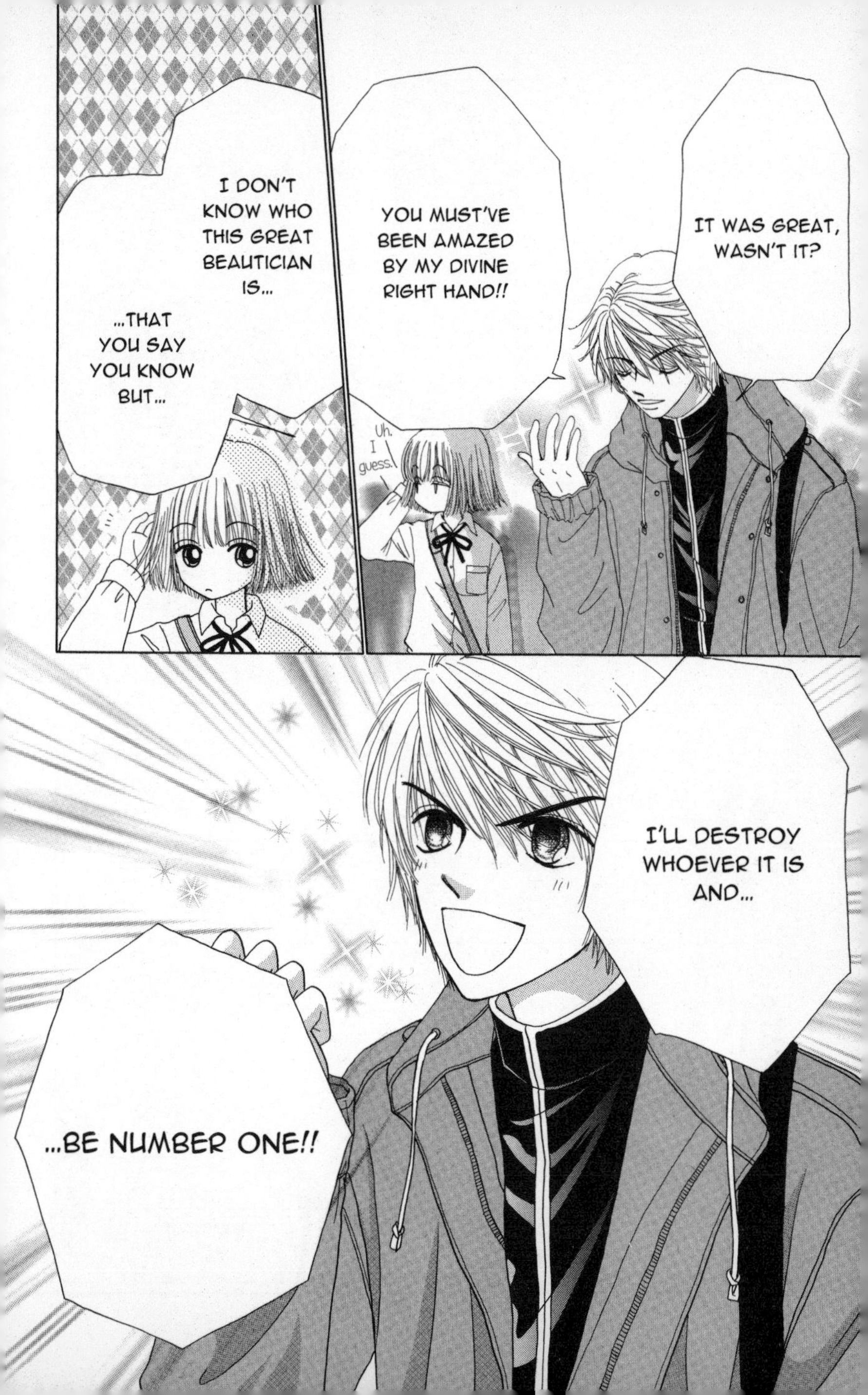
IT WAS GREAT, WASN'T IT?
YOU MUST'VE BEEN AMAZED BY MY DIVINE RIGHT HAND!!
Uh. I guess.
I DON'T KNOW WHO THIS GREAT BEAUTICIAN IS...
...THAT YOU SAY YOU KNOW BUT...
I'LL DESTROY WHOEVER IT IS AND...
...BE NUMBER ONE!!

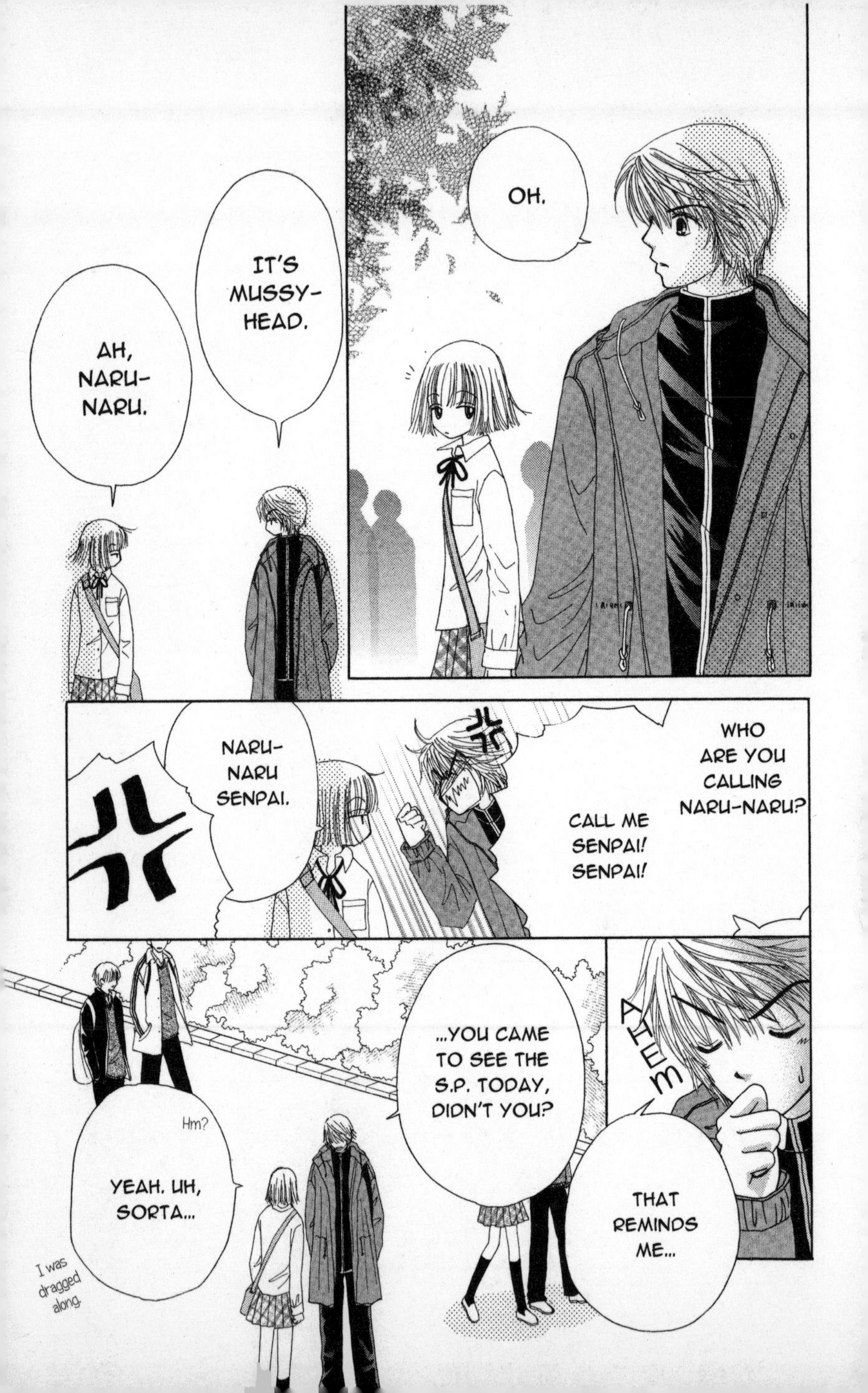
OH.
IT'S MUSSY-HEAD.
AH, NARU-NARU.
WHO ARE YOU CALLING NARU-NARU?
CALL ME SENPAI! SENPAI!
NARU-NARU SENPAI.
AHEM
THAT REMINDS ME...
...YOU CAME TO SEE THE S.P. TODAY, DIDN'T YOU?
Hm?
YEAH. UH, SORTA...
I was dragged along.

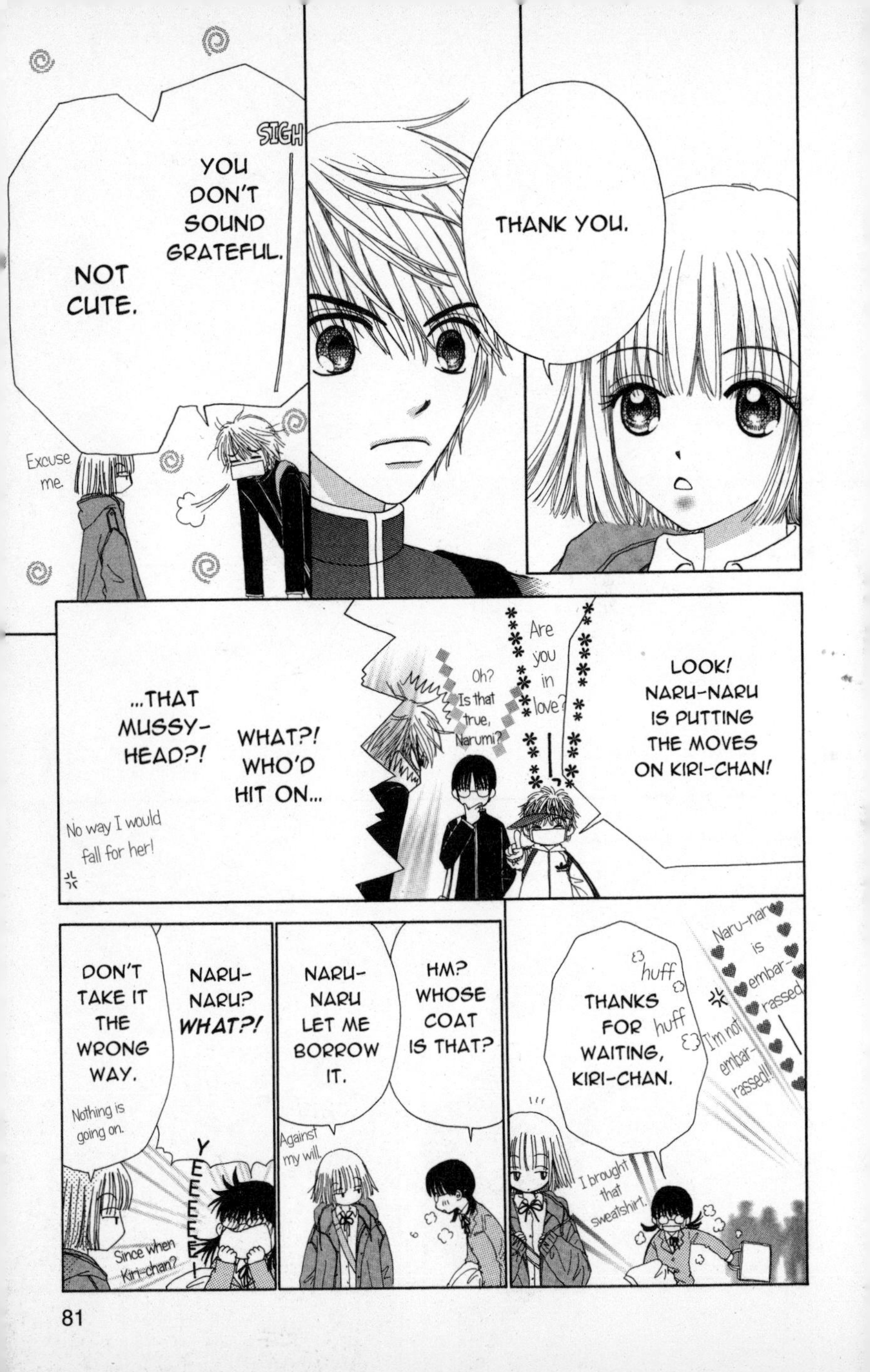
THANK YOU.
YOU DON'T SOUND GRATEFUL.
NOT CUTE.
SIGH
Excuse me.
LOOK! NARU-NARU IS PUTTING THE MOVES ON KIRI-CHAN!
Are you in love?
Oh? Is that true, Narumi?
WHAT?! WHO'D HIT ON...
...THAT MUSSY-HEAD?!
No way I would fall for her!
THANKS FOR WAITING, KIRI-CHAN.
huff huff
Naru-naru is embarrassed
I'm not embarrassed!!
I brought that sweatshirt.
HM? WHOSE COAT IS THAT?
NARU-NARU LET ME BORROW IT.
Against my will.
NARU-NARU? WHAT?!
YEEEEE!
DON'T TAKE IT THE WRONG WAY.
Nothing is going on.
Since when Kiri-chan?

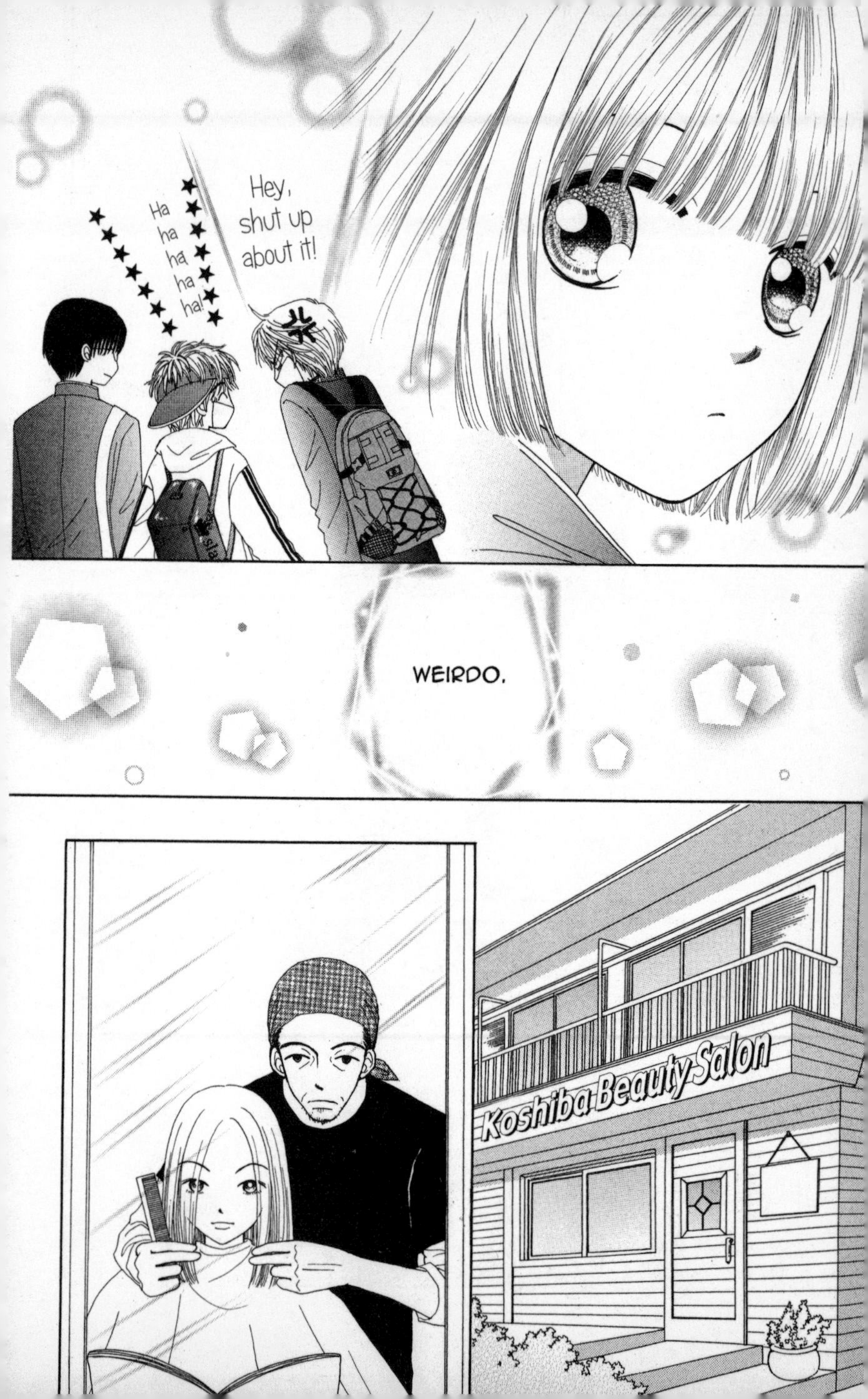
Hey, shut up about it!
Ha ha ha ha ha!
WEIRDO.
Koshiba Beauty Salon

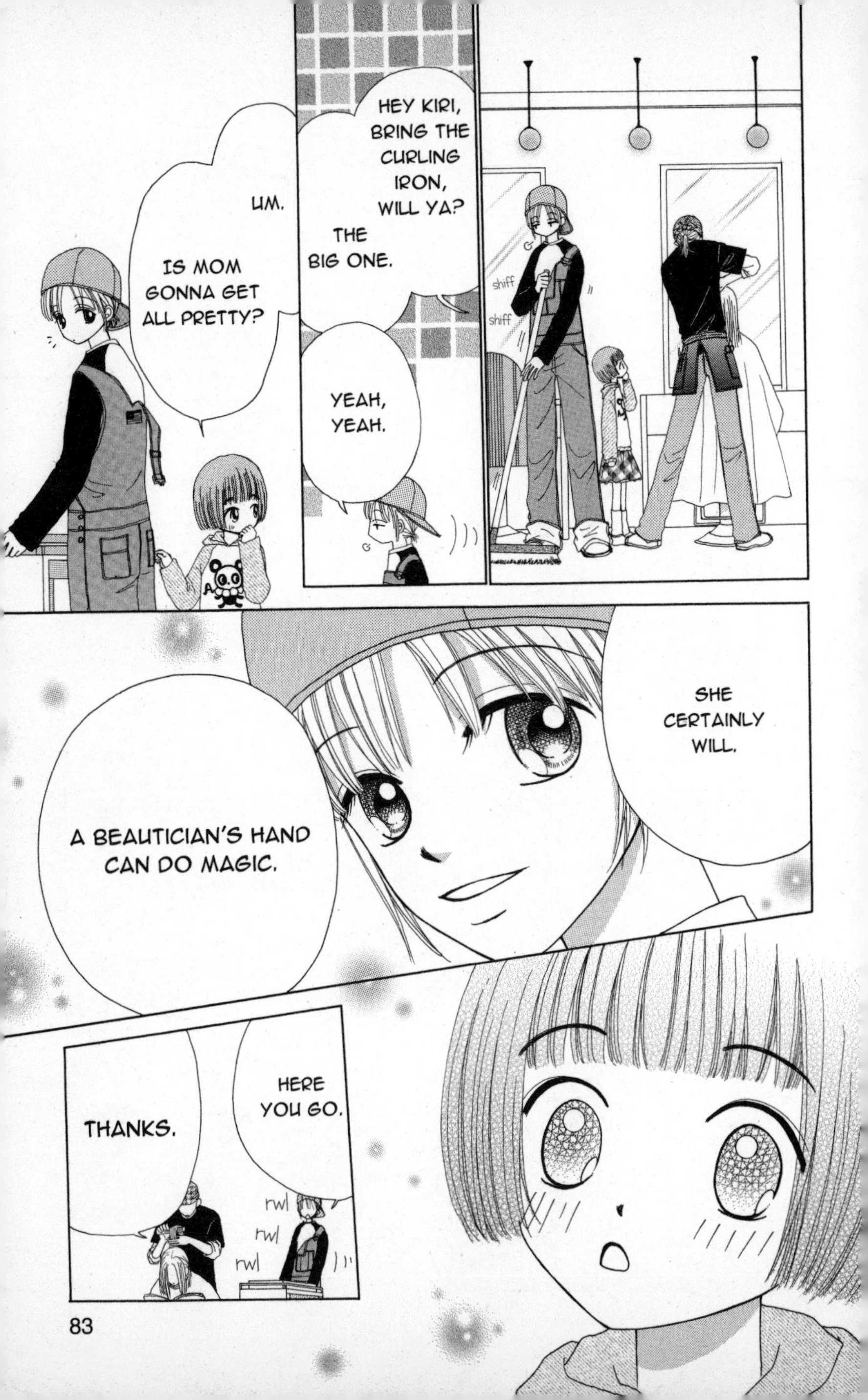
shiff
shiff
HEY KIRI, BRING THE CURLING IRON, WILL YA?
THE BIG ONE.
YEAH, YEAH.
UM.
IS MOM GONNA GET ALL PRETTY?
SHE CERTAINLY WILL.
A BEAUTICIAN'S HAND CAN DO MAGIC.
HERE YOU GO.
THANKS.
rwl
rwl
rwl

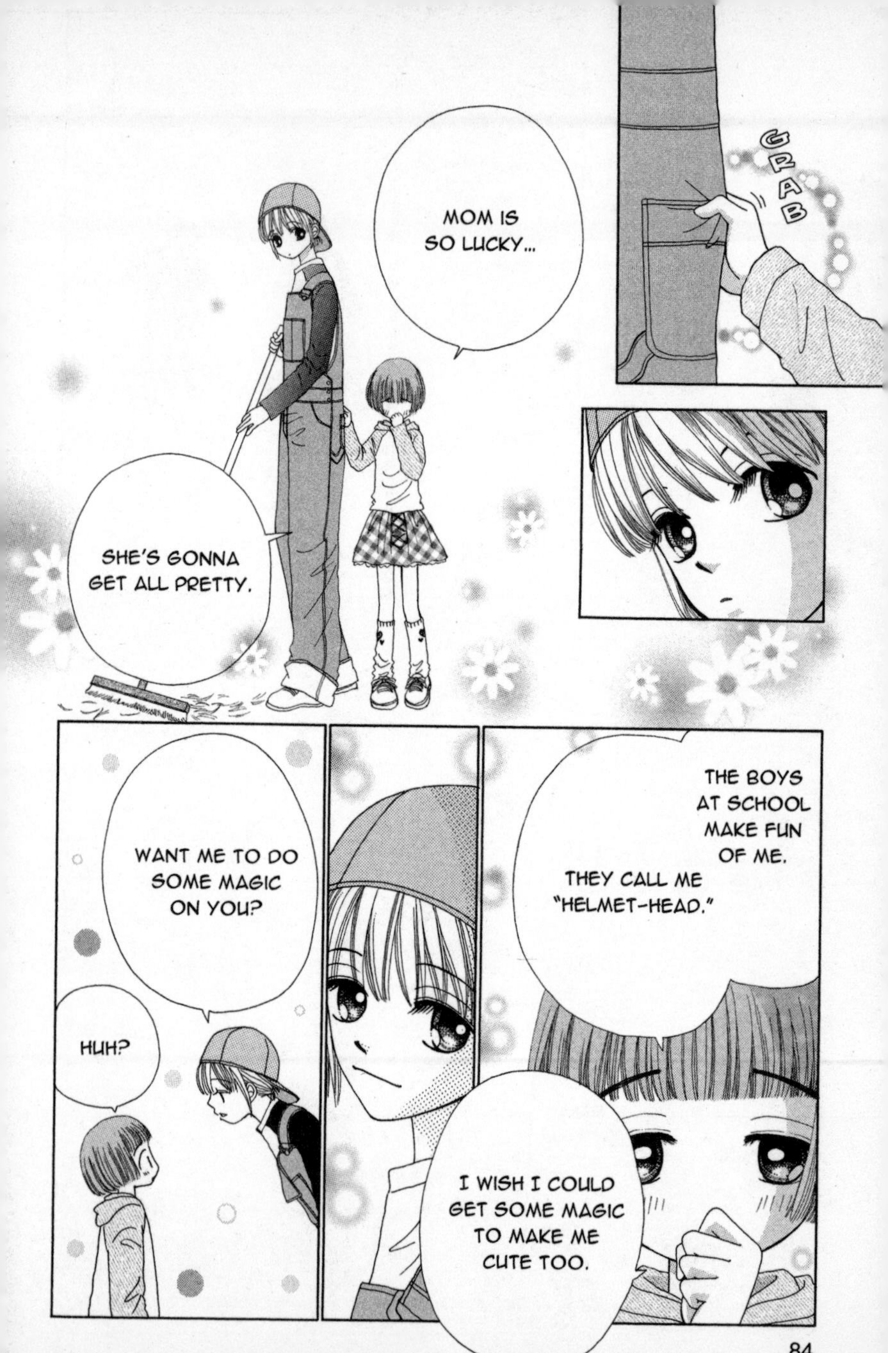
GRAB
MOM IS SO LUCKY...
SHE'S GONNA GET ALL PRETTY.
THE BOYS AT SCHOOL MAKE FUN OF ME.
THEY CALL ME "HELMET-HEAD."
I WISH I COULD GET SOME MAGIC TO MAKE ME CUTE TOO.
WANT ME TO DO SOME MAGIC ON YOU?
HUH?

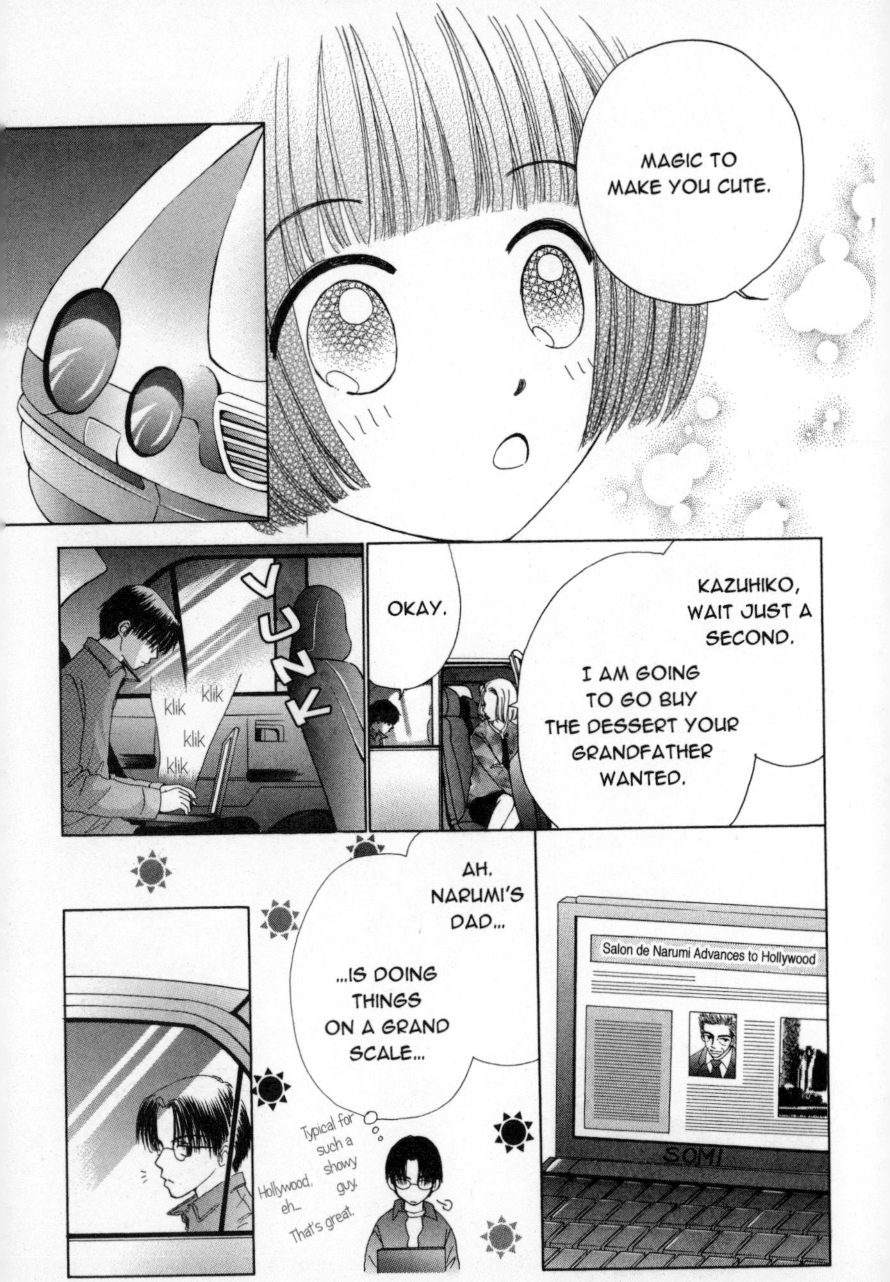
MAGIC TO MAKE YOU CUTE.
KAZUHIKO, WAIT JUST A SECOND.
I AM GOING TO GO BUY THE DESSERT YOUR GRANDFATHER WANTED.
OKAY.
VUNK
klik
klik
klik
klik
Salon de Narumi Advances to Hollywood
SOMI
AH. NARUMI'S DAD...
...IS DOING THINGS ON A GRAND SCALE...
Typical for such a showy guy.
Hollywood, eh... That's great.

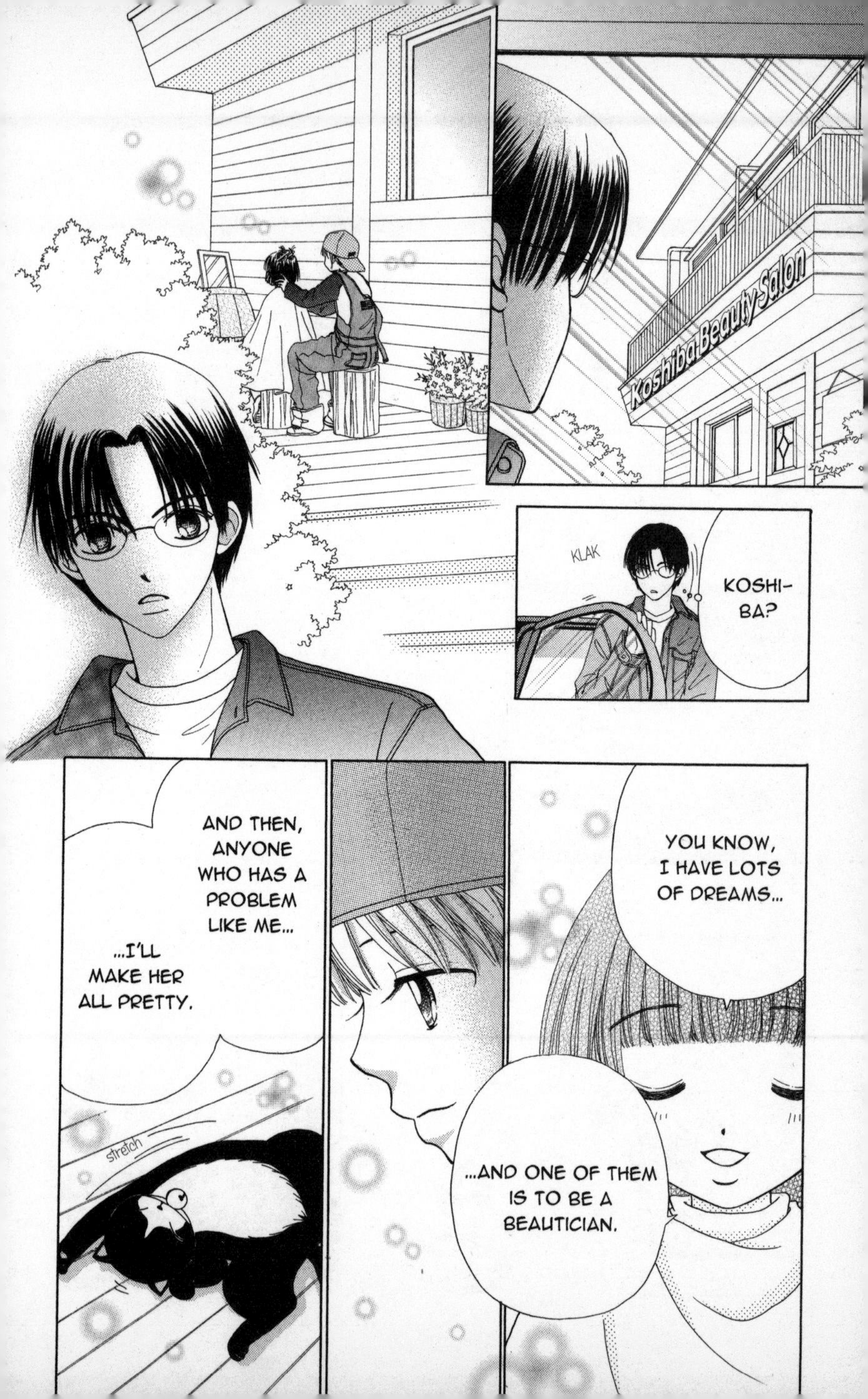
Koshiba Beauty Salon
KLAK
KOSHI-BA?
YOU KNOW, I HAVE LOTS OF DREAMS...
...AND ONE OF THEM IS TO BE A BEAUTICIAN.
AND THEN, ANYONE WHO HAS A PROBLEM LIKE ME...
...I'LL MAKE HER ALL PRETTY.
stretch

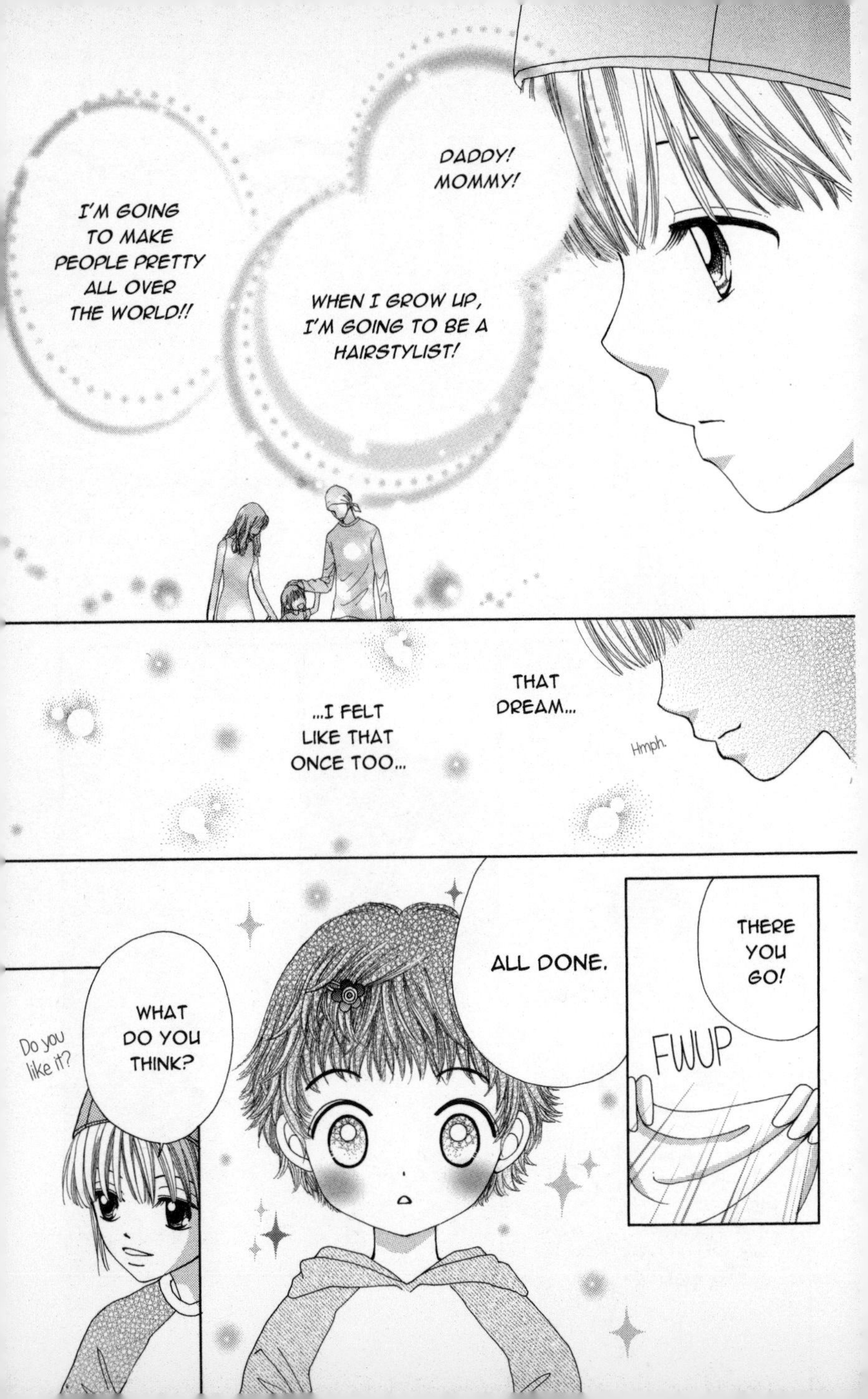
DADDY! MOMMY!
WHEN I GROW UP, I'M GOING TO BE A HAIRSTYLIST!
I'M GOING TO MAKE PEOPLE PRETTY ALL OVER THE WORLD!!
Hmph.
THAT DREAM...
...I FELT LIKE THAT ONCE TOO...
THERE YOU GO!
FWUP
ALL DONE.
WHAT DO YOU THINK?
Do you like it?

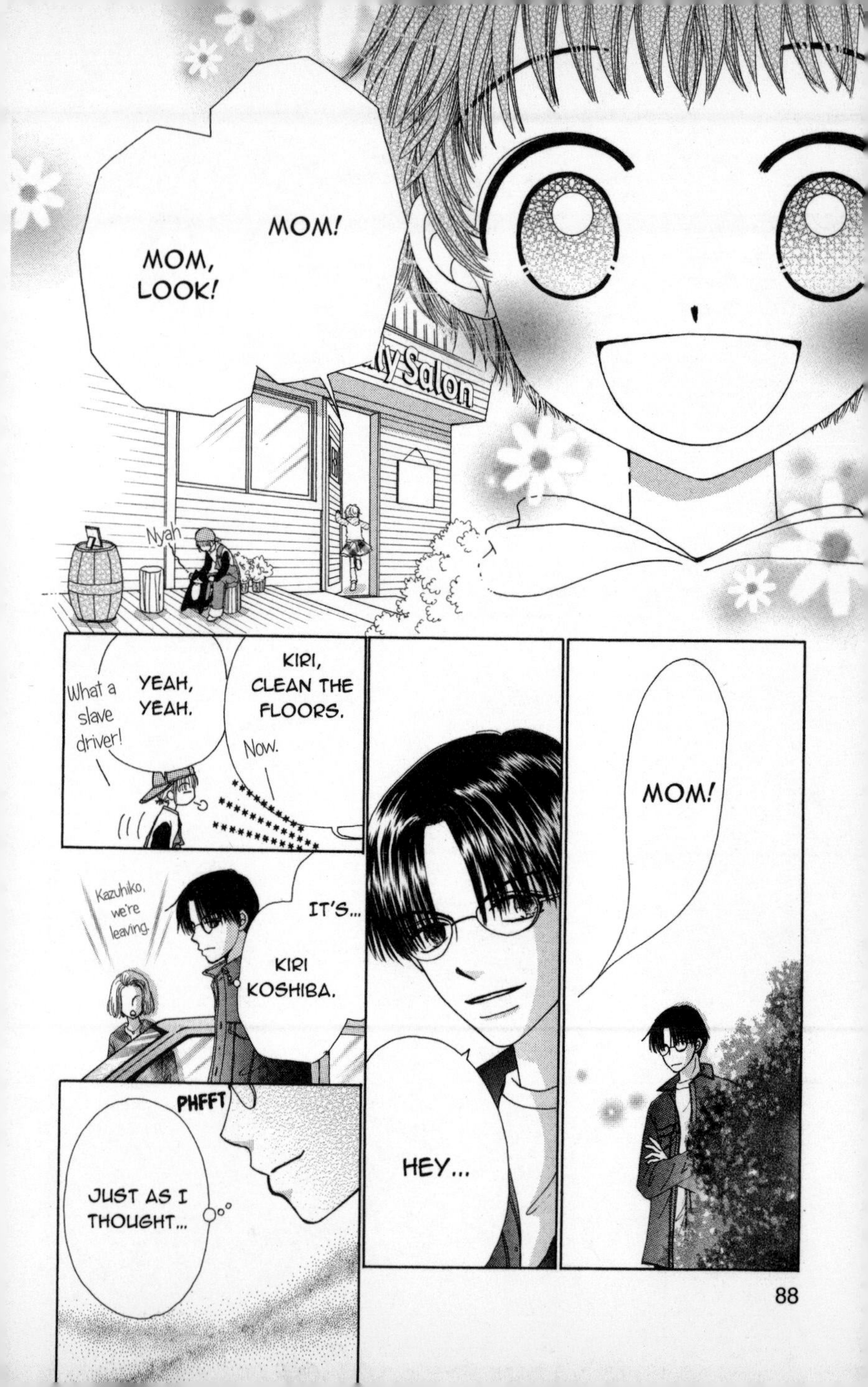
MOM!
MOM, LOOK!
Nyah
MOM!
HEY...
KIRI, CLEAN THE FLOORS.
Now.
YEAH, YEAH.
What a slave driver!
IT'S...
KIRI KOSHIBA.
Kazuhiko, we're leaving.
PHFFT
JUST AS I THOUGHT...

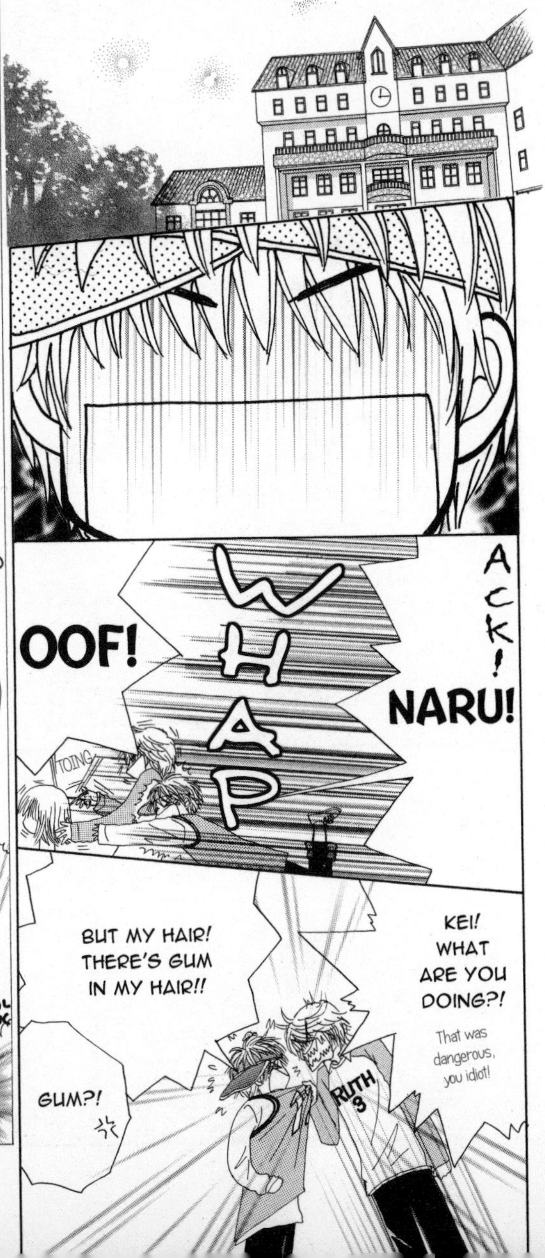
ACK!
NARU!
WHAP
OOF!
TOING
KEI! WHAT ARE YOU DOING?!
That was dangerous, you idiot!
BUT MY HAIR! THERE'S GUM IN MY HAIR!!
GUM?!
RUTH 3

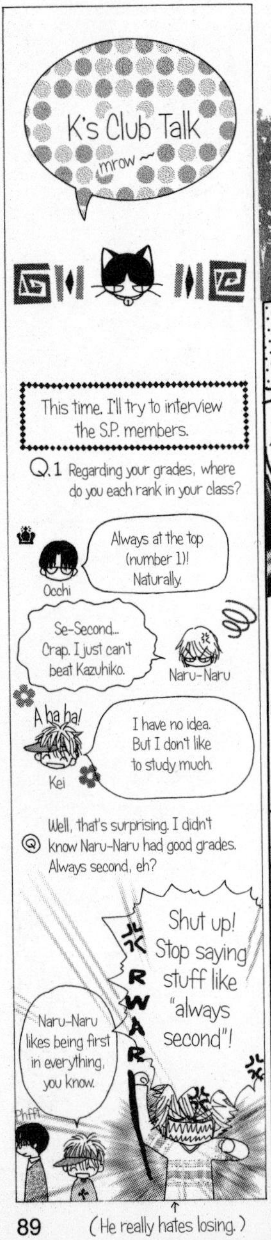
K's Club Talk
mrow~
This time. I'll try to interview the S.P. members.
Q.1 Regarding your grades, where do you each rank in your class?
Always at the top (number 1)! Naturally.
Occhi
Se-Second... Crap. I just can't beat Kazuhiko.
Naru-Naru
A ha ha!
I have no idea. But I don't like to study much.
Kei
Q Well, that's surprising. I didn't know Naru-Naru had good grades. Always second, eh?
Shut up! Stop saying stuff like "always second"!
RWAR
Naru-Naru likes being first in everything, you know.
Phff!

(He really hates losing.)

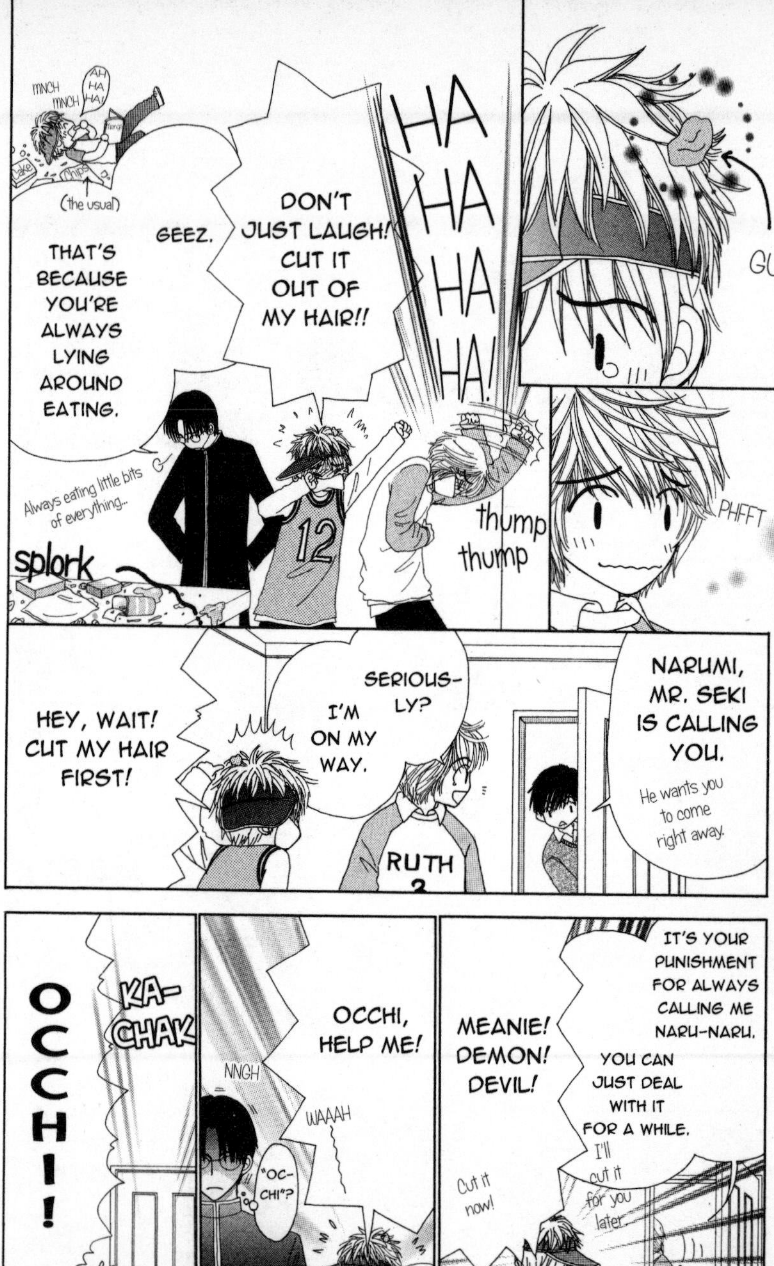
GUM
PHFFT
HA HA HA HA!
DON'T JUST LAUGH! CUT IT OUT OF MY HAIR!!
GEEZ.
THAT'S BECAUSE YOU'RE ALWAYS LYING AROUND EATING.
AH HA HA!
MNCH MNCH
Cake
Chips
(the usual)
Always eating little bits of everything...
splork
thump thump
NARUMI, MR. SEKI IS CALLING YOU.
He wants you to come right away.
SERIOUS-LY?
I'M ON MY WAY.
HEY, WAIT! CUT MY HAIR FIRST!
RUTH
IT'S YOUR PUNISHMENT FOR ALWAYS CALLING ME NARU-NARU.
YOU CAN JUST DEAL WITH IT FOR A WHILE.
I'll cut it for you later.
MEANIE! DEMON! DEVIL!
Cut it now!
OCCHI, HELP ME!
NNGH
WAAAH
"OC-CHI"?
KA-CHAK
OCCHI!

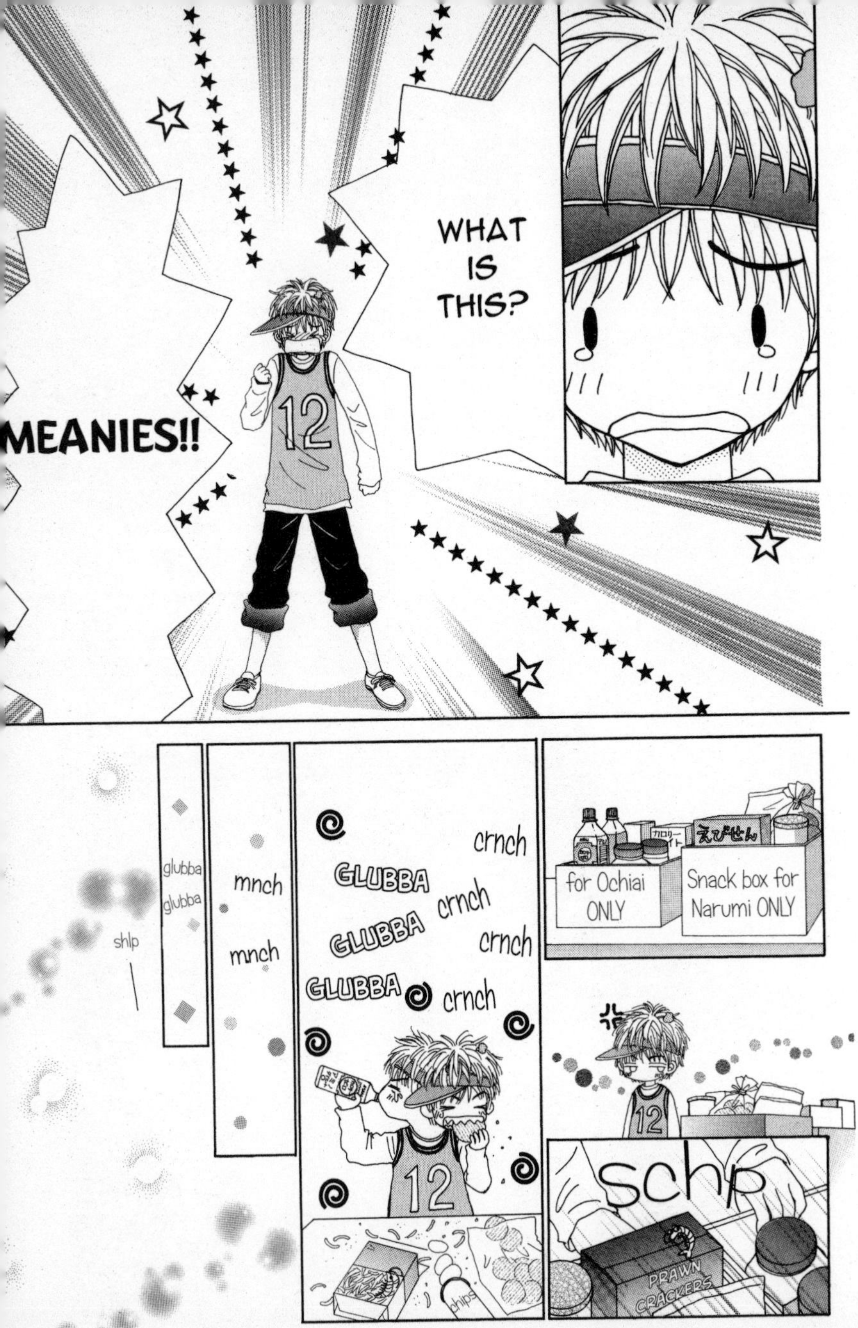
WHAT IS THIS?
MEANIES!!
えびせん
for Ochiai ONLY
Snack box for Narumi ONLY
schp
PRAWN CRACKERS
crnch
GLUBBA
crnch
GLUBBA
crnch
GLUBBA
crnch
chips
mnch
mnch
glubba
glubba
shlp

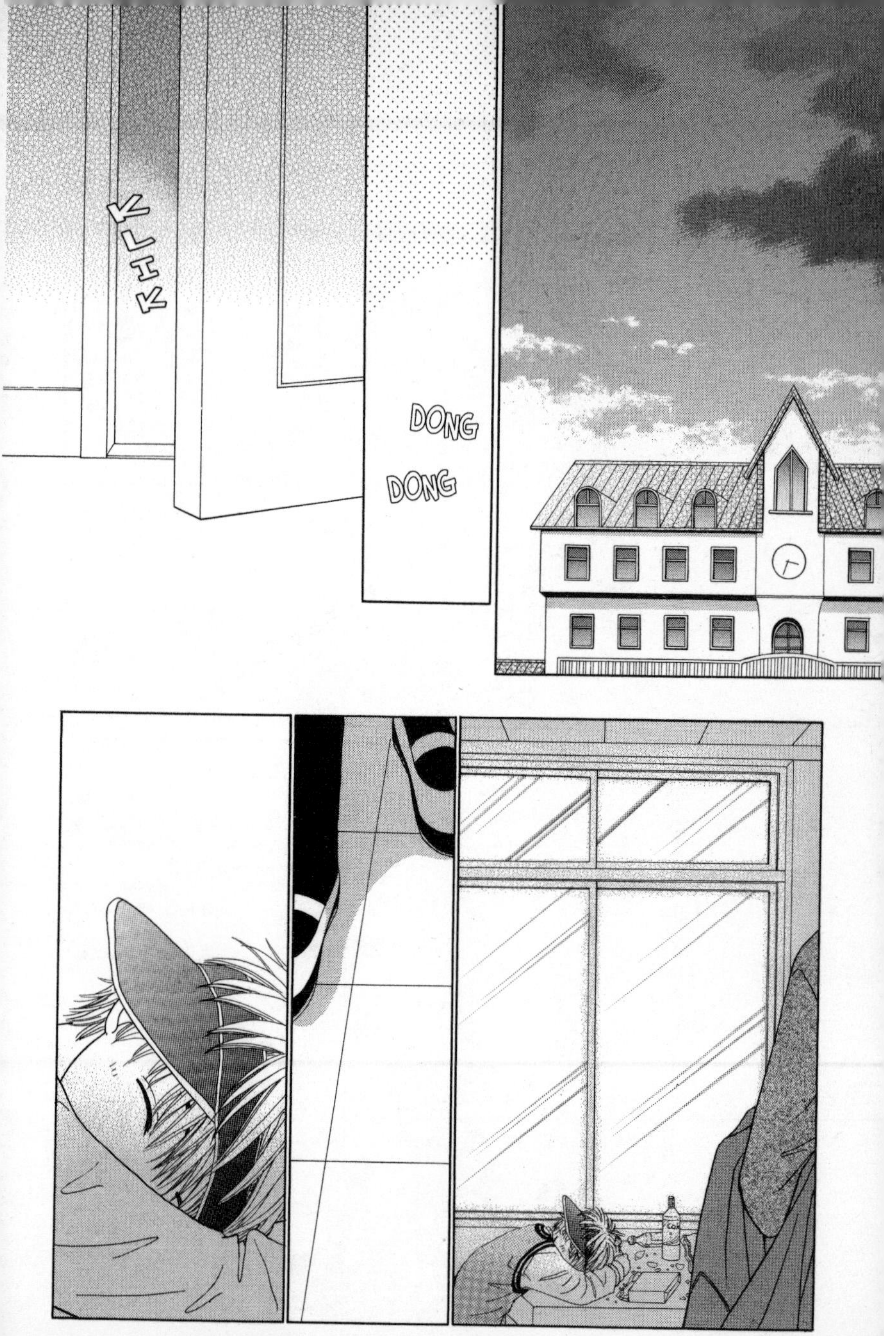
DONG
DONG
KLIK

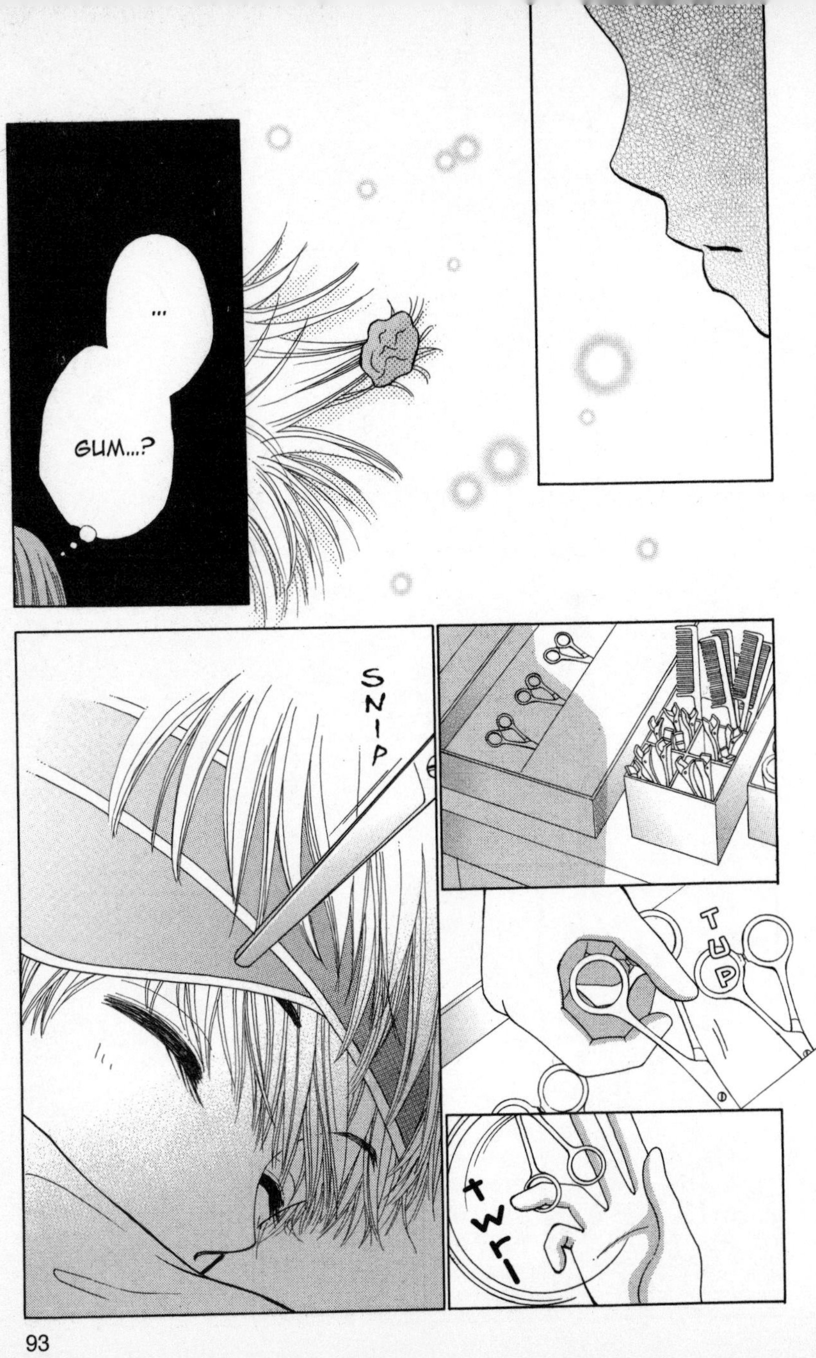
…
GUM…?
TUP
twrl
SNIP

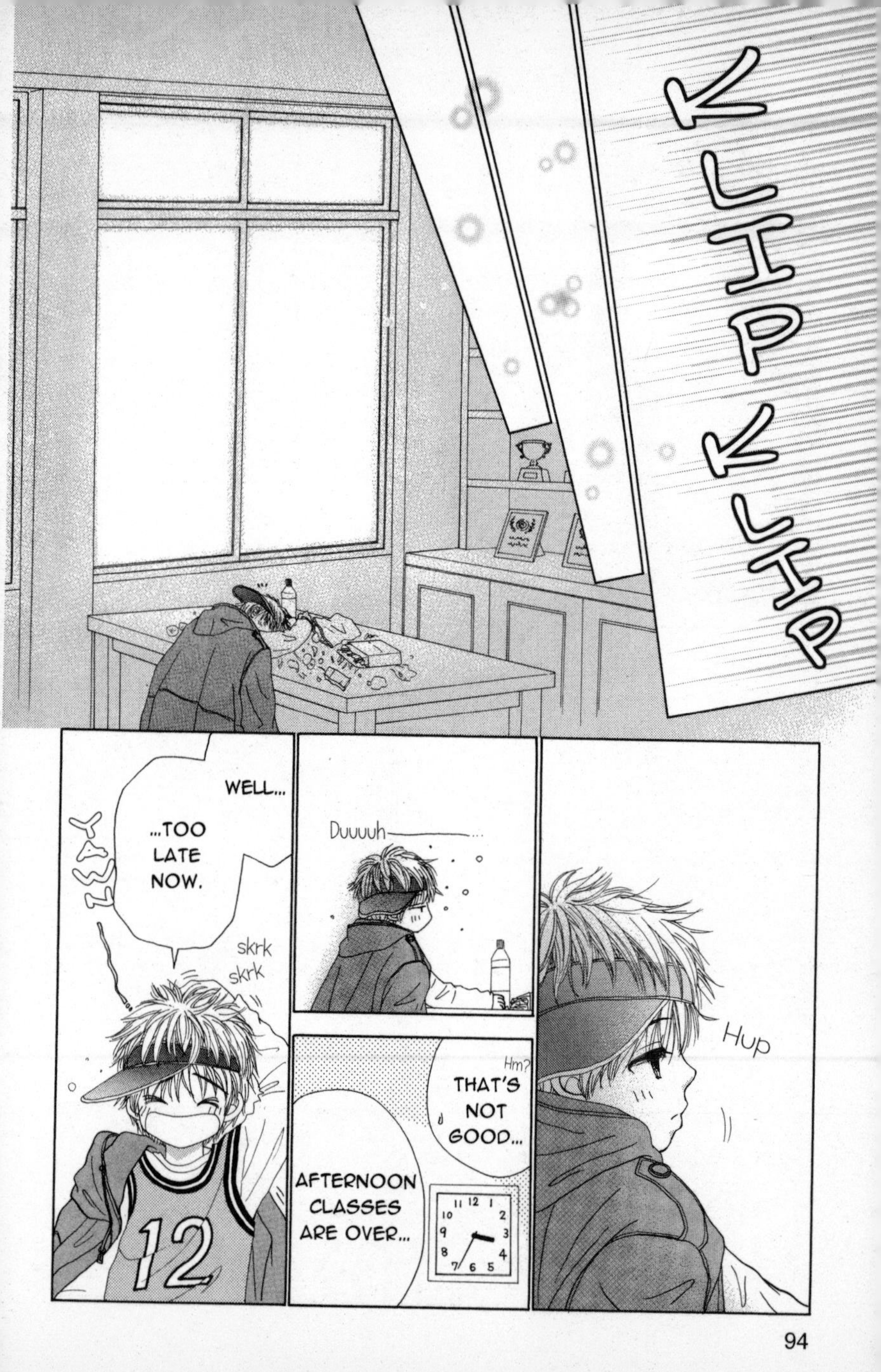
KLIP KLIP
Hup
Duuuuh...
Hm?
THAT'S NOT GOOD...
AFTERNOON CLASSES ARE OVER...
WELL...
...TOO LATE NOW.
YAWN
skrk skrk

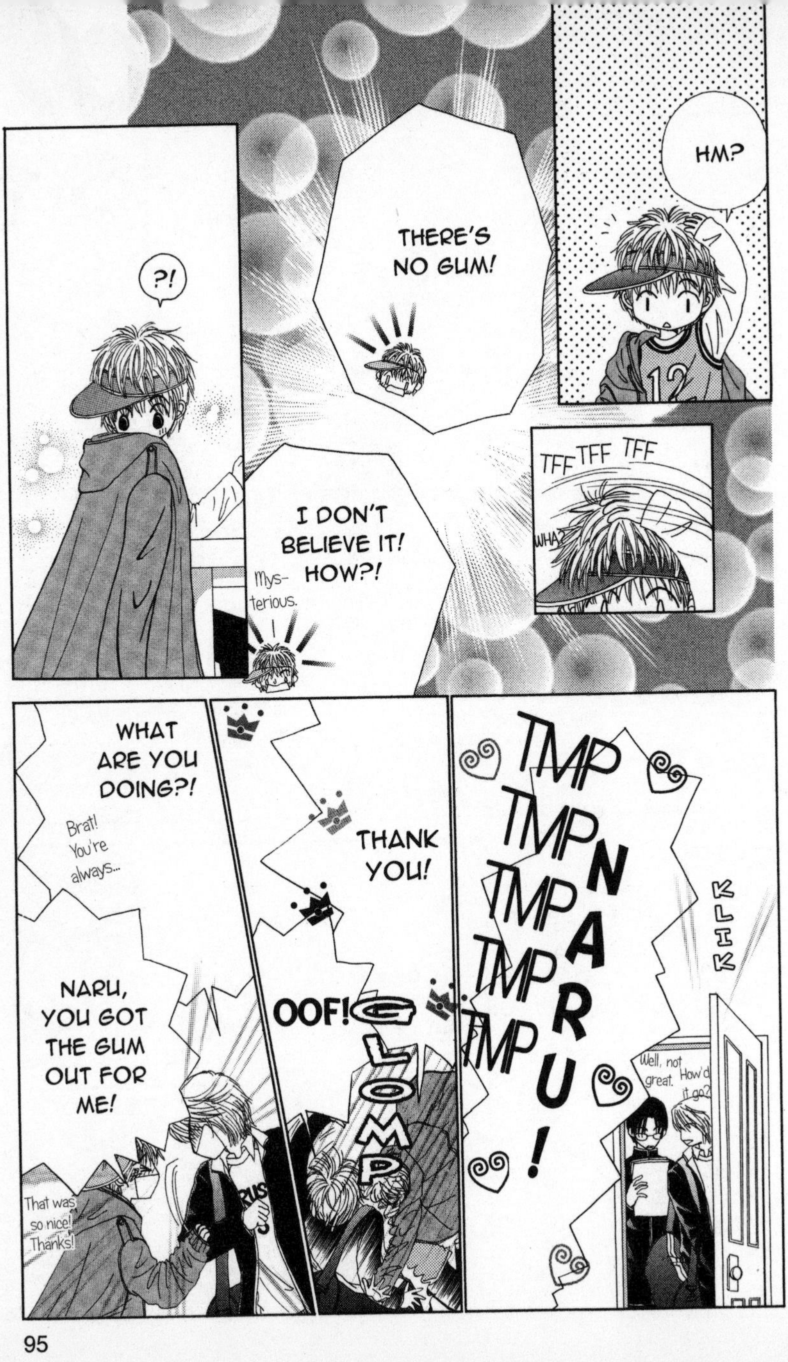
HM?
TFF TFF TFF
WHA
THERE'S NO GUM!
I DON'T BELIEVE IT! HOW?!
Mys-terious.
?!
KLIK
TMP TMP TMP TMP TMP
NARU!
How'd it go?
Well, not great.
THANK YOU!
OOF!
GLOMP
WHAT ARE YOU DOING?!
Brat! You're always...
NARU, YOU GOT THE GUM OUT FOR ME!
That was so nice! Thanks!

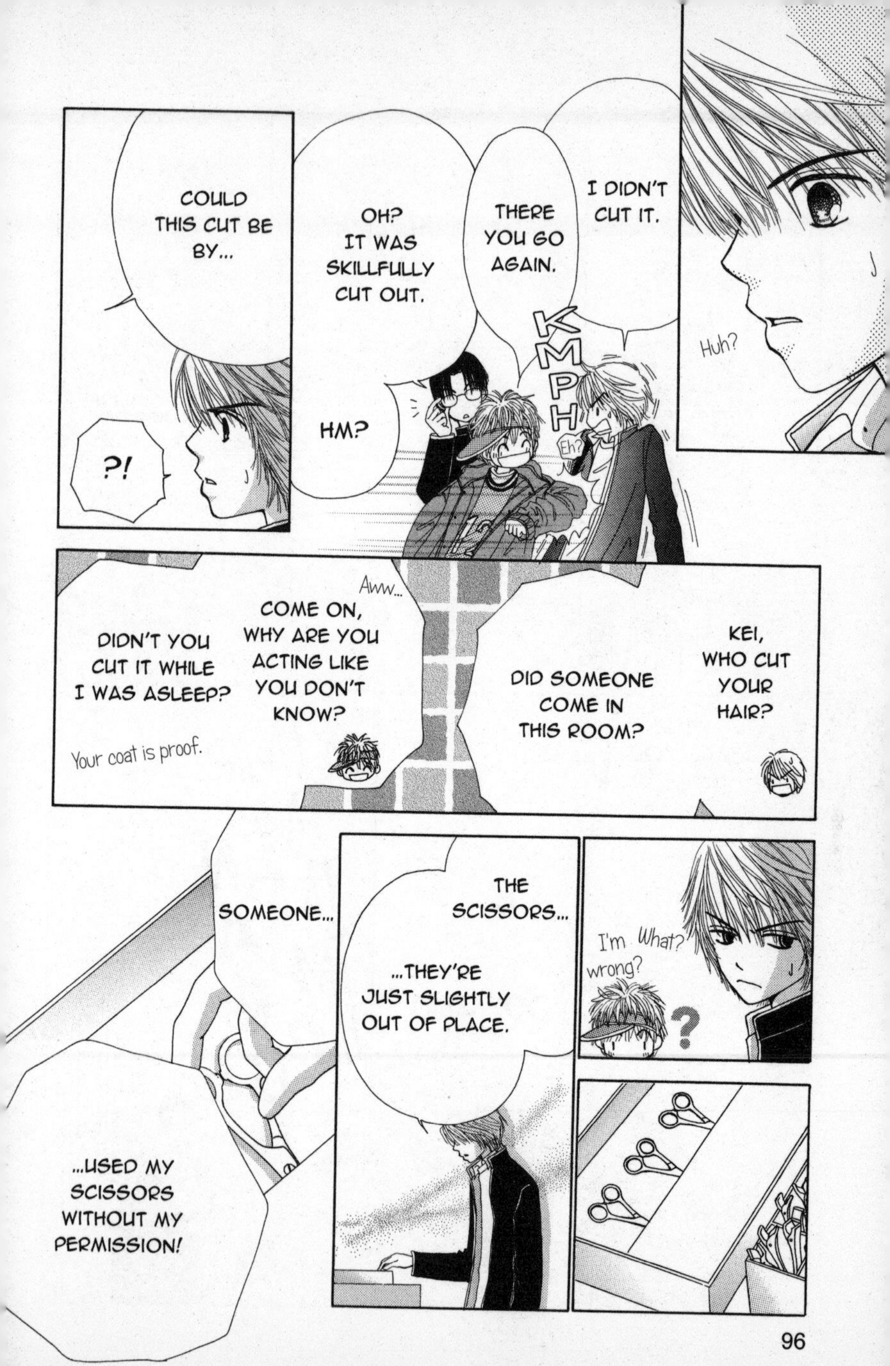
I DIDN'T CUT IT.
Huh?
THERE YOU GO AGAIN.
KMPH
Eh?
OH? IT WAS SKILLFULLY CUT OUT.
HM?
COULD THIS CUT BE BY...
?!
KEI, WHO CUT YOUR HAIR?
DID SOMEONE COME IN THIS ROOM?
Aww...
COME ON, WHY ARE YOU ACTING LIKE YOU DON'T KNOW?
DIDN'T YOU CUT IT WHILE I WAS ASLEEP?
Your coat is proof.
What?
I'm wrong?
?
THE SCISSORS...
...THEY'RE JUST SLIGHTLY OUT OF PLACE.
SOMEONE...
...USED MY SCISSORS WITHOUT MY PERMISSION!

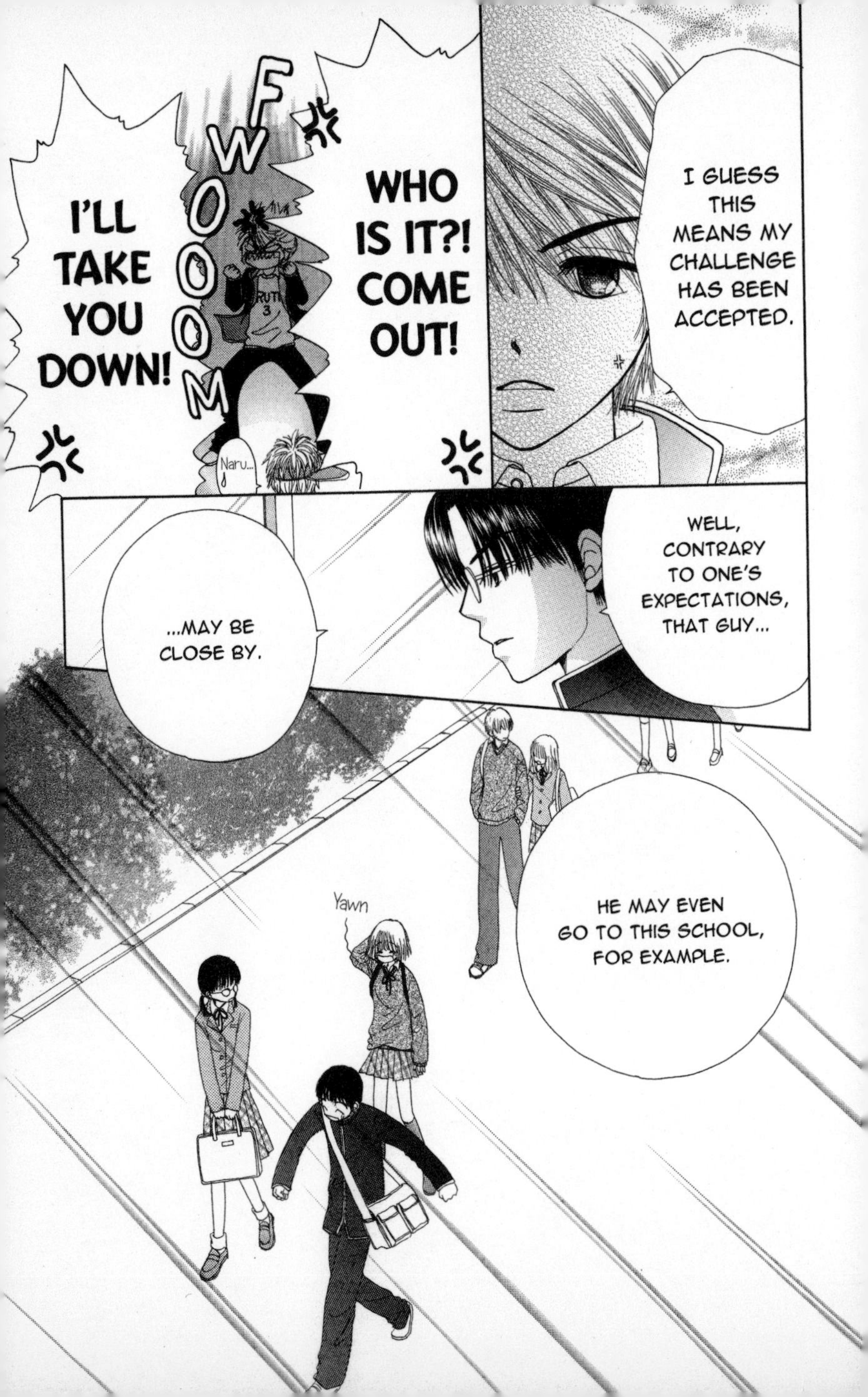
I GUESS THIS MEANS MY CHALLENGE HAS BEEN ACCEPTED.
FWOOOOM
WHO IS IT?! COME OUT!
I'LL TAKE YOU DOWN!
Naru...
WELL, CONTRARY TO ONE'S EXPECTATIONS, THAT GUY...
...MAY BE CLOSE BY.
HE MAY EVEN GO TO THIS SCHOOL, FOR EXAMPLE.
Yawn

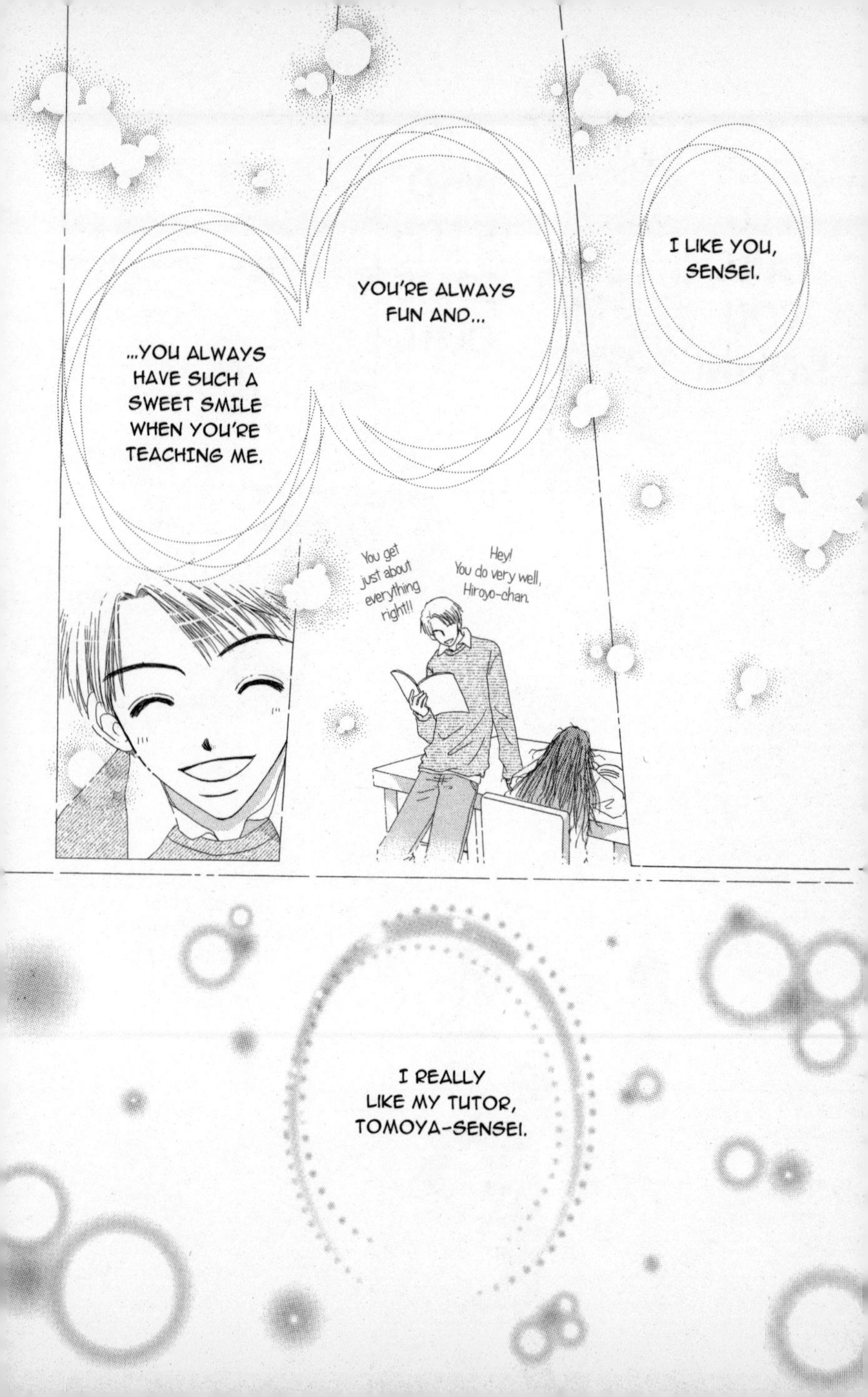
I LIKE YOU, SENSEI.
YOU'RE ALWAYS FUN AND...
Hey! You do very well, Hiroyo-chan.
You get just about everything right!!
...YOU ALWAYS HAVE SUCH A SWEET SMILE WHEN YOU'RE TEACHING ME.
I REALLY LIKE MY TUTOR, TOMOYA-SENSEI.

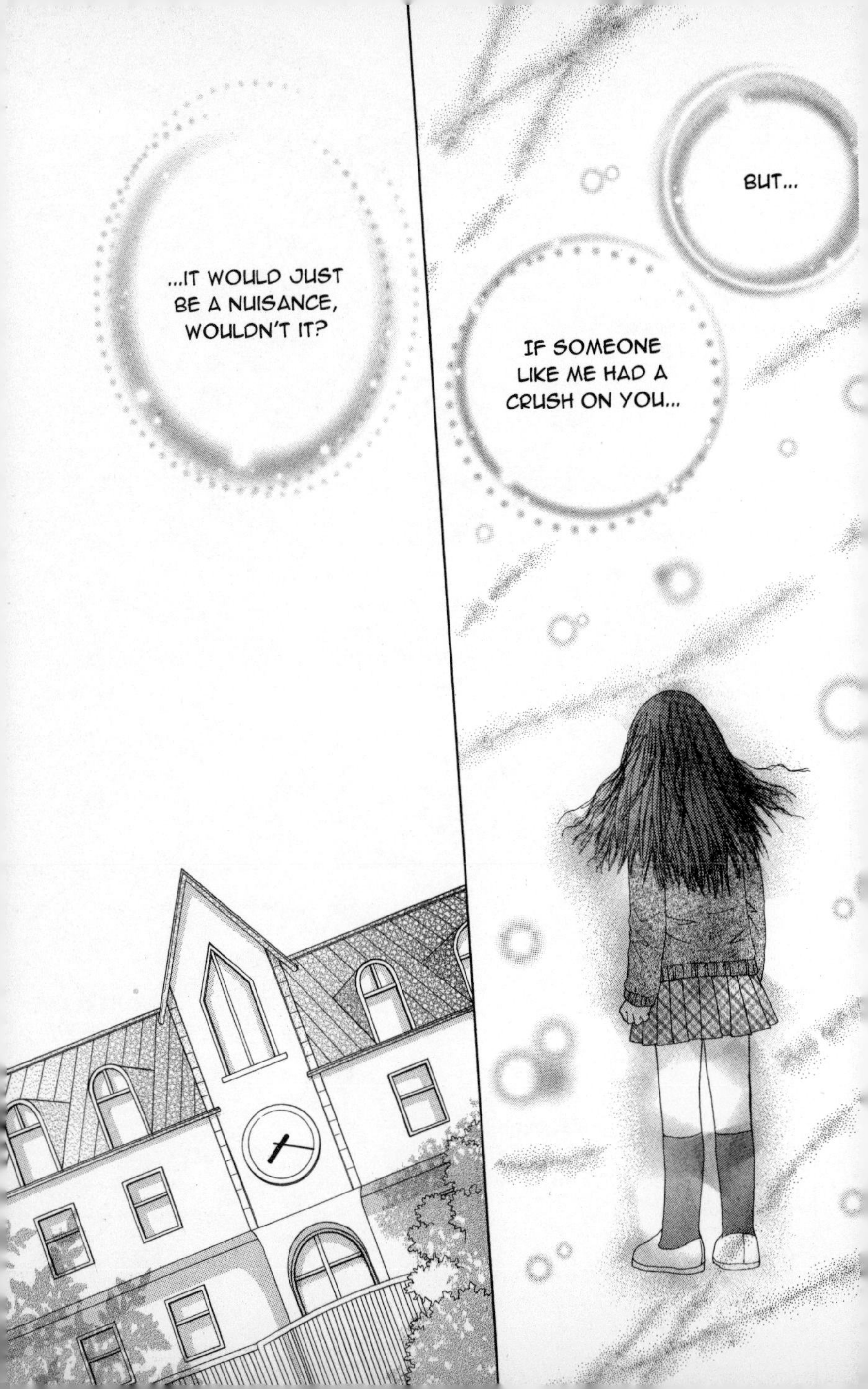
BUT...
IF SOMEONE LIKE ME HAD A CRUSH ON YOU...
...IT WOULD JUST BE A NUISANCE, WOULDN'T IT?

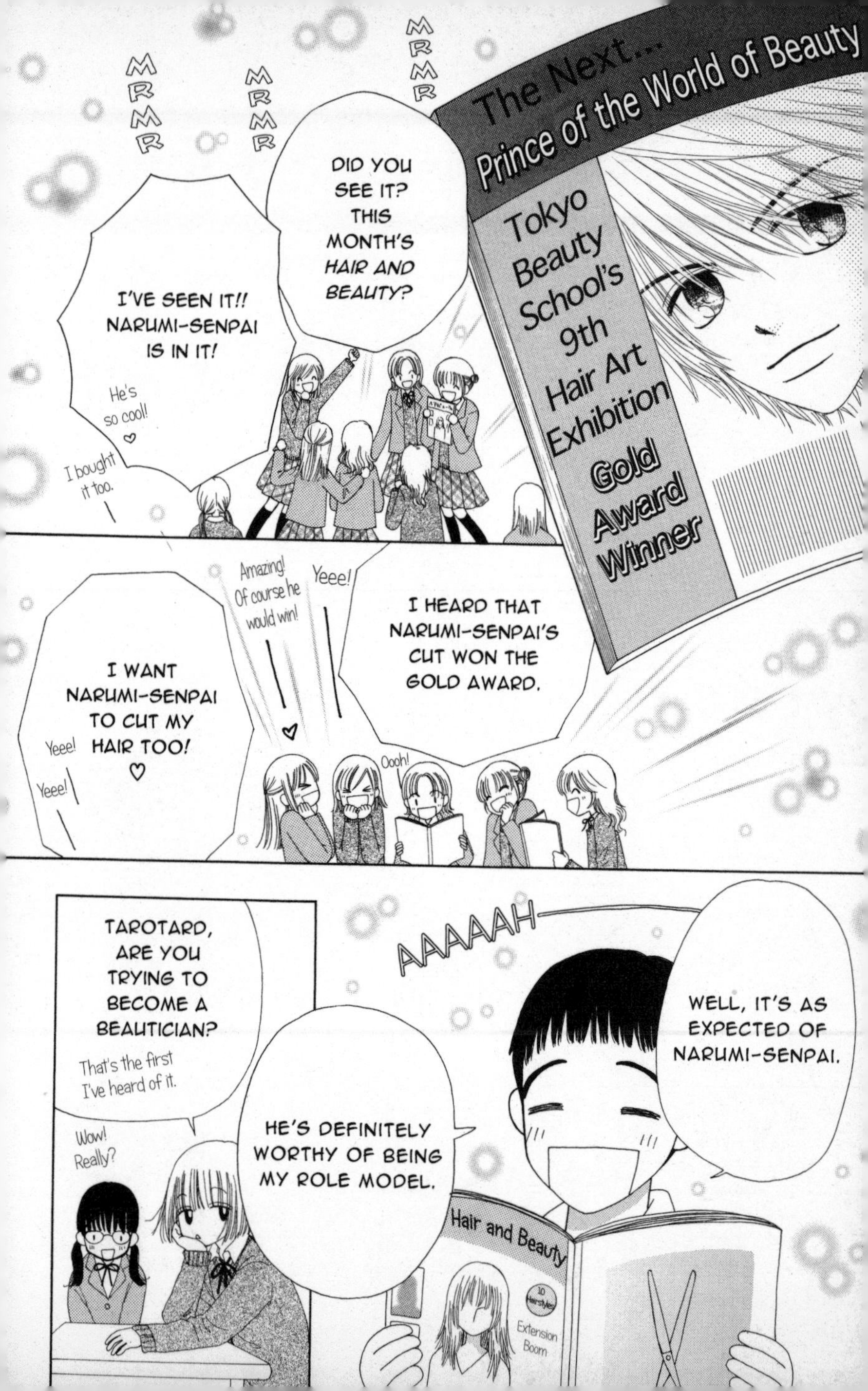

The Next...
Prince of the World of Beauty
Tokyo Beauty School's 9th Hair Art Exhibition
Gold Award Winner
MRMR
MRMR
MRMR
DID YOU SEE IT? THIS MONTH'S HAIR AND BEAUTY?
I'VE SEEN IT!! NARUMI-SENPAI IS IN IT!
He's so cool! ♡
I bought it too.
I HEARD THAT NARUMI-SENPAI'S CUT WON THE GOLD AWARD.
Yeee!
Amazing! Of course he would win! ♡
Oooh!
I WANT NARUMI-SENPAI TO CUT MY HAIR TOO! ♡
Yeee!
Yeee!
AAAAAH—
WELL, IT'S AS EXPECTED OF NARUMI-SENPAI.
HE'S DEFINITELY WORTHY OF BEING MY ROLE MODEL.
TAROTARD, ARE YOU TRYING TO BECOME A BEAUTICIAN?
That's the first I've heard of it.
Wow! Really?
Hair and Beauty
Extension Boom

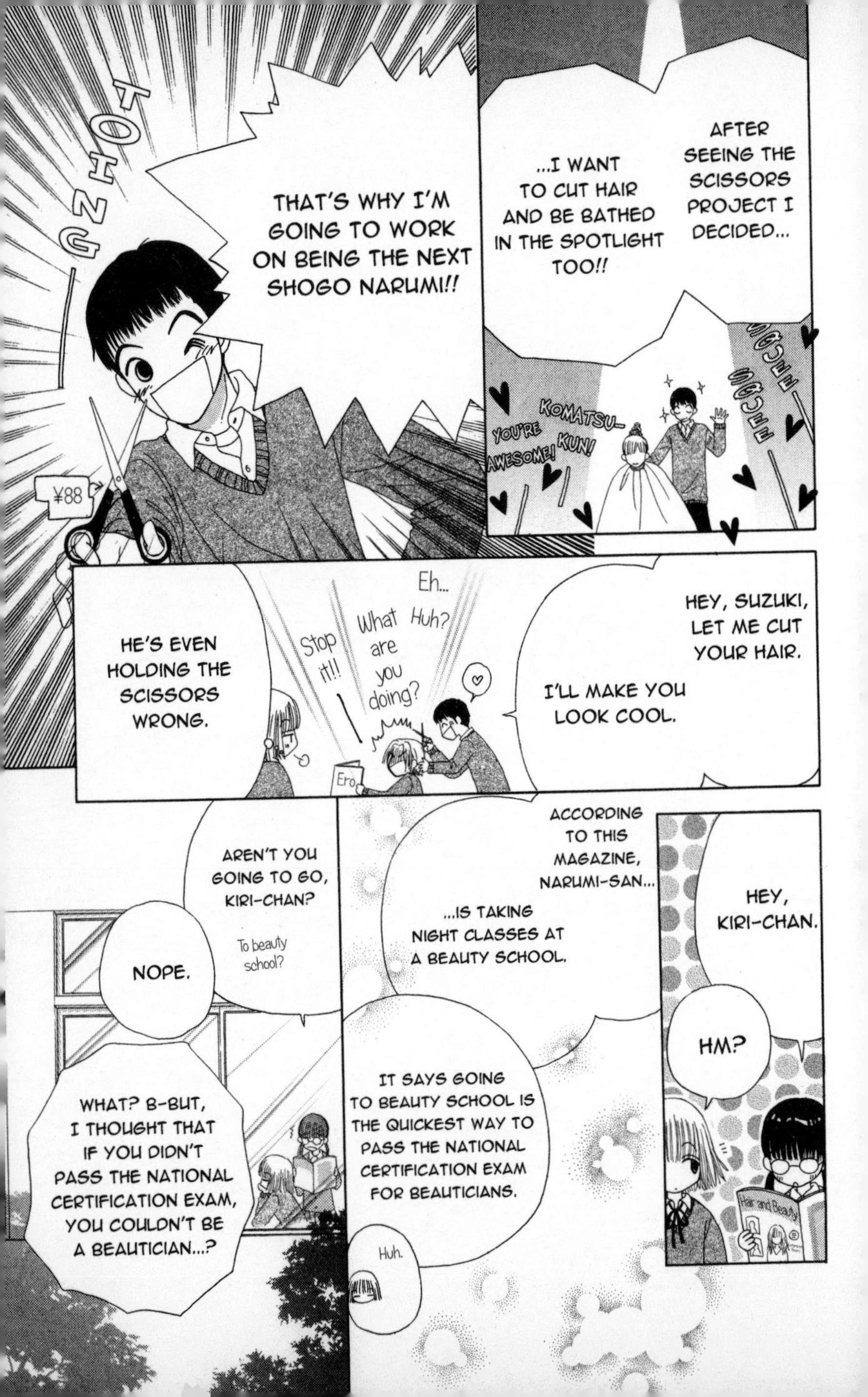
AFTER SEEING THE SCISSORS PROJECT I DECIDED...
...I WANT TO CUT HAIR AND BE BATHED IN THE SPOTLIGHT TOO!!
KOMATSU-KUN!
YOU'RE AWESOME!
TOING
THAT'S WHY I'M GOING TO WORK ON BEING THE NEXT SHOGO NARUMI!!
¥88
HEY, SUZUKI, LET ME CUT YOUR HAIR.
I'LL MAKE YOU LOOK COOL.
Eh...
Huh?
What are you doing?
Stop it!!
Ero
HE'S EVEN HOLDING THE SCISSORS WRONG.
HEY, KIRI-CHAN.
HM?
Hair and Beauty
ACCORDING TO THIS MAGAZINE, NARUMI-SAN...
...IS TAKING NIGHT CLASSES AT A BEAUTY SCHOOL.
IT SAYS GOING TO BEAUTY SCHOOL IS THE QUICKEST WAY TO PASS THE NATIONAL CERTIFICATION EXAM FOR BEAUTICIANS.
Huh.
AREN'T YOU GOING TO GO, KIRI-CHAN?
To beauty school?
NOPE.
WHAT? B-BUT, I THOUGHT THAT IF YOU DIDN'T PASS THE NATIONAL CERTIFICATION EXAM, YOU COULDN'T BE A BEAUTICIAN...?

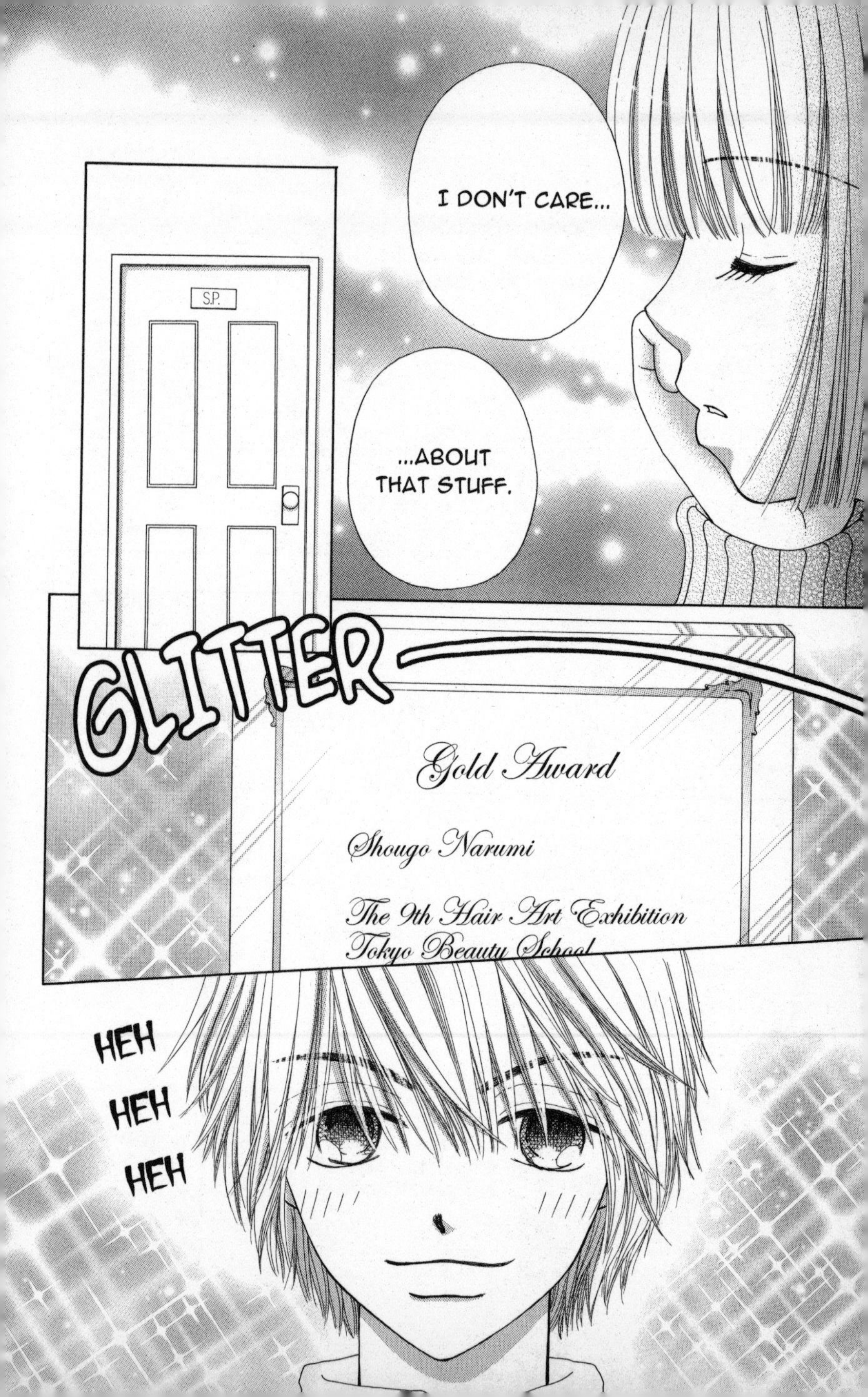
I DON'T CARE...
...ABOUT THAT STUFF.
S.P.
GLITTER
Gold Award
Shougo Narumi
The 9th Hair Art Exhibition
Tokyo Beauty School
HEH HEH HEH

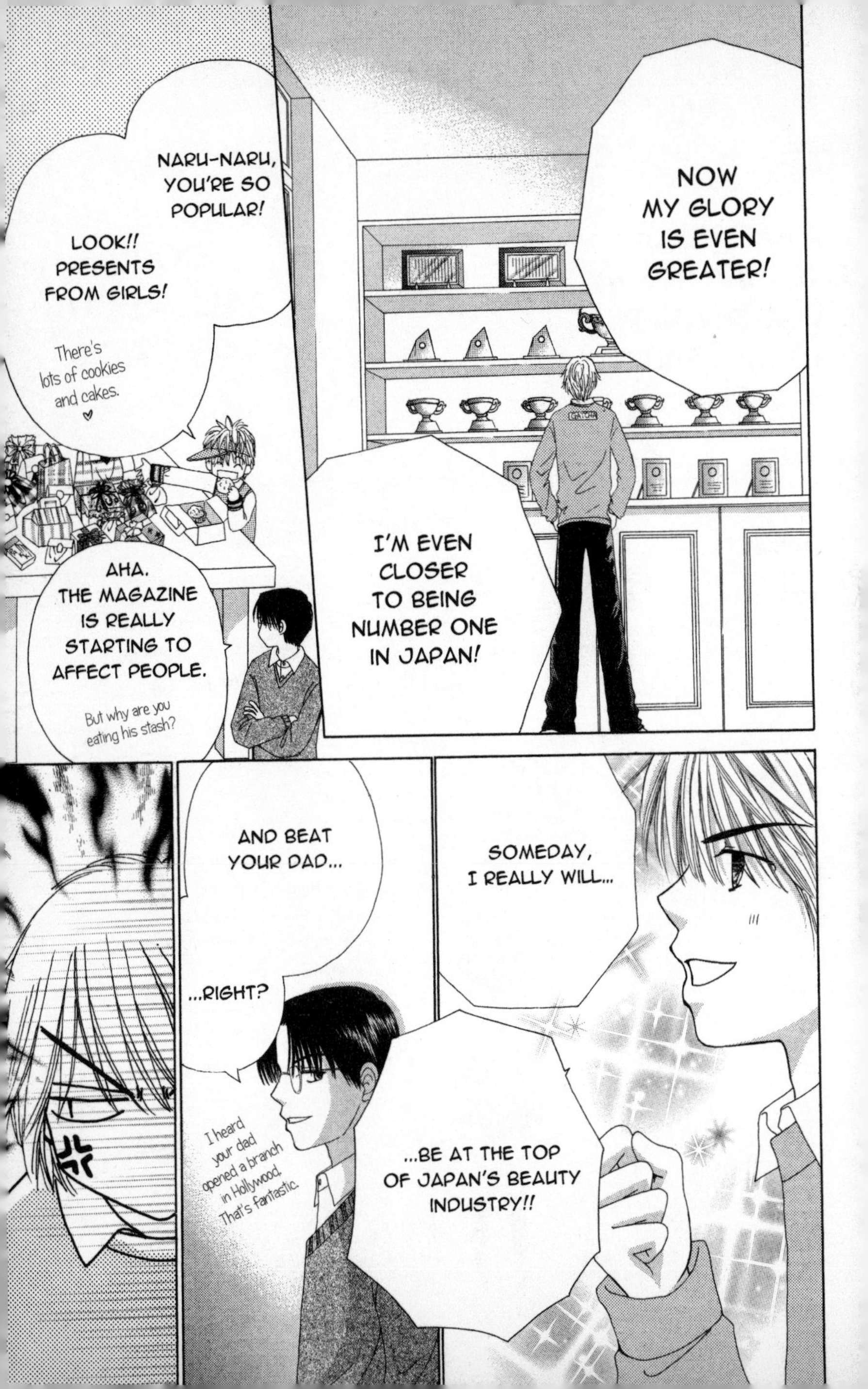
NOW MY GLORY IS EVEN GREATER!
I'M EVEN CLOSER TO BEING NUMBER ONE IN JAPAN!
NARU-NARU, YOU'RE SO POPULAR!
LOOK!! PRESENTS FROM GIRLS!
There's lots of cookies and cakes. ♡
AHA. THE MAGAZINE IS REALLY STARTING TO AFFECT PEOPLE.
But why are you eating his stash?
SOMEDAY, I REALLY WILL...
...BE AT THE TOP OF JAPAN'S BEAUTY INDUSTRY!!
AND BEAT YOUR DAD...
...RIGHT?
I heard your dad opened a branch in Hollywood. That's fantastic.

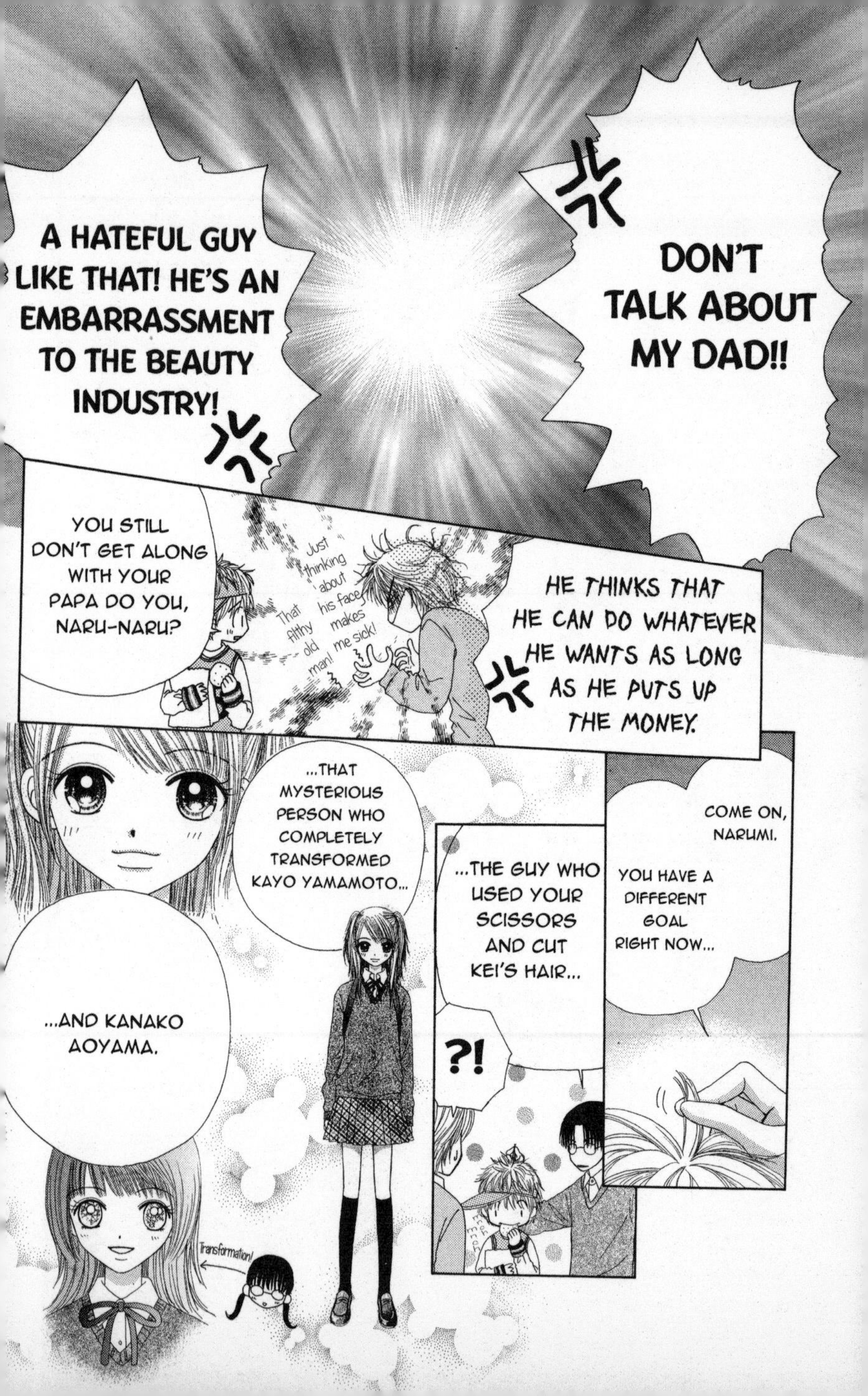
DON'T TALK ABOUT MY DAD!!
A HATEFUL GUY LIKE THAT! HE'S AN EMBARRASSMENT TO THE BEAUTY INDUSTRY!
HE THINKS THAT HE CAN DO WHATEVER HE WANTS AS LONG AS HE PUTS UP THE MONEY.
Just thinking about his face makes me sick!
That filthy old man!
YOU STILL DON'T GET ALONG WITH YOUR PAPA DO YOU, NARU-NARU?
COME ON, NARUMI.
YOU HAVE A DIFFERENT GOAL RIGHT NOW...
...THE GUY WHO USED YOUR SCISSORS AND CUT KEI'S HAIR...
?!
...THAT MYSTERIOUS PERSON WHO COMPLETELY TRANSFORMED KAYO YAMAMOTO...
...AND KANAKO AOYAMA.
Transformation!

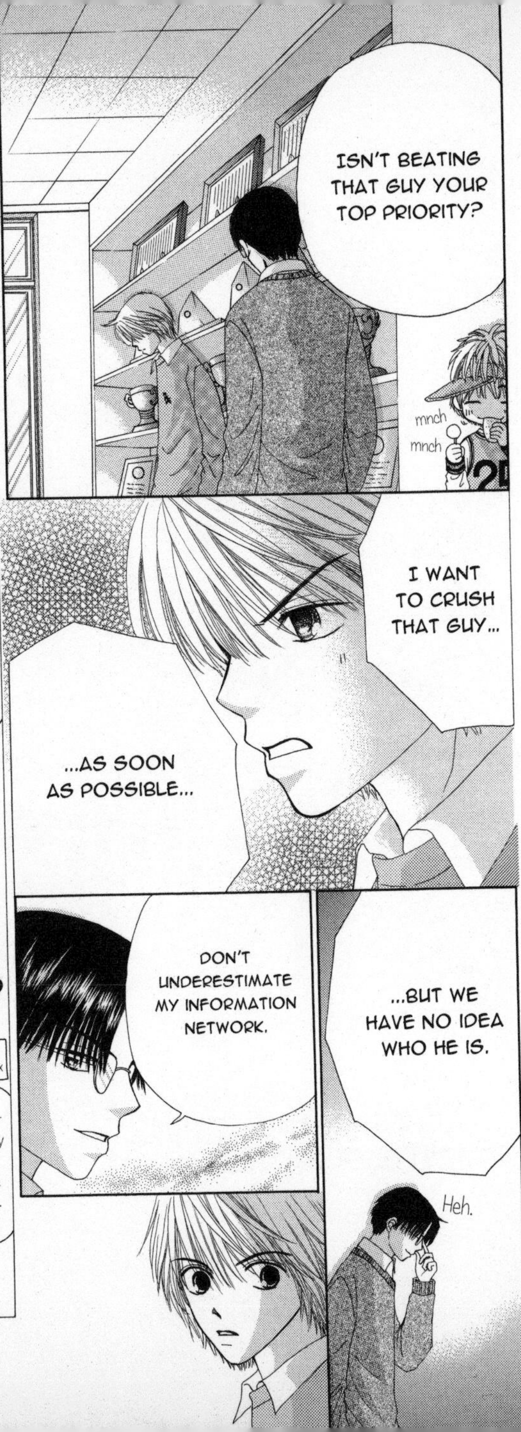
ISN'T BEATING THAT GUY YOUR TOP PRIORITY?
mnch mnch
I WANT TO CRUSH THAT GUY...
...AS SOON AS POSSIBLE...
...BUT WE HAVE NO IDEA WHO HE IS.
DON'T UNDERESTIMATE MY INFORMATION NETWORK.
Heh.

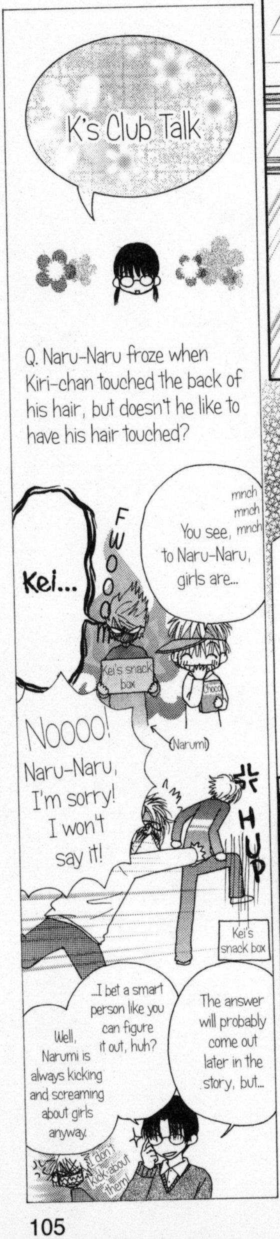
K's Club Talk
Q. Naru-Naru froze when Kiri-chan touched the back of his hair, but doesn't he like to have his hair touched?
mnch mnch mnch
You see, to Naru-Naru, girls are...
Kei...
FWOOOM
Kei's snack box
Choco
Noooo! Naru-Naru, I'm sorry! I won't say it!
(Narumi)
HUP
Kei's snack box
The answer will probably come out later in the story, but...
...I bet a smart person like you can figure it out, huh?
Well, Narumi is always kicking and screaming about girls anyway.
I don't kick about them!

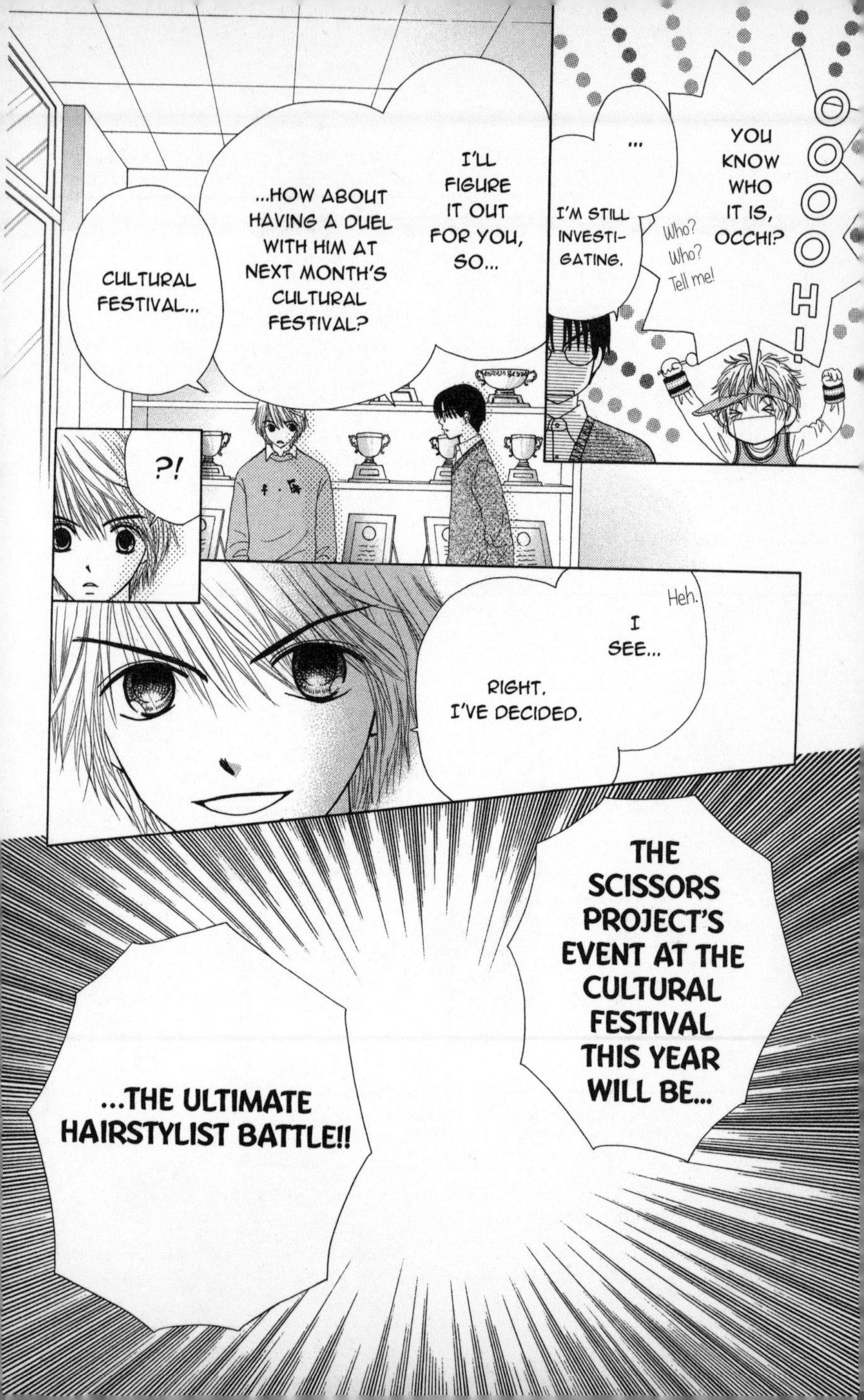
YOU KNOW WHO IT IS, OCCHI?
OOOOH!
Who? Who? Tell me!
...
I'M STILL INVESTIGATING.
I'LL FIGURE IT OUT FOR YOU, SO...
...HOW ABOUT HAVING A DUEL WITH HIM AT NEXT MONTH'S CULTURAL FESTIVAL?
CULTURAL FESTIVAL...
?!
Heh.
I SEE...
RIGHT. I'VE DECIDED.
THE SCISSORS PROJECT'S EVENT AT THE CULTURAL FESTIVAL THIS YEAR WILL BE...
...THE ULTIMATE HAIRSTYLIST BATTLE!!

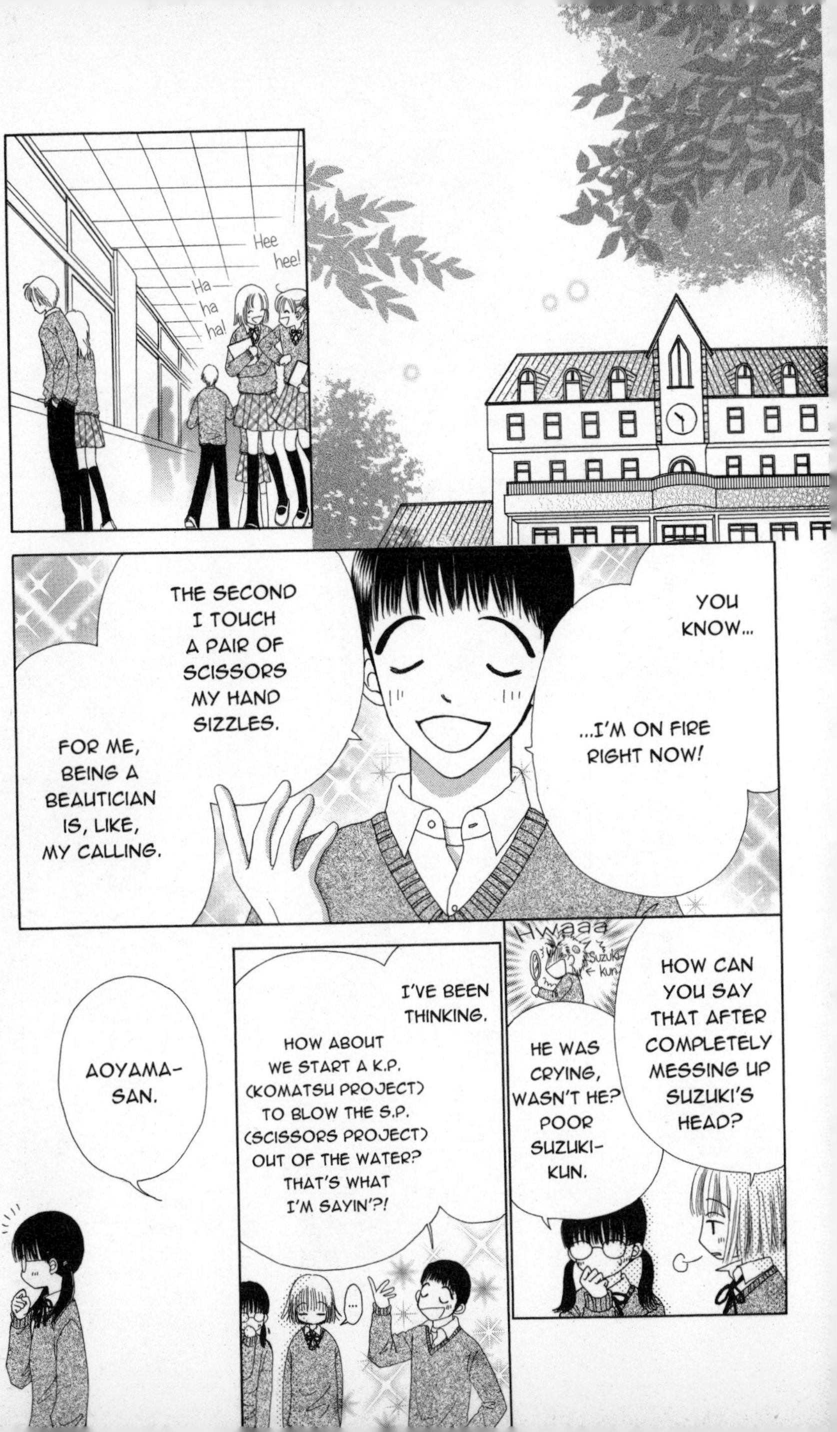
Hee hee!
Ha- ha ha!
YOU KNOW...
...I'M ON FIRE RIGHT NOW!
THE SECOND I TOUCH A PAIR OF SCISSORS MY HAND SIZZLES.
FOR ME, BEING A BEAUTICIAN IS, LIKE, MY CALLING.
Hwaaa
Suzuki-kun
HOW CAN YOU SAY THAT AFTER COMPLETELY MESSING UP SUZUKI'S HEAD?
HE WAS CRYING, WASN'T HE? POOR SUZUKI-KUN.
I'VE BEEN THINKING.
HOW ABOUT WE START A K.P. (KOMATSU PROJECT) TO BLOW THE S.P. (SCISSORS PROJECT) OUT OF THE WATER? THAT'S WHAT I'M SAYIN'?!
...
AOYAMA-SAN.

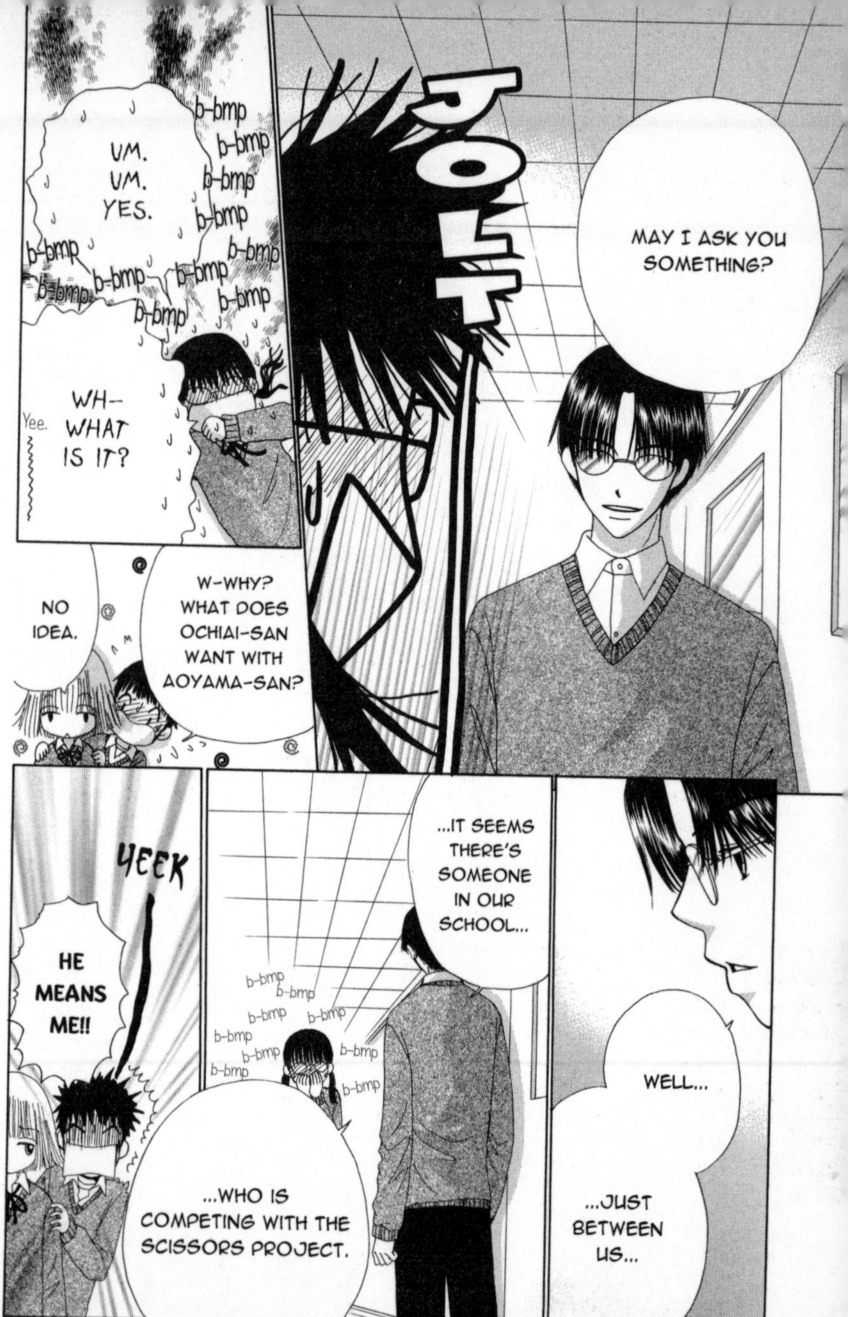

MAY I ASK YOU SOMETHING?
JOLT
b-bmp b-bmp b-bmp b-bmp b-bmp b-bmp b-bmp b-bmp b-bmp b-bmp b-bmp
UM. UM. YES.
WH- WHAT IS IT?
Yee.
W-WHY? WHAT DOES OCHIAI-SAN WANT WITH AOYAMA-SAN?
NO IDEA.
WELL...
...JUST BETWEEN US...
...IT SEEMS THERE'S SOMEONE IN OUR SCHOOL...
b-bmp b-bmp b-bmp b-bmp b-bmp b-bmp b-bmp b-bmp b-bmp
...WHO IS COMPETING WITH THE SCISSORS PROJECT.
YEEK
HE MEANS ME!!

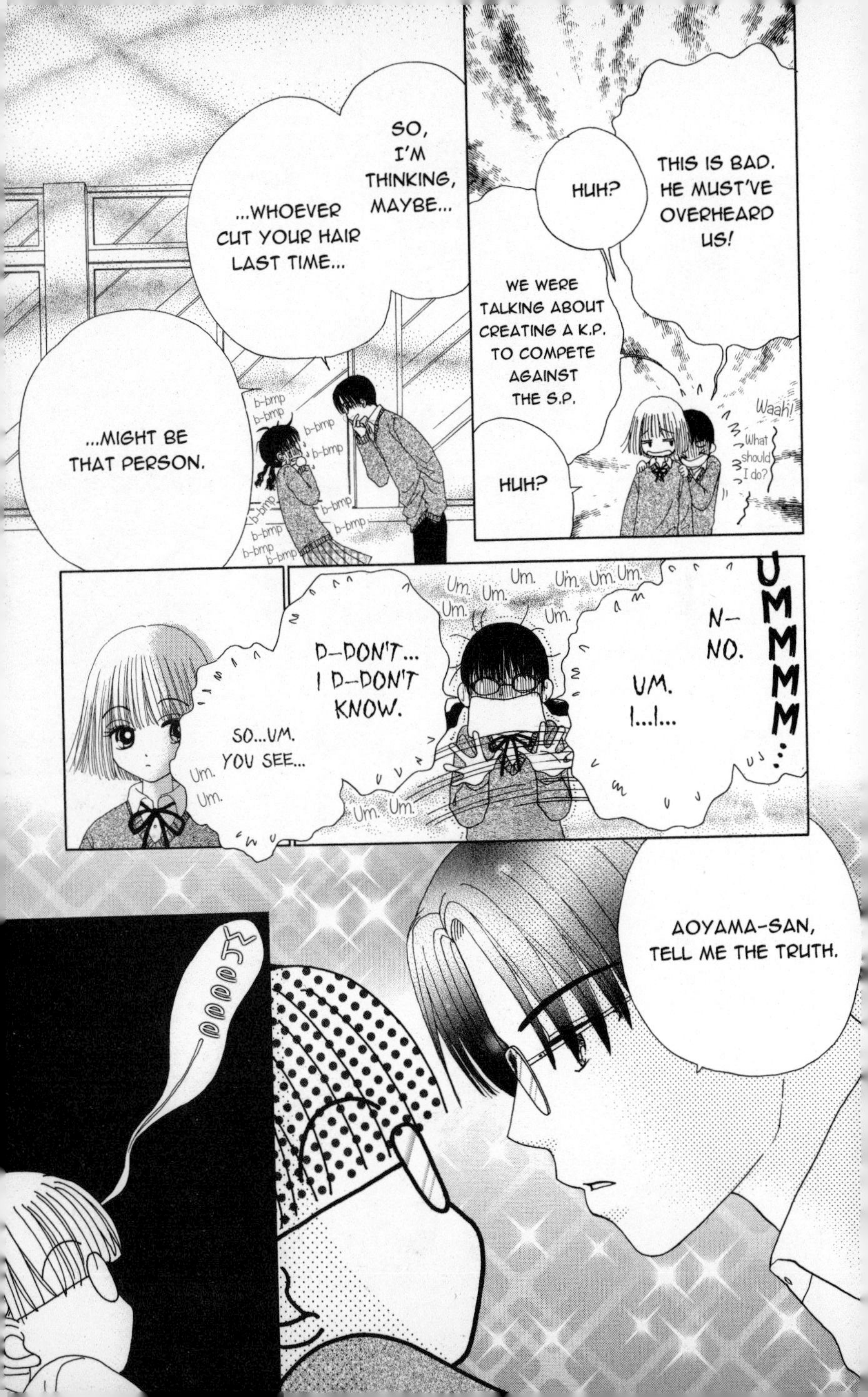
THIS IS BAD. HE MUST'VE OVERHEARD US!
HUH?
WE WERE TALKING ABOUT CREATING A K.P. TO COMPETE AGAINST THE S.P.
Waah!
What should I do?
HUH?
SO, I'M THINKING, MAYBE...
...WHOEVER CUT YOUR HAIR LAST TIME...
b-bmp b-bmp b-bmp b-bmp
...MIGHT BE THAT PERSON.
b-bmp b-bmp b-bmp b-bmp b-bmp b-bmp
UMMMM...
N-NO.
UM. I...I...
Um. Um. Um. Um. Um. Um. Um.
D-DON'T... I D-DON'T KNOW.
SO...UM. YOU SEE...
Um. Um.
Um. Um.
AOYAMA-SAN, TELL ME THE TRUTH.

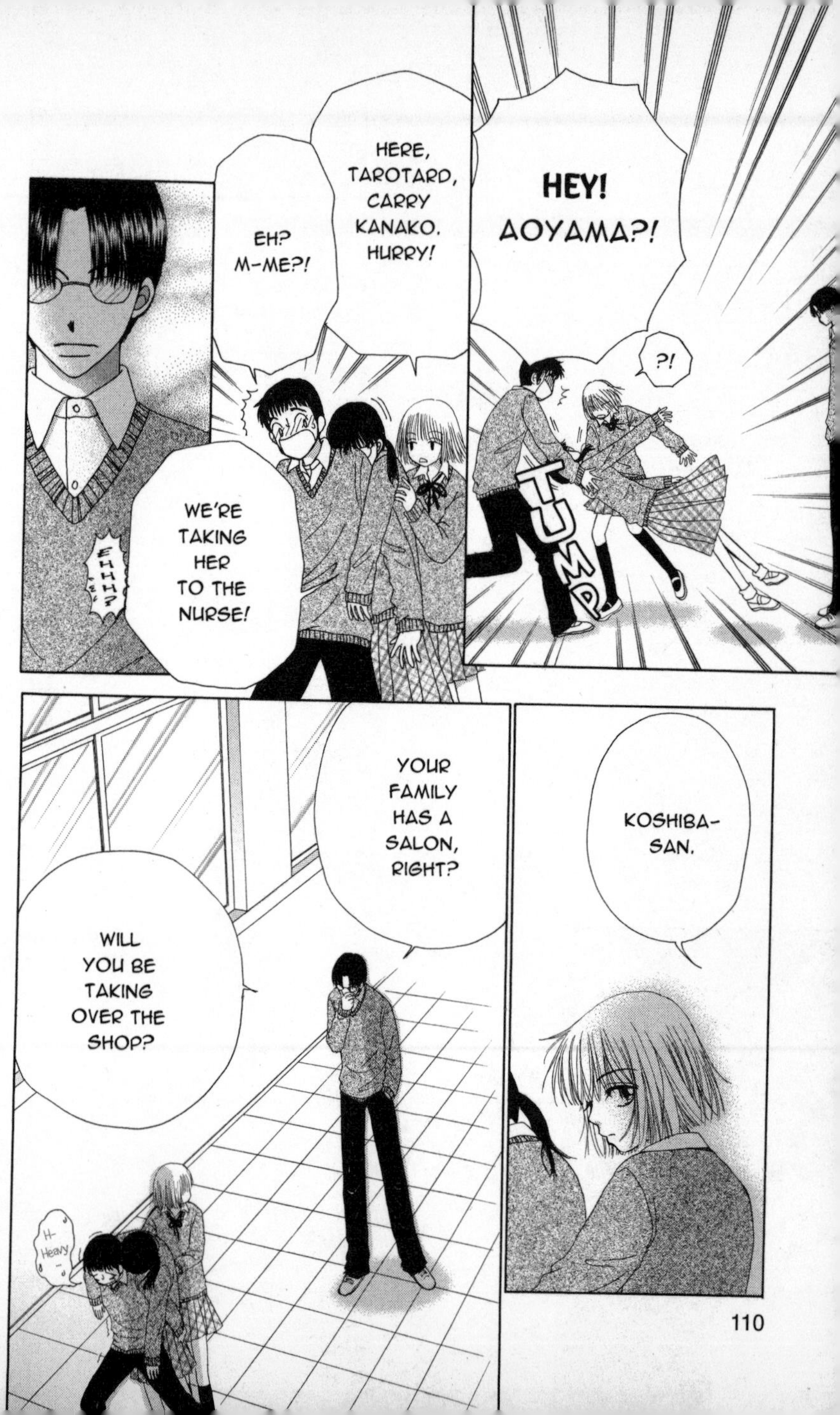
HEY!
AOYAMA?!
?!
TUMP
HERE, TAROTARD, CARRY KANAKO. HURRY!
EH? M-ME?!
WE'RE TAKING HER TO THE NURSE!
EHHH?
KOSHIBA-SAN.
YOUR FAMILY HAS A SALON, RIGHT?
WILL YOU BE TAKING OVER THE SHOP?
H-Heavy...

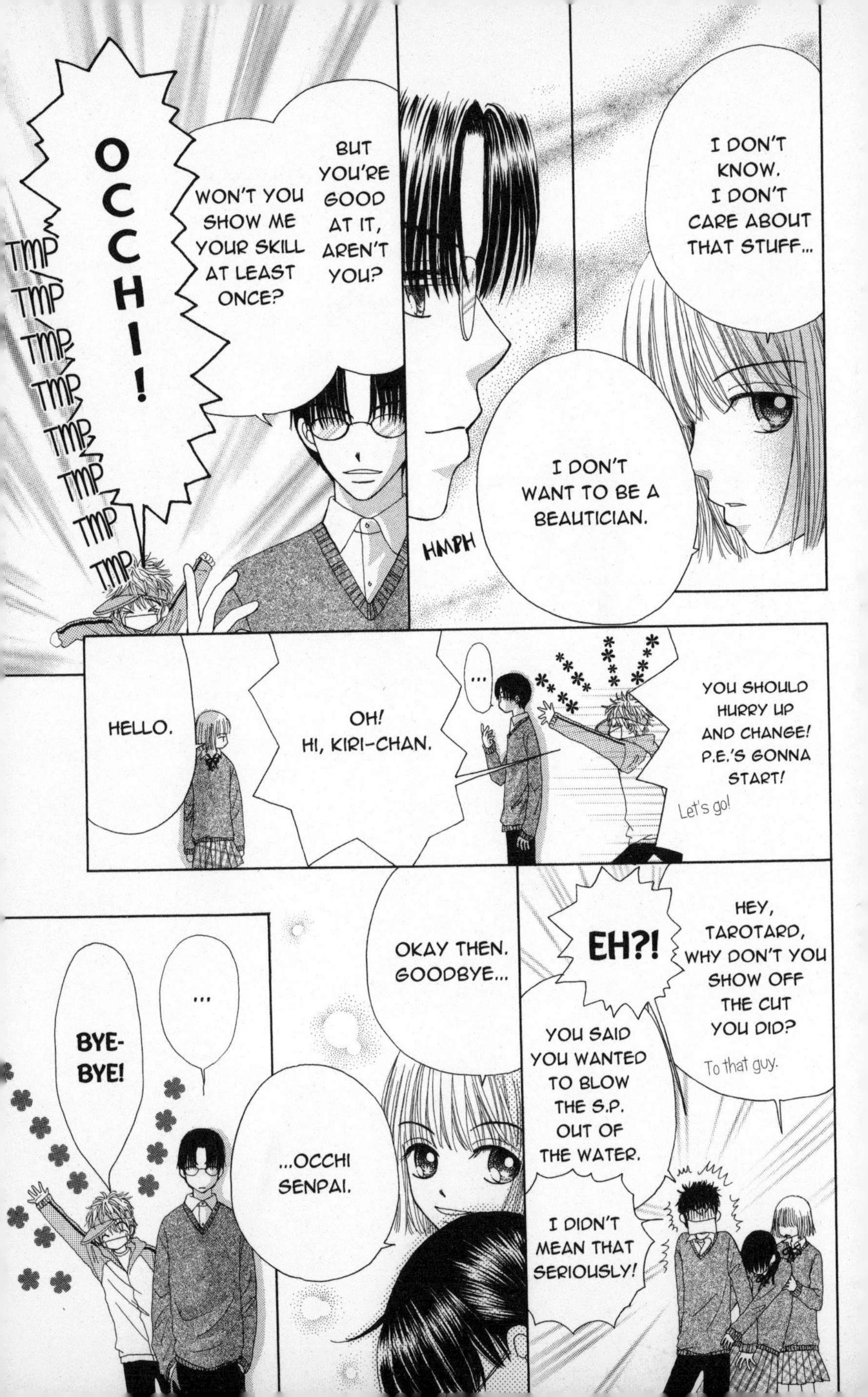
I DON'T KNOW. I DON'T CARE ABOUT THAT STUFF...
I DON'T WANT TO BE A BEAUTICIAN.
HMPH
BUT YOU'RE GOOD AT IT, AREN'T YOU?
WON'T YOU SHOW ME YOUR SKILL AT LEAST ONCE?
OCCHI!
TMP TMP TMP TMP TMP TMP TMP TMP
YOU SHOULD HURRY UP AND CHANGE! P.E.'S GONNA START!
Let's go!
...
OH! HI, KIRI-CHAN.
HELLO.
HEY, TAROTARD, WHY DON'T YOU SHOW OFF THE CUT YOU DID?
To that guy.
EH?!
YOU SAID YOU WANTED TO BLOW THE S.P. OUT OF THE WATER.
I DIDN'T MEAN THAT SERIOUSLY!
OKAY THEN. GOODBYE...
...OCCHI SENPAI.
...
BYE-BYE!

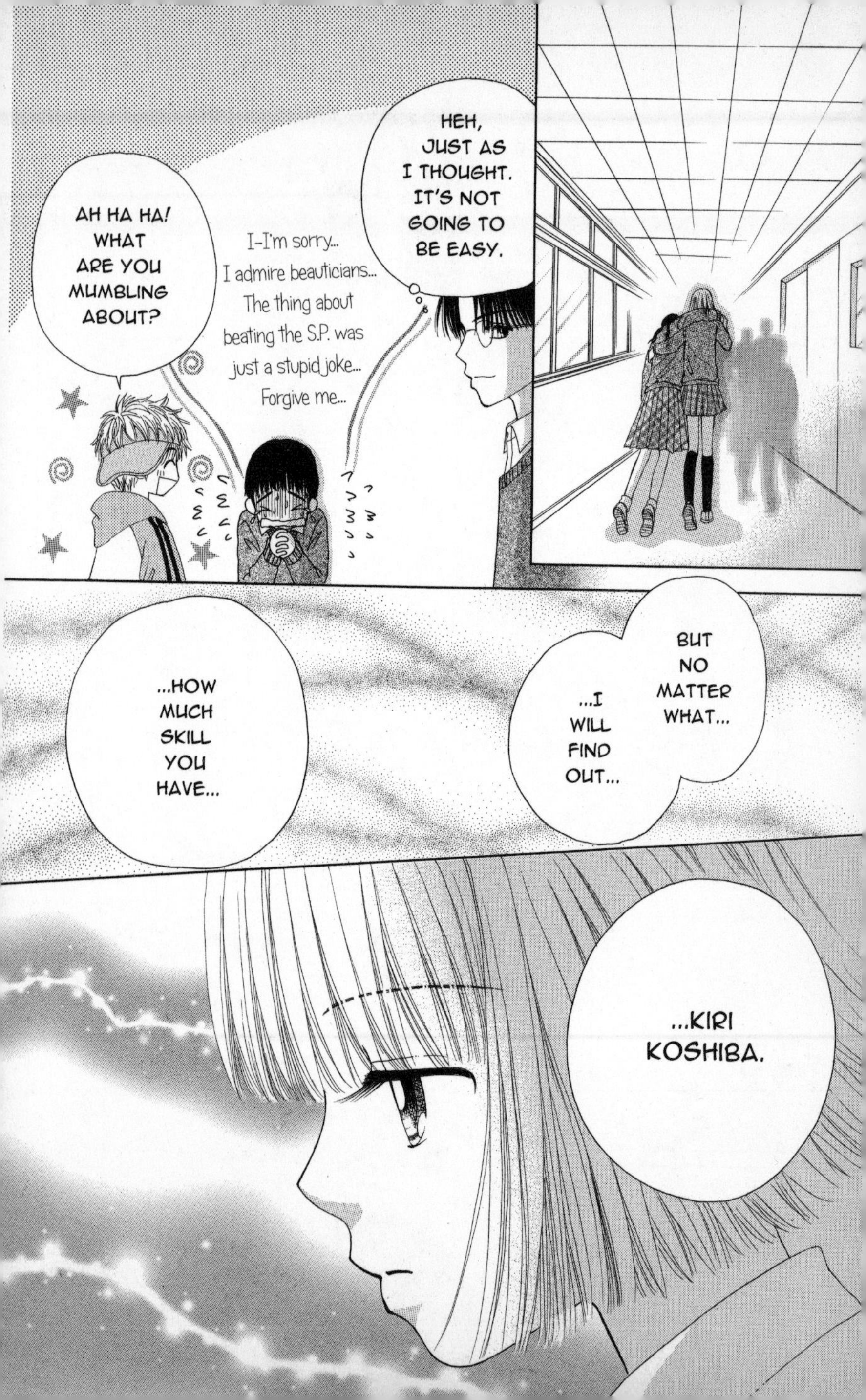
HEH, JUST AS I THOUGHT. IT'S NOT GOING TO BE EASY.
I-I'm sorry... I admire beauticians... The thing about beating the S.P. was just a stupid joke... Forgive me...
AH HA HA! WHAT ARE YOU MUMBLING ABOUT?
BUT NO MATTER WHAT...
...I WILL FIND OUT...
...HOW MUCH SKILL YOU HAVE...
...KIRI KOSHIBA.

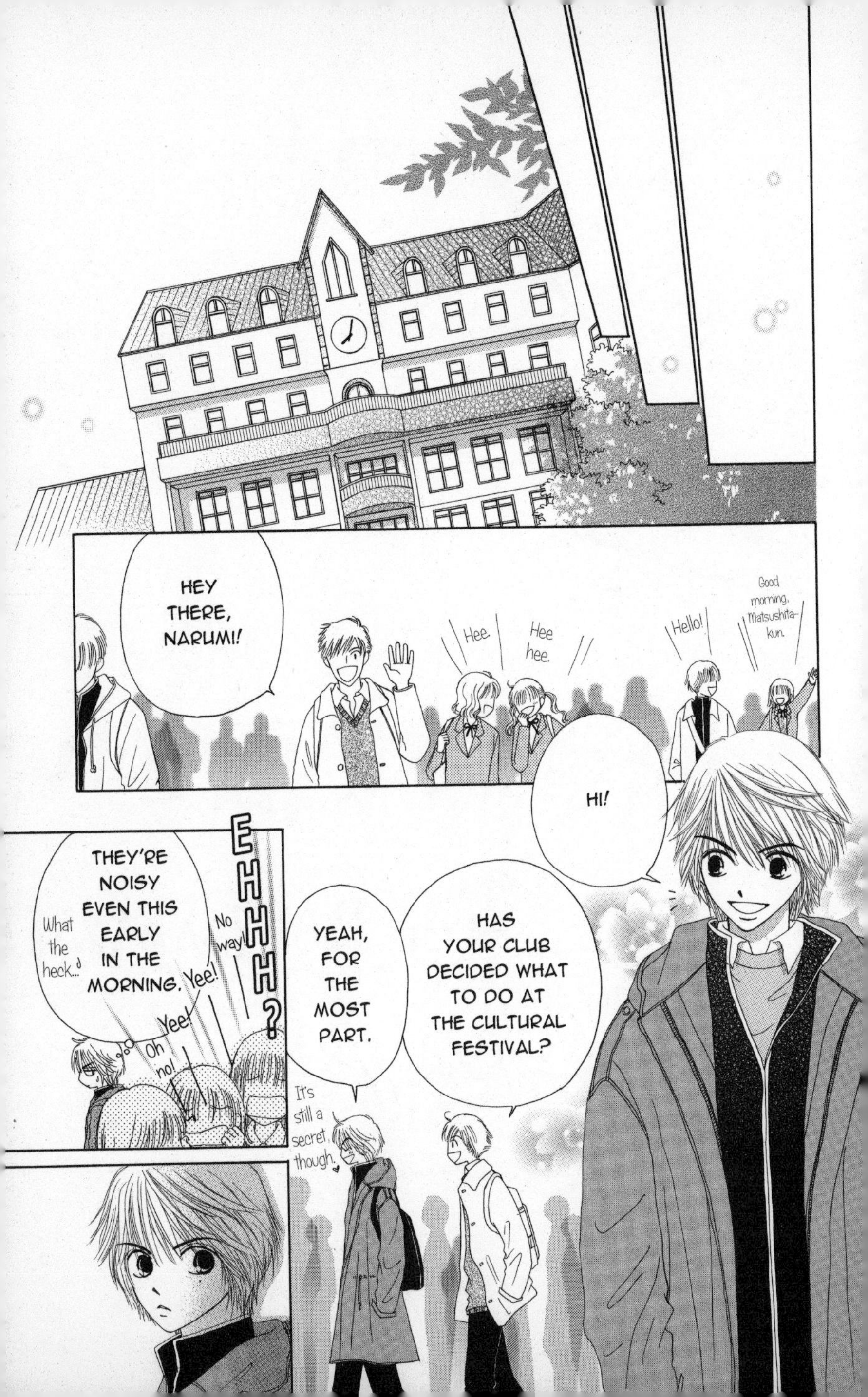
Good morning, Matsushita-kun.
Hello!
Hee hee.
Hee.
HEY THERE, NARUMI!
HI!
HAS YOUR CLUB DECIDED WHAT TO DO AT THE CULTURAL FESTIVAL?
YEAH, FOR THE MOST PART.
It's still a secret, though.
EHHHH?
No way!
THEY'RE NOISY EVEN THIS EARLY IN THE MORNING.
What the heck...
Yee!
Yee!
Oh no!

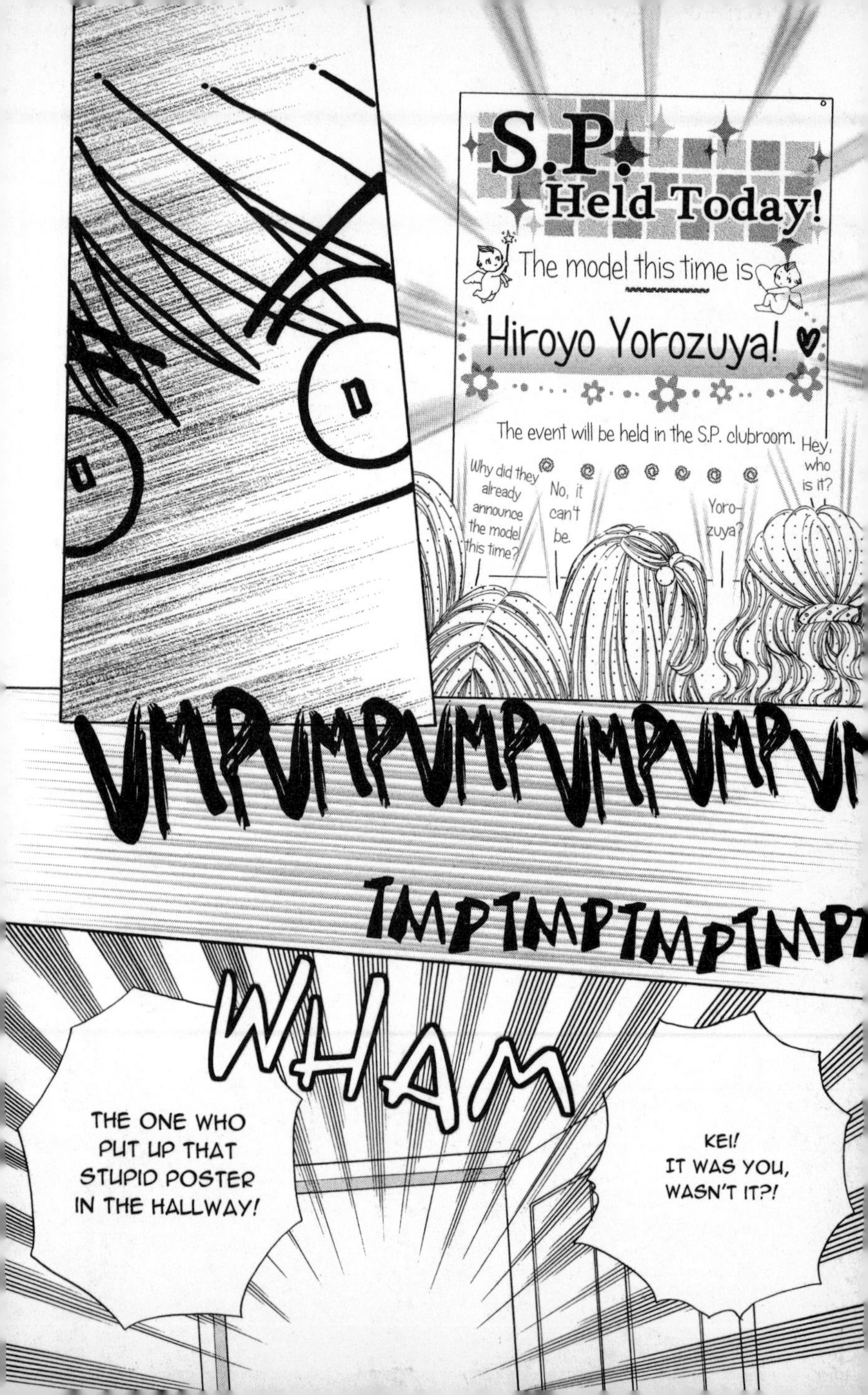
S.P. Held Today!
The model this time is
Hiroyo Yorozuya!
The event will be held in the S.P. clubroom.
Hey, who is it?
Yoro-zuya?
No, it can't be.
Why did they already announce the model this time?
VMPVMPVMPVMPVMPVMP
TMPTMPTMPTMP
WHAM
KEI! IT WAS YOU, WASN'T IT?!
THE ONE WHO PUT UP THAT STUPID POSTER IN THE HALLWAY!

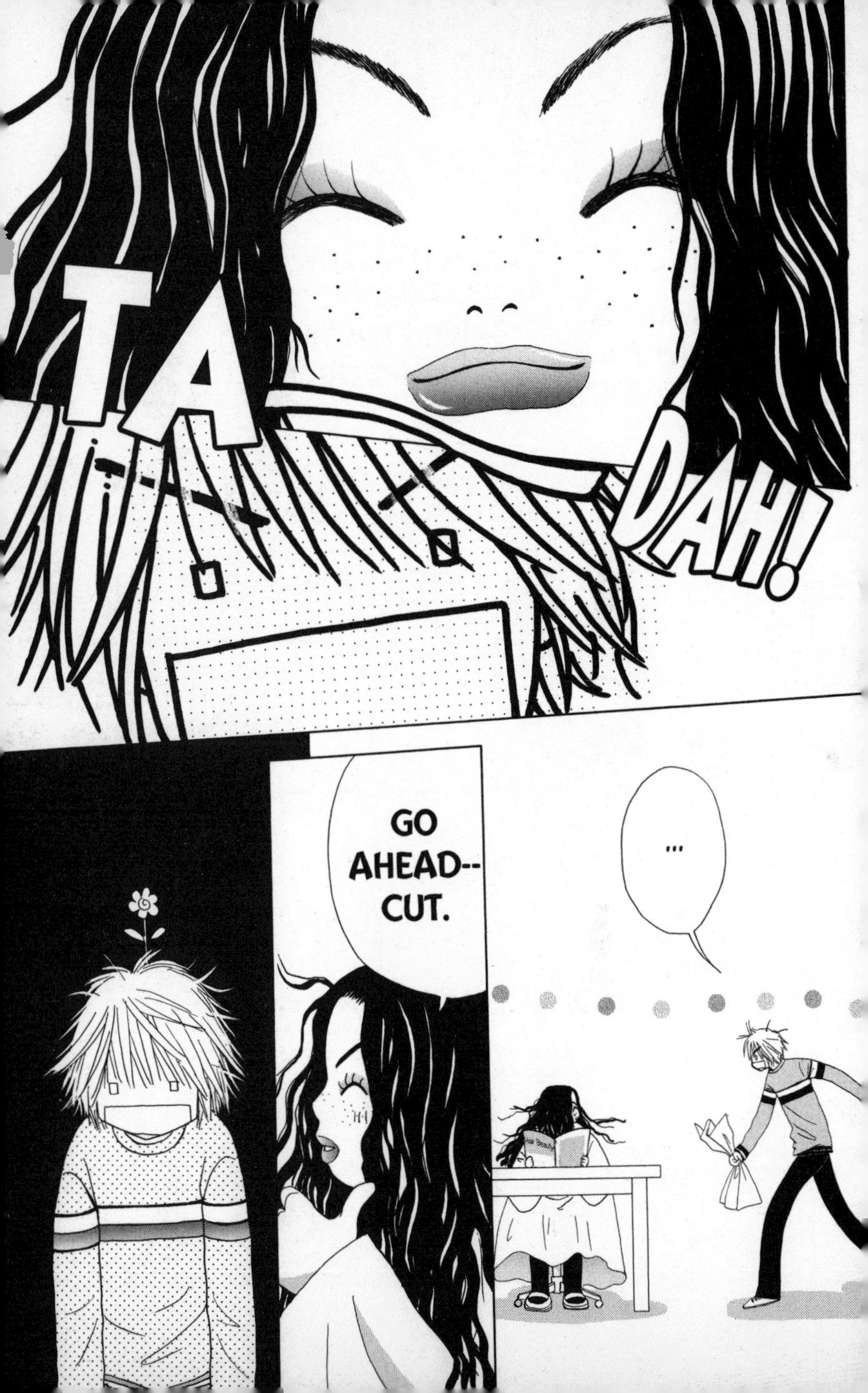
TA
DAH!
...
GO AHEAD-- CUT.

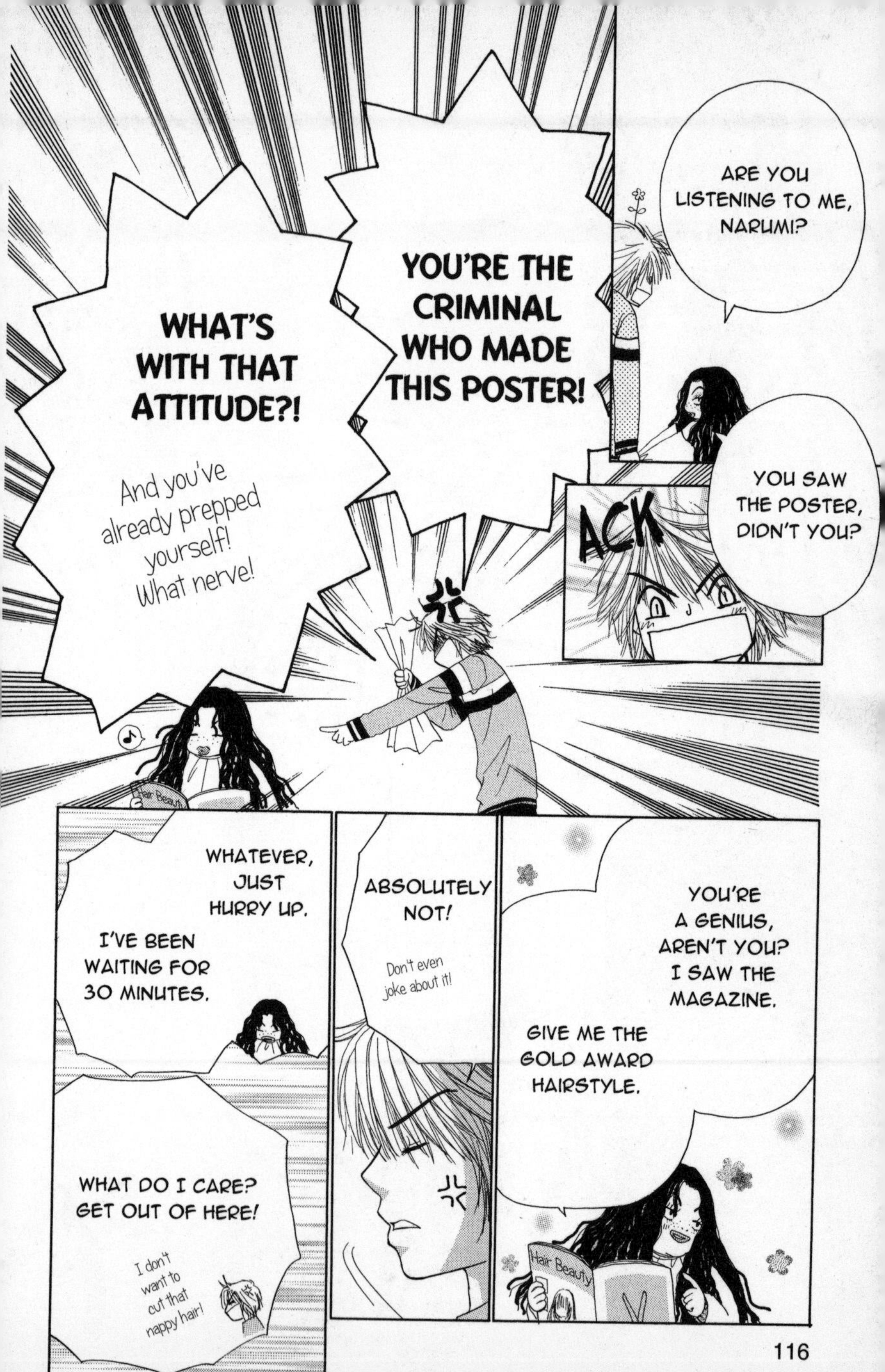
ARE YOU LISTENING TO ME, NARUMI?
YOU SAW THE POSTER, DIDN'T YOU?
ACK
YOU'RE THE CRIMINAL WHO MADE THIS POSTER!
WHAT'S WITH THAT ATTITUDE?!
And you've already prepped yourself! What nerve!
Hair Beauty
YOU'RE A GENIUS, AREN'T YOU? I SAW THE MAGAZINE.
GIVE ME THE GOLD AWARD HAIRSTYLE.
Hair Beauty
ABSOLUTELY NOT!
Don't even joke about it!
WHATEVER, JUST HURRY UP.
I'VE BEEN WAITING FOR 30 MINUTES.
WHAT DO I CARE? GET OUT OF HERE!
I don't want to cut that nappy hair!

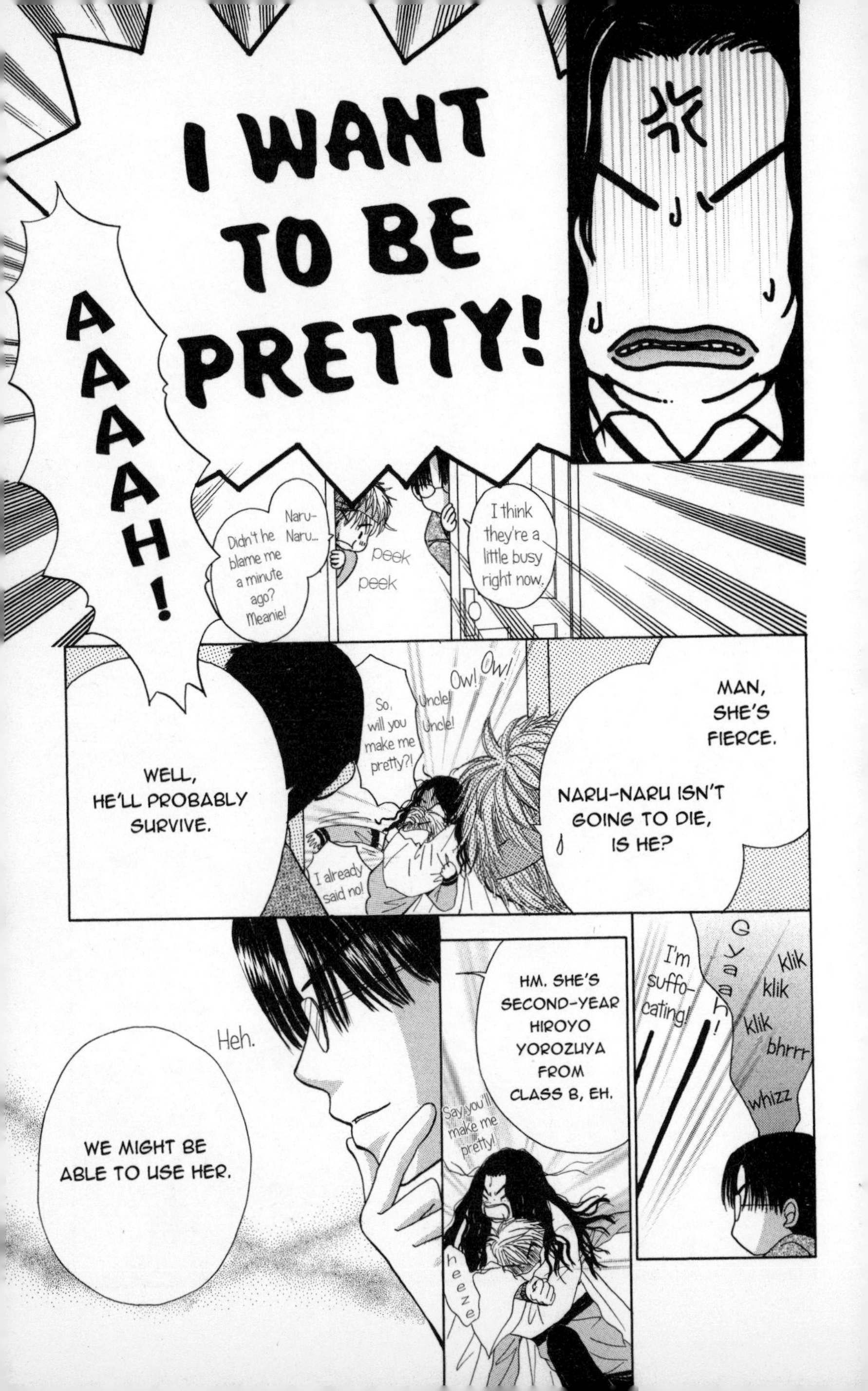
I WANT TO BE PRETTY!
AAAAAH!
I think they're a little busy right now.
Naru-Naru...
Didn't he blame me a minute ago? Meanie!
peek
peek
MAN, SHE'S FIERCE.
NARU-NARU ISN'T GOING TO DIE, IS HE?
Ow! Ow!
Uncle! Uncle!
So, will you make me pretty?!
I already said no!
WELL, HE'LL PROBABLY SURVIVE.
I'm suffocating!
Gyaah!
klik
klik
klik
bhrrr
whizz
HM. SHE'S SECOND-YEAR HIROYO YOROZUYA FROM CLASS B, EH.
Say you'll make me pretty!
heeze
Heh.
WE MIGHT BE ABLE TO USE HER.

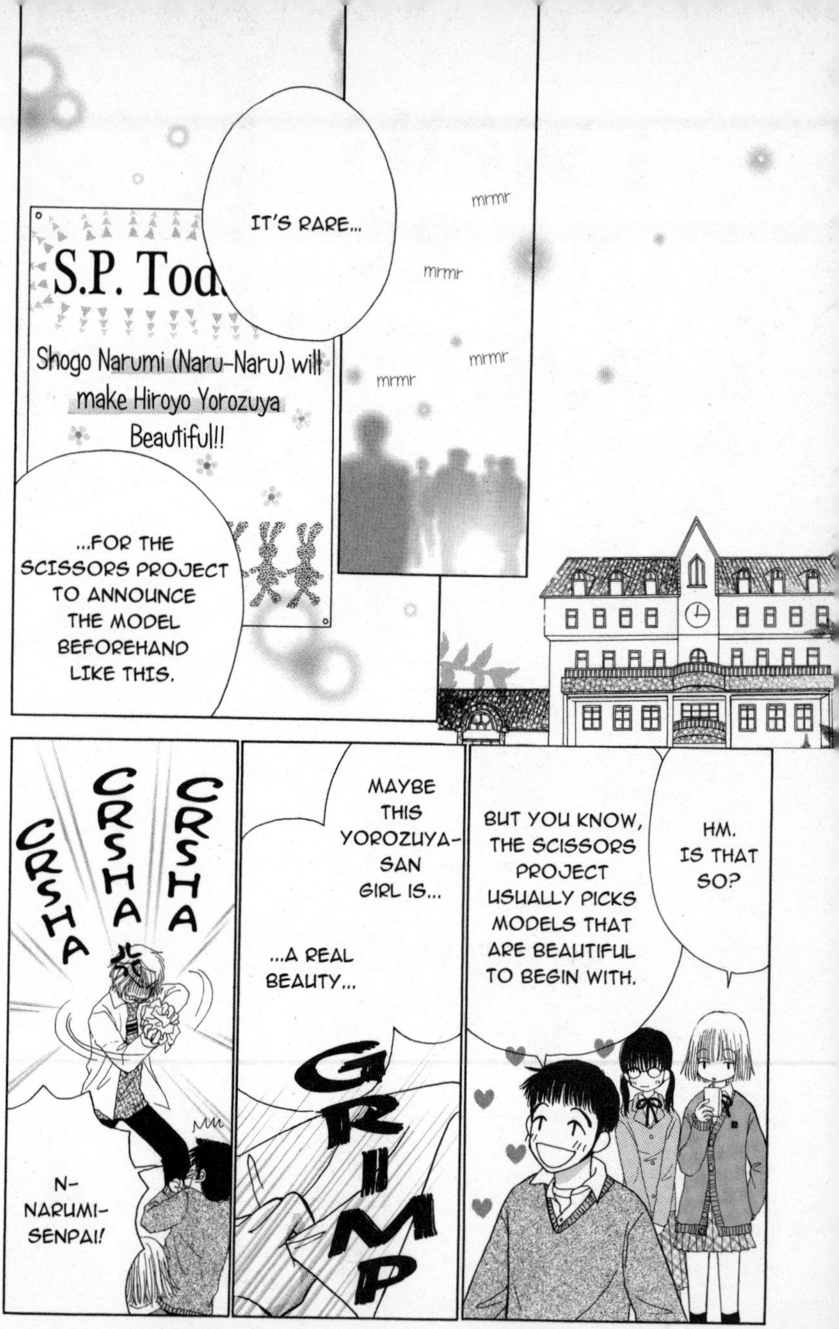
mrmr
mrmr
IT'S RARE...
mrmr
mrmr
S.P. Tod
Shogo Narumi (Naru-Naru) will make Hiroyo Yorozuya Beautiful!!
...FOR THE SCISSORS PROJECT TO ANNOUNCE THE MODEL BEFOREHAND LIKE THIS.
HM. IS THAT SO?
BUT YOU KNOW, THE SCISSORS PROJECT USUALLY PICKS MODELS THAT ARE BEAUTIFUL TO BEGIN WITH.
MAYBE THIS YOROZUYA-SAN GIRL IS...
...A REAL BEAUTY...
GRIMP
CRSHA
CRSHA
CRSHA
N-NARUMI-SENPAI!

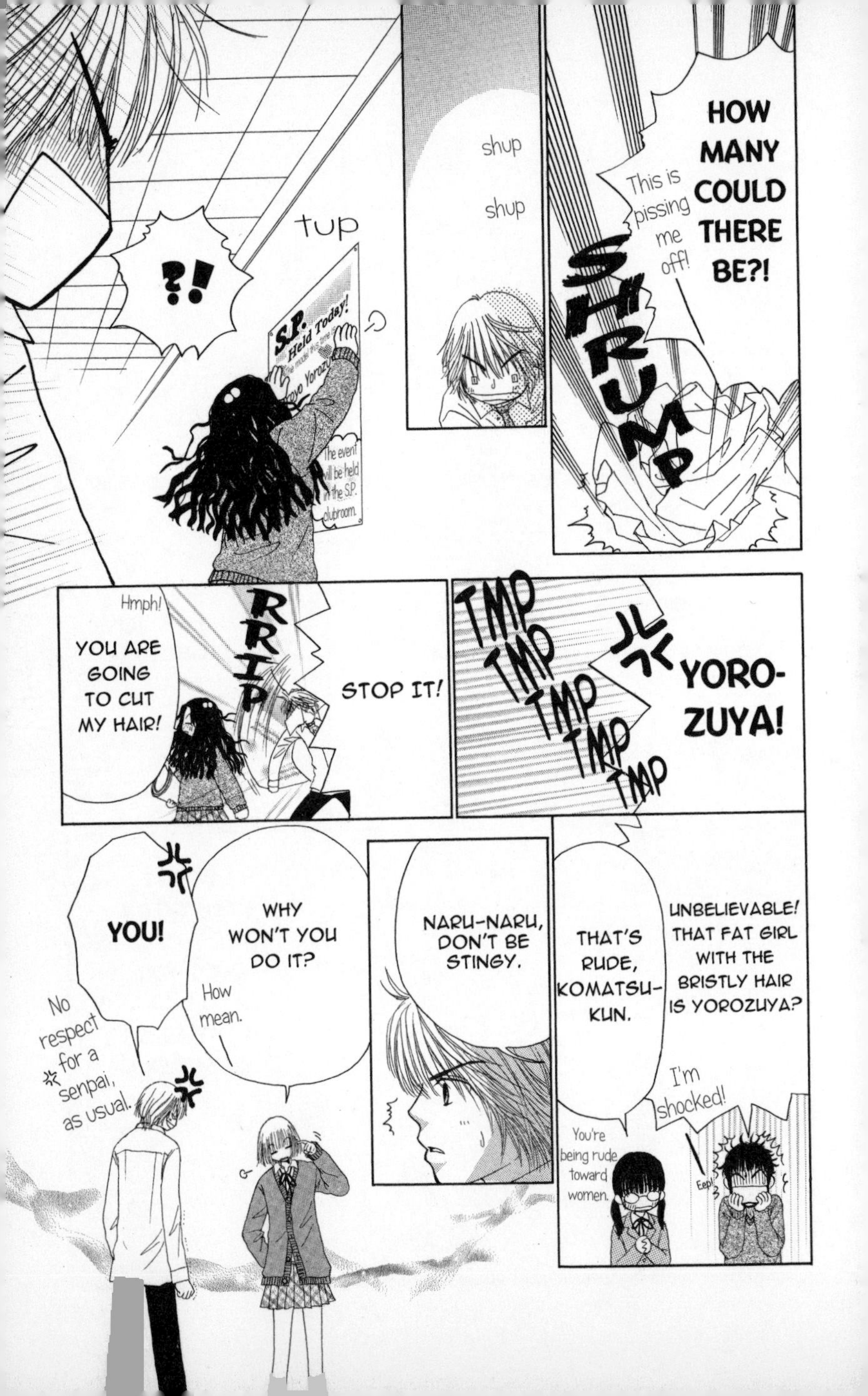
HOW MANY COULD THERE BE?!
This is pissing me off!
SHRUMP
shup
shup
tup
S.P. Held Today!
The event will be held in the S.P. clubroom.
?!
TMP TMP TMP TMP TMP
YORO-ZUYA!
STOP IT!
RRIP
Hmph!
YOU ARE GOING TO CUT MY HAIR!
UNBELIEVABLE! THAT FAT GIRL WITH THE BRISTLY HAIR IS YOROZUYA?
I'm shocked!
Eep!
THAT'S RUDE, KOMATSU-KUN.
You're being rude toward women.
NARU-NARU, DON'T BE STINGY.
WHY WON'T YOU DO IT?
How mean.
YOU!
No respect for a senpai, as usual.

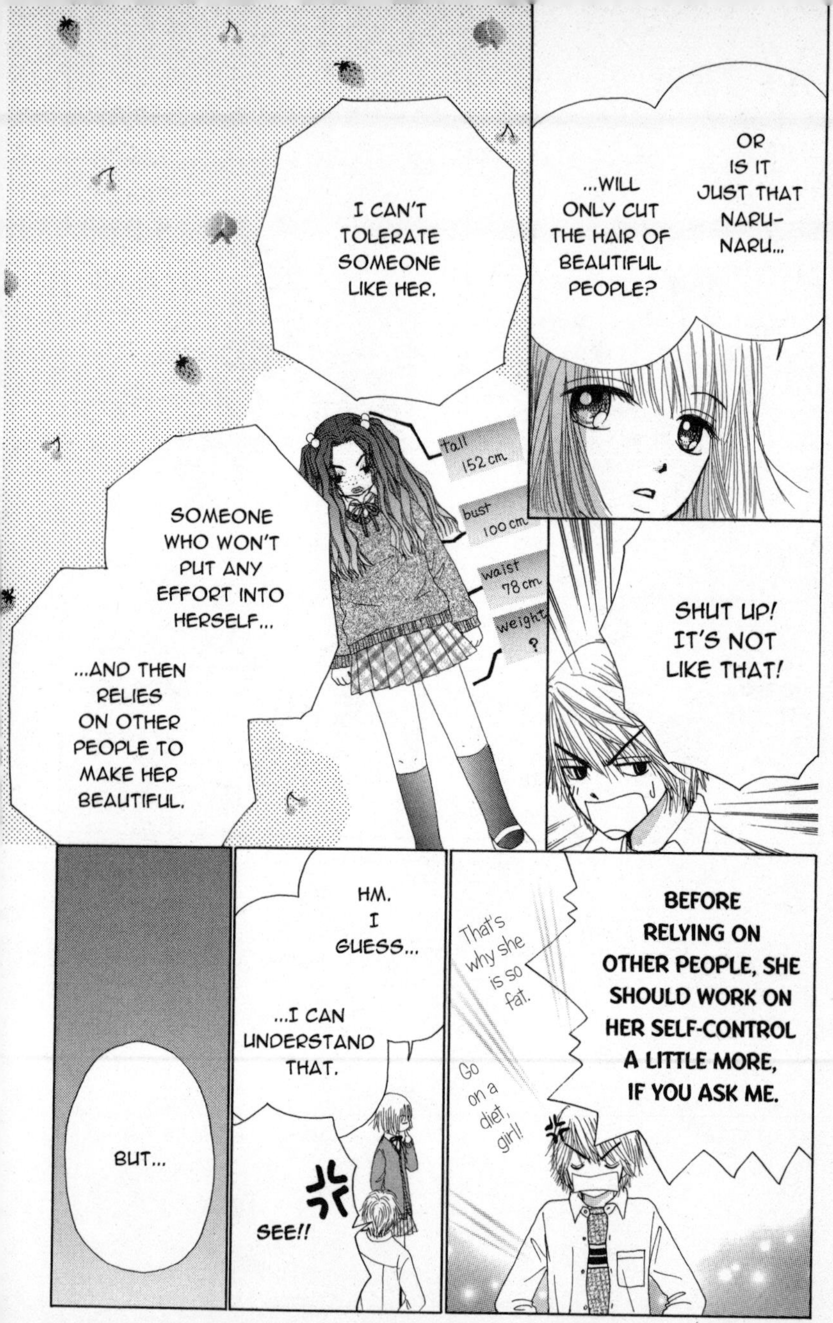
OR IS IT JUST THAT NARU-NARU...
...WILL ONLY CUT THE HAIR OF BEAUTIFUL PEOPLE?
SHUT UP! IT'S NOT LIKE THAT!
I CAN'T TOLERATE SOMEONE LIKE HER.
tall 152 cm
bust 100 cm
waist 78 cm
weight ?
SOMEONE WHO WON'T PUT ANY EFFORT INTO HERSELF...
...AND THEN RELIES ON OTHER PEOPLE TO MAKE HER BEAUTIFUL.
BEFORE RELYING ON OTHER PEOPLE, SHE SHOULD WORK ON HER SELF-CONTROL A LITTLE MORE, IF YOU ASK ME.
That's why she is so fat.
Go on a diet, girl!
HM. I GUESS...
...I CAN UNDERSTAND THAT.
SEE!!
BUT...

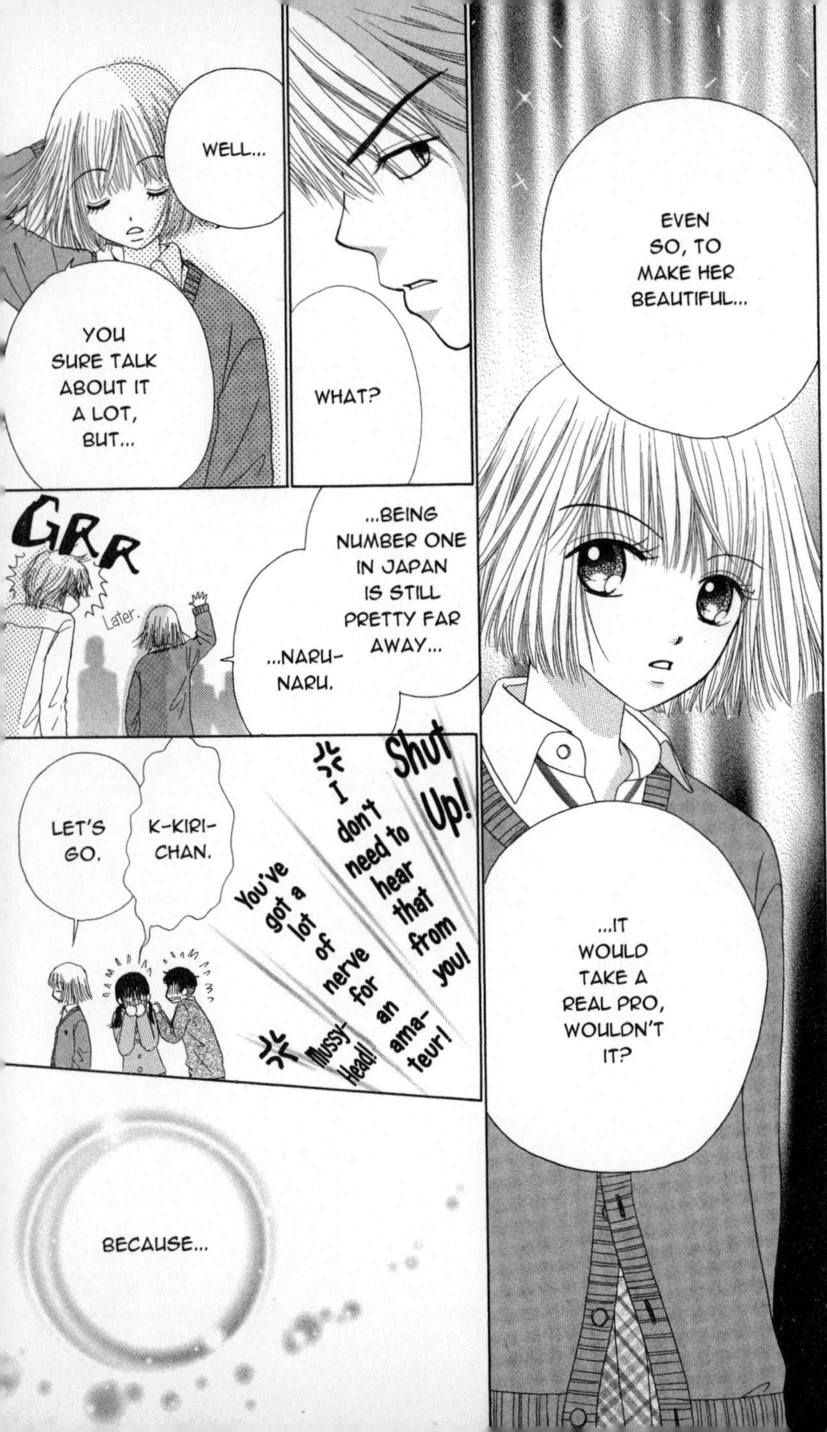
EVEN SO, TO MAKE HER BEAUTIFUL...
...IT WOULD TAKE A REAL PRO, WOULDN'T IT?
WHAT?
WELL...
YOU SURE TALK ABOUT IT A LOT, BUT...
...BEING NUMBER ONE IN JAPAN IS STILL PRETTY FAR AWAY...
...NARU-NARU.
GRR
Later.
Shut Up!
I don't need to hear that from you!
You've got a lot of nerve for an amateur!
Mussy-Head!
K-KIRI-CHAN.
LET'S GO.
BECAUSE...

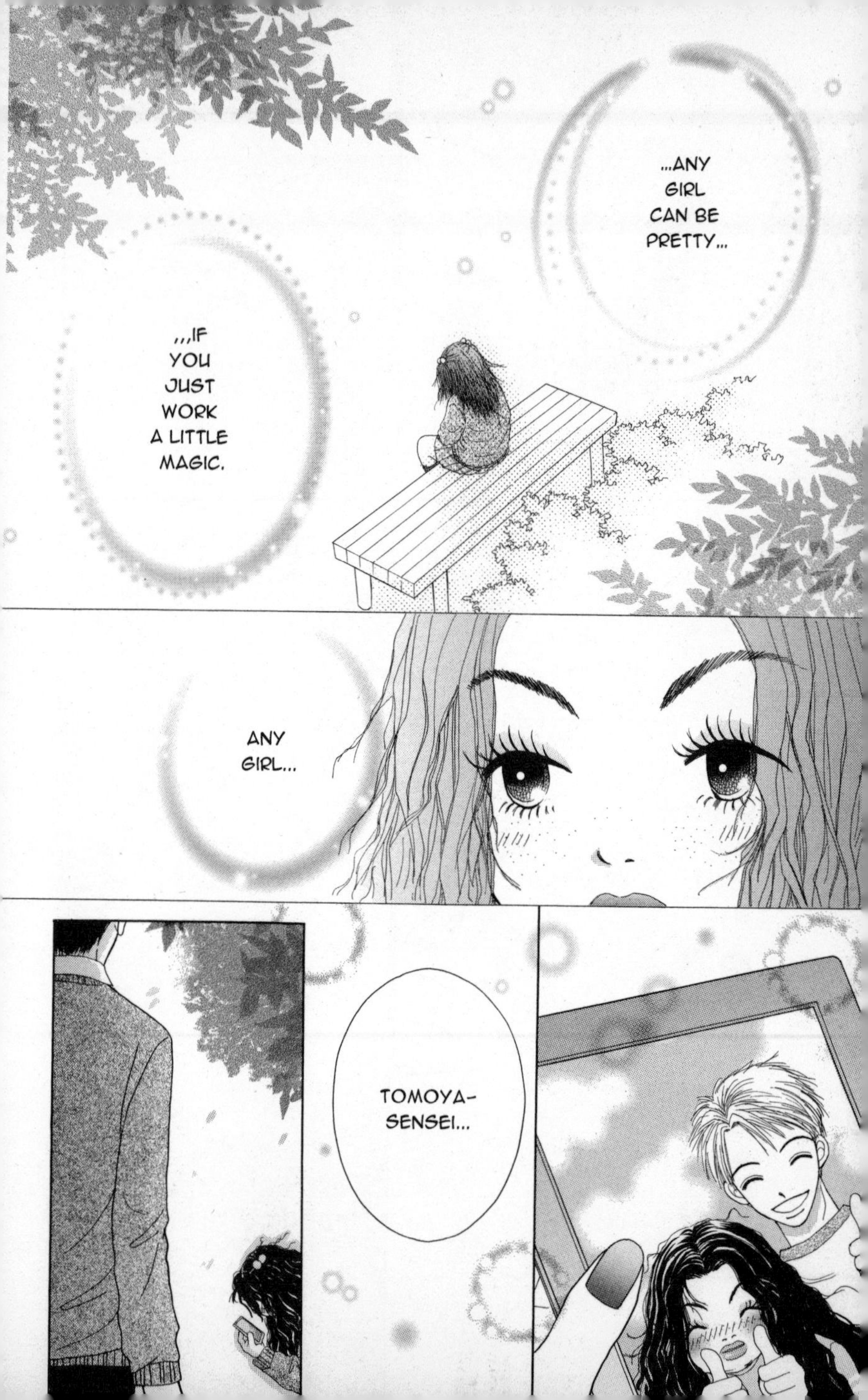
...ANY GIRL CAN BE PRETTY...
,,,IF YOU JUST WORK A LITTLE MAGIC.
ANY GIRL...
TOMOYA-SENSEI...

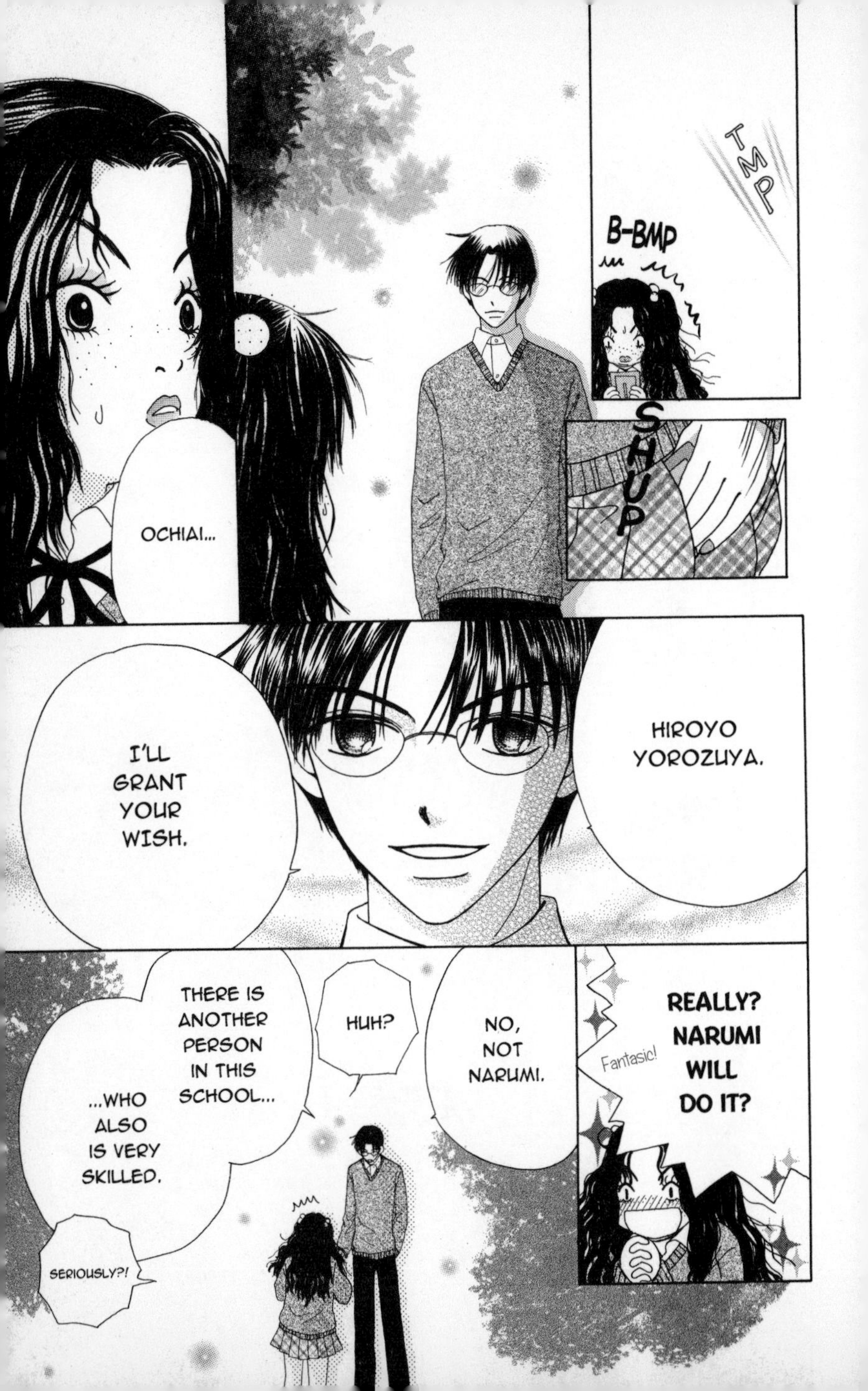
TMP
B-BMP
SHUP
OCHIAI...
HIROYO YOROZUYA.
I'LL GRANT YOUR WISH.
REALLY? NARUMI WILL DO IT?
Fantasic!
NO, NOT NARUMI.
HUH?
THERE IS ANOTHER PERSON IN THIS SCHOOL...
...WHO ALSO IS VERY SKILLED.
SERIOUSLY?!

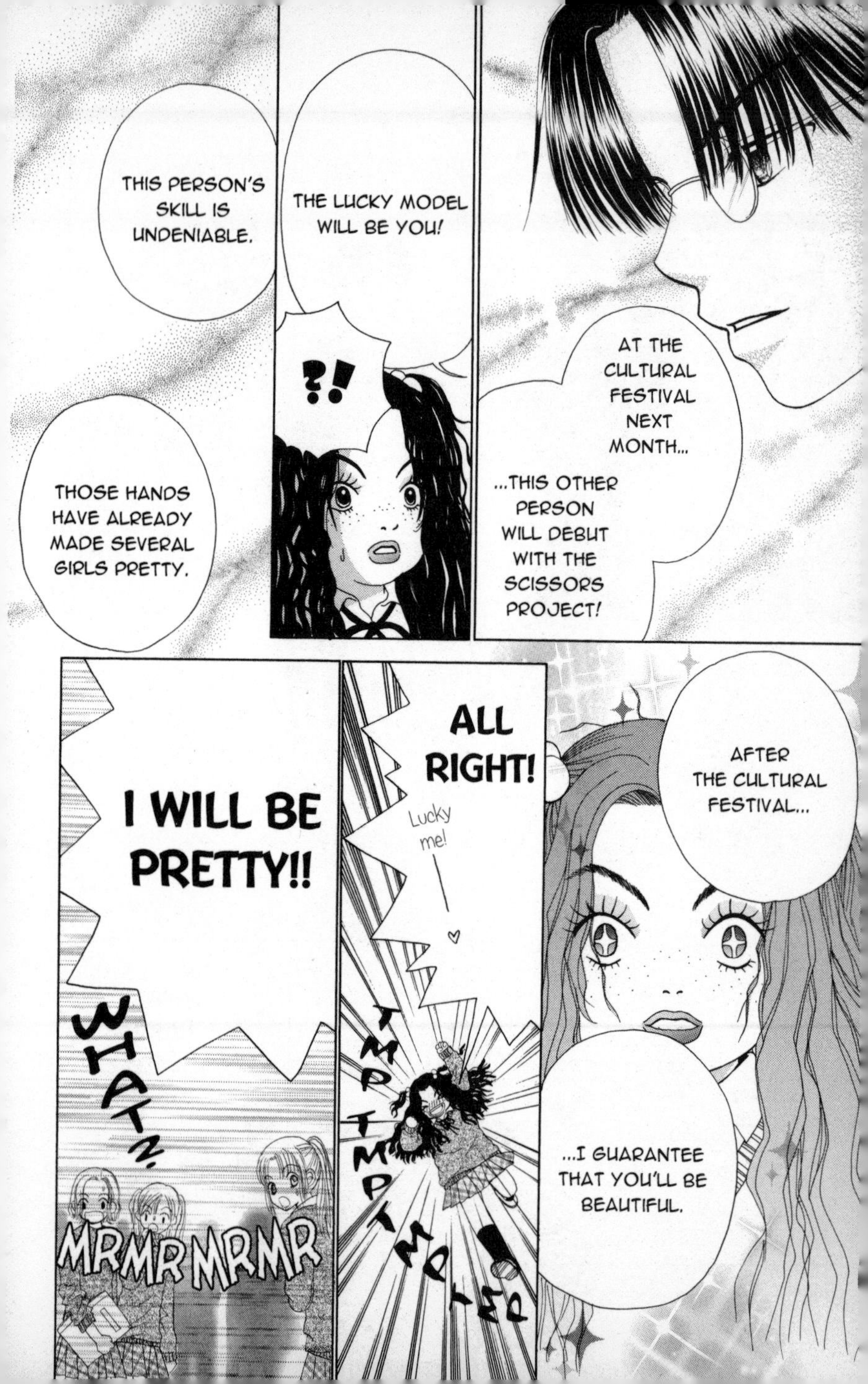

AT THE CULTURAL FESTIVAL NEXT MONTH...
...THIS OTHER PERSON WILL DEBUT WITH THE SCISSORS PROJECT!
THE LUCKY MODEL WILL BE YOU!
?!
THIS PERSON'S SKILL IS UNDENIABLE.
THOSE HANDS HAVE ALREADY MADE SEVERAL GIRLS PRETTY.
AFTER THE CULTURAL FESTIVAL...
...I GUARANTEE THAT YOU'LL BE BEAUTIFUL.
ALL RIGHT!
Lucky me!
TMP
TMP
TMP
I WILL BE PRETTY!!
WHAT?
MRMRMRMR

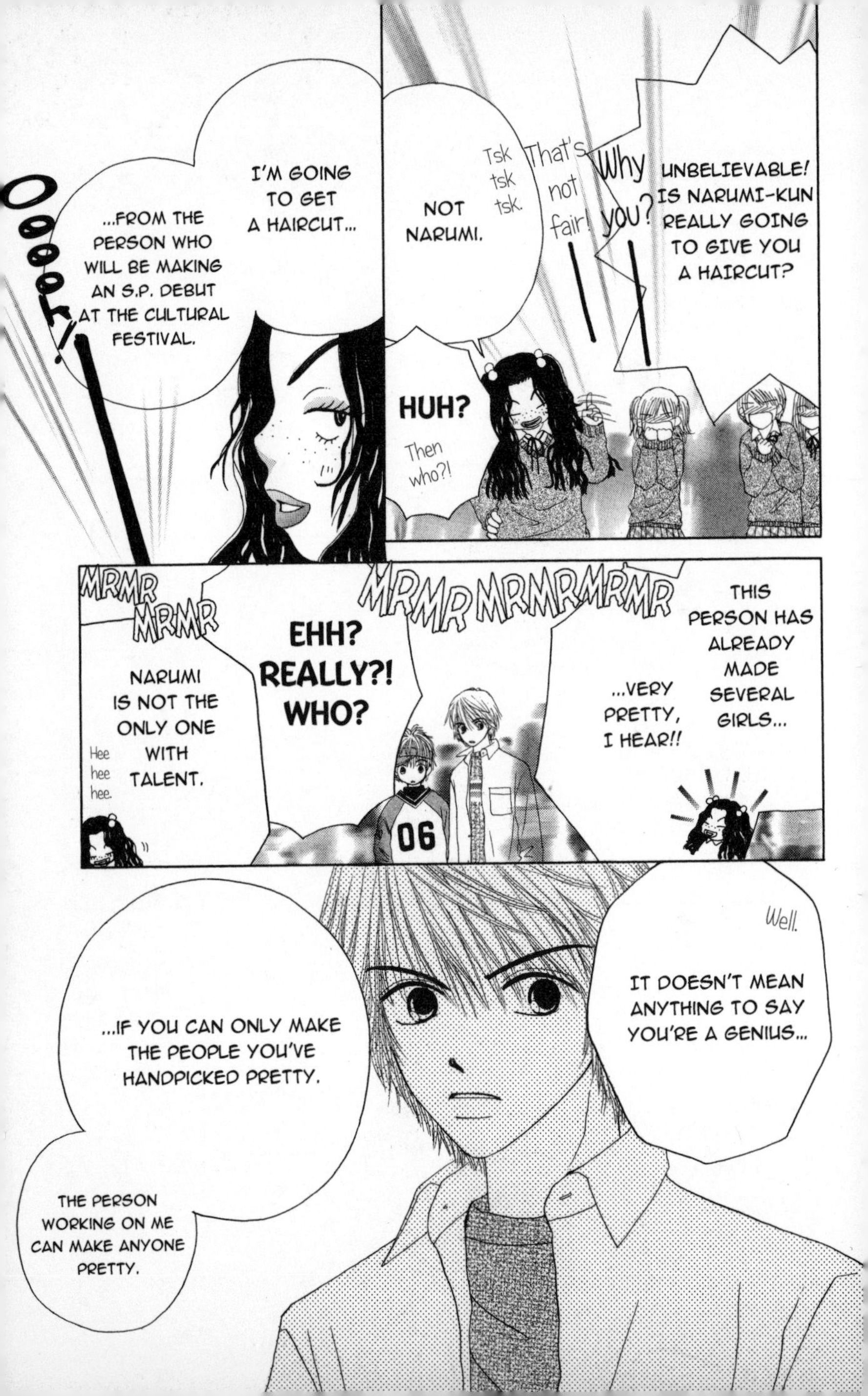
UNBELIEVABLE! IS NARUMI-KUN REALLY GOING TO GIVE YOU A HAIRCUT?
Why you?
That's not fair!
Tsk tsk tsk.
NOT NARUMI.
HUH?
Then who?!
I'M GOING TO GET A HAIRCUT...
...FROM THE PERSON WHO WILL BE MAKING AN S.P. DEBUT AT THE CULTURAL FESTIVAL.
Oooor!
THIS PERSON HAS ALREADY MADE SEVERAL GIRLS...
...VERY PRETTY, I HEAR!!
MRMR MRMRMRMR
EHH? REALLY?! WHO?
NARUMI IS NOT THE ONLY ONE WITH TALENT.
Hee hee hee.
MRMR MRMR
Well.
IT DOESN'T MEAN ANYTHING TO SAY YOU'RE A GENIUS...
...IF YOU CAN ONLY MAKE THE PEOPLE YOU'VE HANDPICKED PRETTY.
THE PERSON WORKING ON ME CAN MAKE ANYONE PRETTY.

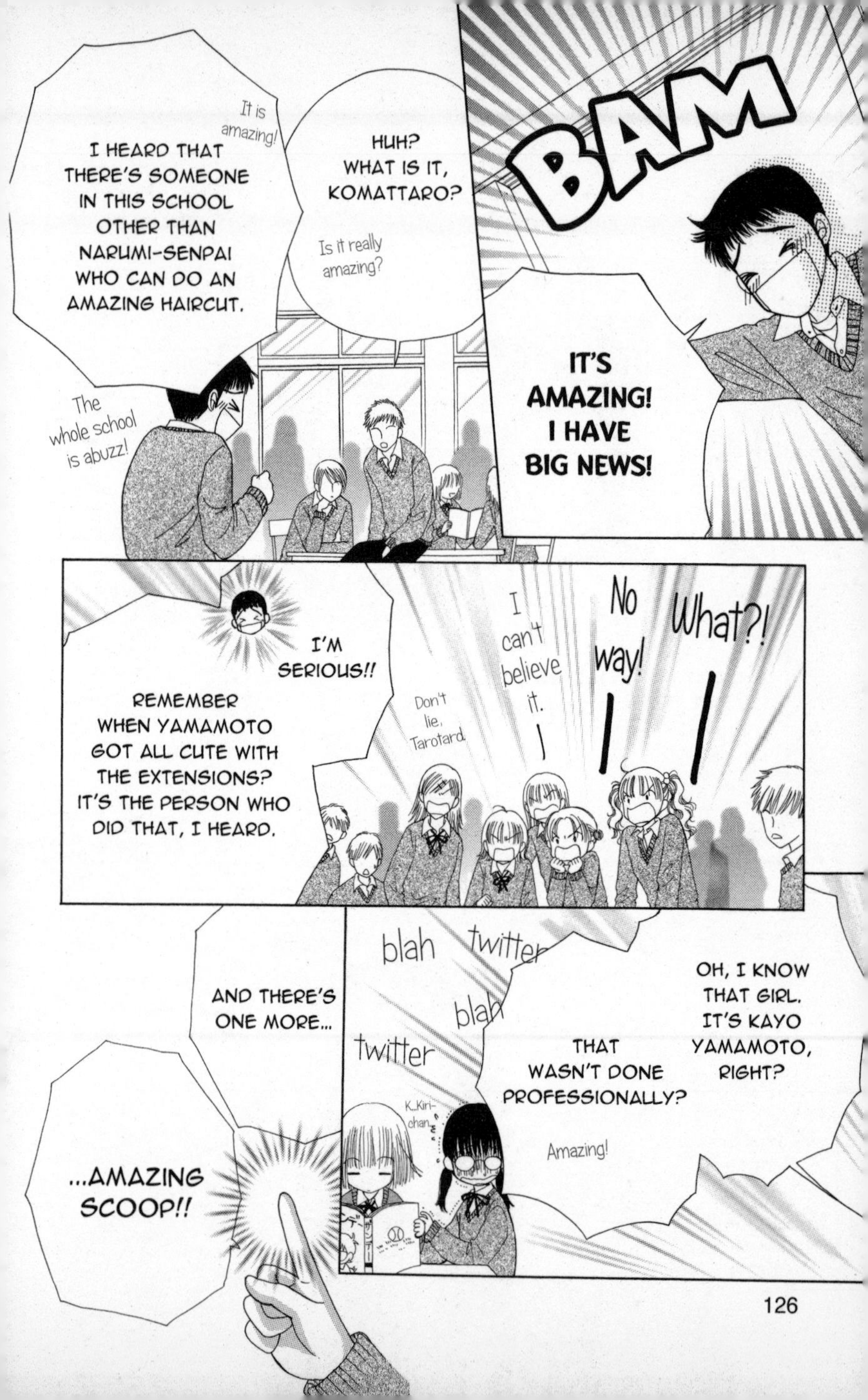
BAM
IT'S AMAZING! I HAVE BIG NEWS!
HUH? WHAT IS IT, KOMATTARO?
Is it really amazing?
I HEARD THAT THERE'S SOMEONE IN THIS SCHOOL OTHER THAN NARUMI-SENPAI WHO CAN DO AN AMAZING HAIRCUT.
It is amazing!
The whole school is abuzz!
What?!
No way!
I can't believe it.
Don't lie, Tarotard.
I'M SERIOUS!!
REMEMBER WHEN YAMAMOTO GOT ALL CUTE WITH THE EXTENSIONS? IT'S THE PERSON WHO DID THAT, I HEARD.
OH, I KNOW THAT GIRL. IT'S KAYO YAMAMOTO, RIGHT?
THAT WASN'T DONE PROFESSIONALLY?
blah
twitter
blah
twitter
Amazing!
K...Kiri-chan...
AND THERE'S ONE MORE...
...AMAZING SCOOP!!

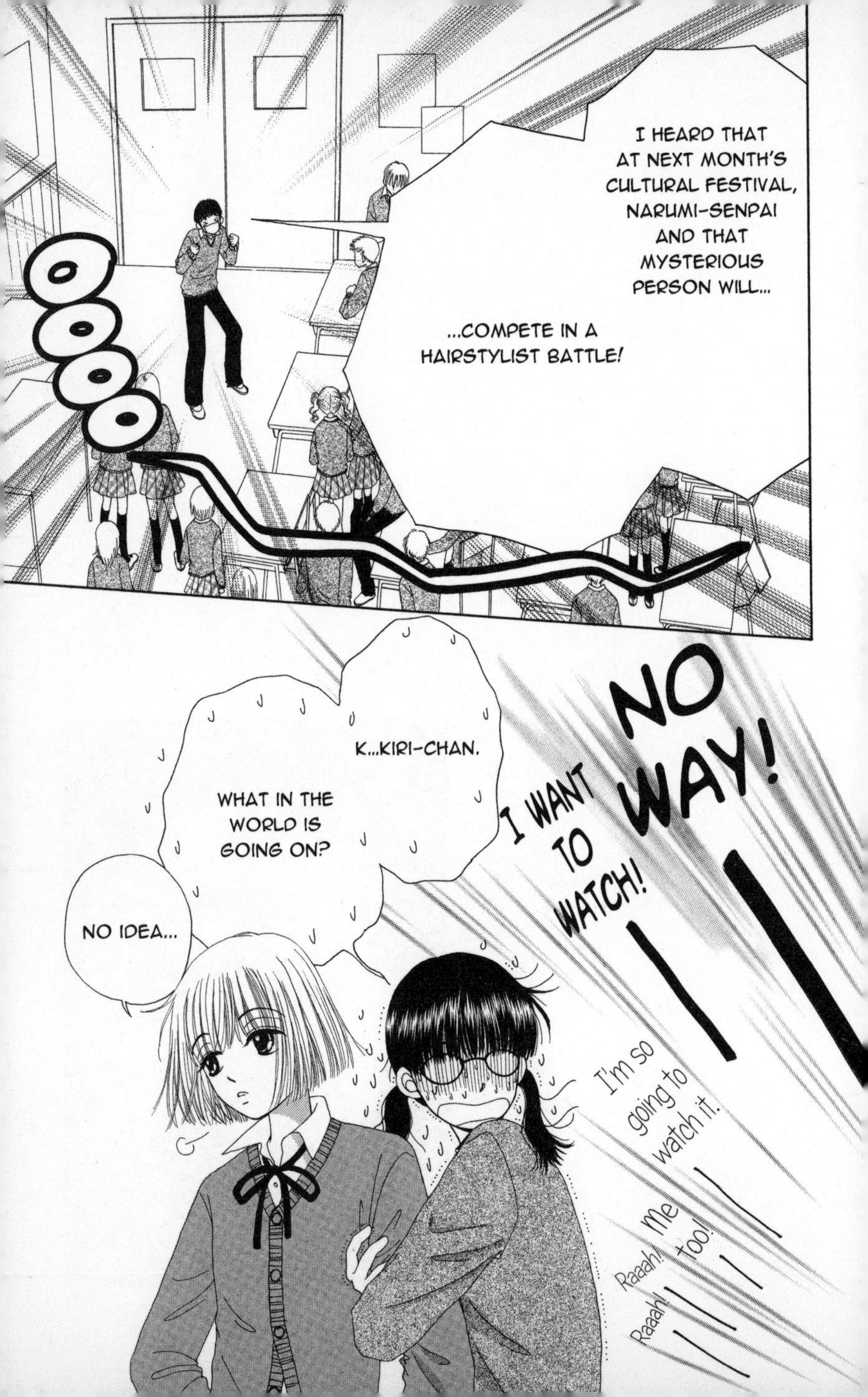
I HEARD THAT AT NEXT MONTH'S CULTURAL FESTIVAL, NARUMI-SENPAI AND THAT MYSTERIOUS PERSON WILL...
...COMPETE IN A HAIRSTYLIST BATTLE!
OOOO
NO WAY!
I WANT TO WATCH!
K...KIRI-CHAN.
WHAT IN THE WORLD IS GOING ON?
NO IDEA...
I'm so going to watch it.
Me too!
Raaah! Raaah!

Beauty Pop

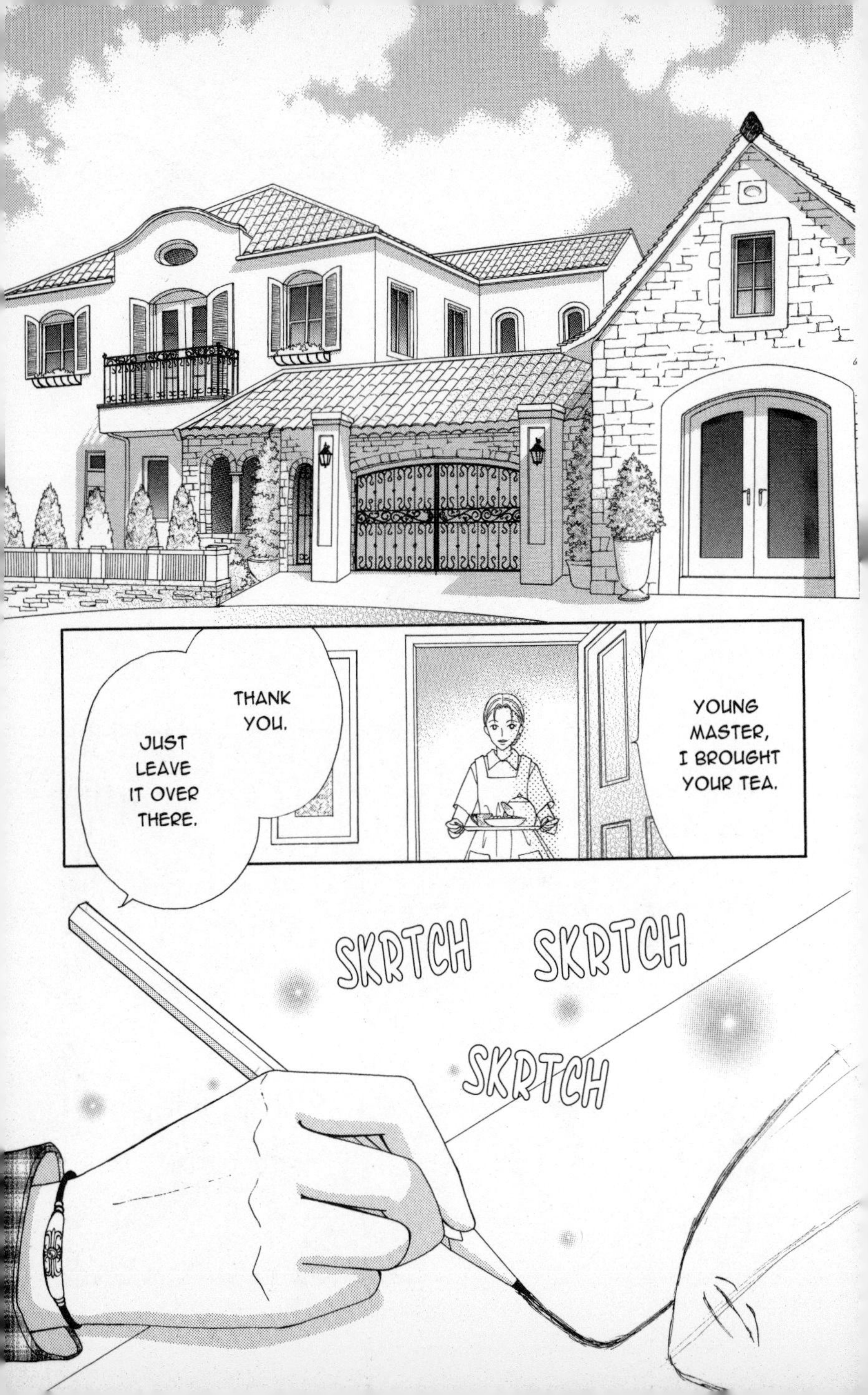
YOUNG MASTER, I BROUGHT YOUR TEA.
THANK YOU. JUST LEAVE IT OVER THERE.
SKRTCH
SKRTCH
SKRTCH

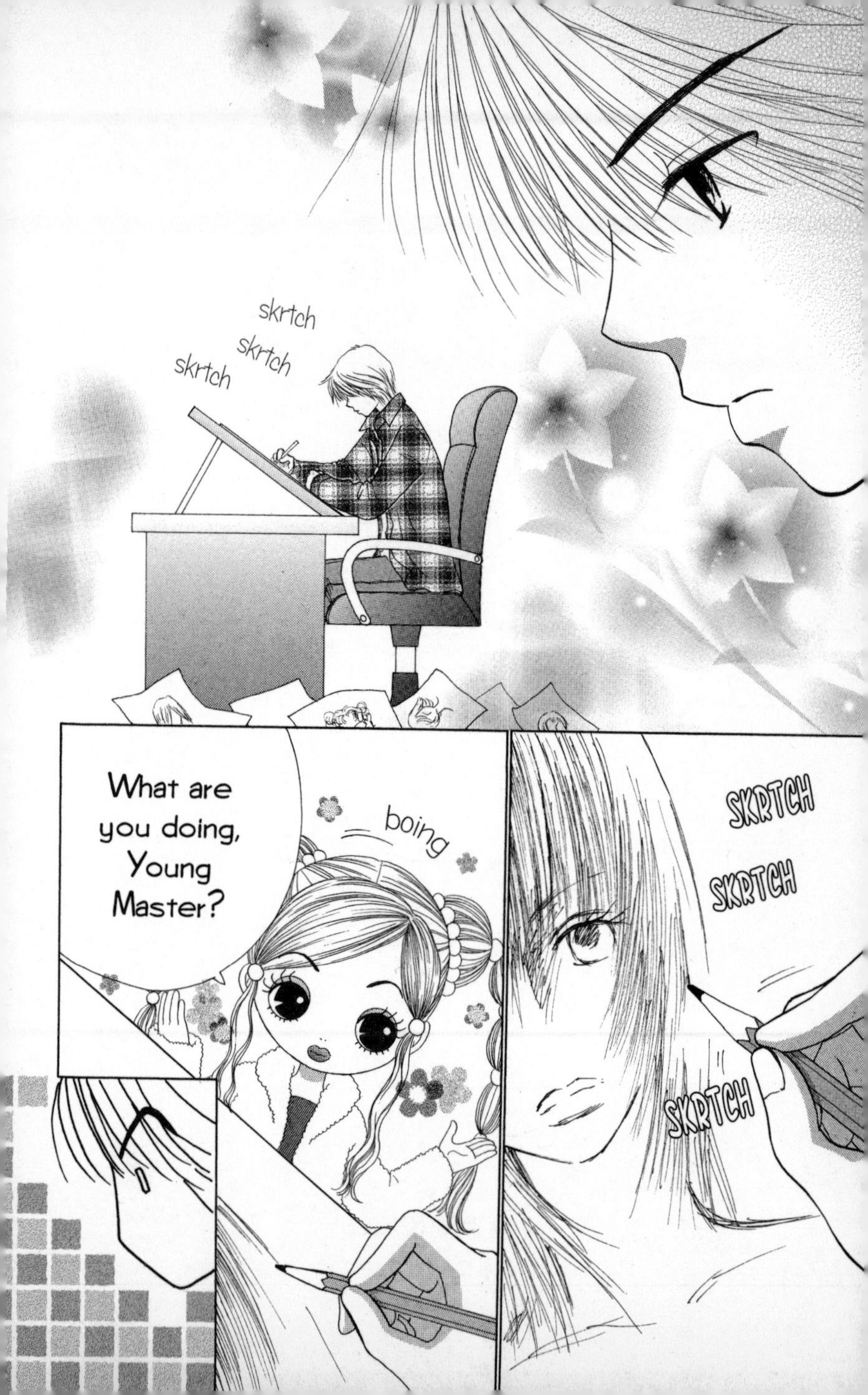
skrtch
skrtch
skrtch
SKRTCH
SKRTCH
SKRTCH
What are you doing, Young Master?
boing

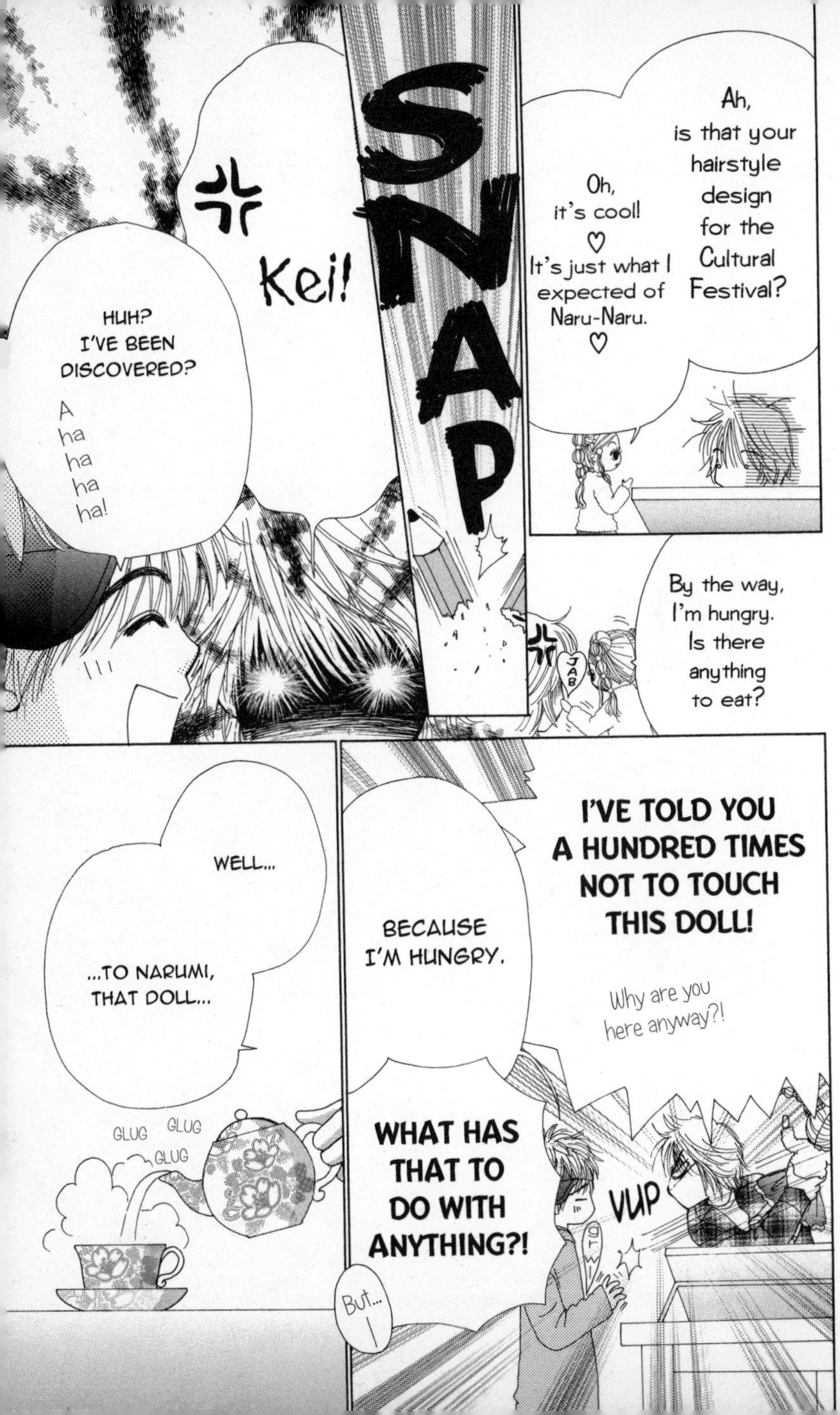
Ah, is that your hairstyle design for the Cultural Festival?
Oh, it's cool! ♡ It's just what I expected of Naru-Naru. ♡
By the way, I'm hungry. Is there anything to eat?
JAB
SNAP
Kei!
HUH? I'VE BEEN DISCOVERED?
A ha ha ha ha!
I'VE TOLD YOU A HUNDRED TIMES NOT TO TOUCH THIS DOLL!
Why are you here anyway?!
BECAUSE I'M HUNGRY.
WHAT HAS THAT TO DO WITH ANYTHING?!
VUP
But...
WELL...
...TO NARUMI, THAT DOLL...
GLUG GLUG GLUG

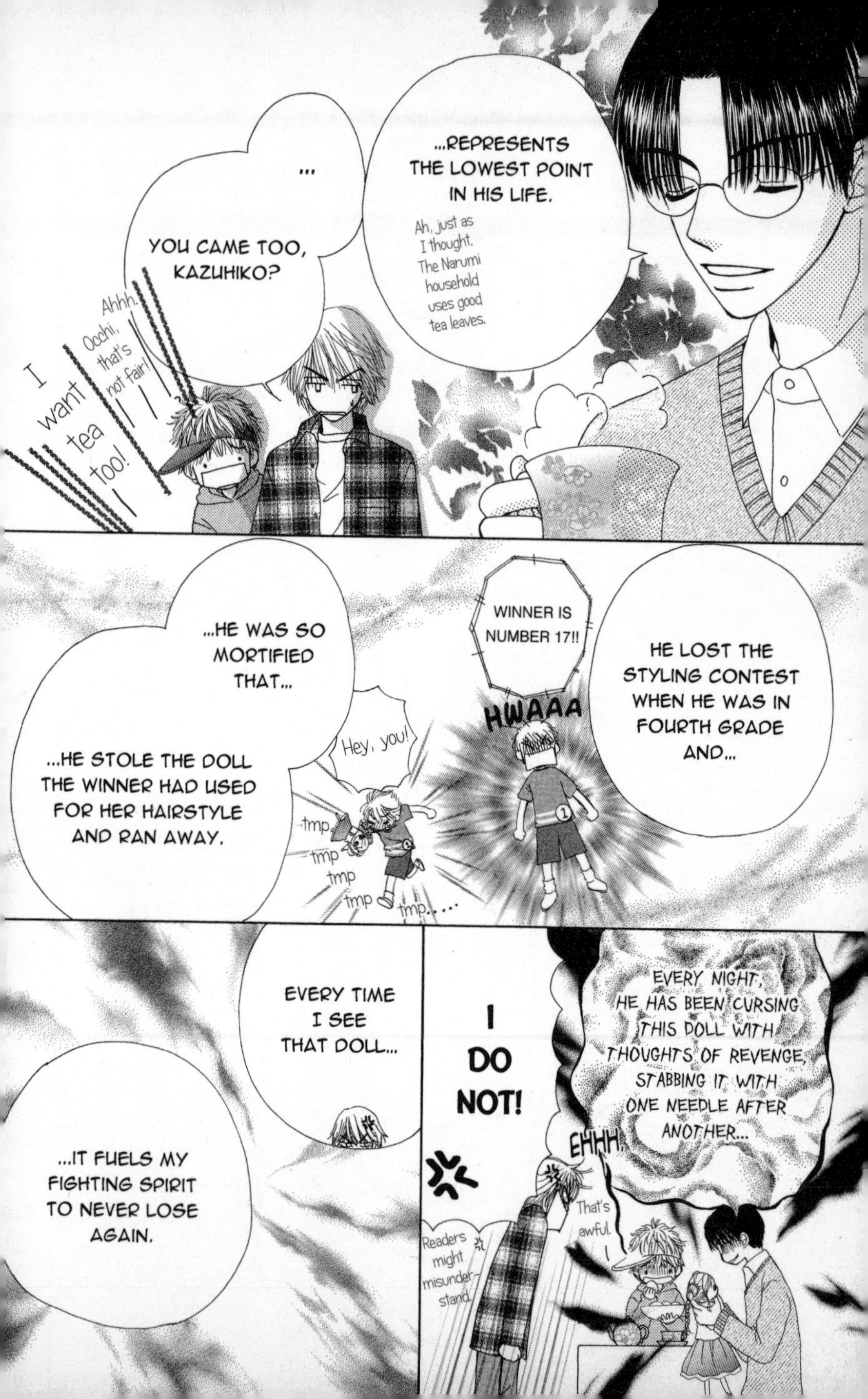
...REPRESENTS THE LOWEST POINT IN HIS LIFE.
Ah, just as I thought. The Narumi household uses good tea leaves.
...
YOU CAME TOO, KAZUHIKO?
Ahhh! Oochi, that's not fair!
I want tea too!
HE LOST THE STYLING CONTEST WHEN HE WAS IN FOURTH GRADE AND...
WINNER IS NUMBER 17!!
HWAAA
...HE WAS SO MORTIFIED THAT...
Hey, you!
...HE STOLE THE DOLL THE WINNER HAD USED FOR HER HAIRSTYLE AND RAN AWAY.
tmp tmp tmp tmp tmp...
EVERY NIGHT, HE HAS BEEN CURSING THIS DOLL WITH THOUGHTS OF REVENGE, STABBING IT WITH ONE NEEDLE AFTER ANOTHER...
I DO NOT!
EHHH
That's awful.
Readers might misunderstand.
EVERY TIME I SEE THAT DOLL...
...IT FUELS MY FIGHTING SPIRIT TO NEVER LOSE AGAIN.

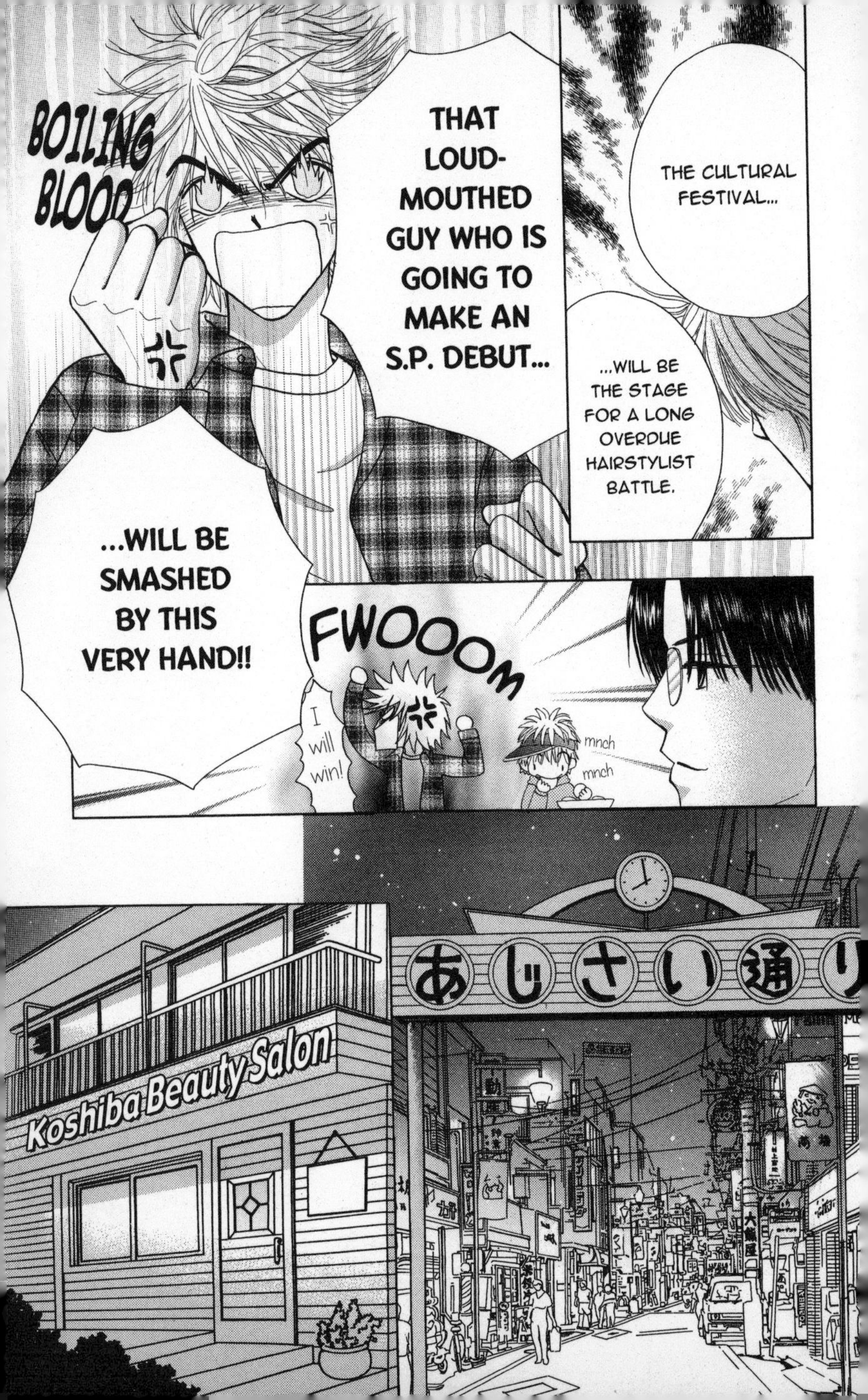
THE CULTURAL FESTIVAL...
...WILL BE THE STAGE FOR A LONG OVERDUE HAIRSTYLIST BATTLE.
THAT LOUD-MOUTHED GUY WHO IS GOING TO MAKE AN S.P. DEBUT...
BOILING BLOOD
...WILL BE SMASHED BY THIS VERY HAND!!
FWOOOM
mnch mnch
I will win!
あじさい通り
Koshiba Beauty Salon

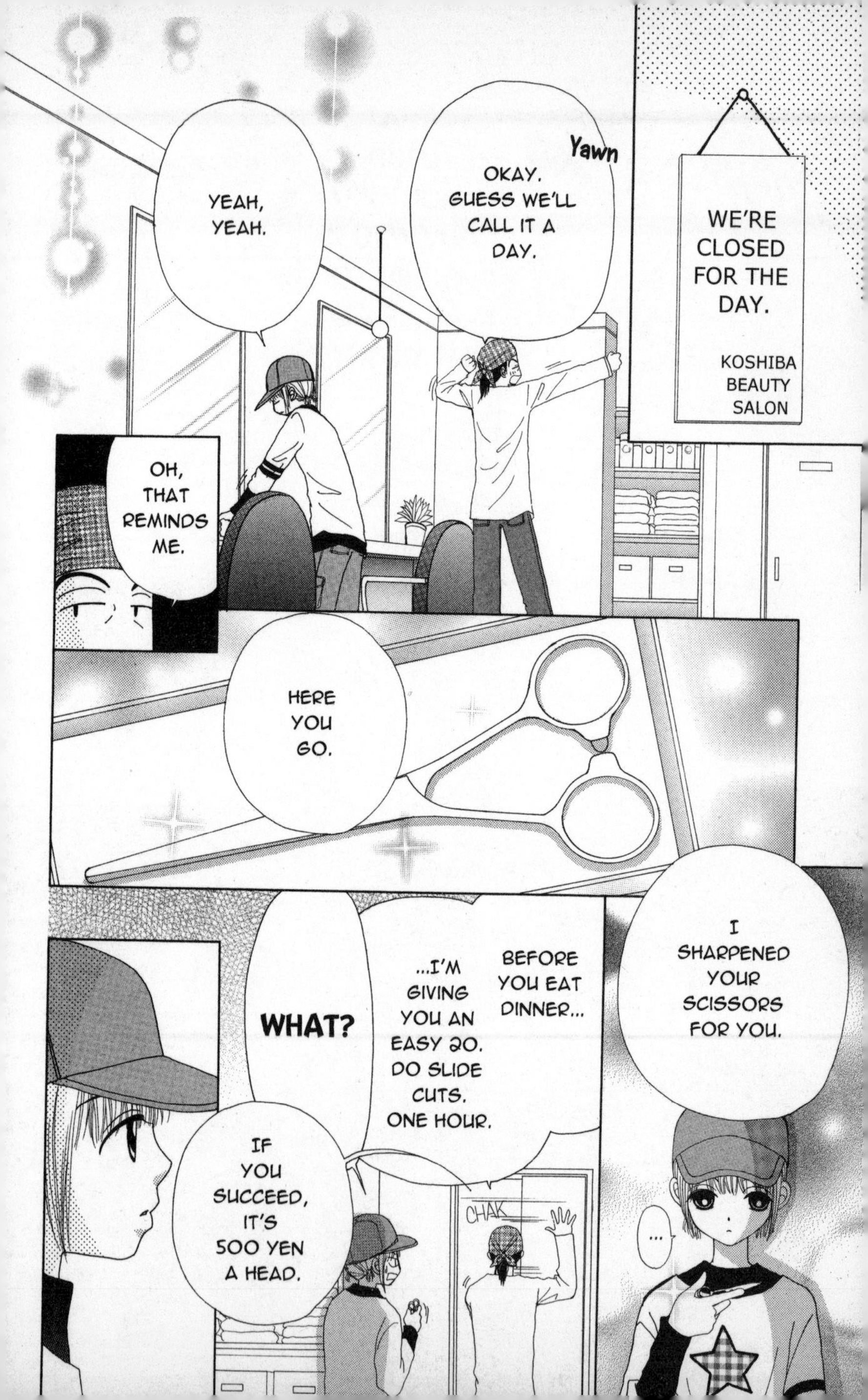
WE'RE CLOSED FOR THE DAY.
KOSHIBA BEAUTY SALON
Yawn
OKAY. GUESS WE'LL CALL IT A DAY.
YEAH, YEAH.
OH, THAT REMINDS ME.
HERE YOU GO.
I SHARPENED YOUR SCISSORS FOR YOU.
...
BEFORE YOU EAT DINNER...
...I'M GIVING YOU AN EASY 20. DO SLIDE CUTS. ONE HOUR.
WHAT?
IF YOU SUCCEED, IT'S 500 YEN A HEAD.
CHAK

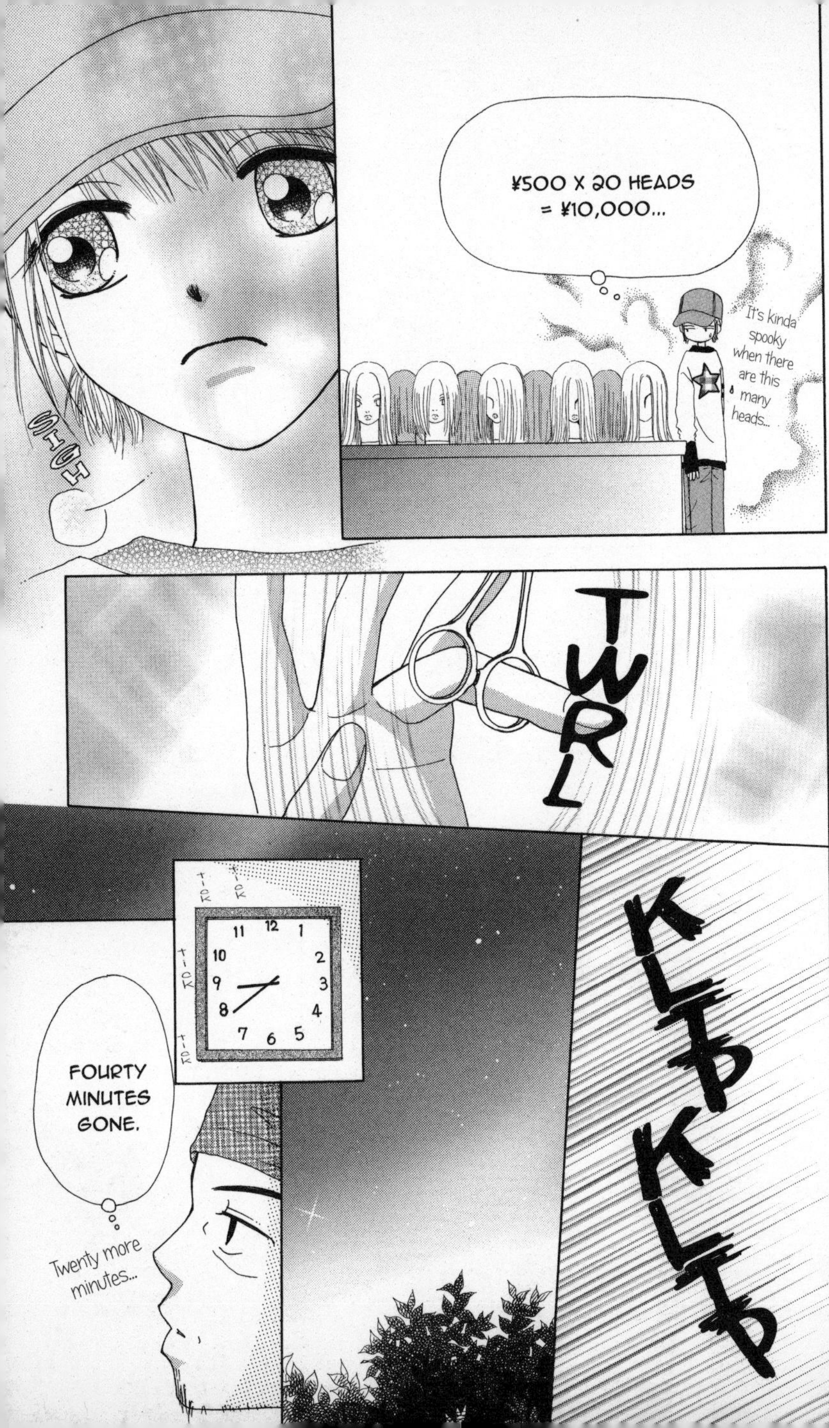
¥500 X 20 HEADS = ¥10,000...
It's kinda spooky when there are this many heads...
SIGH
TWRL
KLIP KLIP
tick tick tick tick
FOURTY MINUTES GONE.
Twenty more minutes...

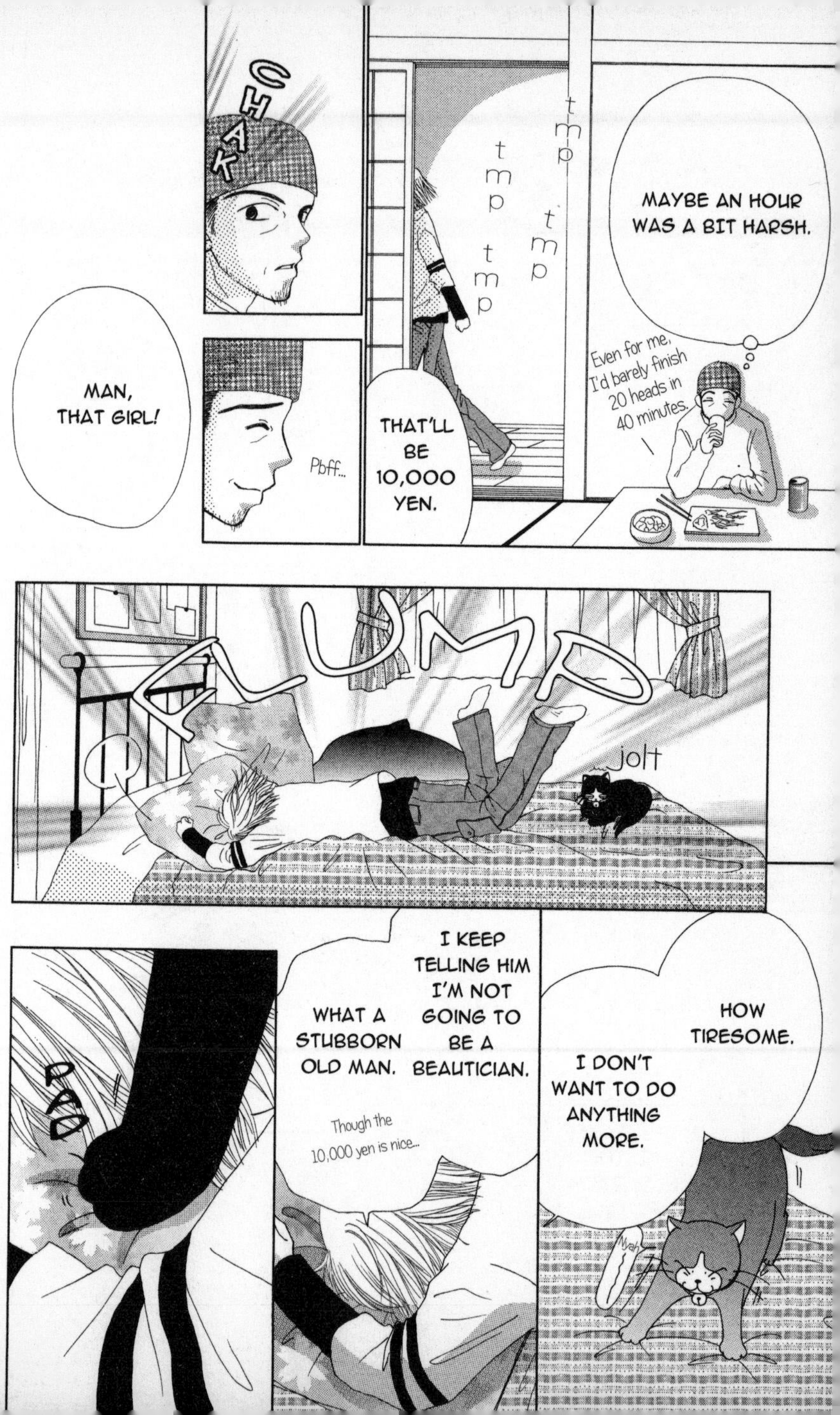
MAYBE AN HOUR WAS A BIT HARSH.
Even for me, I'd barely finish 20 heads in 40 minutes.
tmp tmp tmp tmp
THAT'LL BE 10,000 YEN.
CHAK
Pbff...
MAN, THAT GIRL!
FLUMP
jolt
HOW TIRESOME.
I DON'T WANT TO DO ANYTHING MORE.
Nyah
I KEEP TELLING HIM I'M NOT GOING TO BE A BEAUTICIAN.
WHAT A STUBBORN OLD MAN.
Though the 10,000 yen is nice...
PAD

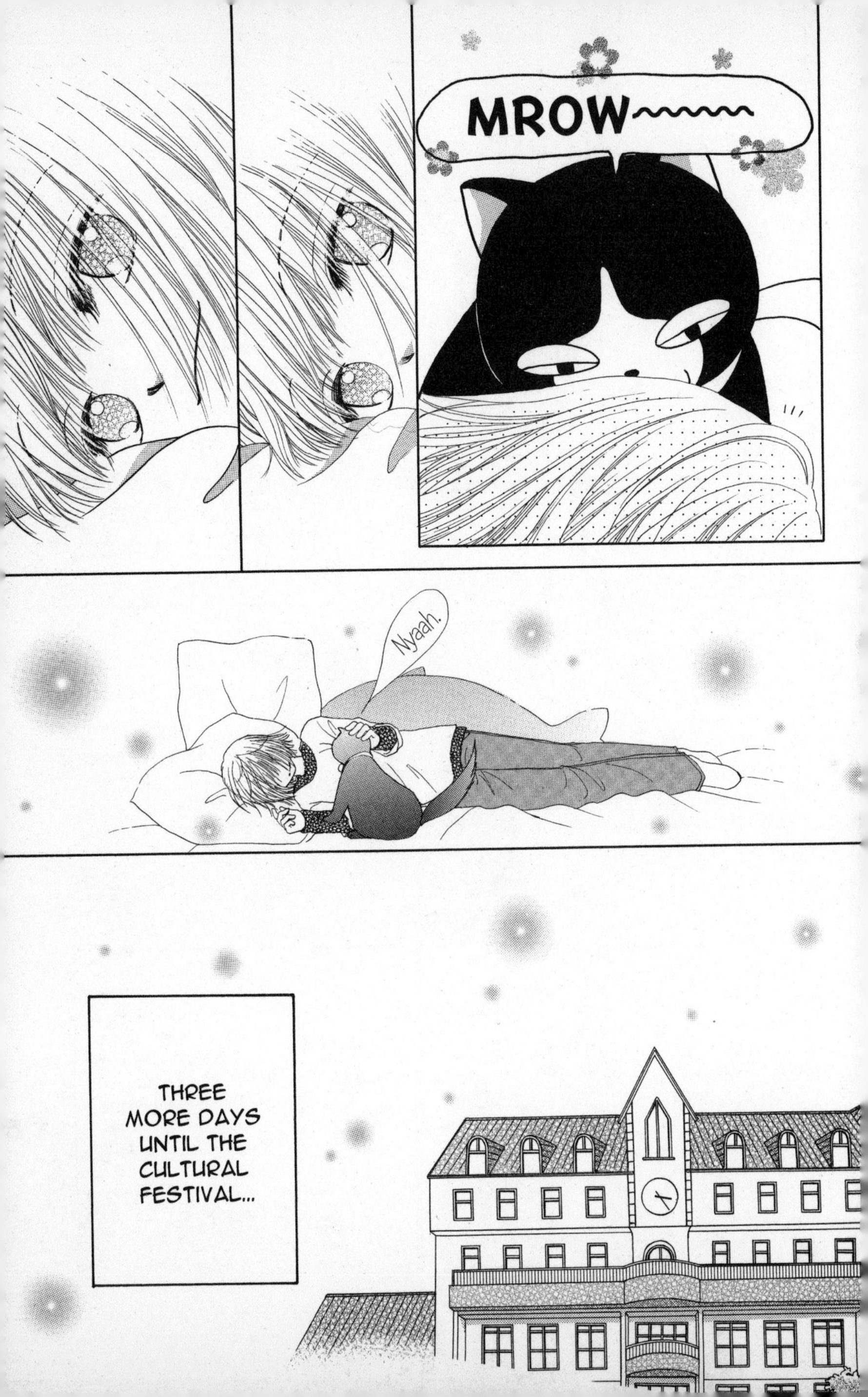
MROW~~~~
Nyaah.
THREE MORE DAYS UNTIL THE CULTURAL FESTIVAL...

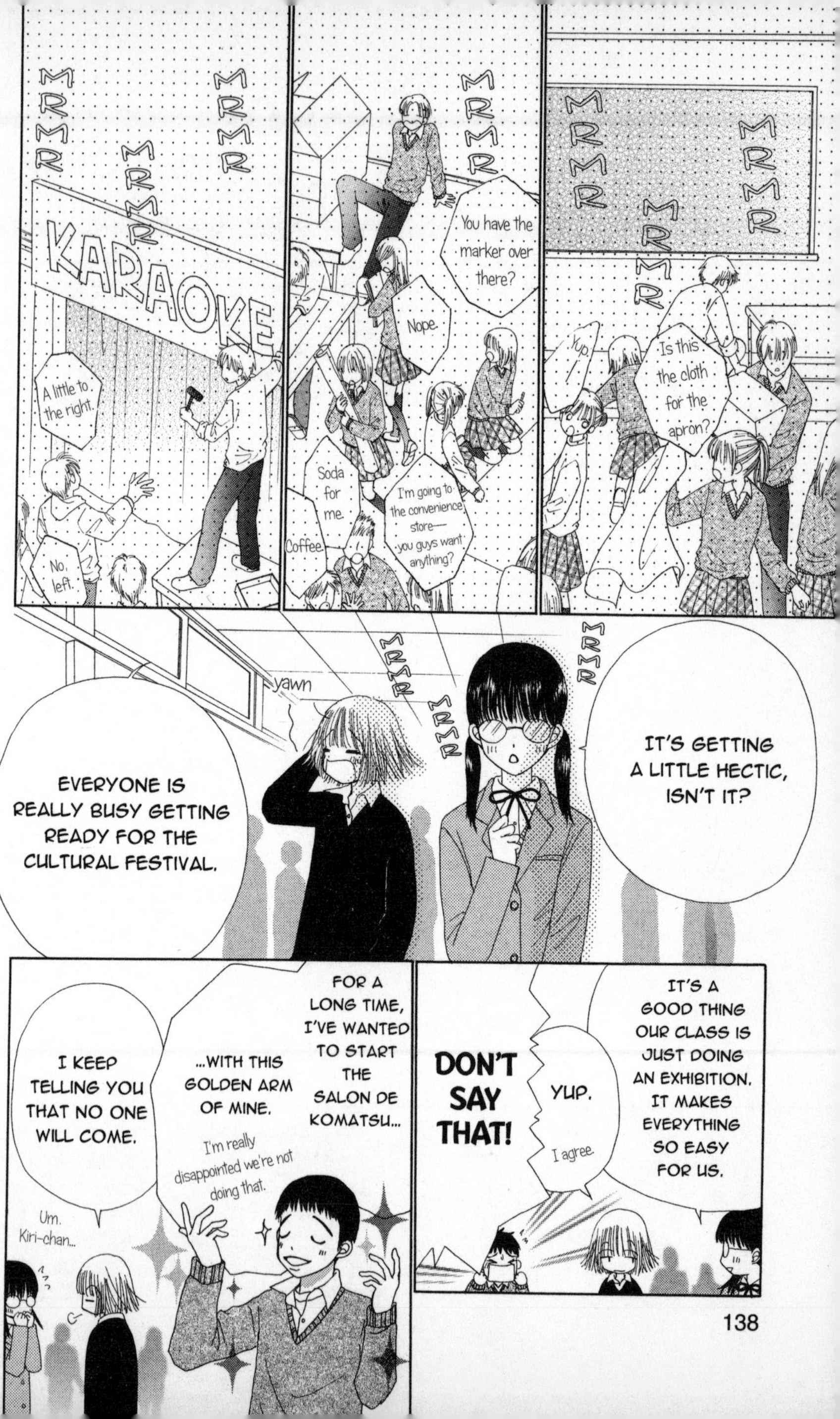
MRMR
MRMR
MRMR
Is this the cloth for the apron?
Yup.
MRMR
You have the marker over there?
Nope.
I'm going to the convenience store— you guys want anything?
Soda for me.
Coffee.
MRMR
MRMR
MRMR
KARAOKE
A little to the right.
No, left.
MRMR
IT'S GETTING A LITTLE HECTIC, ISN'T IT?
MRMR
MRMR
yawn
EVERYONE IS REALLY BUSY GETTING READY FOR THE CULTURAL FESTIVAL.
IT'S A GOOD THING OUR CLASS IS JUST DOING AN EXHIBITION. IT MAKES EVERYTHING SO EASY FOR US.
YUP.
I agree.
DON'T SAY THAT!
FOR A LONG TIME, I'VE WANTED TO START THE SALON DE KOMATSU...
...WITH THIS GOLDEN ARM OF MINE.
I'm really disappointed we're not doing that.
I KEEP TELLING YOU THAT NO ONE WILL COME.
Um. Kiri-chan...

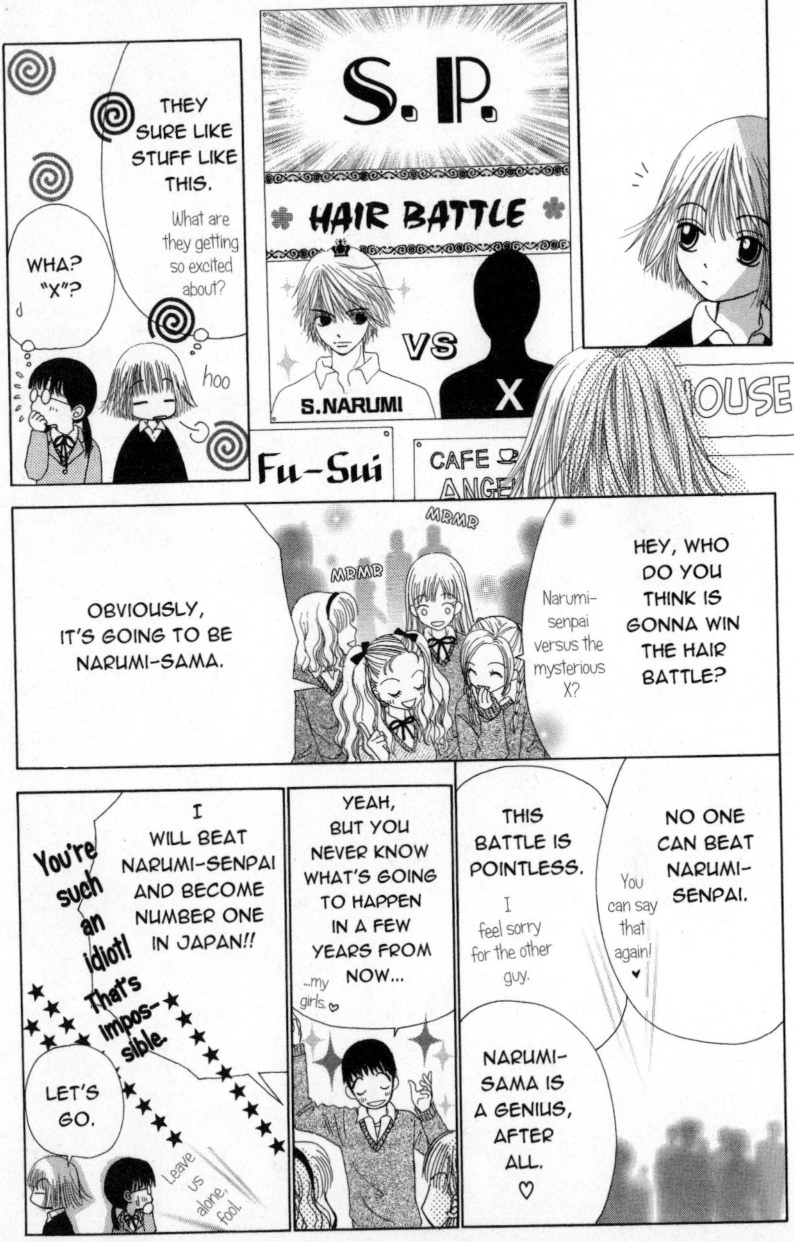
OUSE
CAFE
ANGE
S.P.
HAIR BATTLE
S.NARUMI
VS
X
Fu-Sui
THEY SURE LIKE STUFF LIKE THIS.
What are they getting so excited about?
WHA? "X"?
hoo
HEY, WHO DO YOU THINK IS GONNA WIN THE HAIR BATTLE?
Narumi-senpai versus the mysterious X?
MRMR
MRMR
OBVIOUSLY, IT'S GOING TO BE NARUMI-SAMA.
NO ONE CAN BEAT NARUMI-SENPAI.
You can say that again! ♥
THIS BATTLE IS POINTLESS.
I feel sorry for the other guy.
NARUMI-SAMA IS A GENIUS, AFTER ALL. ♡
YEAH, BUT YOU NEVER KNOW WHAT'S GOING TO HAPPEN IN A FEW YEARS FROM NOW...
...my girls. ♡
I WILL BEAT NARUMI-SENPAI AND BECOME NUMBER ONE IN JAPAN!!
You're such an idiot! That's impossible.
LET'S GO.
Leave us alone, fool.

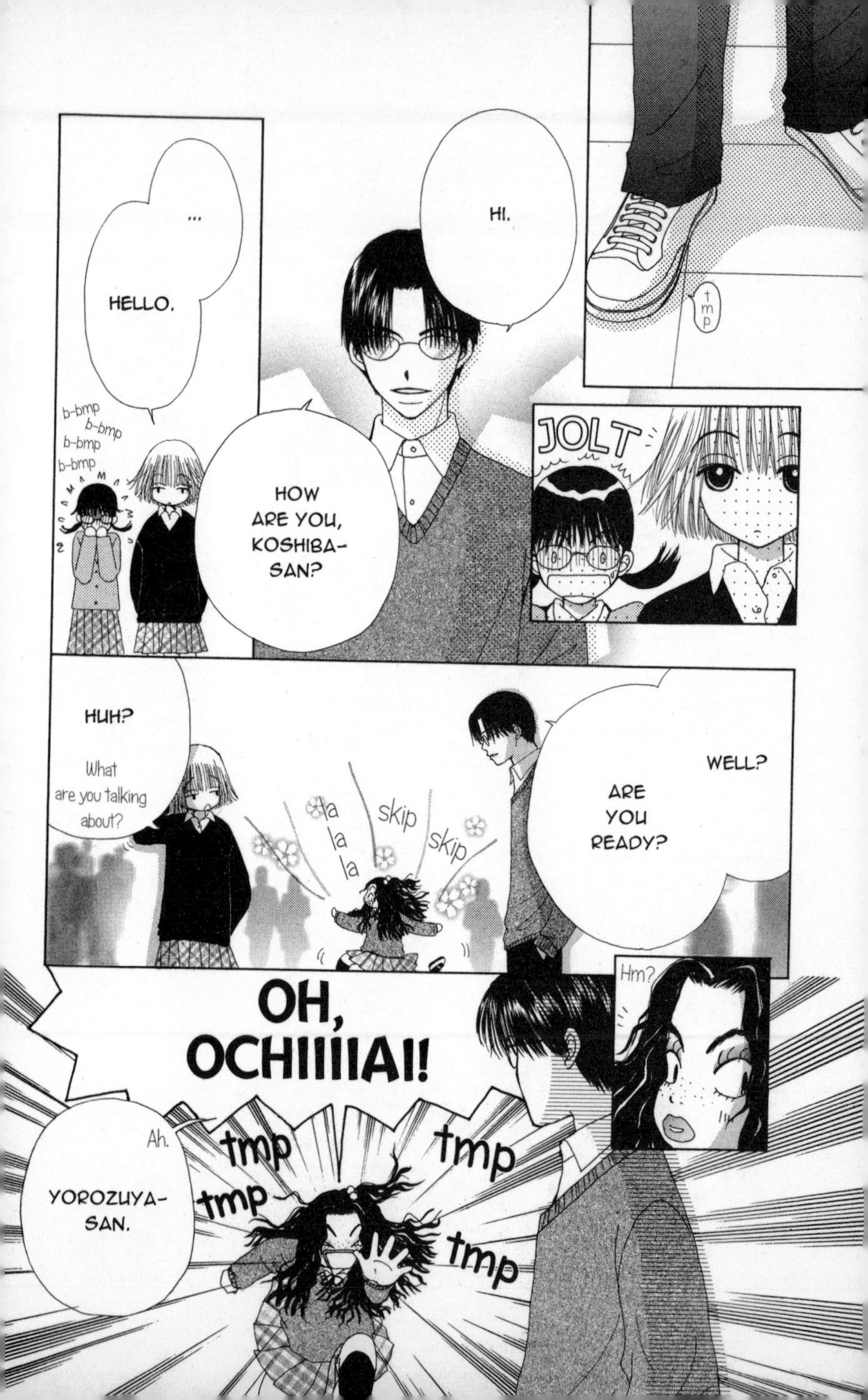

tmp
JOLT
HI.
HOW ARE YOU, KOSHIBA-SAN?
...
HELLO.
b-bmp b-bmp b-bmp b-bmp
WELL?
ARE YOU READY?
skip skip
la la la
HUH?
What are you talking about?
Hm?
OH, OCHIIIIAI!
tmp tmp tmp tmp
Ah.
YOROZUYA-SAN.

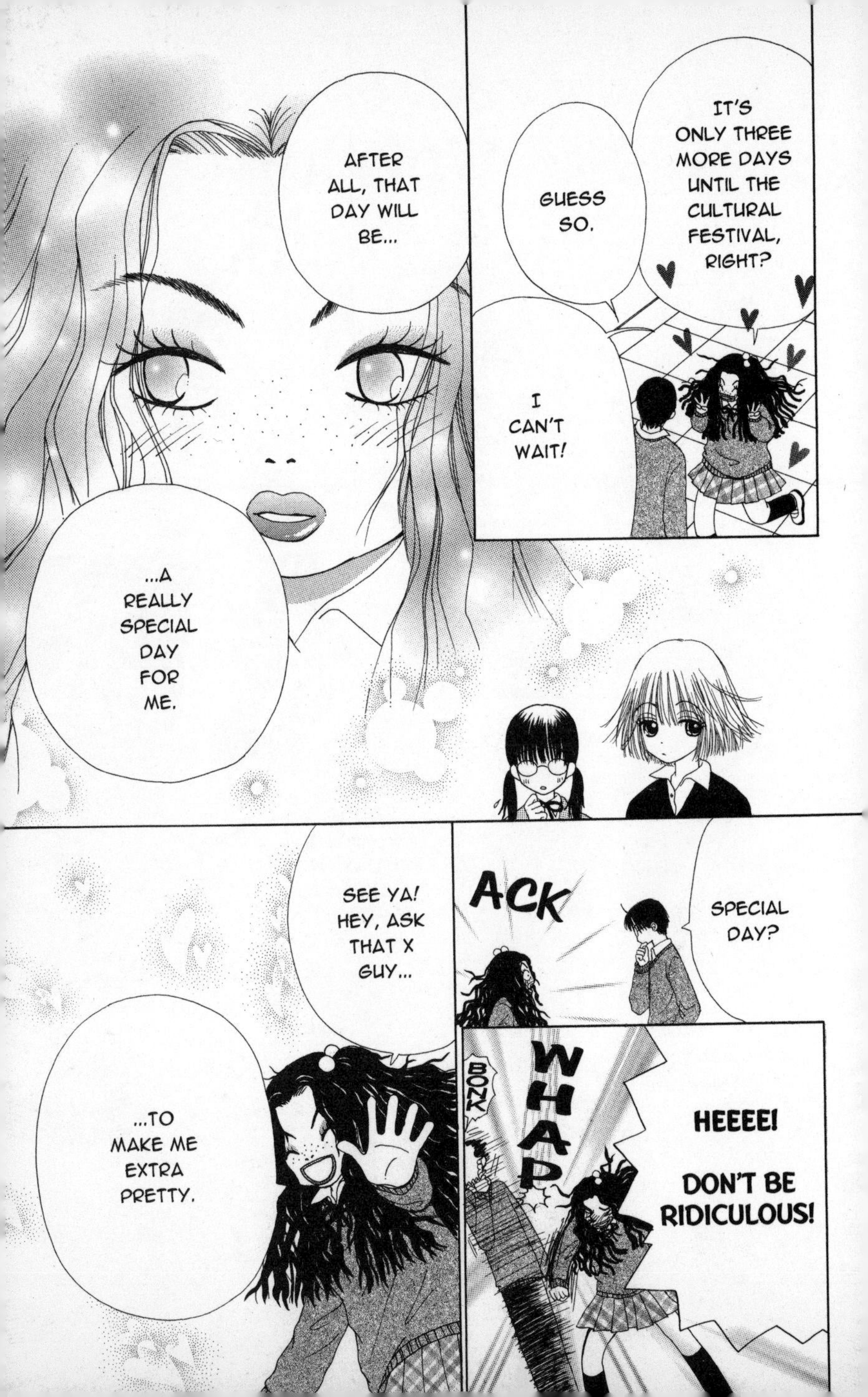
IT'S ONLY THREE MORE DAYS UNTIL THE CULTURAL FESTIVAL, RIGHT?
GUESS SO.
I CAN'T WAIT!
AFTER ALL, THAT DAY WILL BE...
...A REALLY SPECIAL DAY FOR ME.
SPECIAL DAY?
ACK
WHAP
BONK
HEEEE!
DON'T BE RIDICULOUS!
SEE YA! HEY, ASK THAT X GUY...
...TO MAKE ME EXTRA PRETTY.

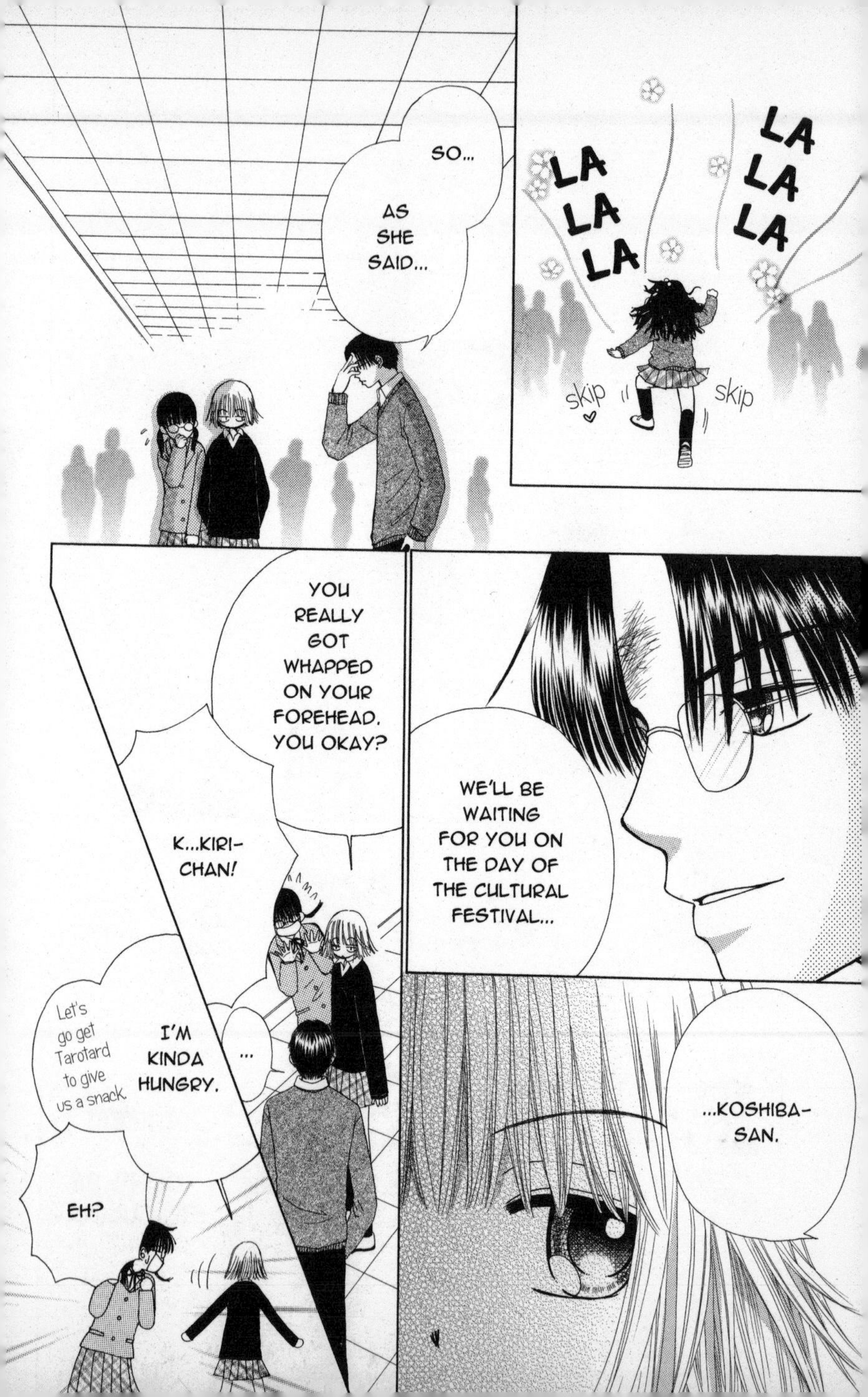

LA LA LA
LA LA LA
skip skip
SO...
AS SHE SAID...
WE'LL BE WAITING FOR YOU ON THE DAY OF THE CULTURAL FESTIVAL...
...KOSHIBA-SAN.
YOU REALLY GOT WHAPPED ON YOUR FOREHEAD. YOU OKAY?
K...KIRI-CHAN!
...
I'M KINDA HUNGRY.
Let's go get Tarotard to give us a snack.
EH?

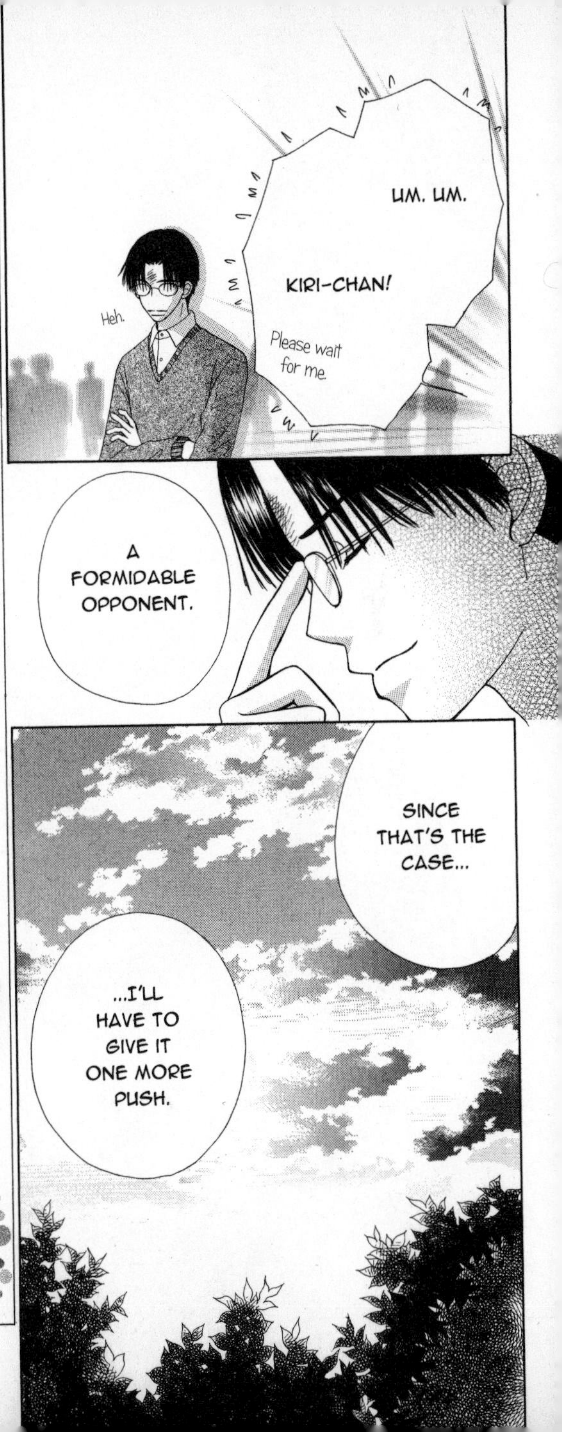
UM. UM.
KIRI-CHAN!
Please wait for me.
Heh.
A FORMIDABLE OPPONENT.
SINCE THAT'S THE CASE...
...I'LL HAVE TO GIVE IT ONE MORE PUSH.

K's Club Talk

Well now, here's a silhouette quiz. Which of the following is Kei-kun?

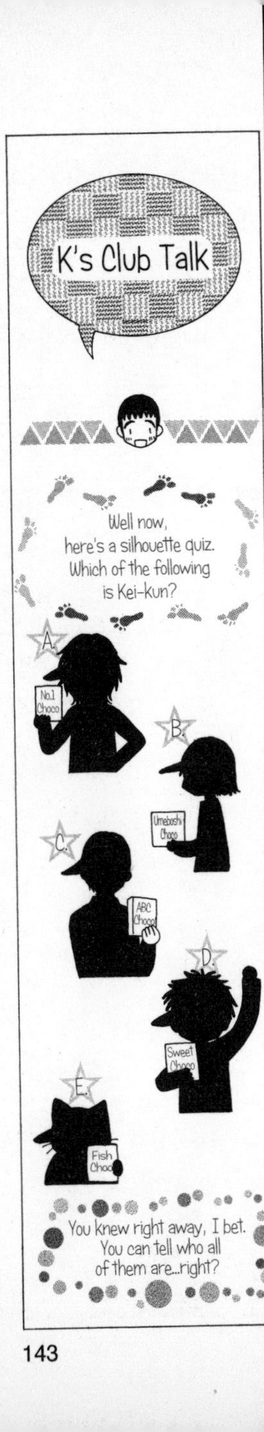
A.
No.1 Choco
B.
Umeboshi Choco
C.
ABC Choco
D.
Sweet Choco
E.
Fish Choco

You knew right away, I bet. You can tell who all of them are...right?

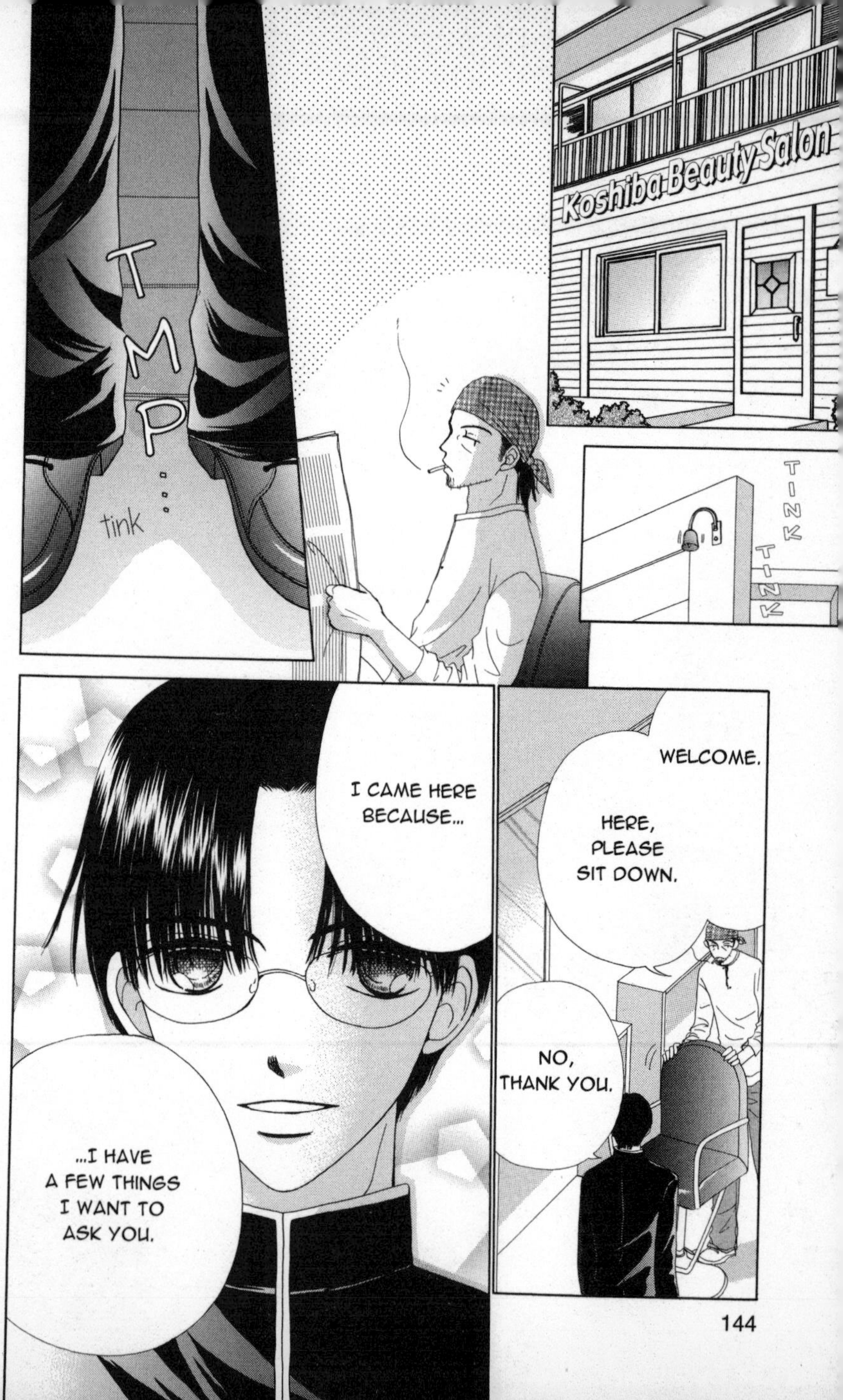

Koshiba Beauty Salon
TINK
TINK
TMP...
tink
WELCOME.
HERE, PLEASE SIT DOWN.
NO, THANK YOU.
I CAME HERE BECAUSE...
...I HAVE A FEW THINGS I WANT TO ASK YOU.

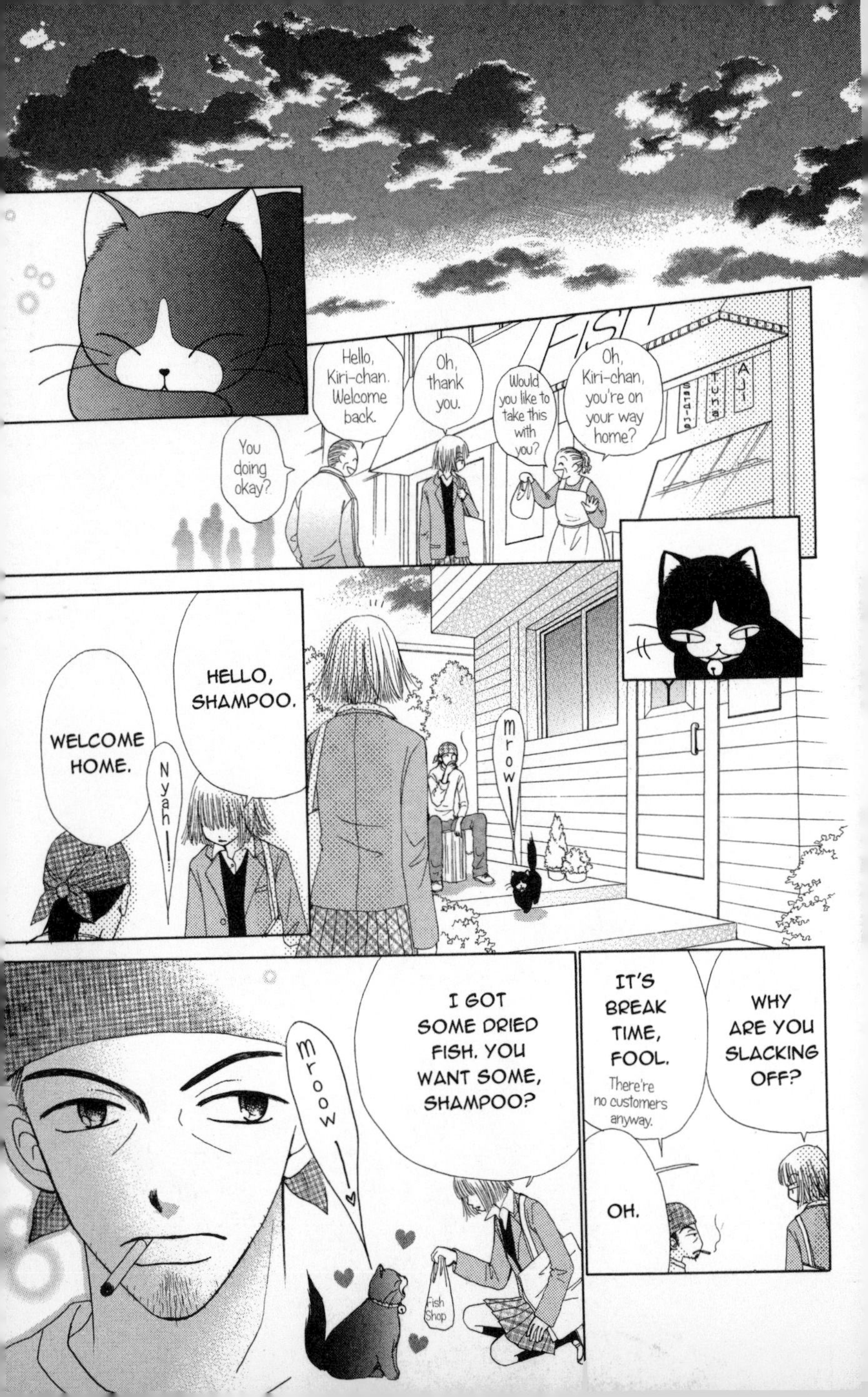
FISH
Aji
Tuna
Sardine
Oh, Kiri-chan, you're on your way home?
Would you like to take this with you?
Oh, thank you.
Hello, Kiri-chan. Welcome back.
You doing okay?
mrow
HELLO, SHAMPOO.
WELCOME HOME.
Nyah
WHY ARE YOU SLACKING OFF?
IT'S BREAK TIME, FOOL.
There're no customers anyway.
OH.
I GOT SOME DRIED FISH. YOU WANT SOME, SHAMPOO?
mroow
Fish Shop

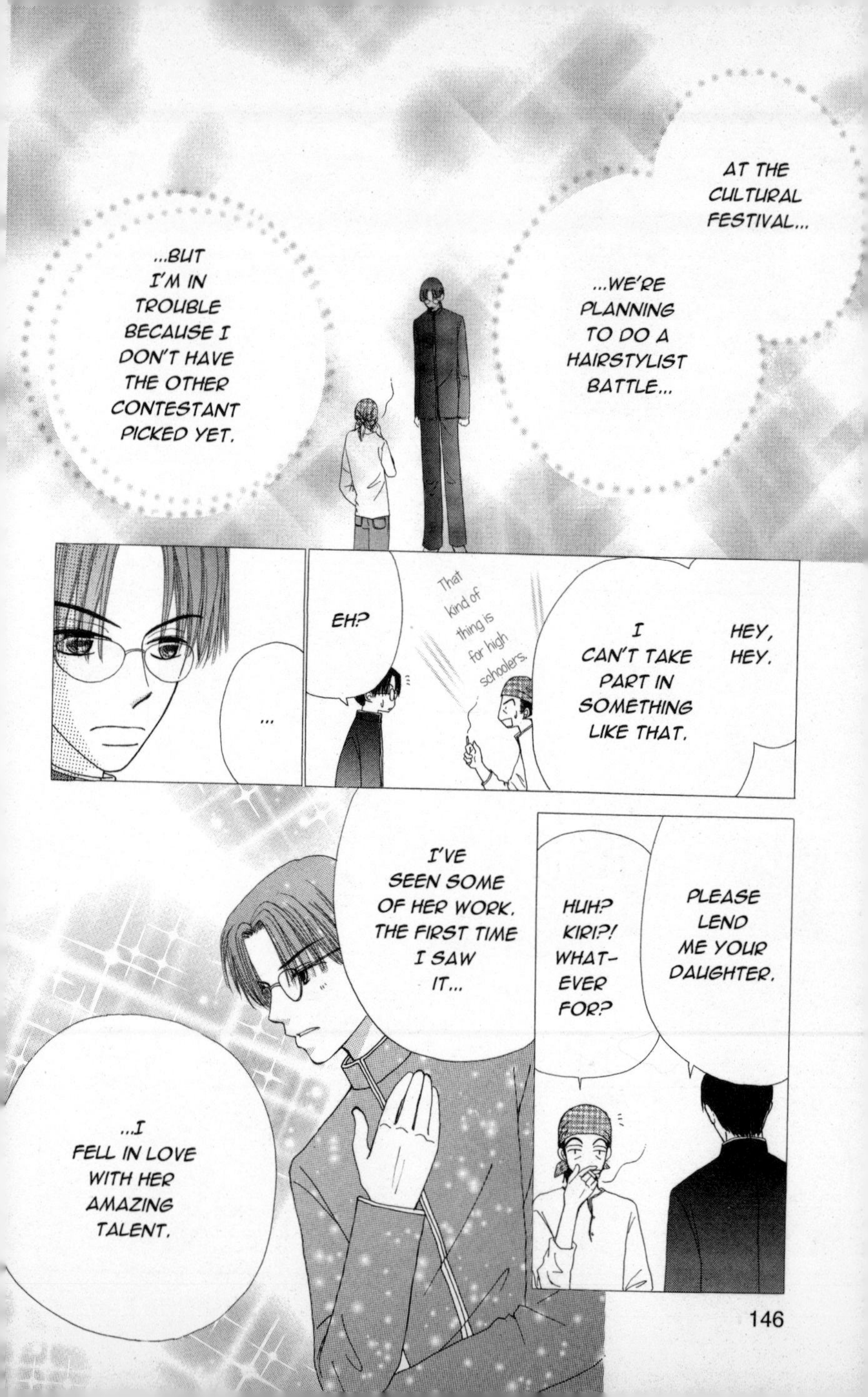
AT THE CULTURAL FESTIVAL...
...WE'RE PLANNING TO DO A HAIRSTYLIST BATTLE...
...BUT I'M IN TROUBLE BECAUSE I DON'T HAVE THE OTHER CONTESTANT PICKED YET.
HEY, HEY.
I CAN'T TAKE PART IN SOMETHING LIKE THAT.
That kind of thing is for high schoolers.
EH?
...
PLEASE LEND ME YOUR DAUGHTER.
HUH? KIRI?! WHAT-EVER FOR?
I'VE SEEN SOME OF HER WORK. THE FIRST TIME I SAW IT...
...I FELL IN LOVE WITH HER AMAZING TALENT.

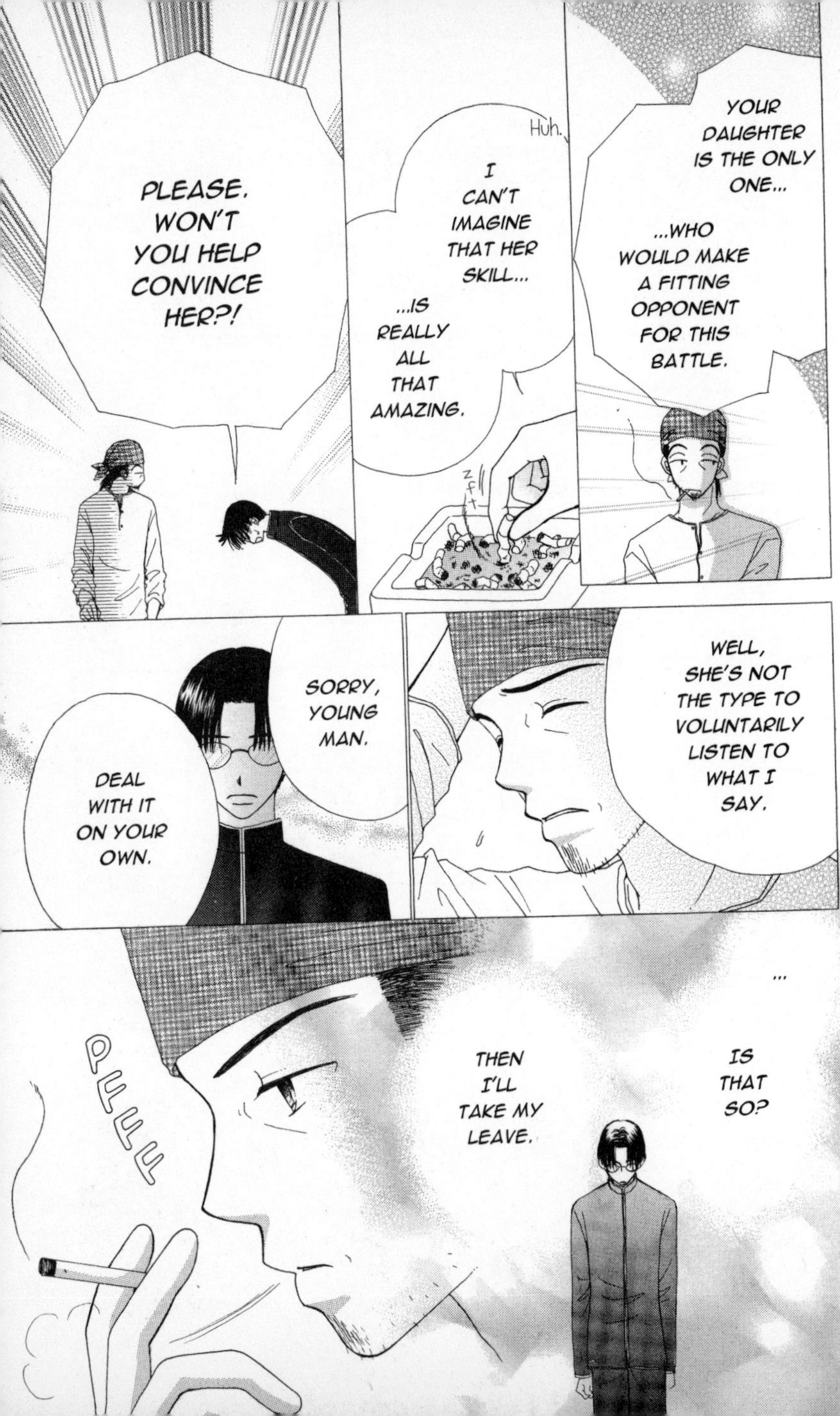
Huh.
YOUR DAUGHTER IS THE ONLY ONE...
...WHO WOULD MAKE A FITTING OPPONENT FOR THIS BATTLE.
I CAN'T IMAGINE THAT HER SKILL...
...IS REALLY ALL THAT AMAZING.
ZFT
PLEASE. WON'T YOU HELP CONVINCE HER?!
WELL, SHE'S NOT THE TYPE TO VOLUNTARILY LISTEN TO WHAT I SAY.
SORRY, YOUNG MAN.
DEAL WITH IT ON YOUR OWN.
...
IS THAT SO?
THEN I'LL TAKE MY LEAVE.
PFFFF

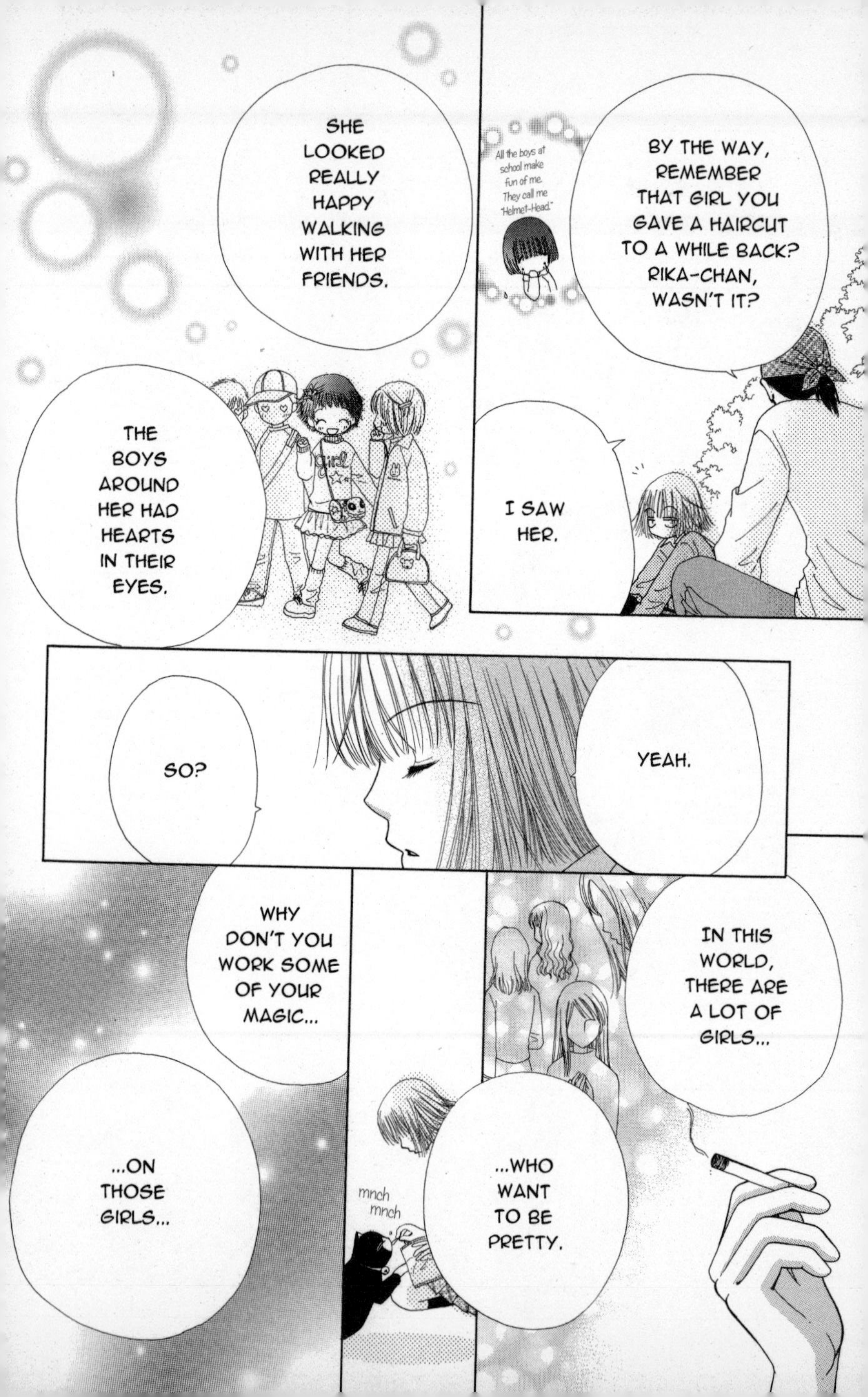
BY THE WAY, REMEMBER THAT GIRL YOU GAVE A HAIRCUT TO A WHILE BACK? RIKA-CHAN, WASN'T IT?
All the boys at school make fun of me. They call me "Helmet-Head."
I SAW HER.
SHE LOOKED REALLY HAPPY WALKING WITH HER FRIENDS.
THE BOYS AROUND HER HAD HEARTS IN THEIR EYES.
YEAH.
SO?
IN THIS WORLD, THERE ARE A LOT OF GIRLS...
...WHO WANT TO BE PRETTY.
mnch mnch
WHY DON'T YOU WORK SOME OF YOUR MAGIC...
...ON THOSE GIRLS...

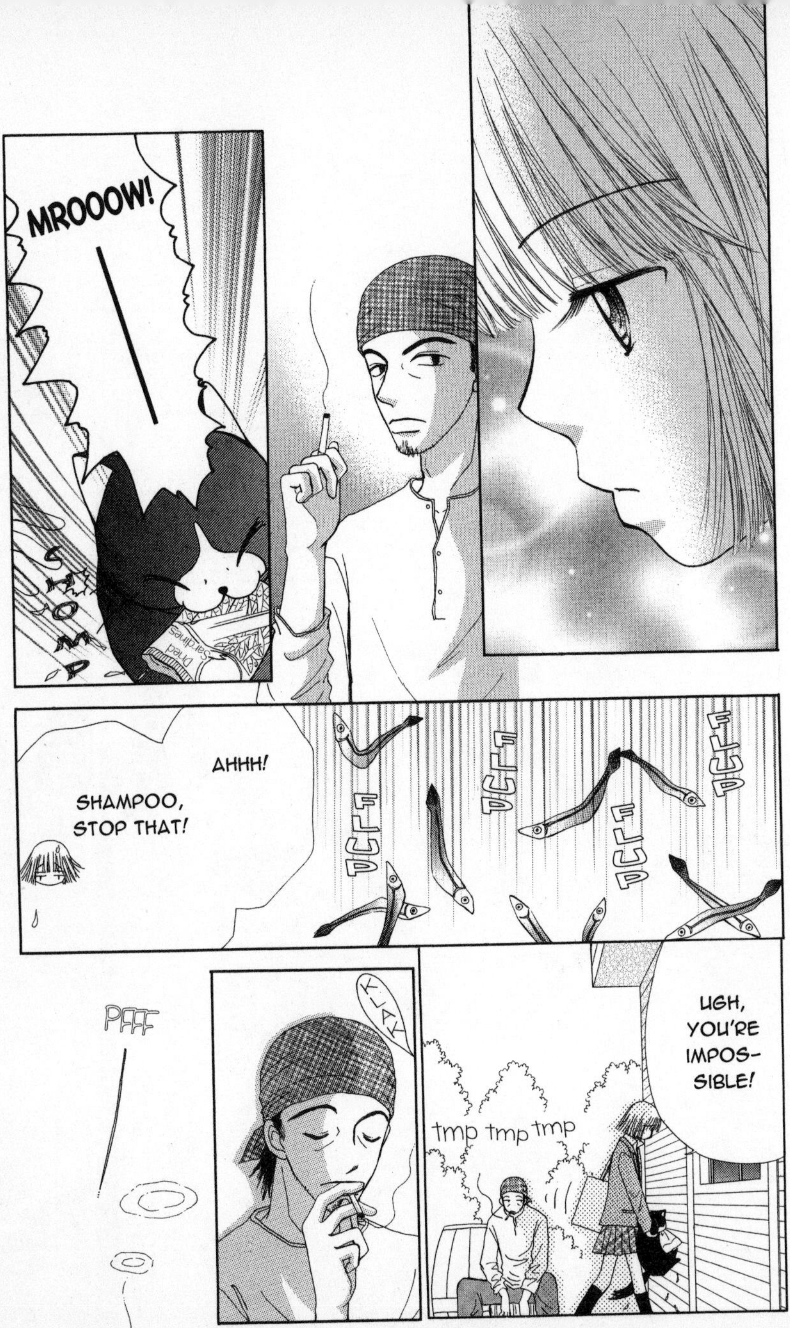
MROOOW!
SHOMP
Dried Sardines
FLUP
FLUP
FLUP
FLUP
AHHH!
SHAMPOO, STOP THAT!
UGH, YOU'RE IMPOS-SIBLE!
tmp tmp tmp
KLAK
PFFF

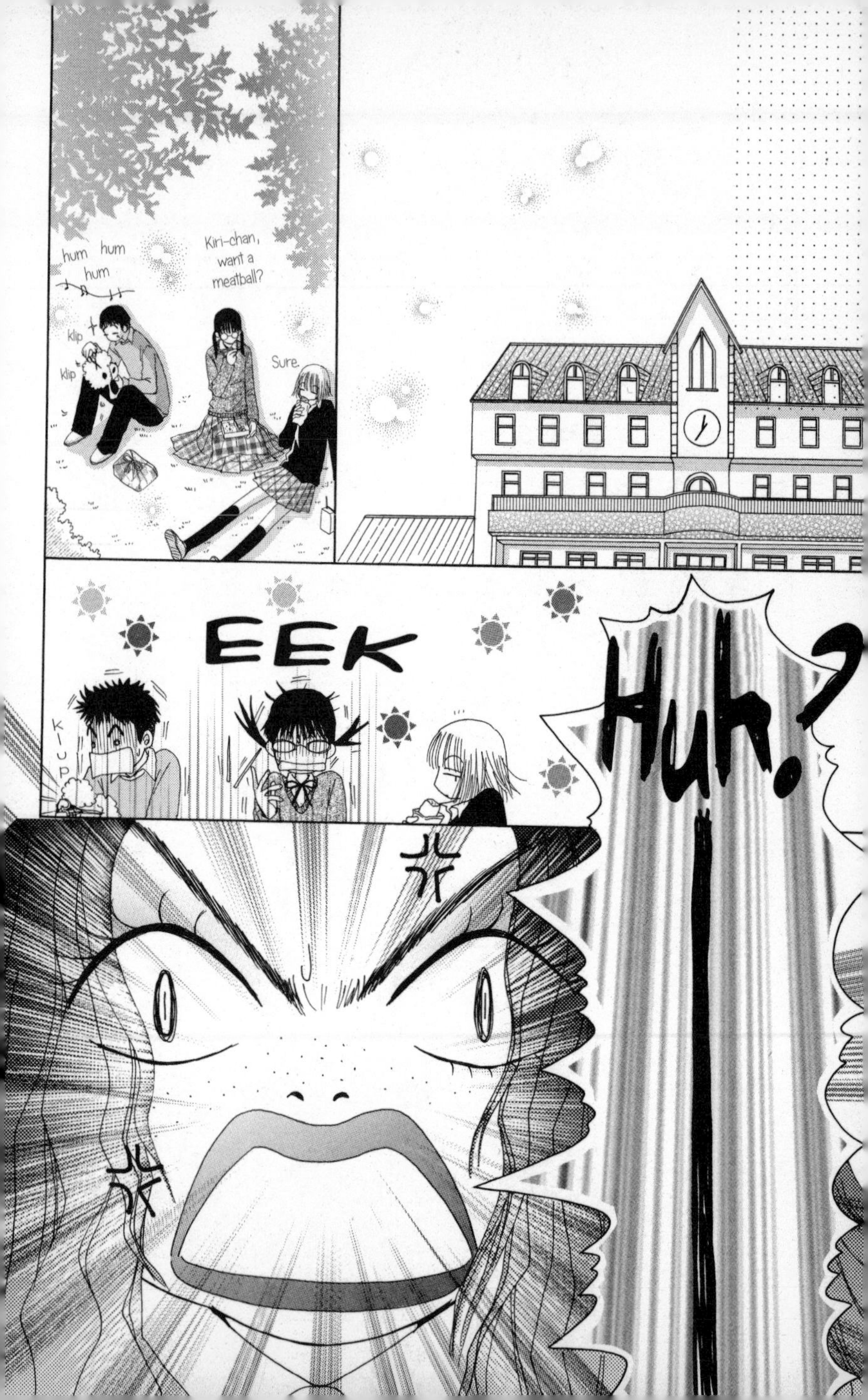
Kiri-chan, want a meatball?
hum hum hum
Sure.
klip klip
EEK
KLIUP
Huk?

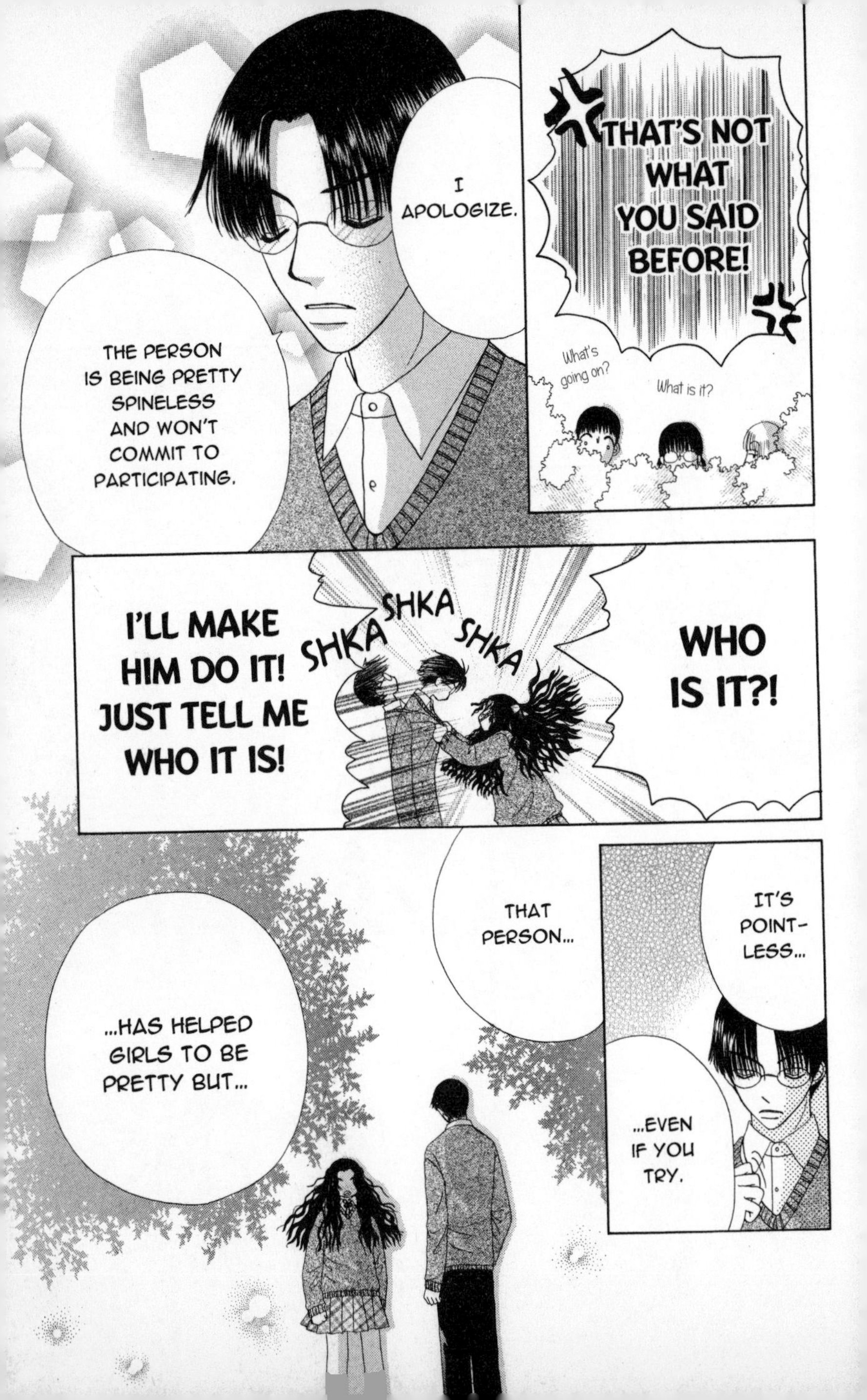
THAT'S NOT WHAT YOU SAID BEFORE!
What's going on?
What is it?
I APOLOGIZE.
THE PERSON IS BEING PRETTY SPINELESS AND WON'T COMMIT TO PARTICIPATING.
WHO IS IT?!
SHKA SHKA SHKA
I'LL MAKE HIM DO IT! JUST TELL ME WHO IT IS!
IT'S POINT-LESS...
...EVEN IF YOU TRY.
THAT PERSON...
...HAS HELPED GIRLS TO BE PRETTY BUT...

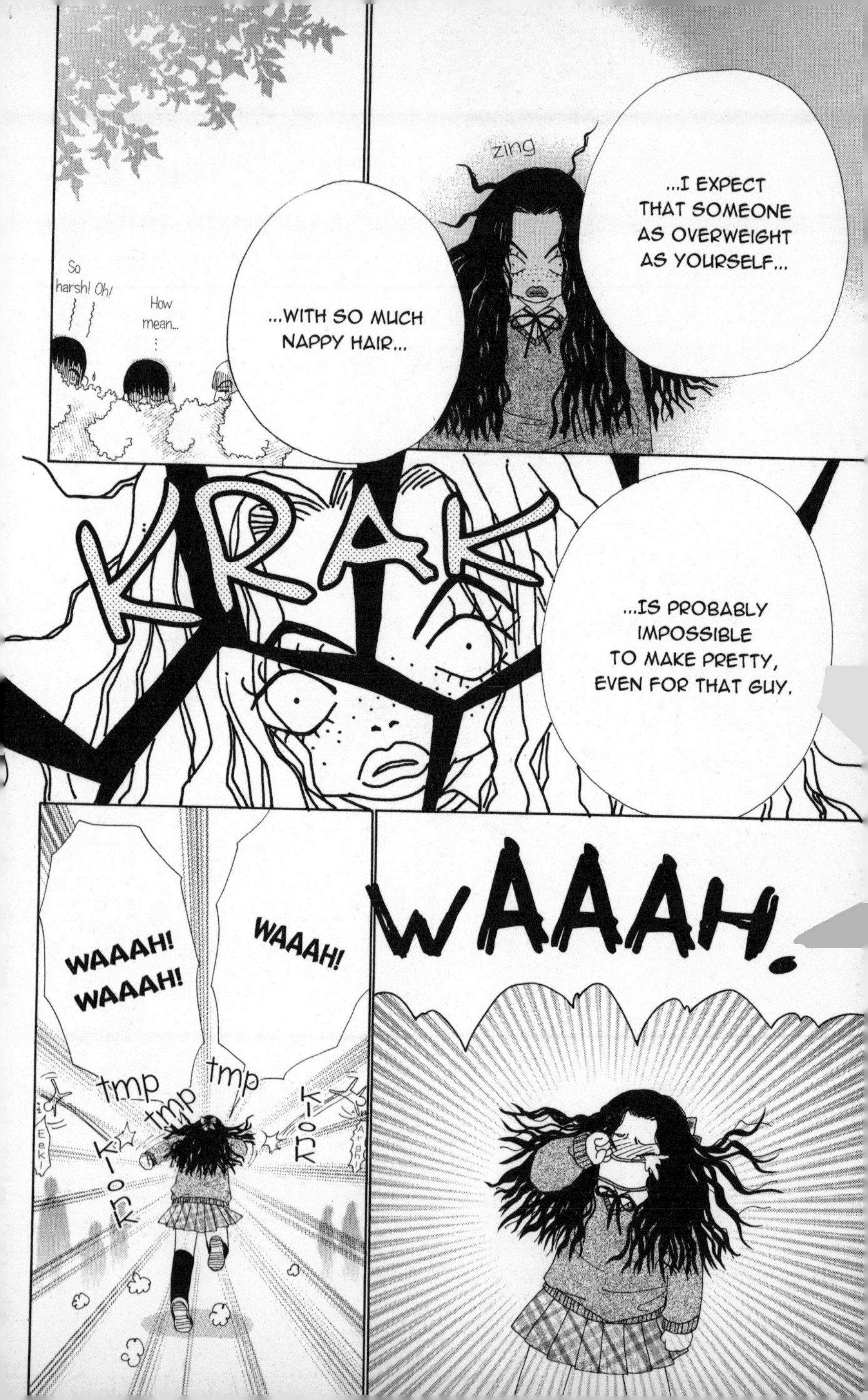
zing
...I EXPECT THAT SOMEONE AS OVERWEIGHT AS YOURSELF...
...WITH SO MUCH NAPPY HAIR...
So harsh! Oh!
How mean...
...IS PROBABLY IMPOSSIBLE TO MAKE PRETTY, EVEN FOR THAT GUY.
KRAK
WAAAH.
WAAAH!
WAAAH! WAAAH!
tmp
tmp
tmp
klonk
Argh!
Eek!
klonk

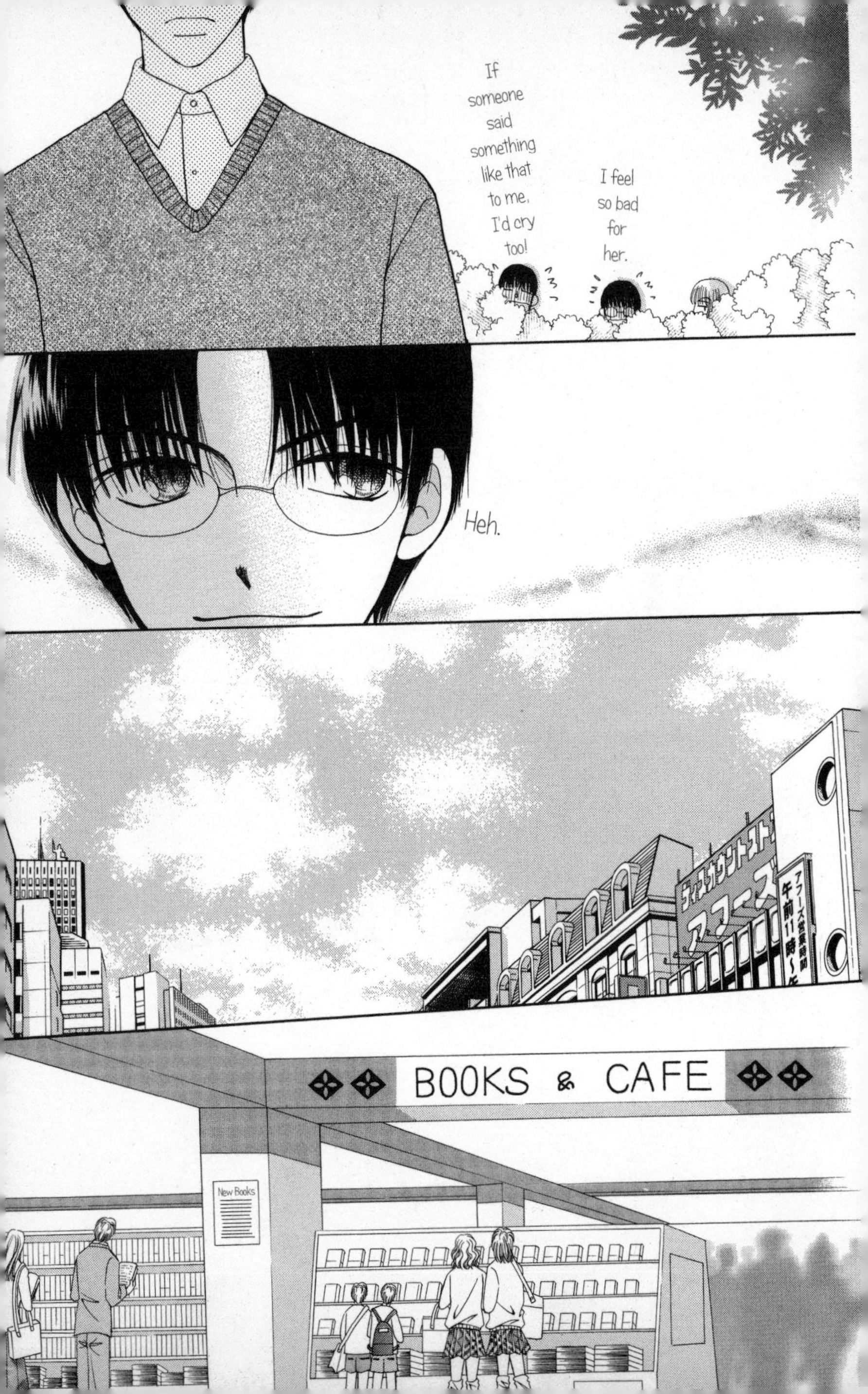
I feel so bad for her.
If someone said something like that to me, I'd cry too!
Heh.
BOOKS & CAFE
New Books

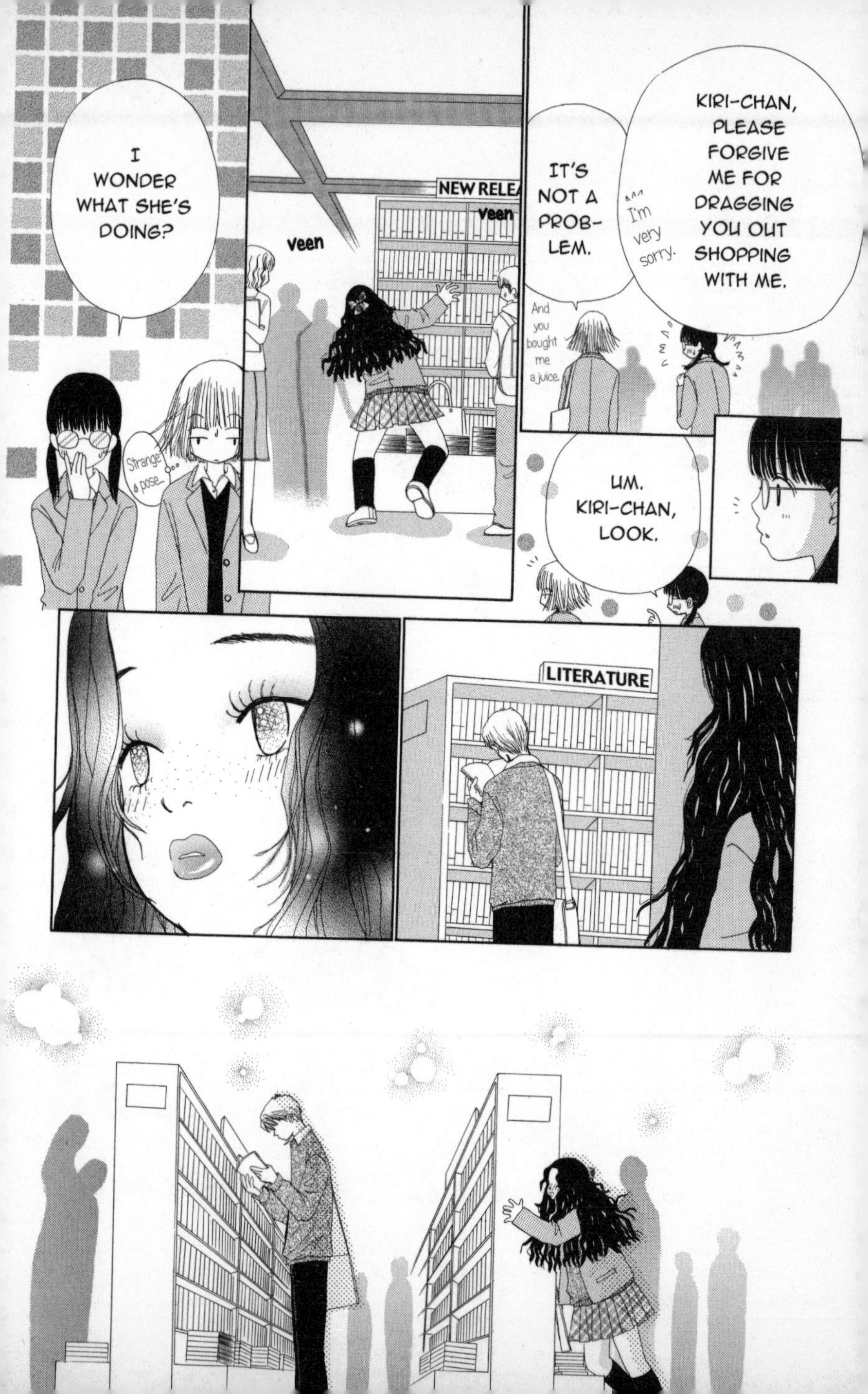
KIRI-CHAN, PLEASE FORGIVE ME FOR DRAGGING YOU OUT SHOPPING WITH ME.
I'm very sorry.
IT'S NOT A PROB-LEM.
And you bought me a juice.
UM. KIRI-CHAN, LOOK.
NEW RELEA
veen
veen
I WONDER WHAT SHE'S DOING?
Strange pose...
LITERATURE

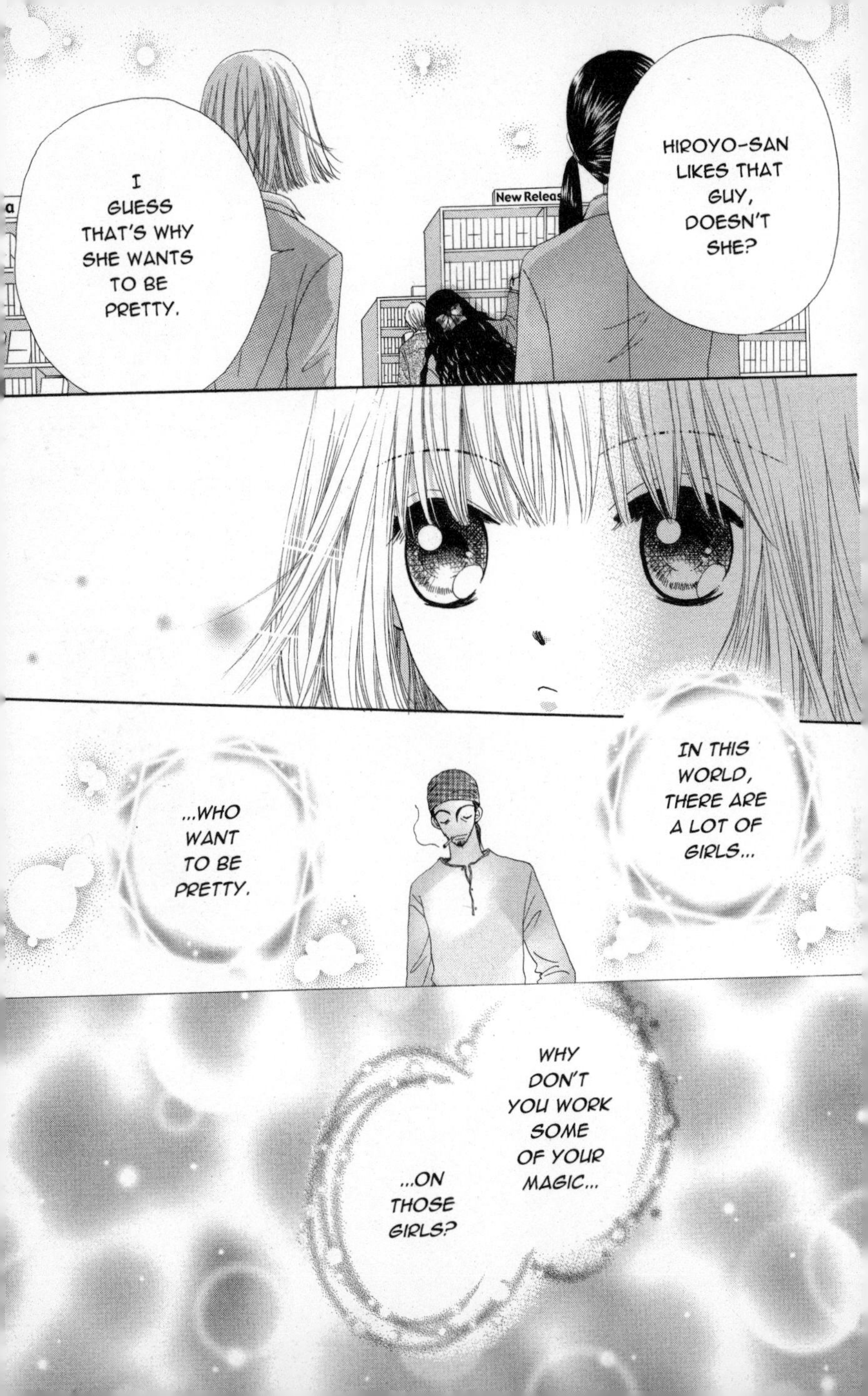

HIROYO-SAN LIKES THAT GUY, DOESN'T SHE?
I GUESS THAT'S WHY SHE WANTS TO BE PRETTY.
New Releas
IN THIS WORLD, THERE ARE A LOT OF GIRLS...
...WHO WANT TO BE PRETTY.
WHY DON'T YOU WORK SOME OF YOUR MAGIC...
...ON THOSE GIRLS?

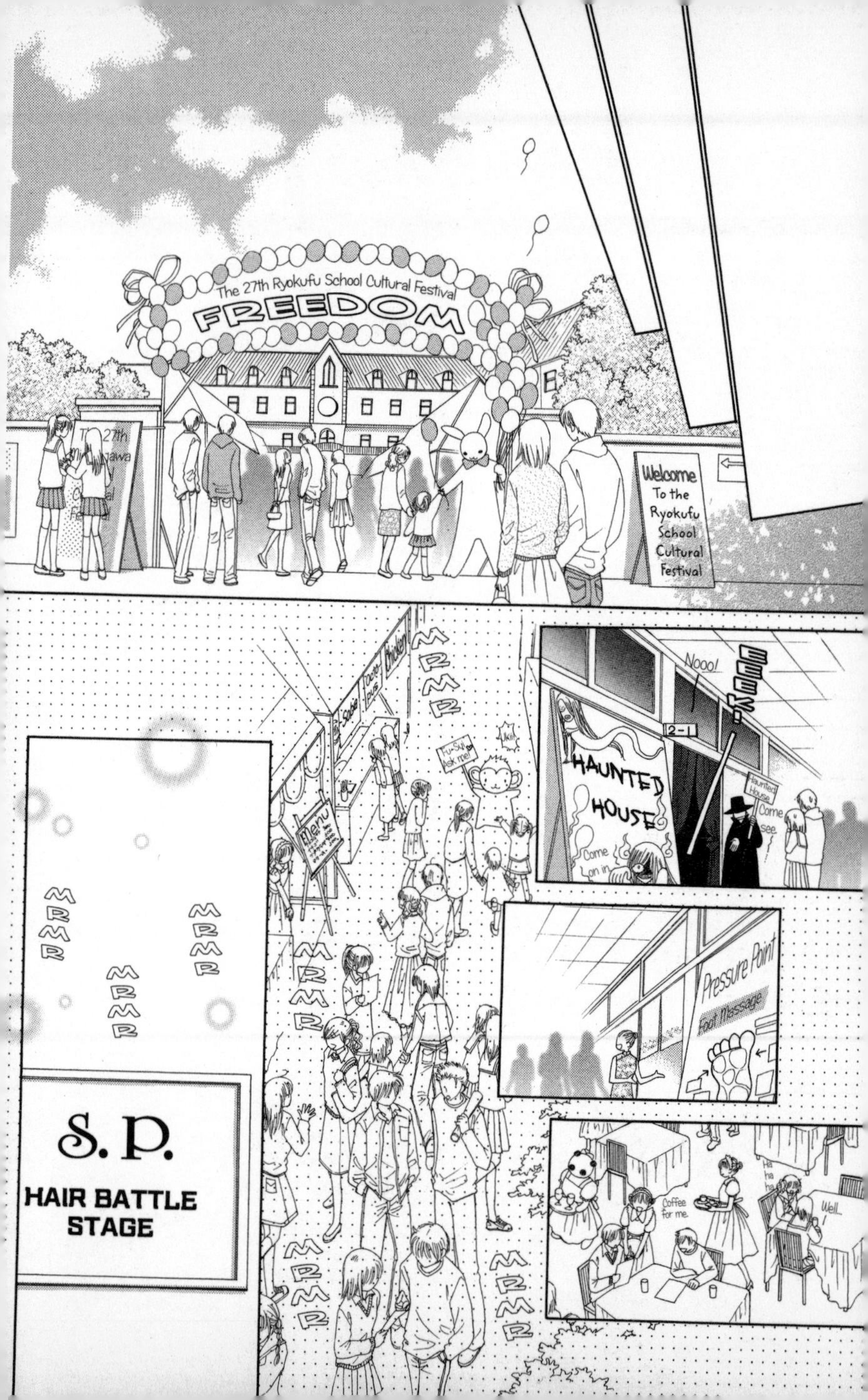
The 27th Ryokufu School Cultural Festival
FREEDOM
Welcome To the Ryokufu School Cultural Festival
EEEK!
Nooo!
2-1
HAUNTED HOUSE
Haunted House
Come see
Come on in
Pressure Point
Foot Massage
Ha ha ha
Well...!
Coffee for me.
Chicken
MRMR
Ukii!
Fu~Su!! Ask me!
Menu
MRMR
MRMR
MRMR
MRMR
MRMR
MRMR
MRMR
S.P.
HAIR BATTLE STAGE

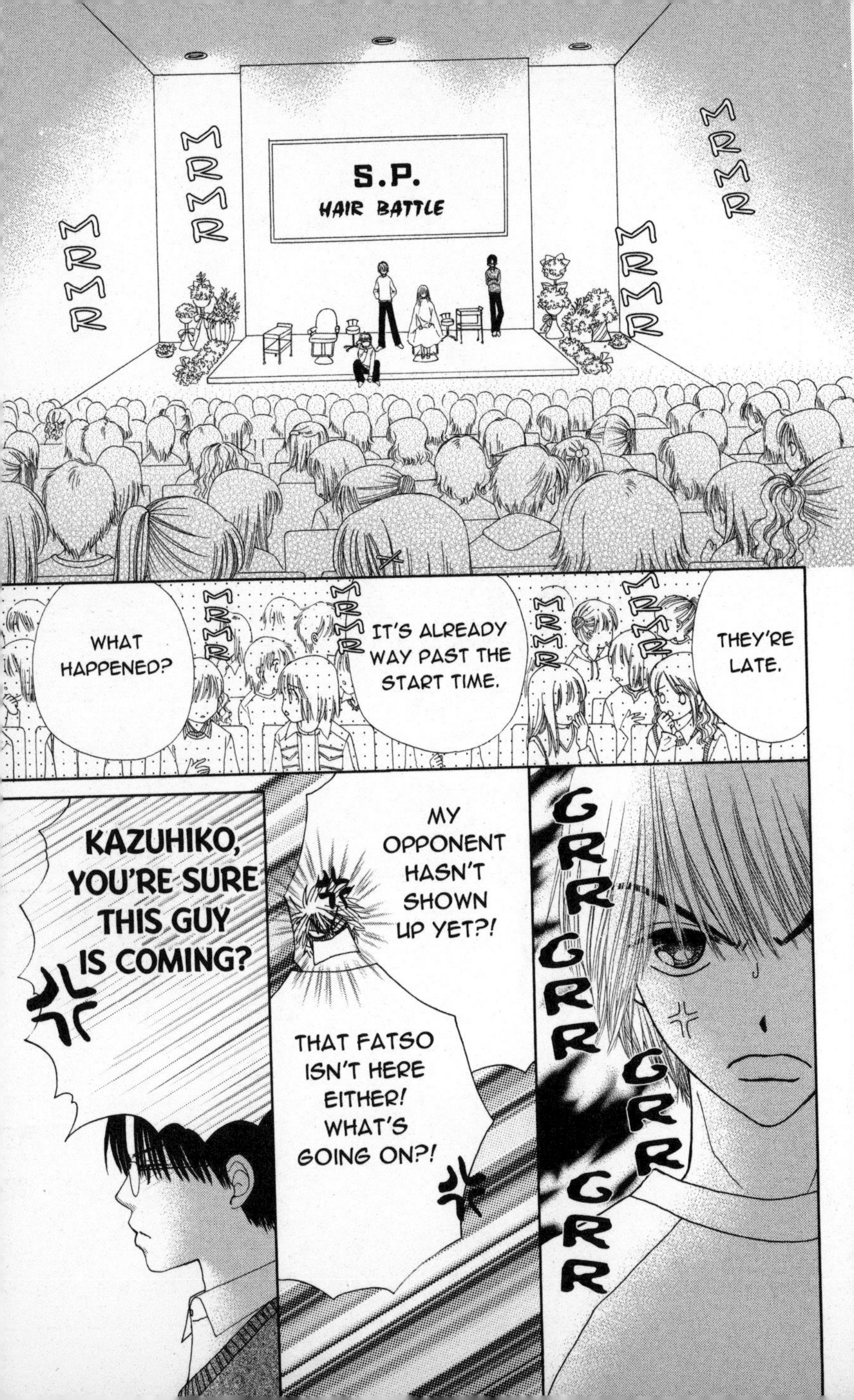
MRMR
MRMR
S.P.
HAIR BATTLE
MRMR
MRMR
THEY'RE LATE.
MRMR
MRMR
IT'S ALREADY WAY PAST THE START TIME.
MRMR
MRMR
WHAT HAPPENED?
GRR GRR
GRR GRR
GRR GRR
MY OPPONENT HASN'T SHOWN UP YET?!
THAT FATSO ISN'T HERE EITHER! WHAT'S GOING ON?!
KAZUHIKO, YOU'RE SURE THIS GUY IS COMING?

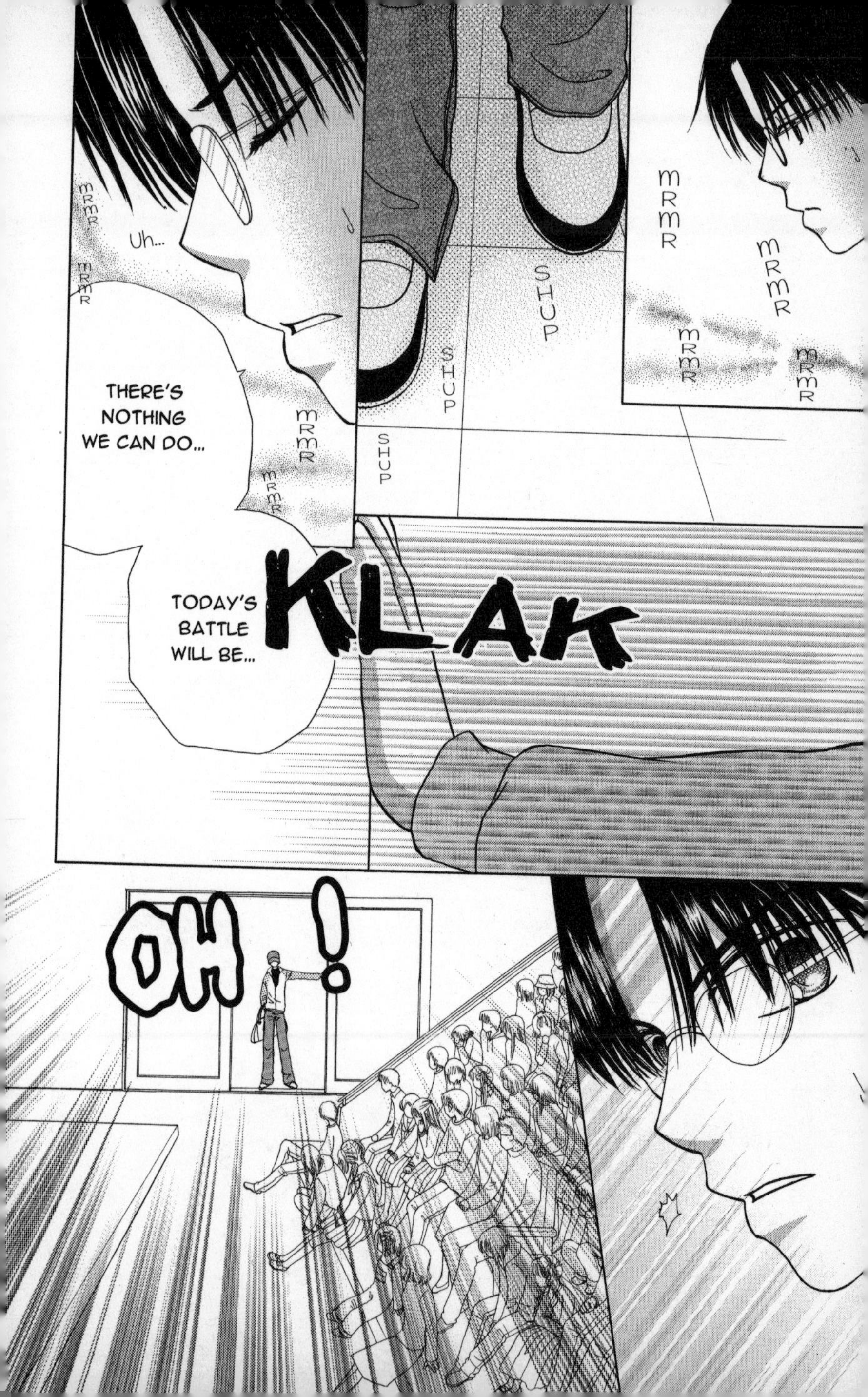
MRMR
MRMR
MRMR
MRMR
SHUP
SHUP
SHUP
MRMR
Uh...
MRMR
THERE'S NOTHING WE CAN DO...
MRMR
MRMR
TODAY'S BATTLE WILL BE...
KLAK
OH!

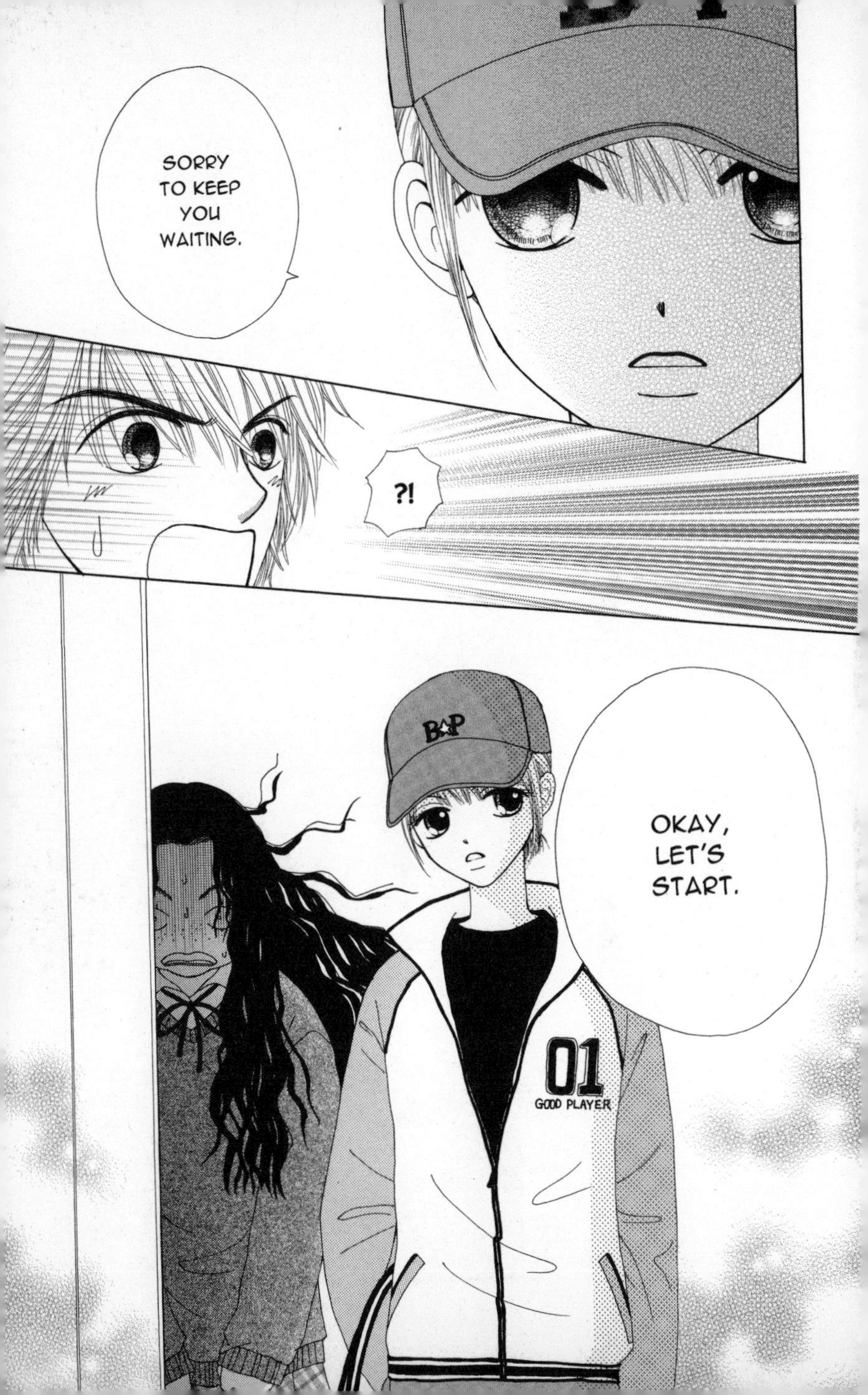
SORRY TO KEEP YOU WAITING.
?!
OKAY, LET'S START.
B☆P
01
GOOD PLAYER

Beauty Pop

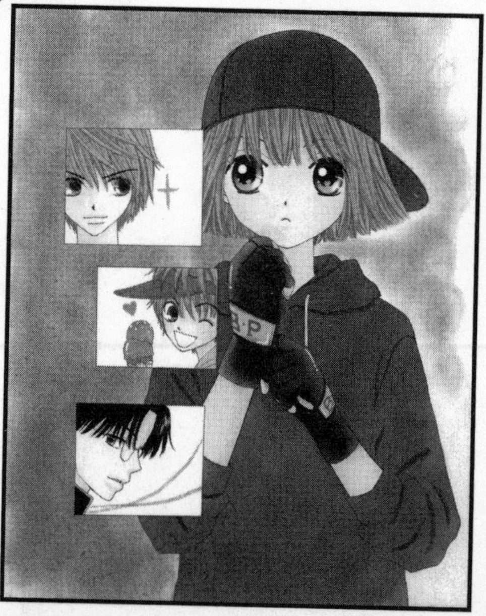

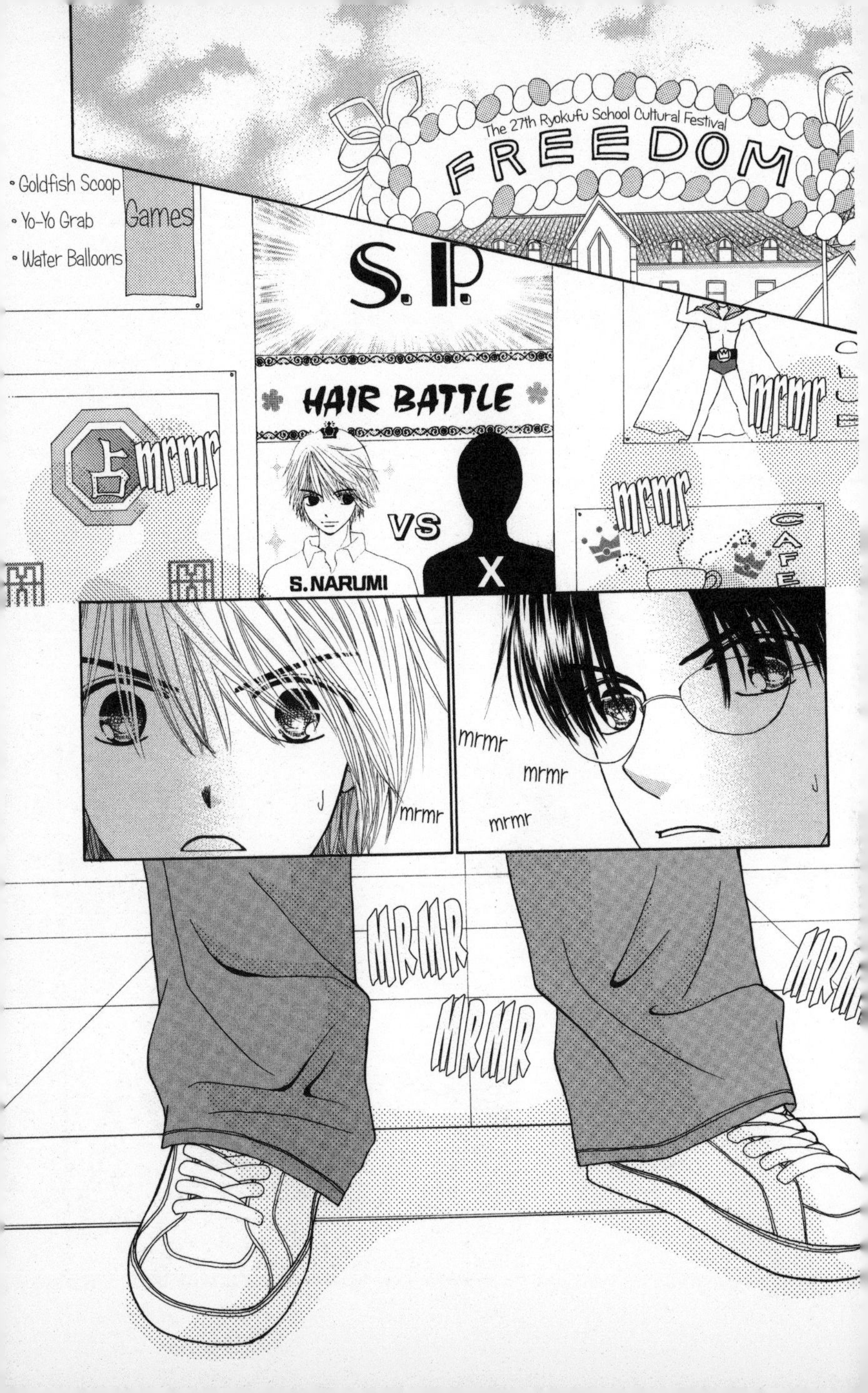
The 27th Ryokufu School Cultural Festival
FREEDOM
Games
• Goldfish Scoop
• Yo-Yo Grab
• Water Balloons
mrmr
mrmr
CAFE
S.P.
HAIR BATTLE
S. NARUMI
VS
X
mrmr
mrmr
mrmr
mrmr
mrmr
MRMR
MRMR
MRMR

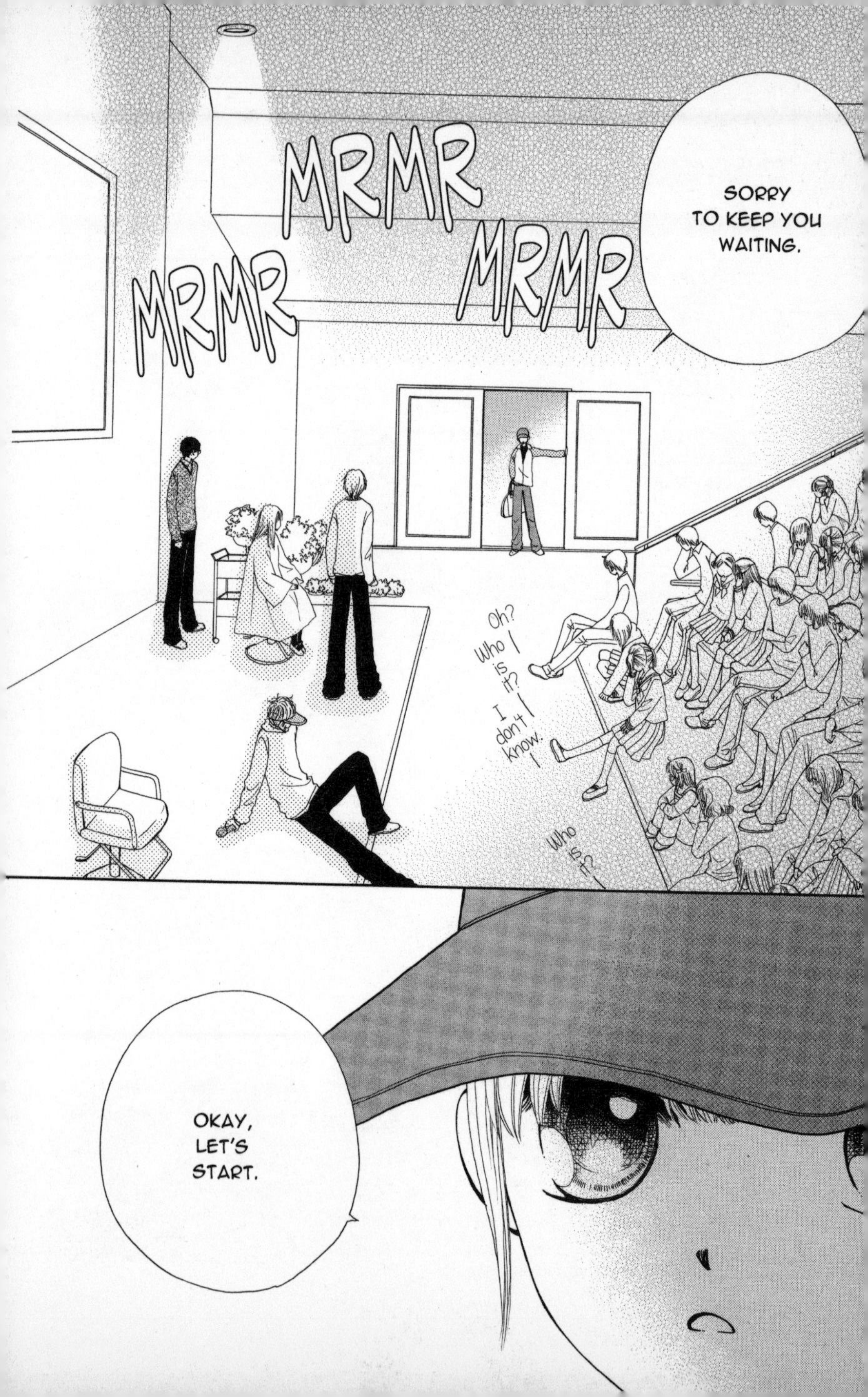
SORRY TO KEEP YOU WAITING.
MRMR
MRMR
MRMR
Oh? Who is it?
I don't know.
Who is it?
OKAY, LET'S START.

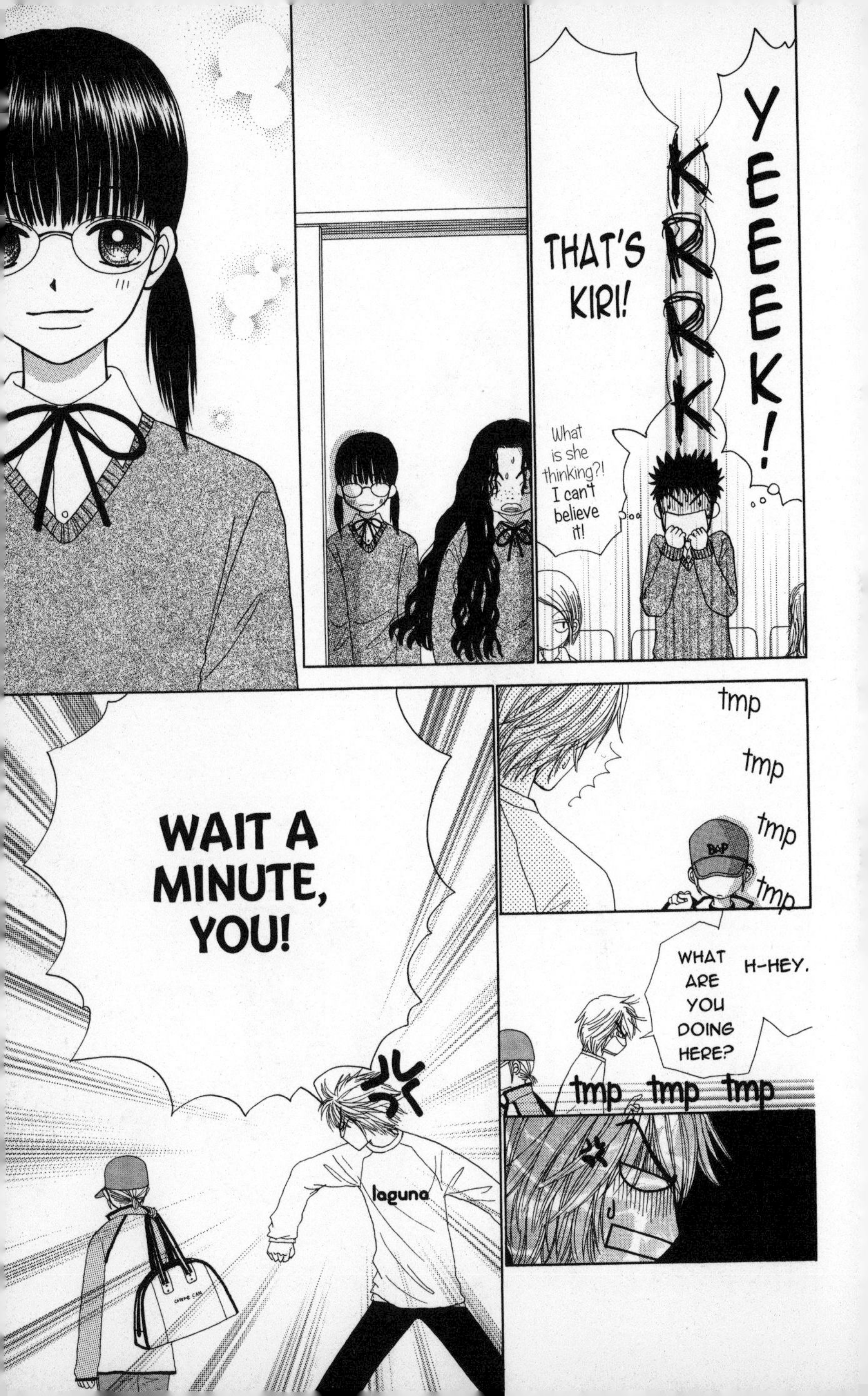
YEEEK!
KRRRK
THAT'S KIRI!
What is she thinking?! I can't believe it!
tmp
tmp
tmp
tmp
H-HEY.
WHAT ARE YOU DOING HERE?
tmp tmp tmp
WAIT A MINUTE, YOU!
laguna

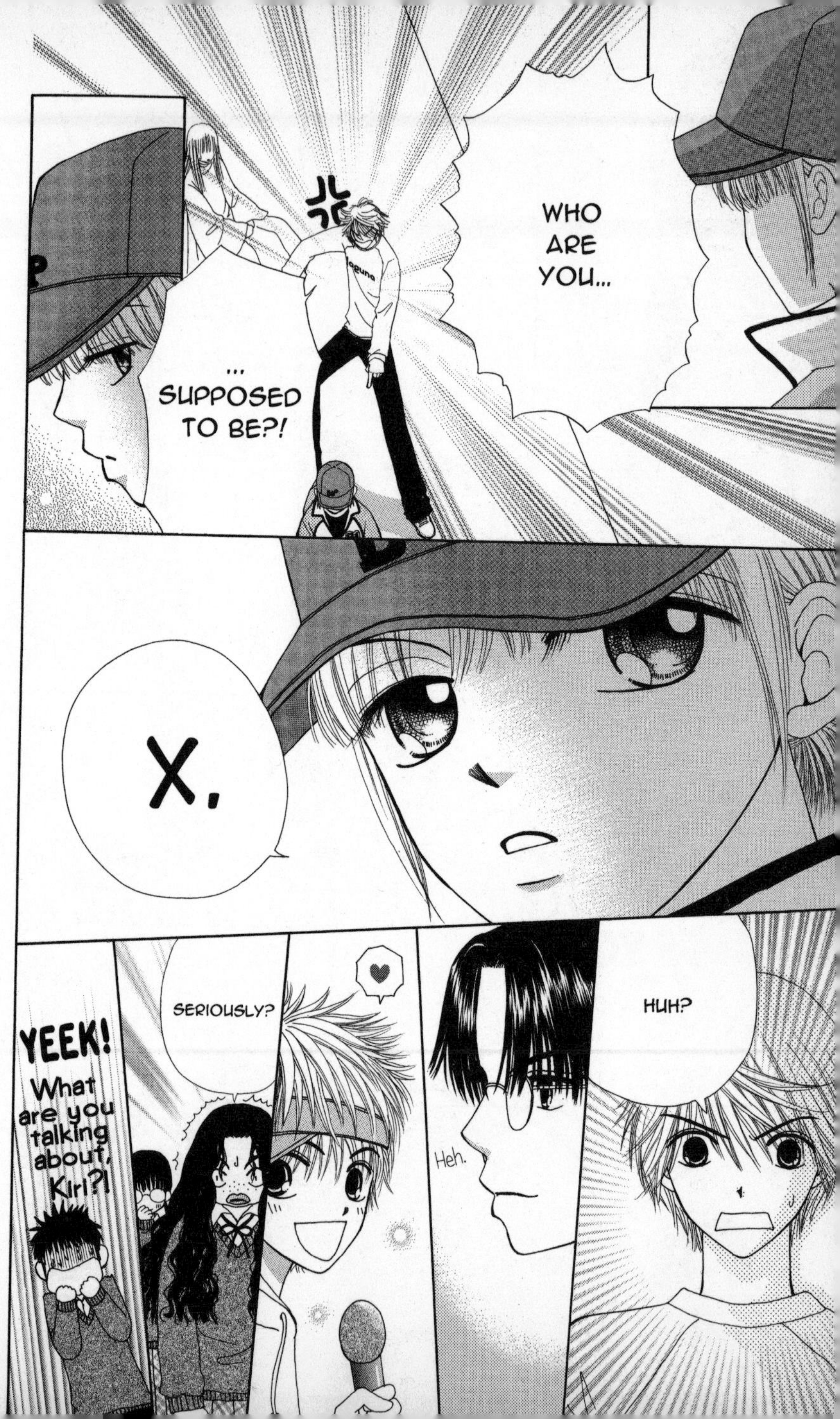
WHO ARE YOU...
... SUPPOSED TO BE?!
X.
HUH?
Heh.
SERIOUSLY?
YEEK! What are you talking about, Kiri?!

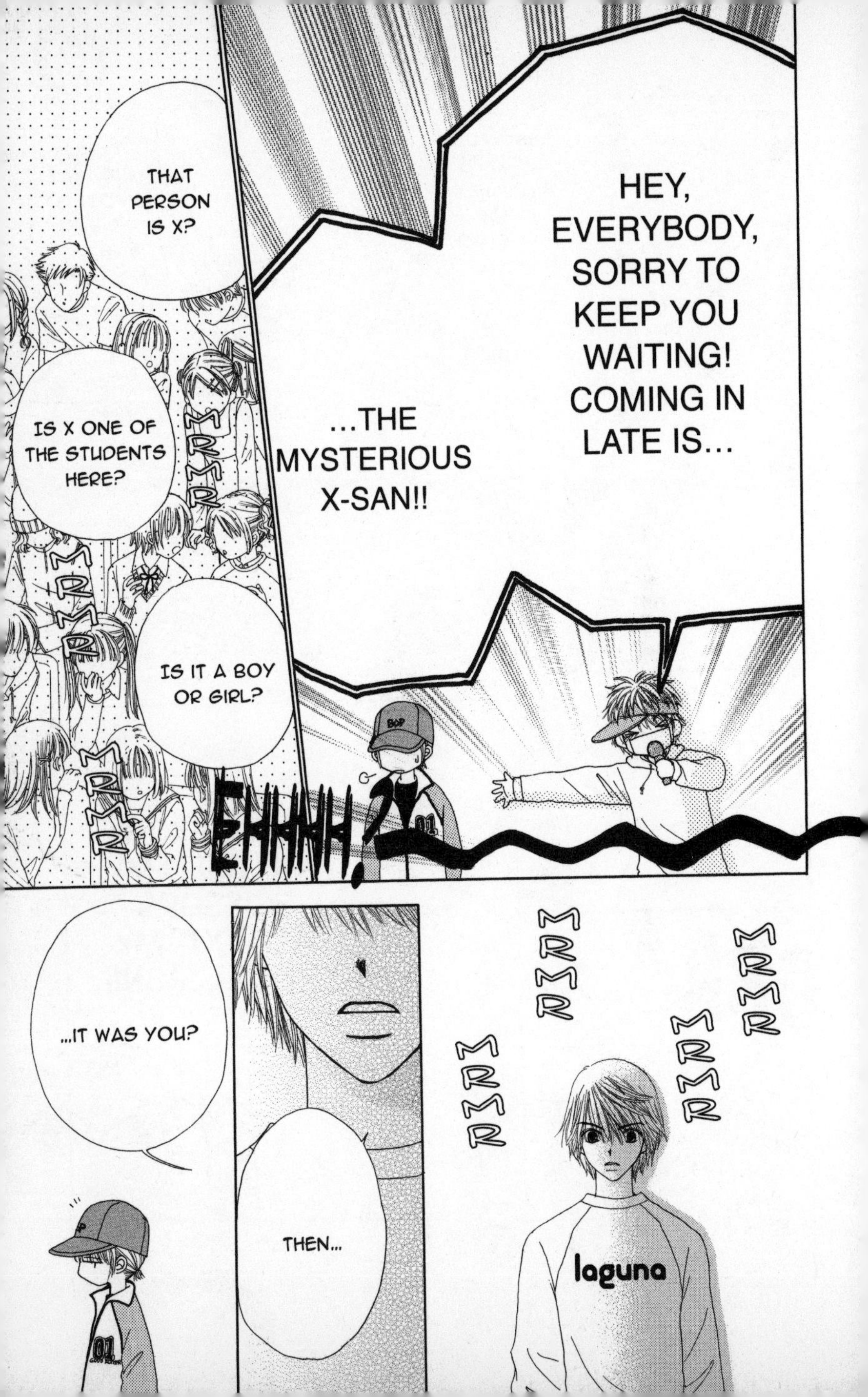
HEY, EVERYBODY, SORRY TO KEEP YOU WAITING! COMING IN LATE IS...
...THE MYSTERIOUS X-SAN!!
THAT PERSON IS X?
MRMR
IS X ONE OF THE STUDENTS HERE?
MRMR
IS IT A BOY OR GIRL?
MRMR
EHHHH!?
MRMR
MRMR
MRMR
MRMR
laguna
THEN...
...IT WAS YOU?

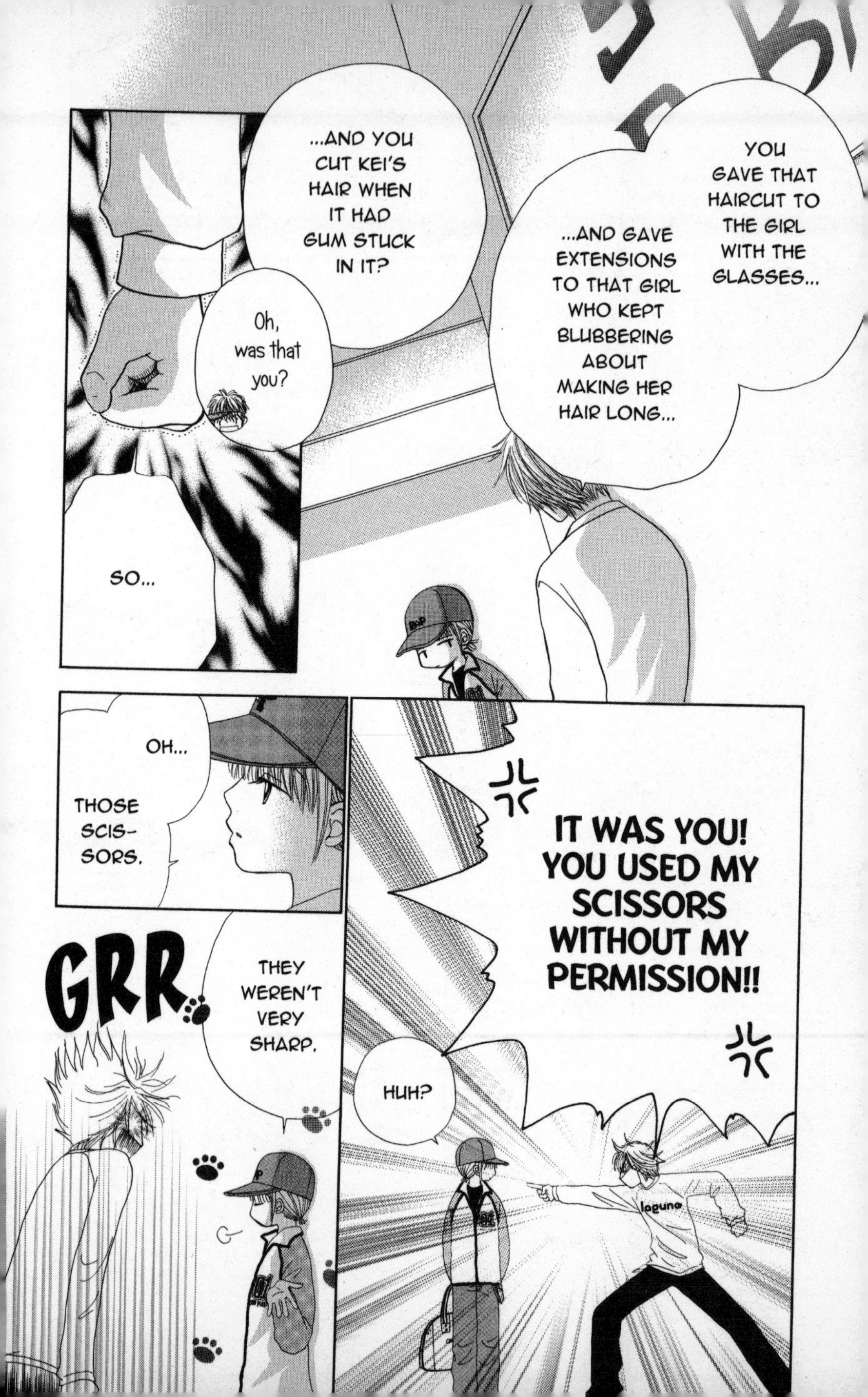
YOU GAVE THAT HAIRCUT TO THE GIRL WITH THE GLASSES...
...AND GAVE EXTENSIONS TO THAT GIRL WHO KEPT BLUBBERING ABOUT MAKING HER HAIR LONG...
...AND YOU CUT KEI'S HAIR WHEN IT HAD GUM STUCK IN IT?
Oh, was that you?
SO...
IT WAS YOU! YOU USED MY SCISSORS WITHOUT MY PERMISSION!!
HUH?
OH...
THOSE SCIS-SORS.
THEY WEREN'T VERY SHARP.
GRR

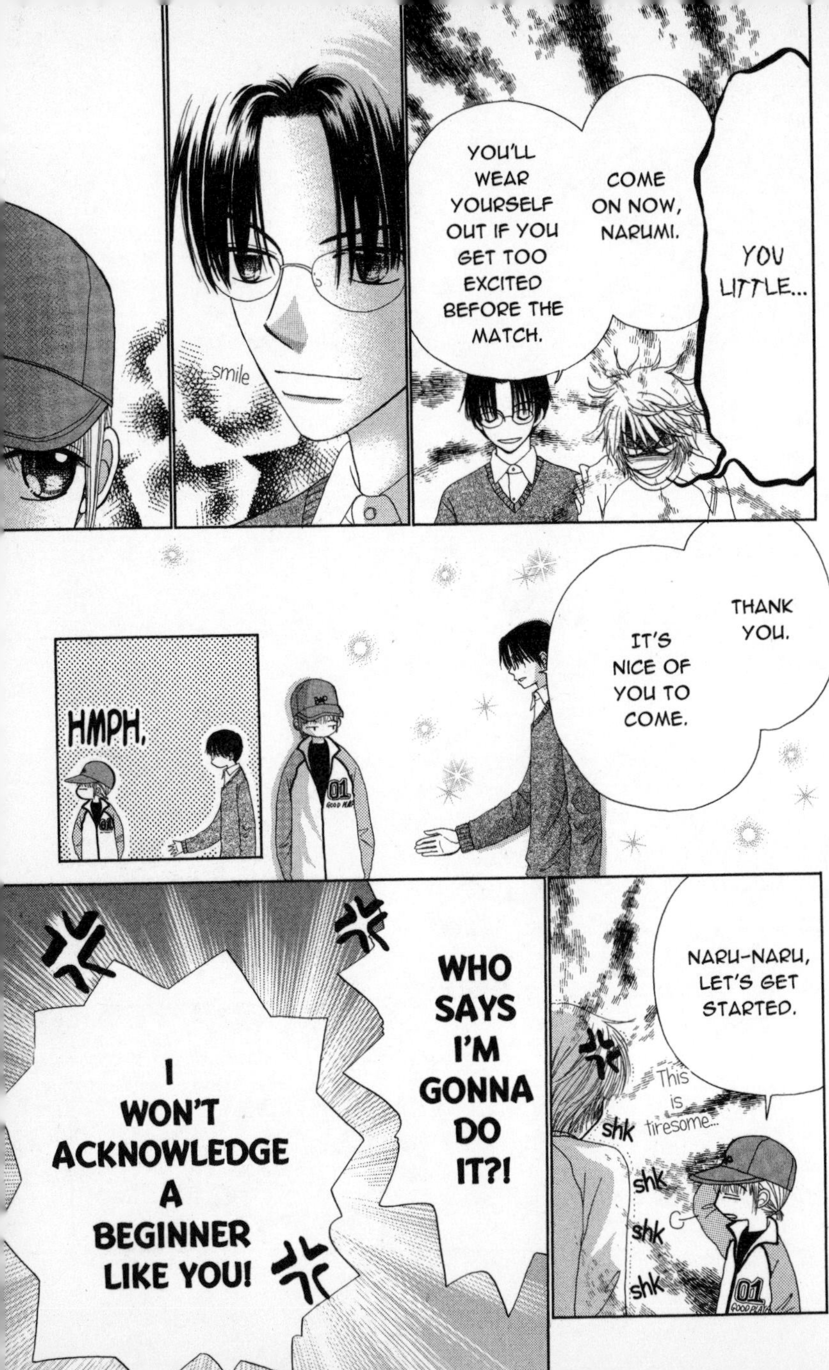
YOU LITTLE...
COME ON NOW, NARUMI.
YOU'LL WEAR YOURSELF OUT IF YOU GET TOO EXCITED BEFORE THE MATCH.
smile
THANK YOU.
IT'S NICE OF YOU TO COME.
HMPH.
NARU-NARU, LET'S GET STARTED.
This is tiresome...
shk
shk
shk
shk
WHO SAYS I'M GONNA DO IT?!
I WON'T ACKNOWLEDGE A BEGINNER LIKE YOU!

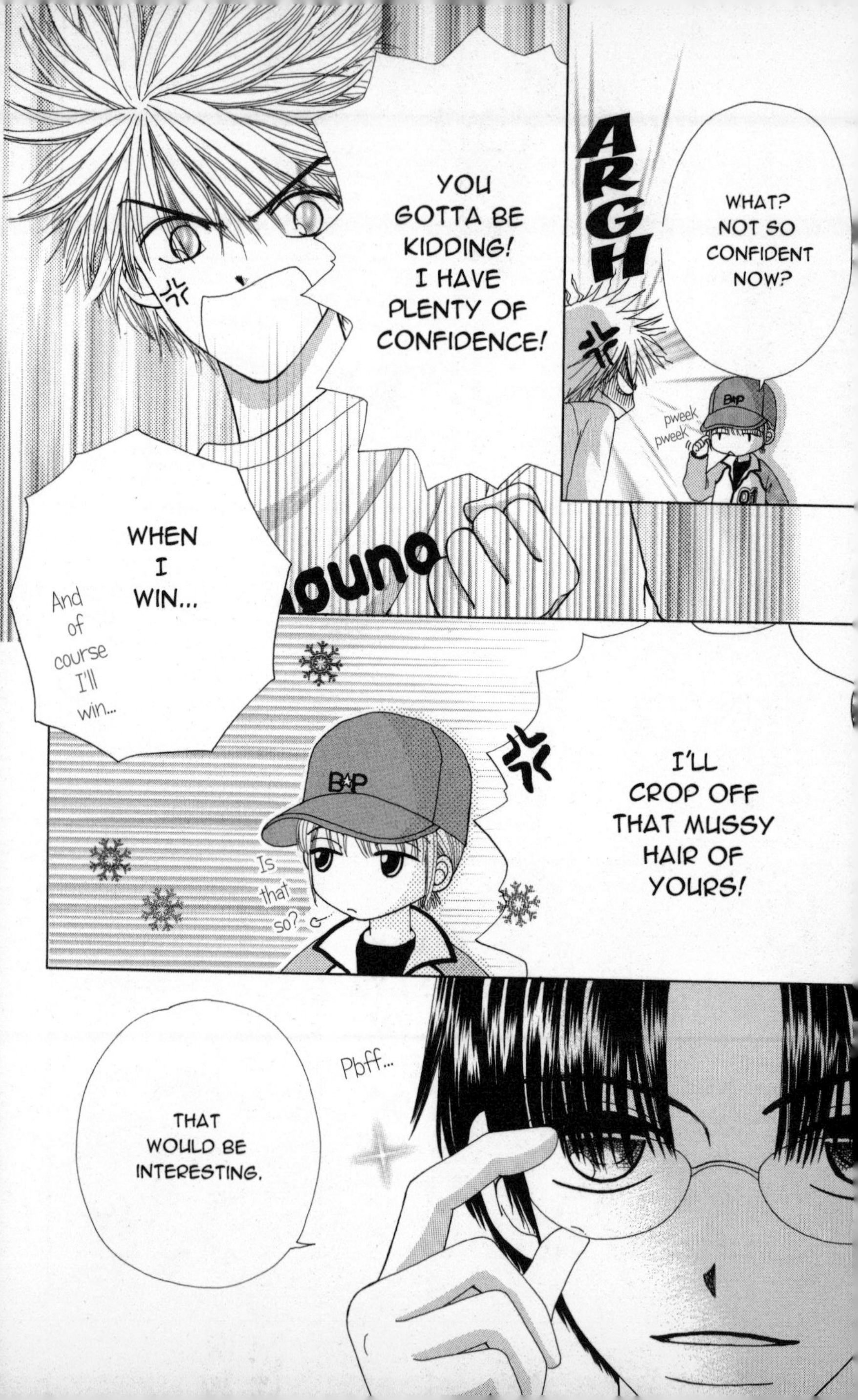
WHAT? NOT SO CONFIDENT NOW?
ARGH
pweek pweek
YOU GOTTA BE KIDDING! I HAVE PLENTY OF CONFIDENCE!
WHEN I WIN...
And of course I'll win...
I'LL CROP OFF THAT MUSSY HAIR OF YOURS!
Is that so?
Pbff...
THAT WOULD BE INTERESTING.

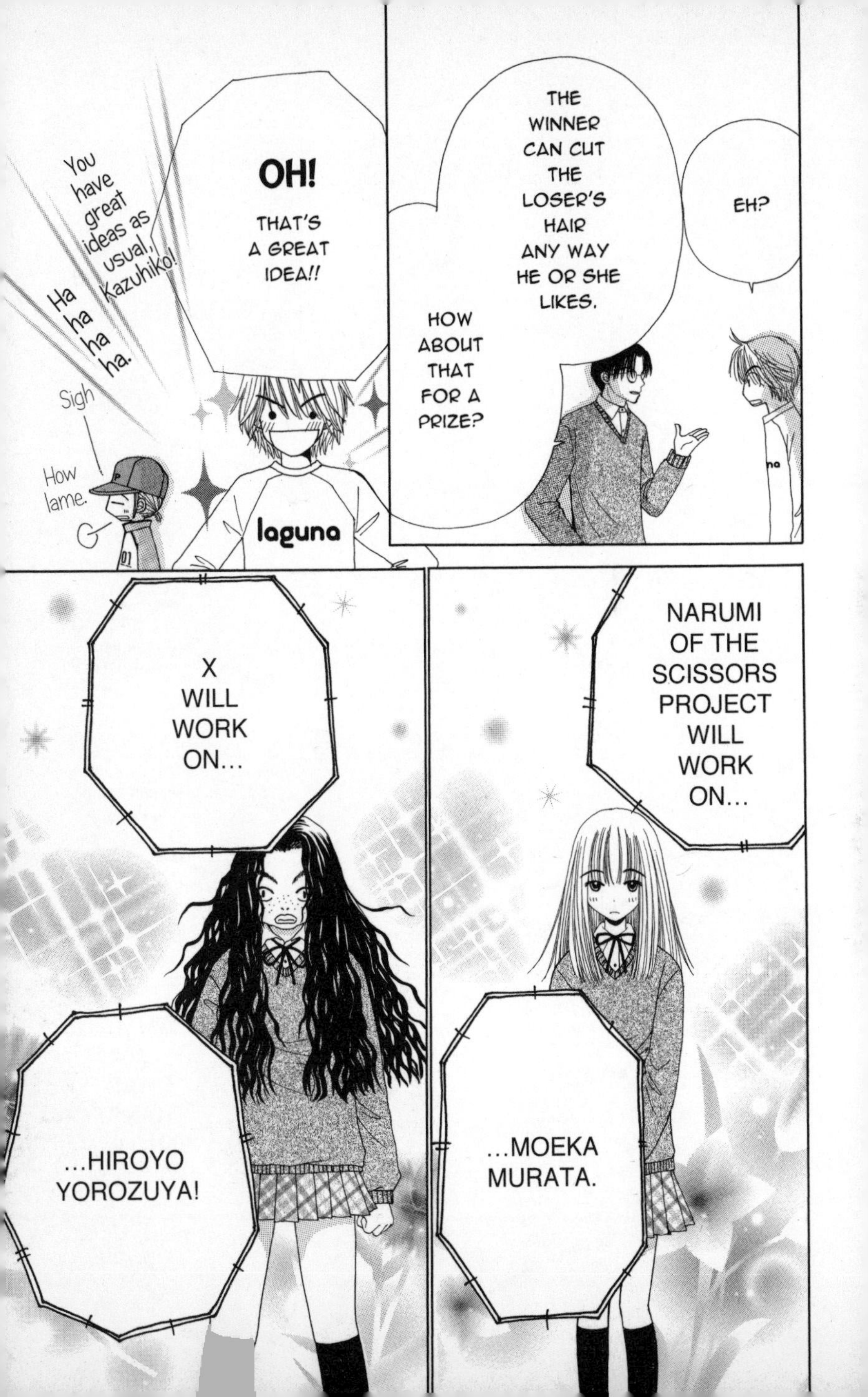
EH?
THE WINNER CAN CUT THE LOSER'S HAIR ANY WAY HE OR SHE LIKES.
HOW ABOUT THAT FOR A PRIZE?
OH!
THAT'S A GREAT IDEA!!
You have great ideas as usual, Kazuhiko!
Ha ha ha ha.
Sigh
How lame.
laguna
NARUMI OF THE SCISSORS PROJECT WILL WORK ON...
...MOEKA MURATA.
X WILL WORK ON...
...HIROYO YOROZUYA!

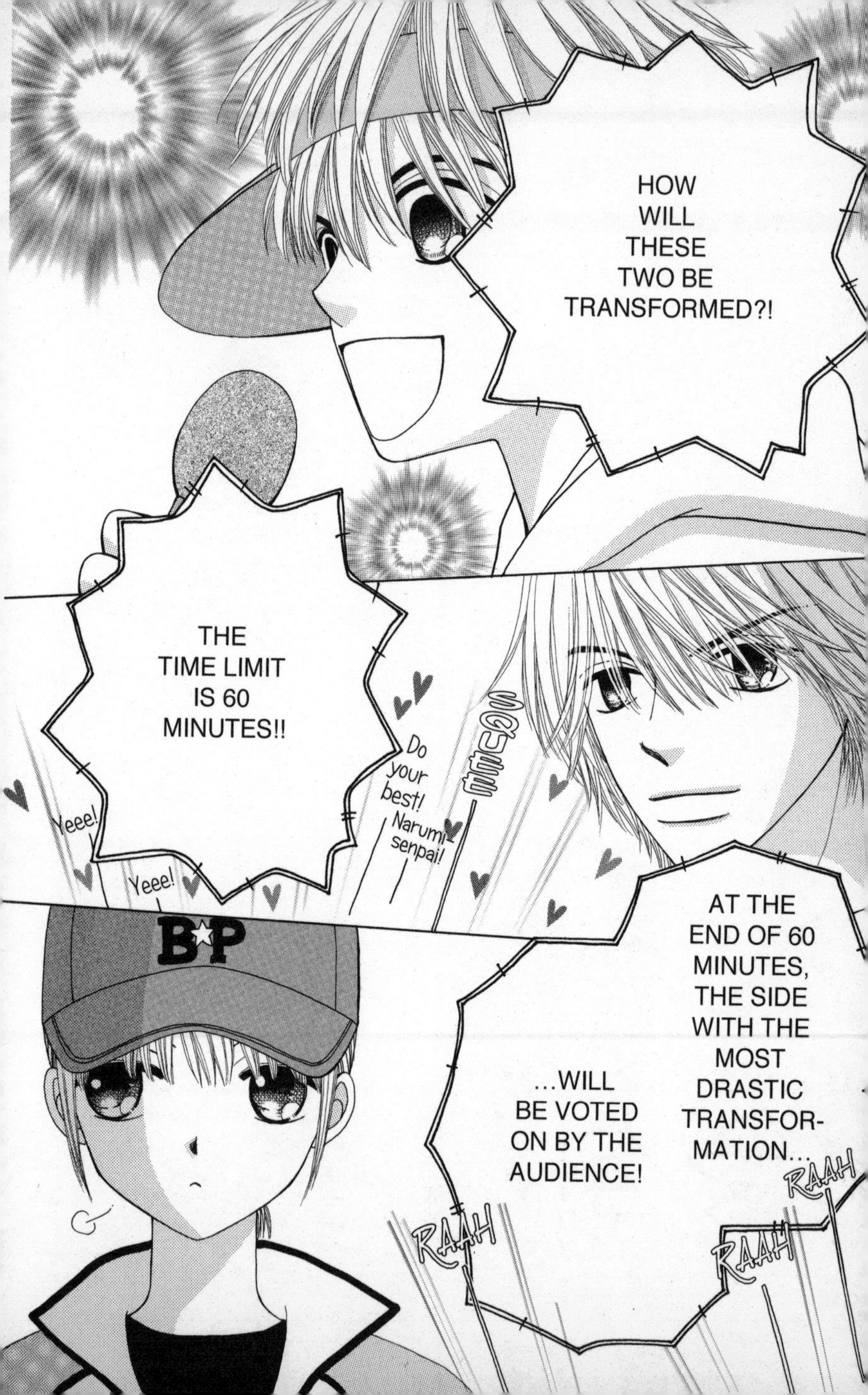
HOW WILL THESE TWO BE TRANSFORMED?!
THE TIME LIMIT IS 60 MINUTES!!
SQUEE
Do your best! Narumi-senpai!
Yeee!
Yeee!
AT THE END OF 60 MINUTES, THE SIDE WITH THE MOST DRASTIC TRANSFORMATION...
...WILL BE VOTED ON BY THE AUDIENCE!
RAAH
RAAH
RAAH

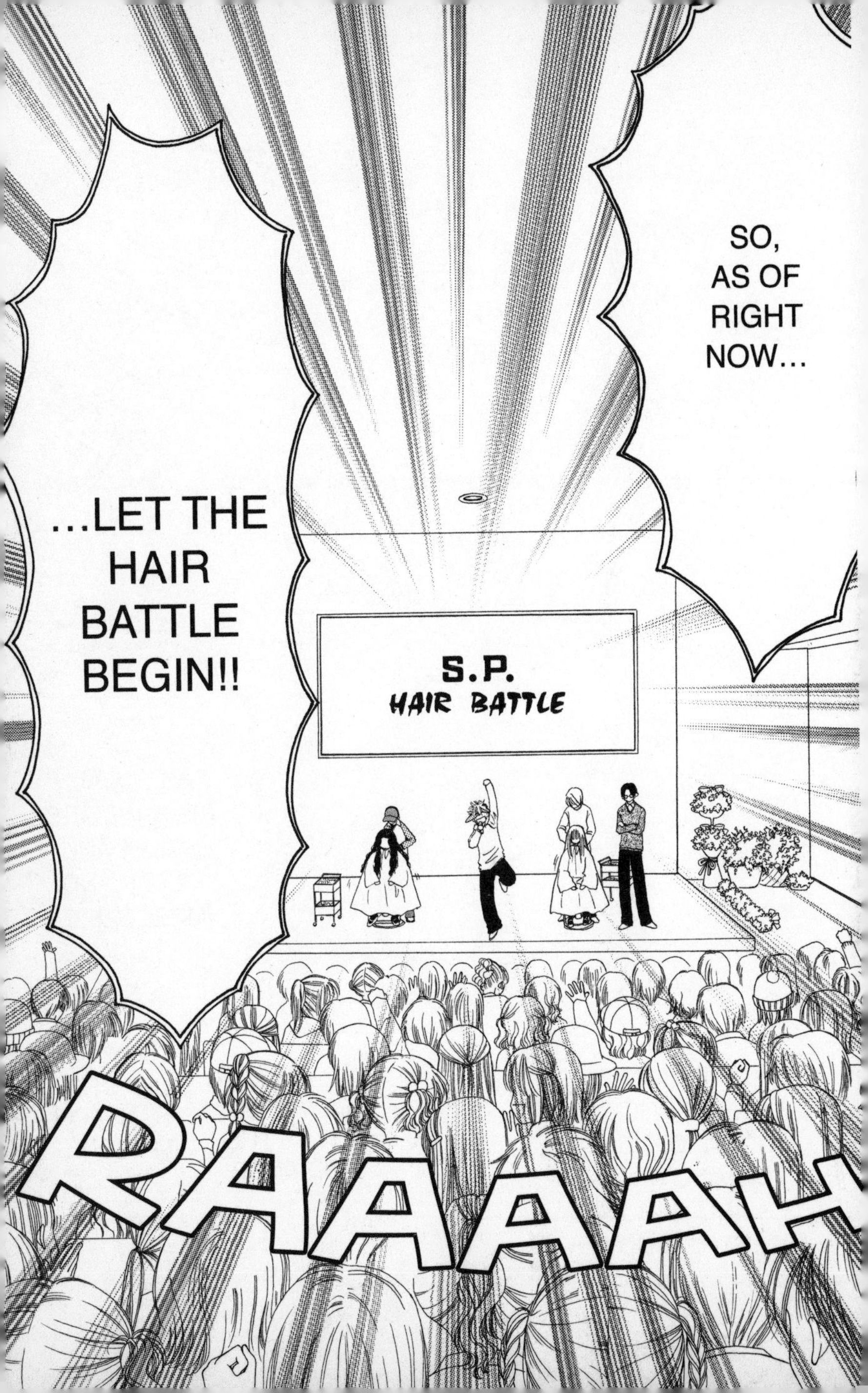
SO, AS OF RIGHT NOW...
...LET THE HAIR BATTLE BEGIN!!
S.P.
HAIR BATTLE
RAAAAH

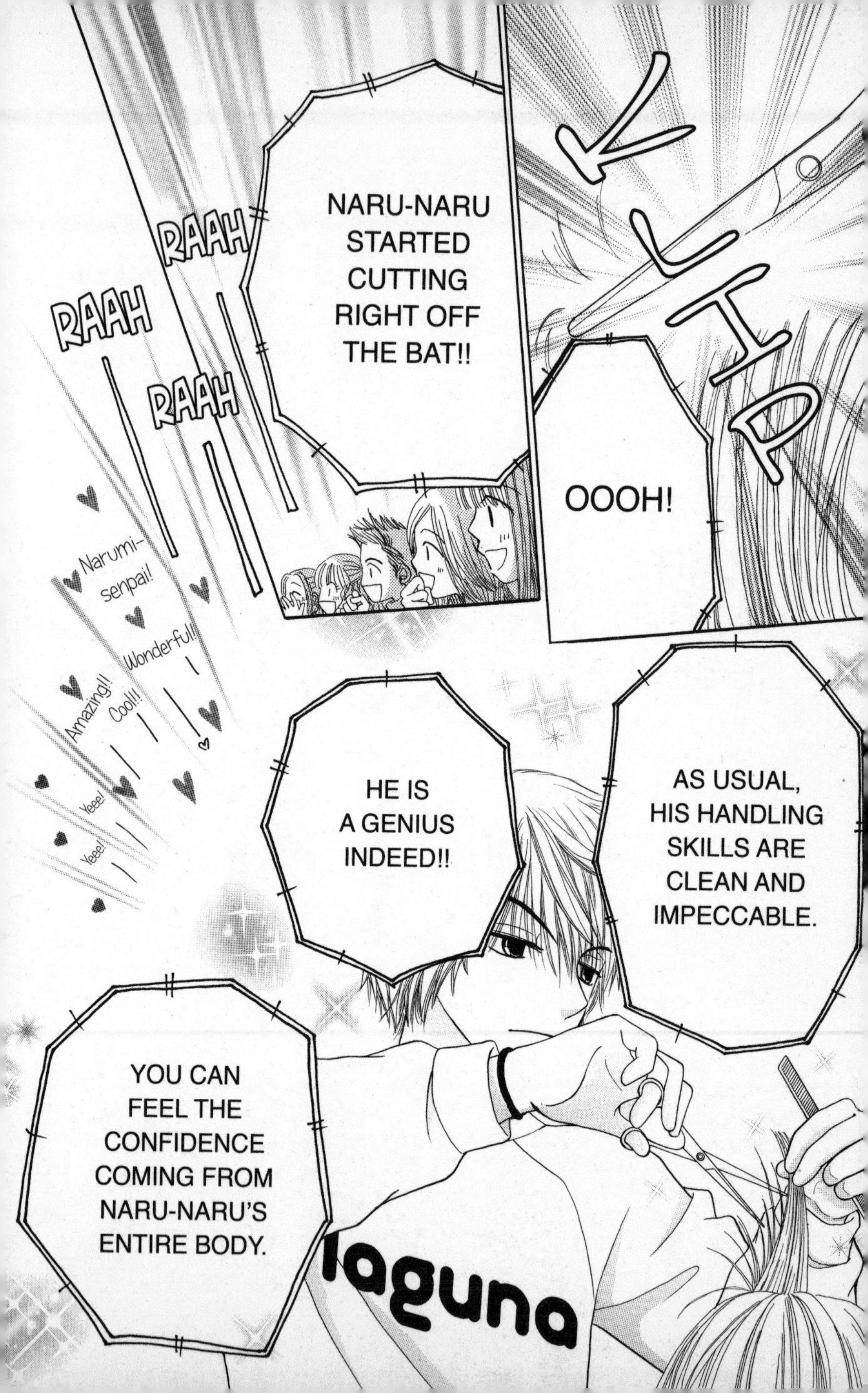
KLIP
OOOH!
NARU-NARU STARTED CUTTING RIGHT OFF THE BAT!!
RAAH
RAAH
RAAH
AS USUAL, HIS HANDLING SKILLS ARE CLEAN AND IMPECCABLE.
HE IS A GENIUS INDEED!!
Wonderful!!
Narumi-senpai!
Cool!!
Amazing!!
Yeee!
Yeee!
YOU CAN FEEL THE CONFIDENCE COMING FROM NARU-NARU'S ENTIRE BODY.
laguna

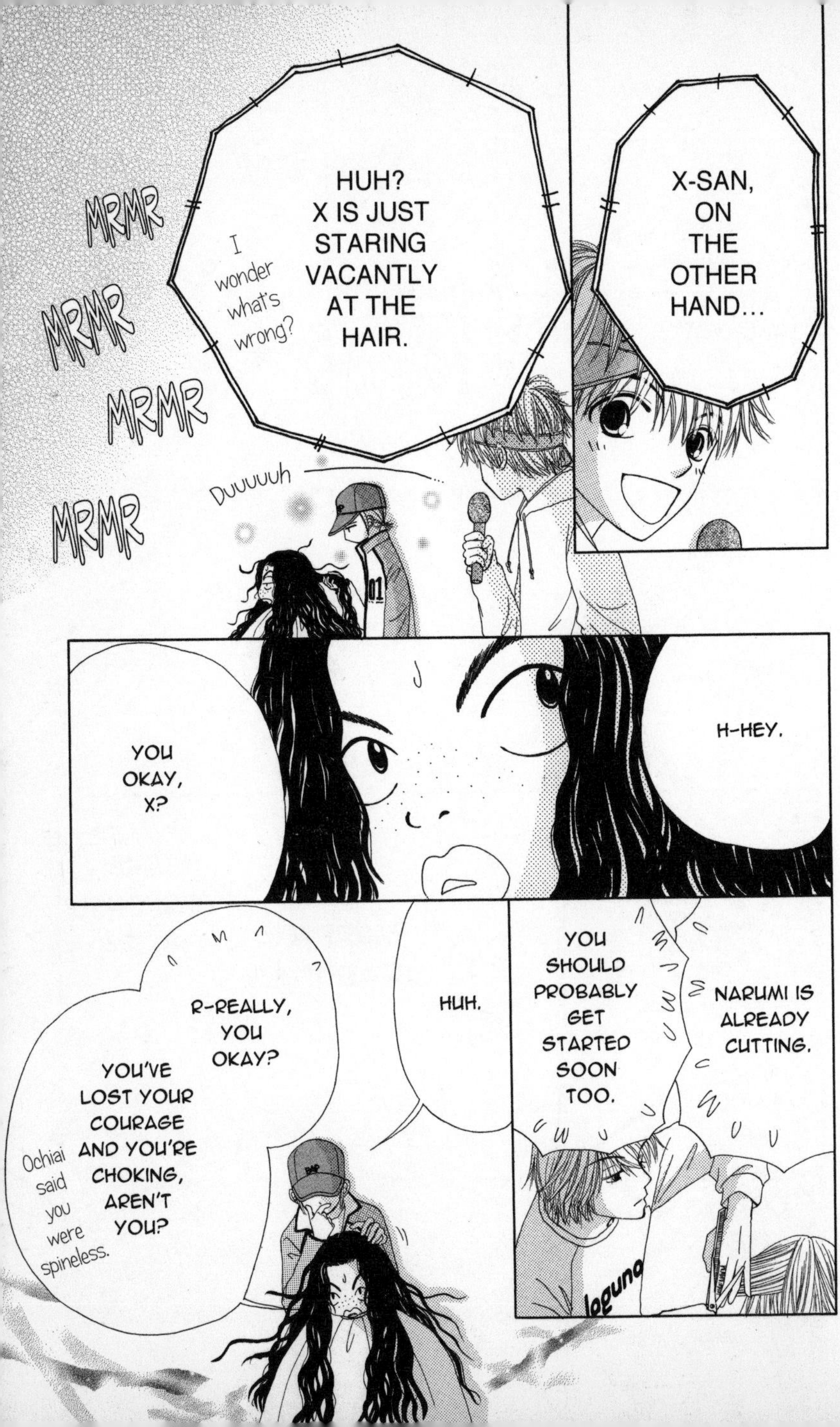
X-SAN, ON THE OTHER HAND...
HUH? X IS JUST STARING VACANTLY AT THE HAIR.
I wonder what's wrong?
MRMR
MRMR
MRMR
MRMR
Duuuuuh
H-HEY.
YOU OKAY, X?
NARUMI IS ALREADY CUTTING.
YOU SHOULD PROBABLY GET STARTED SOON TOO.
HUH.
R-REALLY, YOU OKAY?
YOU'VE LOST YOUR COURAGE AND YOU'RE CHOKING, AREN'T YOU?
Ochiai said you were spineless.

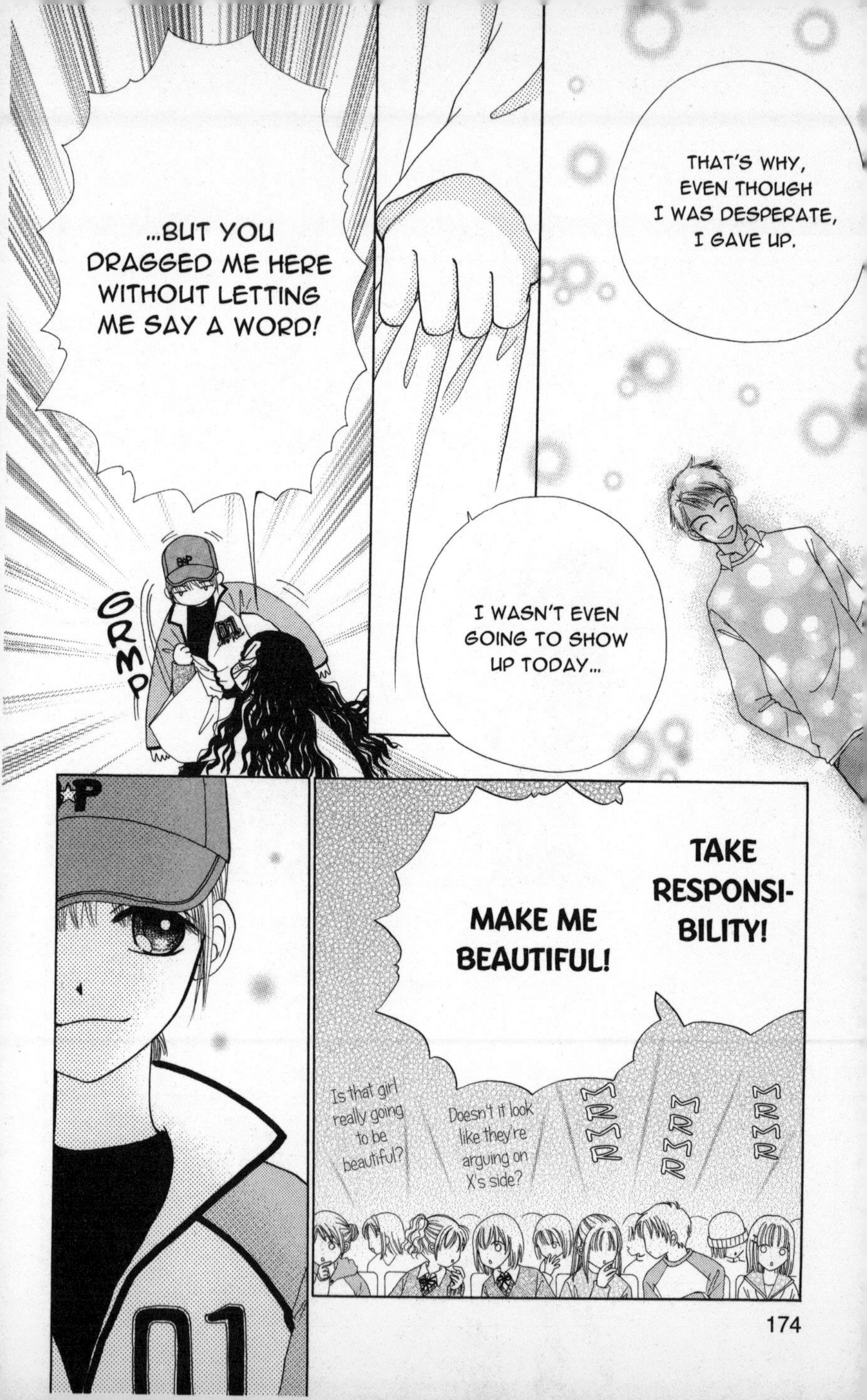
THAT'S WHY, EVEN THOUGH I WAS DESPERATE, I GAVE UP.
I WASN'T EVEN GOING TO SHOW UP TODAY...
...BUT YOU DRAGGED ME HERE WITHOUT LETTING ME SAY A WORD!
GRMP
TAKE RESPONSI-BILITY!
MAKE ME BEAUTIFUL!
MRMR
MRMR
MRMR
Doesn't it look like they're arguing on X's side?
Is that girl really going to be beautiful?

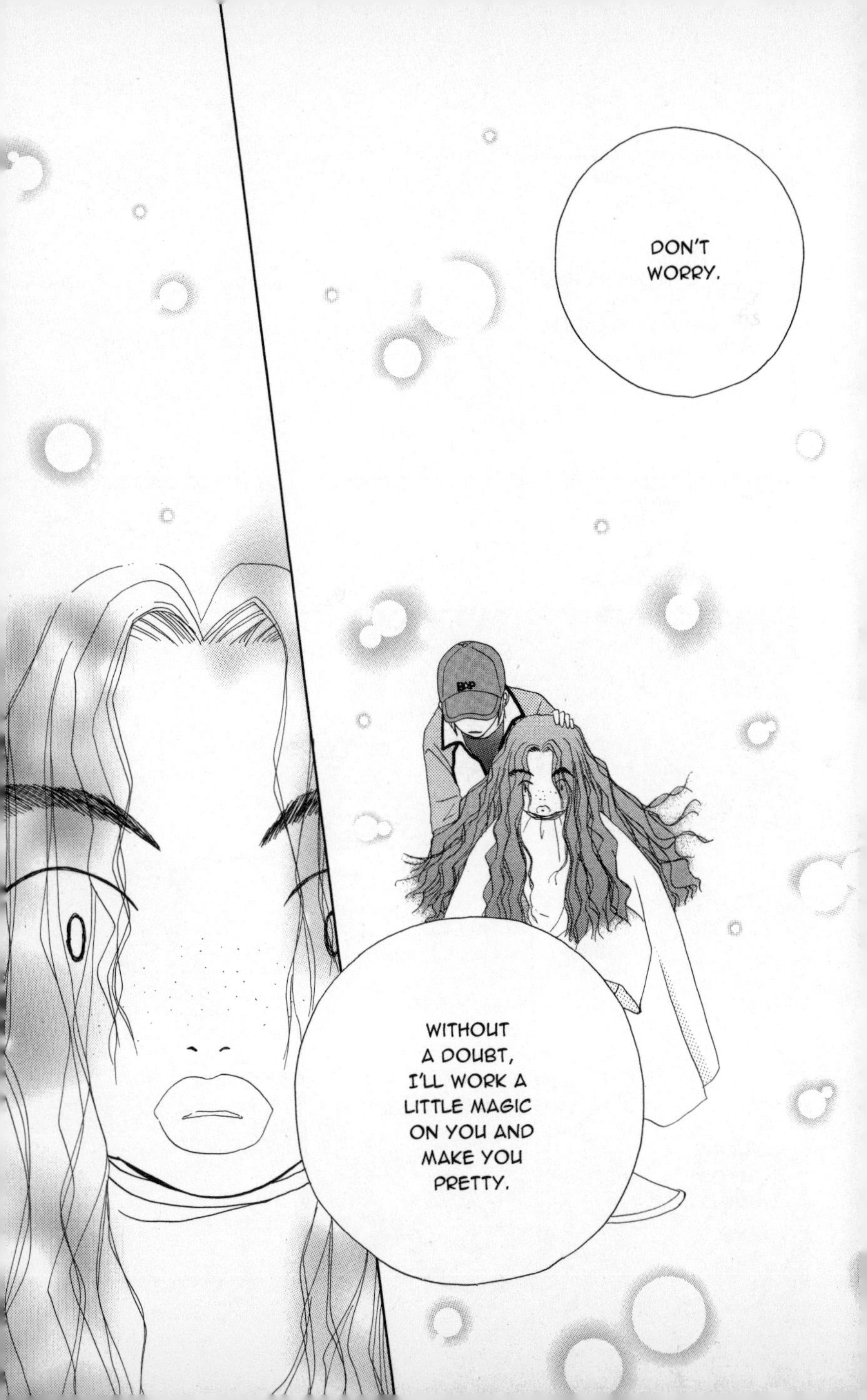
DON'T WORRY.
WITHOUT A DOUBT, I'LL WORK A LITTLE MAGIC ON YOU AND MAKE YOU PRETTY.

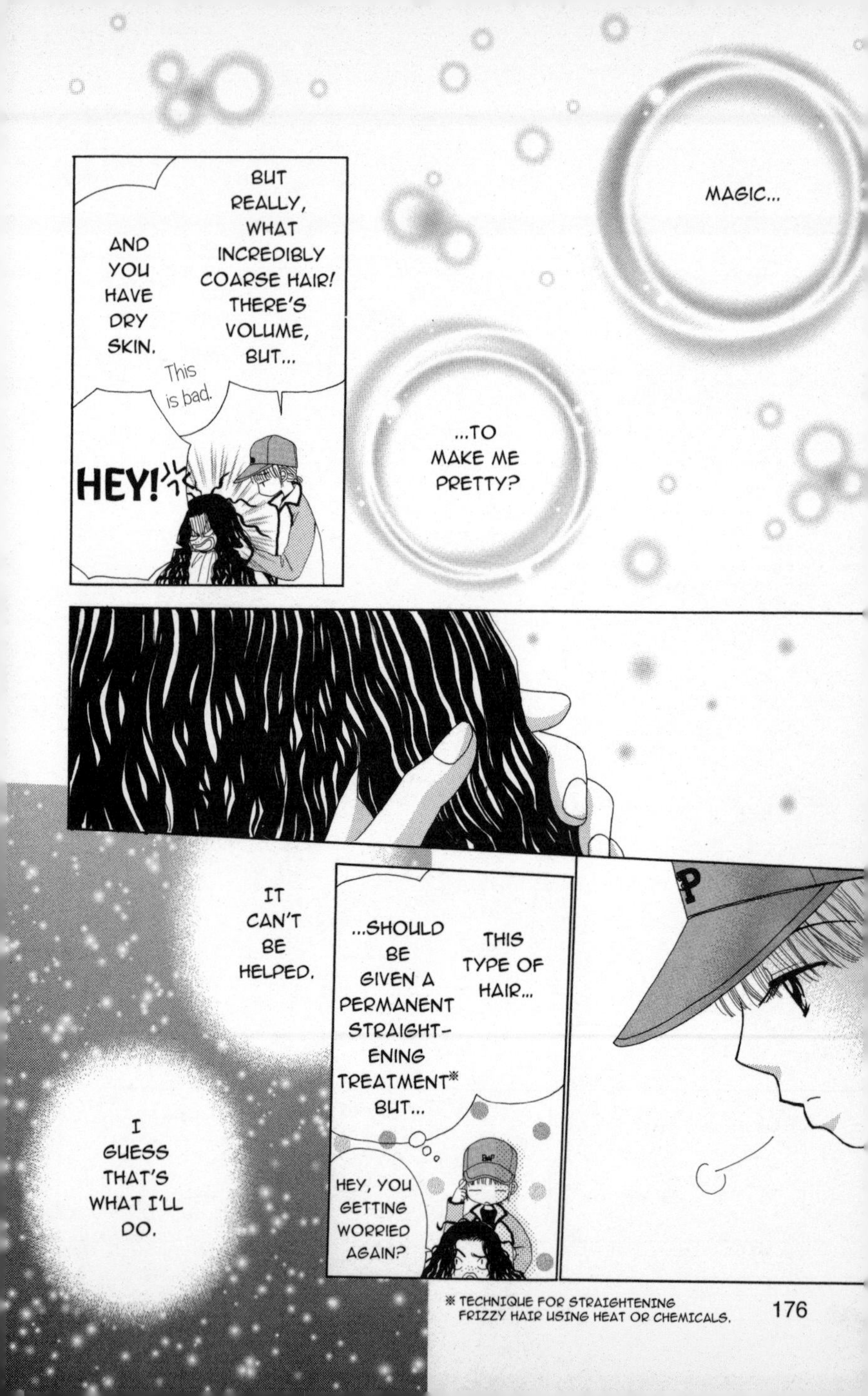
MAGIC...
...TO MAKE ME PRETTY?
BUT REALLY, WHAT INCREDIBLY COARSE HAIR! THERE'S VOLUME, BUT...
AND YOU HAVE DRY SKIN.
This is bad.
HEY!
THIS TYPE OF HAIR...
...SHOULD BE GIVEN A PERMANENT STRAIGHTENING TREATMENT※ BUT...
HEY, YOU GETTING WORRIED AGAIN?
IT CAN'T BE HELPED.
I GUESS THAT'S WHAT I'LL DO.

※ TECHNIQUE FOR STRAIGHTENING FRIZZY HAIR USING HEAT OR CHEMICALS.

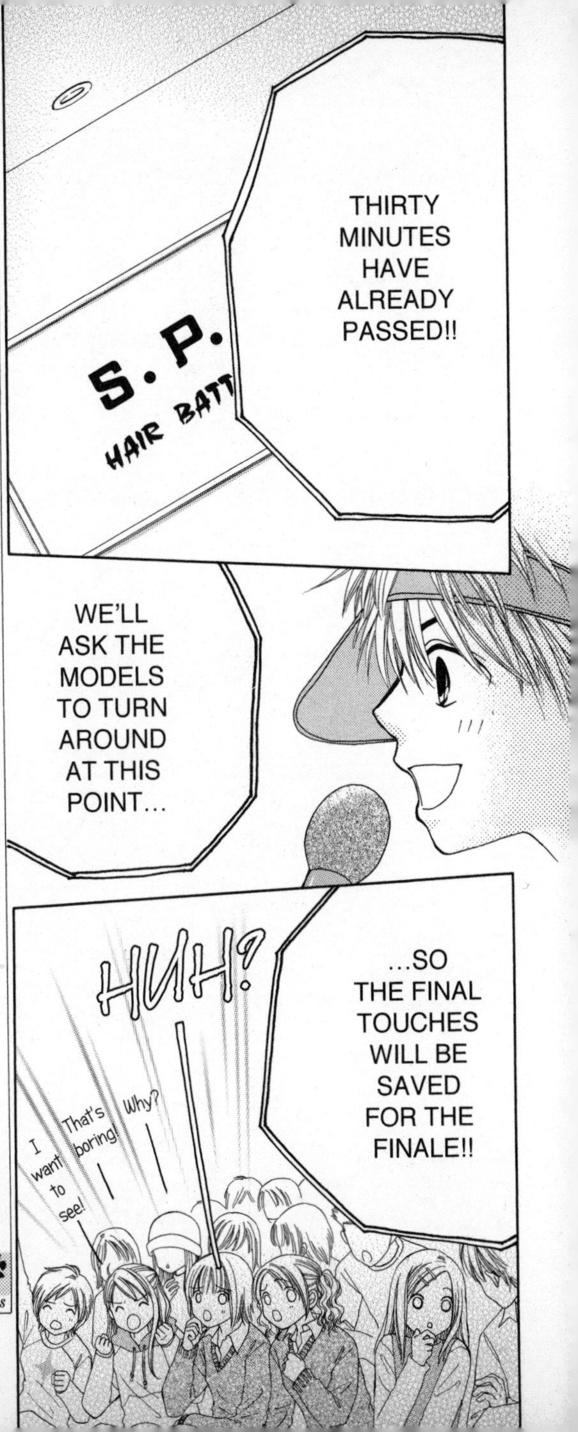
S.P.
HAIR BATT
THIRTY MINUTES HAVE ALREADY PASSED!!
WE'LL ASK THE MODELS TO TURN AROUND AT THIS POINT...
...SO THE FINAL TOUCHES WILL BE SAVED FOR THE FINALE!!
HUH?
Why?
That's boring!
I want to see!

K's Club Talk

Finally, we've come to the last "K's Club Talk" for this volume. In this episode, Kiri is seen cutting hair with her left hand.
As a matter of fact, I saw Mako Morie-sensei, who I had asked to come help me....

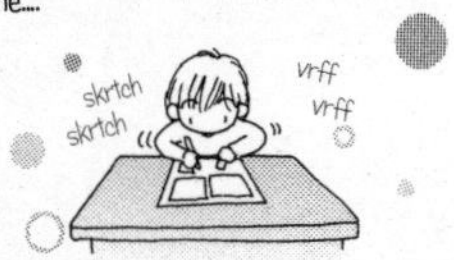
skrtch
skrtch
vrff
vrff

...writing with her right hand and erasing with her left. I thought, "I can use this!!". Morie-sensei is ambidextrous. Amazing!
How convenient!
So, that's why I made Kiri ambidextrous.

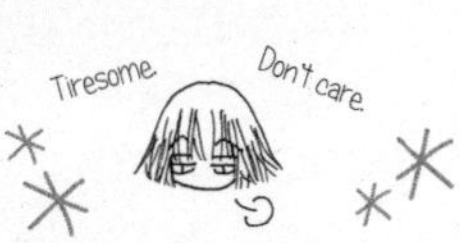
Tiresome
Don't care

♥ Well then, see you again in BP 2!

Kiyoko Arai

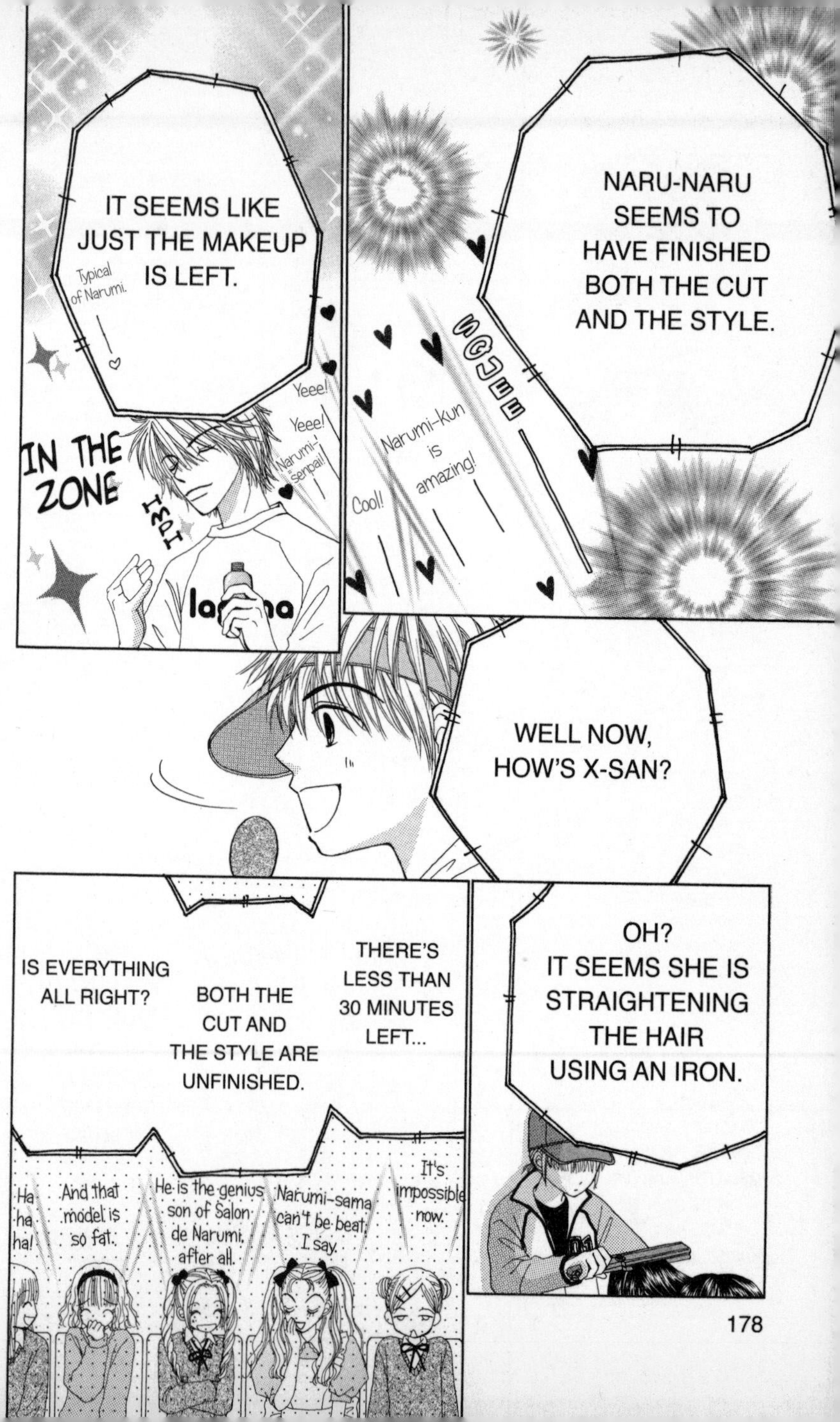
NARU-NARU SEEMS TO HAVE FINISHED BOTH THE CUT AND THE STYLE.
Narumi-kun is amazing!
Cool!
IT SEEMS LIKE JUST THE MAKEUP IS LEFT.
Typical of Narumi.
Yeee!
Yeee!
Narumi-senpai!
IN THE ZONE
WELL NOW, HOW'S X-SAN?
OH? IT SEEMS SHE IS STRAIGHTENING THE HAIR USING AN IRON.
THERE'S LESS THAN 30 MINUTES LEFT...
BOTH THE CUT AND THE STYLE ARE UNFINISHED.
IS EVERYTHING ALL RIGHT?
It's impossible now.
Narumi-sama can't be beat, I say.
He is the genius son of Salon de Narumi, after all.
And that model is so fat.
Ha ha ha!

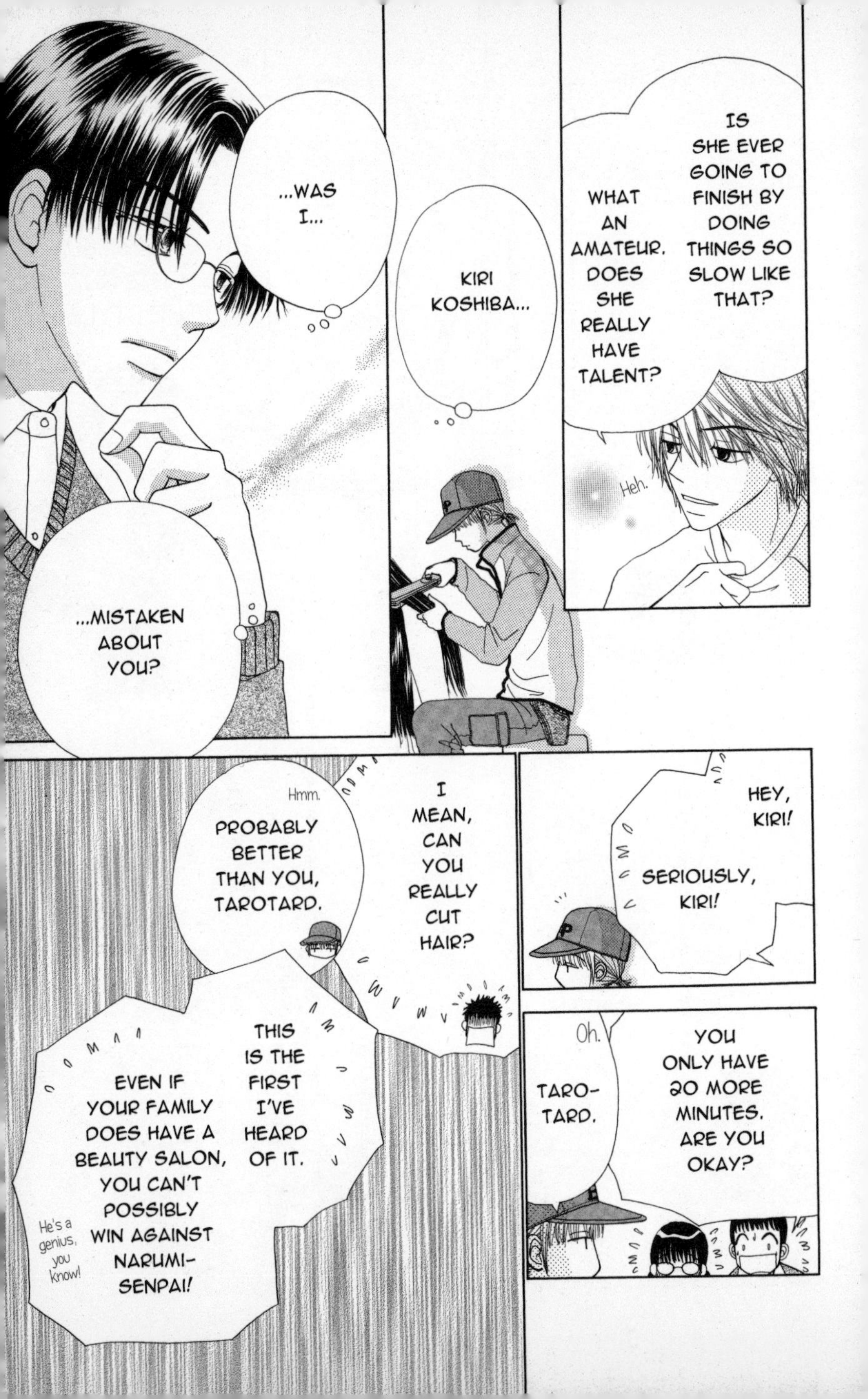
Heh.
IS SHE EVER GOING TO FINISH BY DOING THINGS SO SLOW LIKE THAT?
WHAT AN AMATEUR. DOES SHE REALLY HAVE TALENT?
KIRI KOSHIBA...
...WAS I...
...MISTAKEN ABOUT YOU?
HEY, KIRI!
SERIOUSLY, KIRI!
YOU ONLY HAVE 20 MORE MINUTES. ARE YOU OKAY?
Oh.
TARO-TARD.
I MEAN, CAN YOU REALLY CUT HAIR?
Hmm.
PROBABLY BETTER THAN YOU, TAROTARD.
THIS IS THE FIRST I'VE HEARD OF IT.
EVEN IF YOUR FAMILY DOES HAVE A BEAUTY SALON, YOU CAN'T POSSIBLY WIN AGAINST NARUMI-SENPAI!
He's a genius, you know!

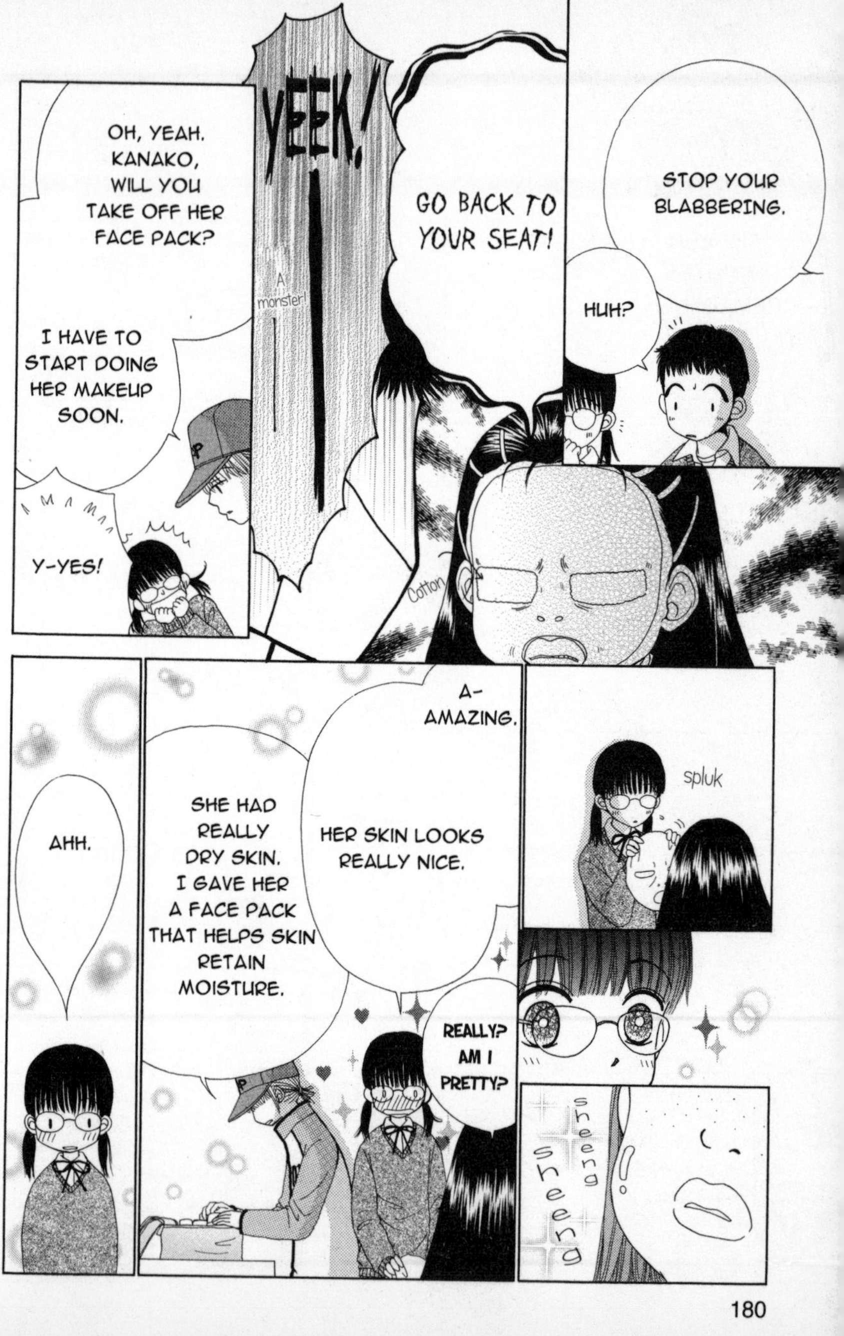
STOP YOUR BLABBERING.
HUH?
GO BACK TO YOUR SEAT!
YEEK!
A monster!
Cotton
OH, YEAH. KANAKO, WILL YOU TAKE OFF HER FACE PACK?
I HAVE TO START DOING HER MAKEUP SOON.
Y-YES!
spluk
sheeng sheeng
A- AMAZING.
HER SKIN LOOKS REALLY NICE.
SHE HAD REALLY DRY SKIN. I GAVE HER A FACE PACK THAT HELPS SKIN RETAIN MOISTURE.
REALLY? AM I PRETTY?
AHH.

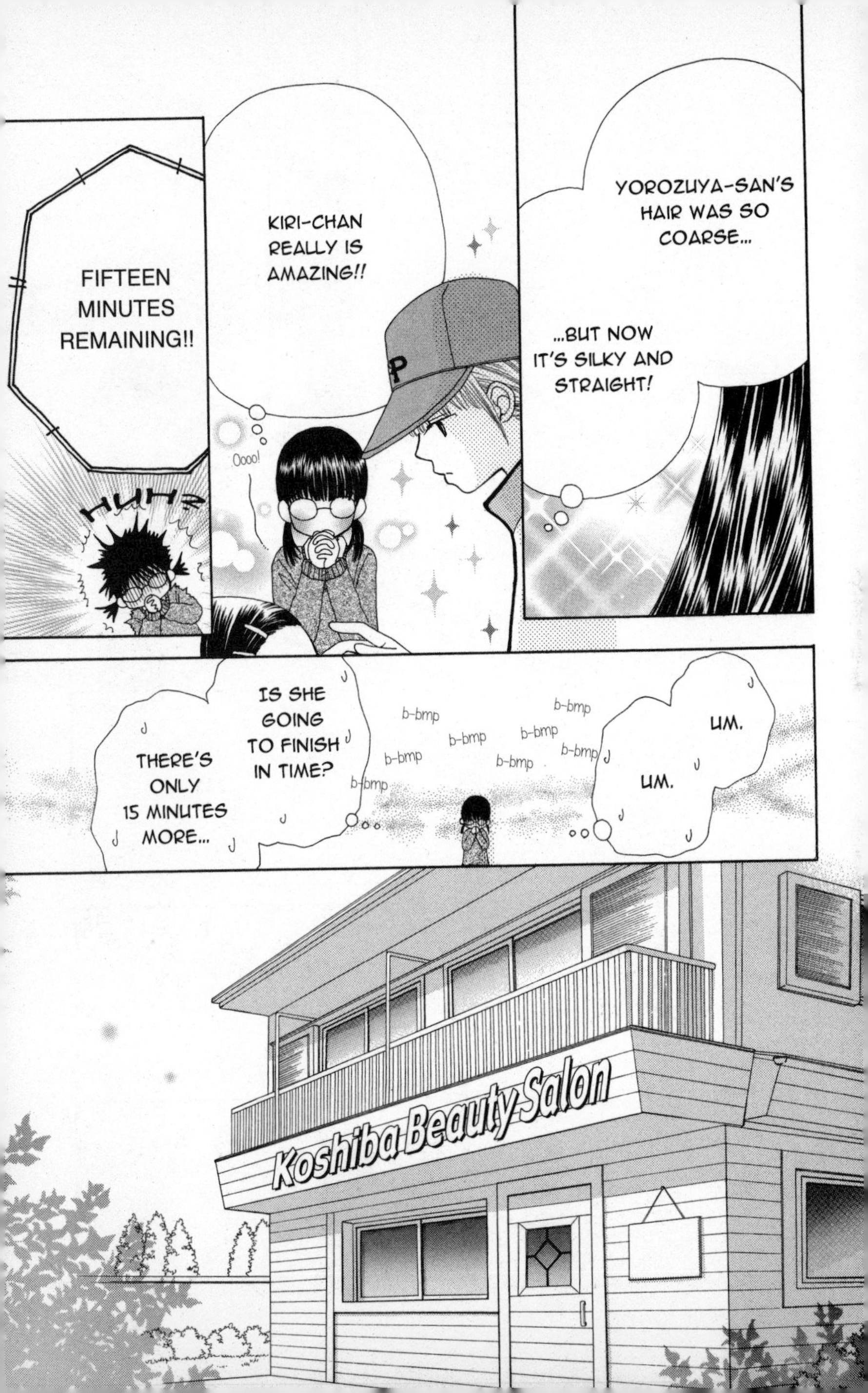
YOROZUYA-SAN'S HAIR WAS SO COARSE...
...BUT NOW IT'S SILKY AND STRAIGHT!
KIRI-CHAN REALLY IS AMAZING!!
Oooo!
FIFTEEN MINUTES REMAINING!!
HUH?
UM.
UM.
b-bmp
b-bmp
b-bmp
b-bmp
b-bmp
b-bmp
b-bmp
IS SHE GOING TO FINISH IN TIME?
THERE'S ONLY 15 MINUTES MORE...
Koshiba Beauty Salon

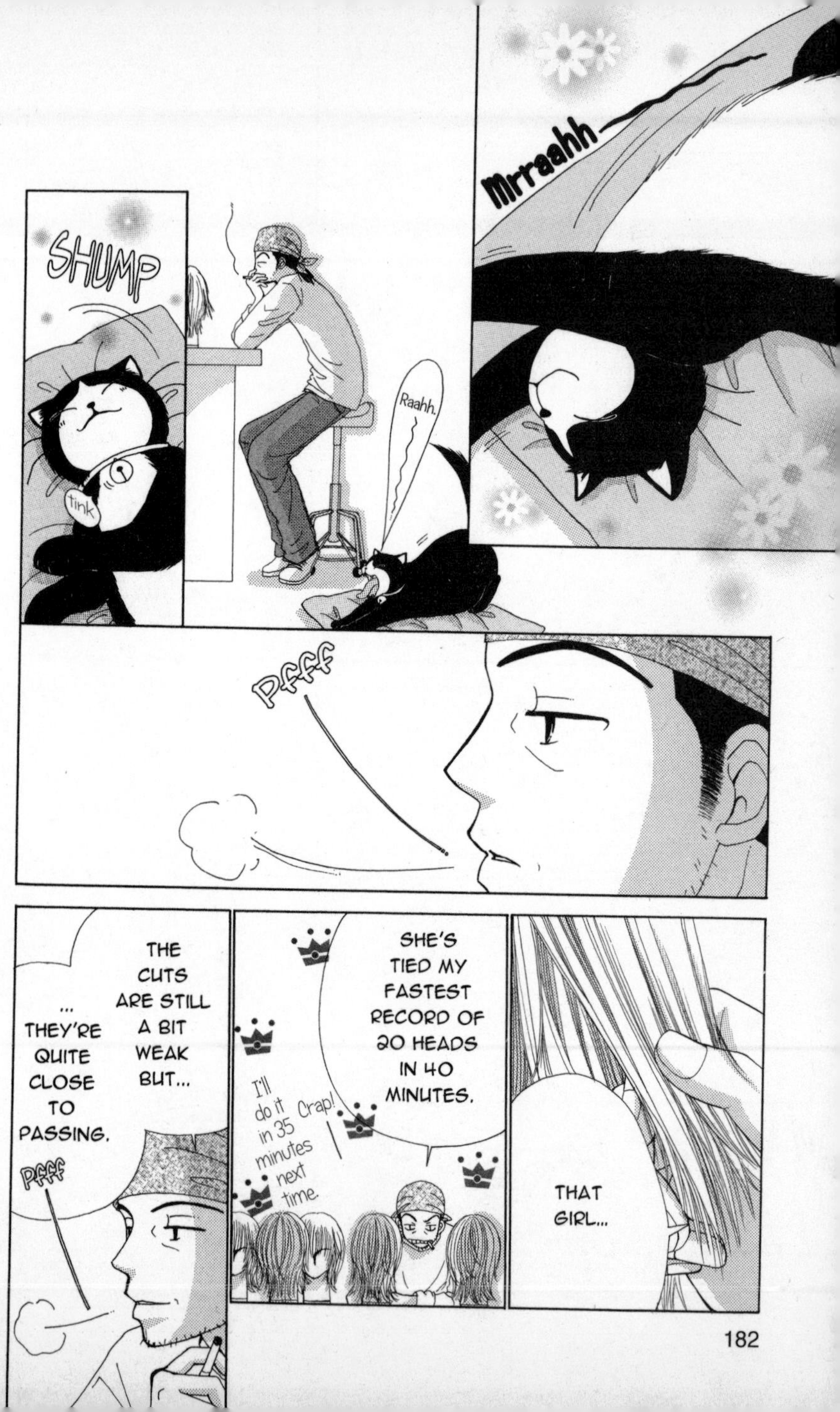
Mrraahh
SHUMP
tink
Raahh.
Pfff
THAT GIRL...
SHE'S TIED MY FASTEST RECORD OF 20 HEADS IN 40 MINUTES.
Crap!
I'll do it in 35 minutes next time.
THE CUTS ARE STILL A BIT WEAK BUT...
... THEY'RE QUITE CLOSE TO PASSING.
Pfff

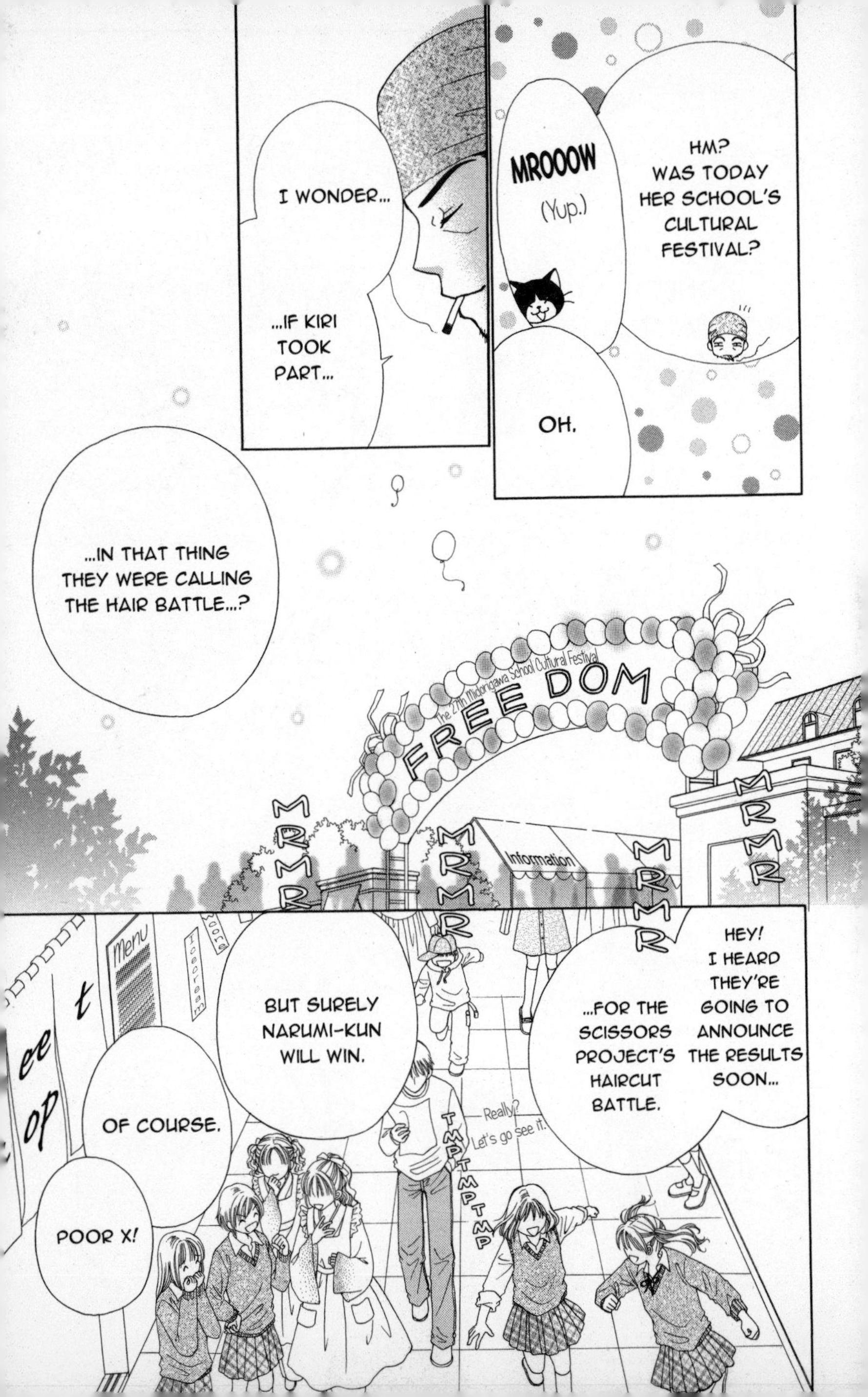
HM? WAS TODAY HER SCHOOL'S CULTURAL FESTIVAL?
MROOOW
(Yup.)
OH.
I WONDER...
...IF KIRI TOOK PART...
...IN THAT THING THEY WERE CALLING THE HAIR BATTLE...?
The 27th Midorigawa School Cultural Festival
FREE DOM
Information
MRMR
MRMR
MRMR
MRMR
HEY! I HEARD THEY'RE GOING TO ANNOUNCE THE RESULTS SOON...
...FOR THE SCISSORS PROJECT'S HAIRCUT BATTLE.
Really?
Let's go see it.
TMPTMPTMPTMP
BUT SURELY NARUMI-KUN WILL WIN.
Menu
Ice cream
OF COURSE.
POOR X!

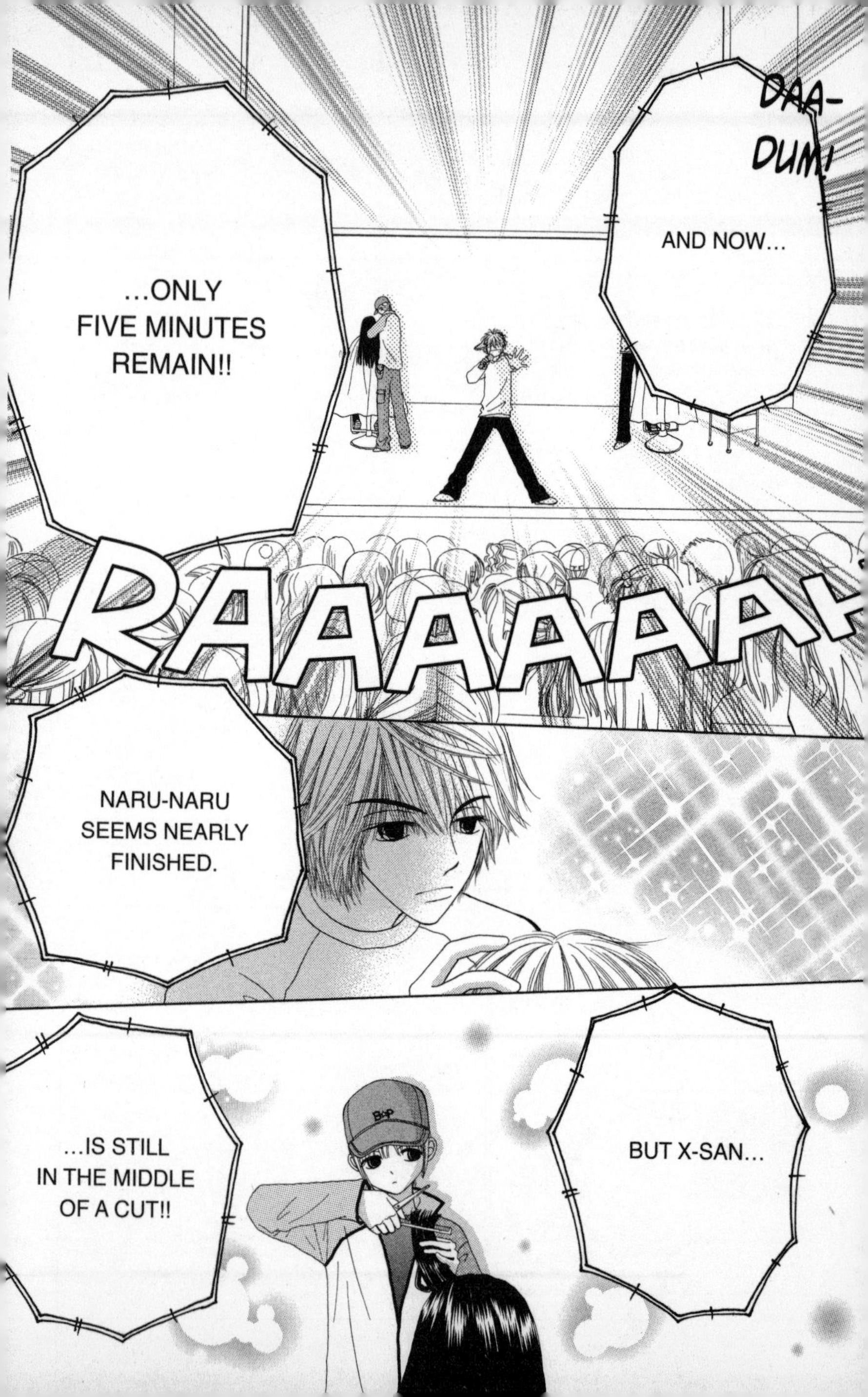
DAA-DUM!
AND NOW...
...ONLY FIVE MINUTES REMAIN!!
RAAAAAAH
NARU-NARU SEEMS NEARLY FINISHED.
BUT X-SAN...
...IS STILL IN THE MIDDLE OF A CUT!!

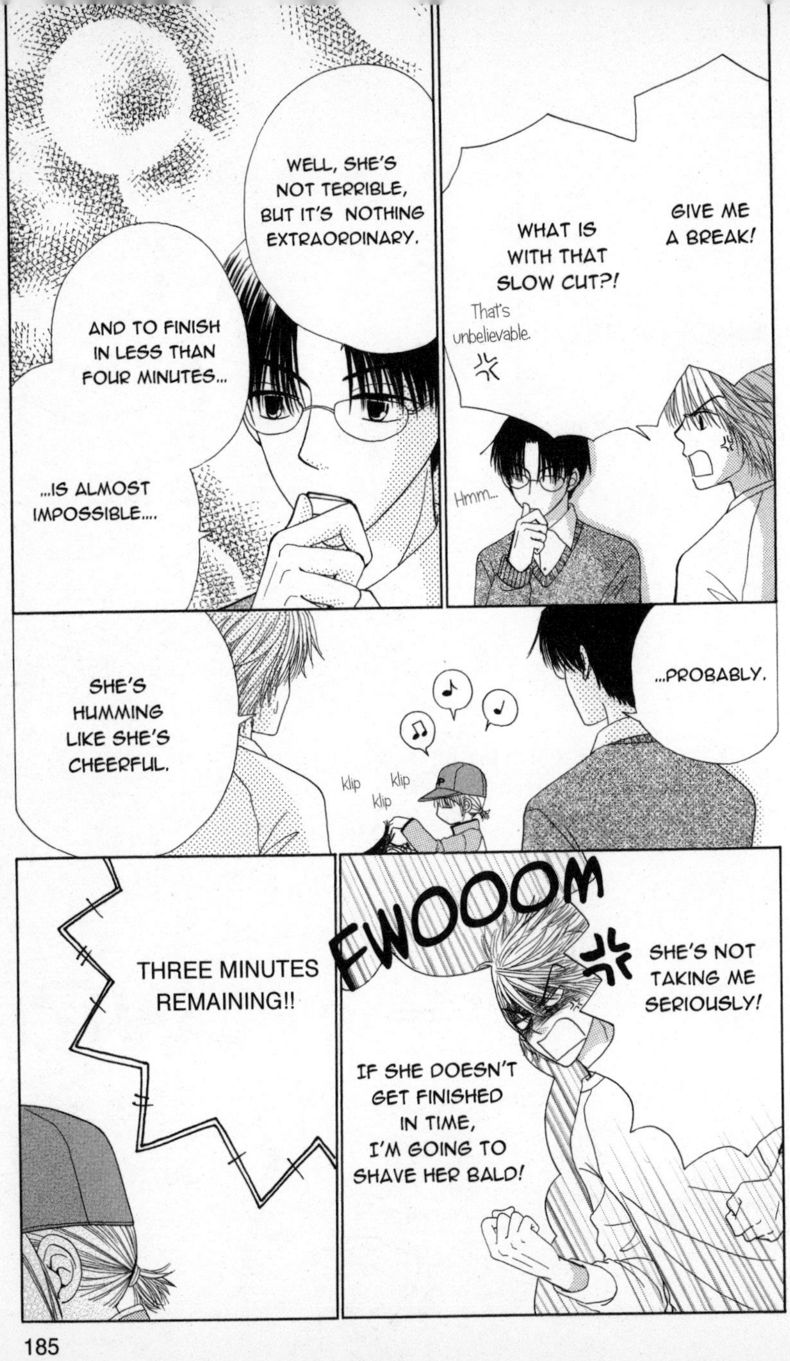
GIVE ME A BREAK!
WHAT IS WITH THAT SLOW CUT?!
That's unbelievable.
Hmm...
WELL, SHE'S NOT TERRIBLE, BUT IT'S NOTHING EXTRAORDINARY.
AND TO FINISH IN LESS THAN FOUR MINUTES...
...IS ALMOST IMPOSSIBLE....
...PROBABLY.
klip
klip
klip
SHE'S HUMMING LIKE SHE'S CHEERFUL.
EWOOOM
SHE'S NOT TAKING ME SERIOUSLY!
IF SHE DOESN'T GET FINISHED IN TIME, I'M GOING TO SHAVE HER BALD!
THREE MINUTES REMAINING!!

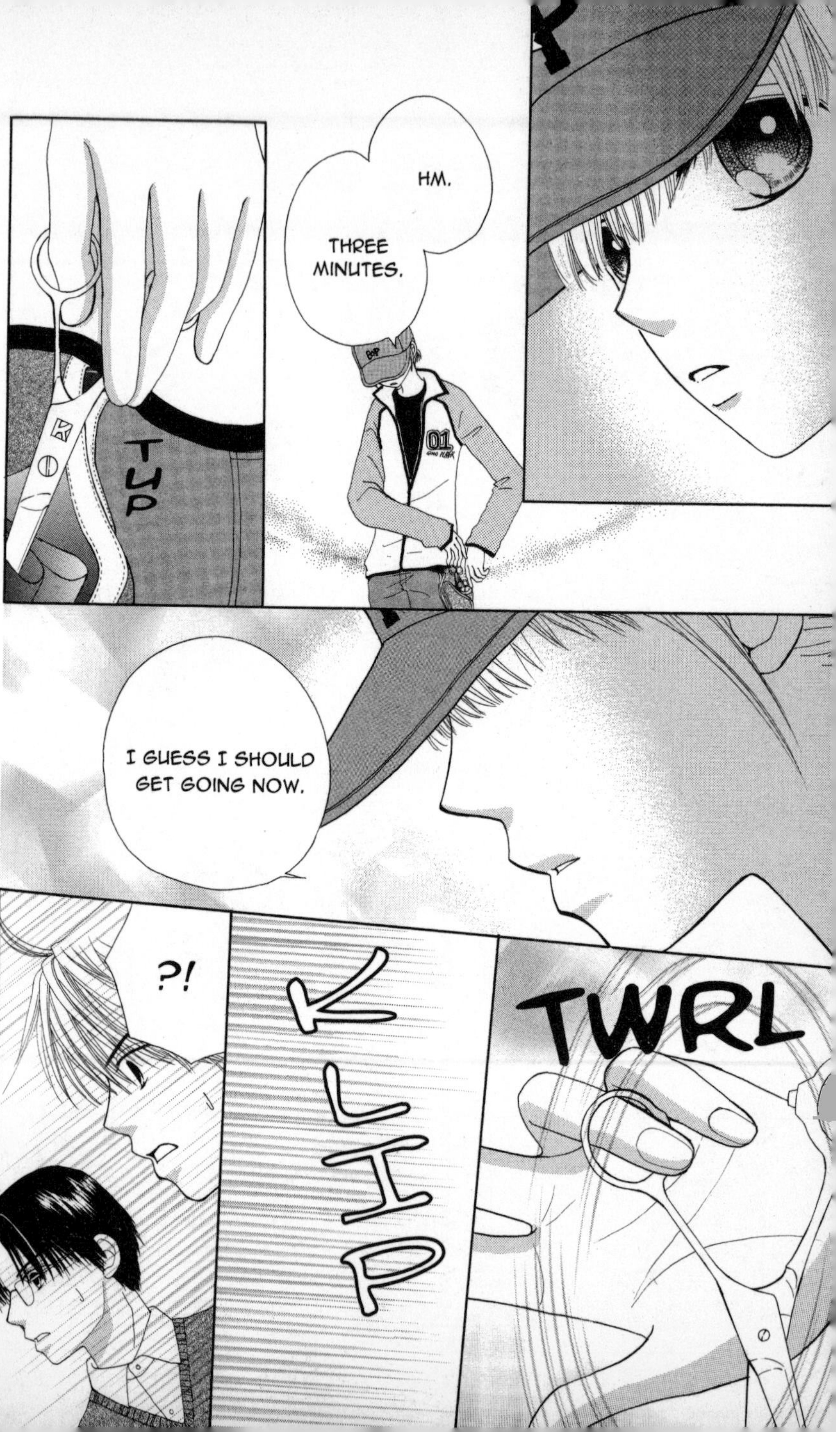
HM.
THREE MINUTES.
TUP
I GUESS I SHOULD GET GOING NOW.
TWRL
KLIP
?!

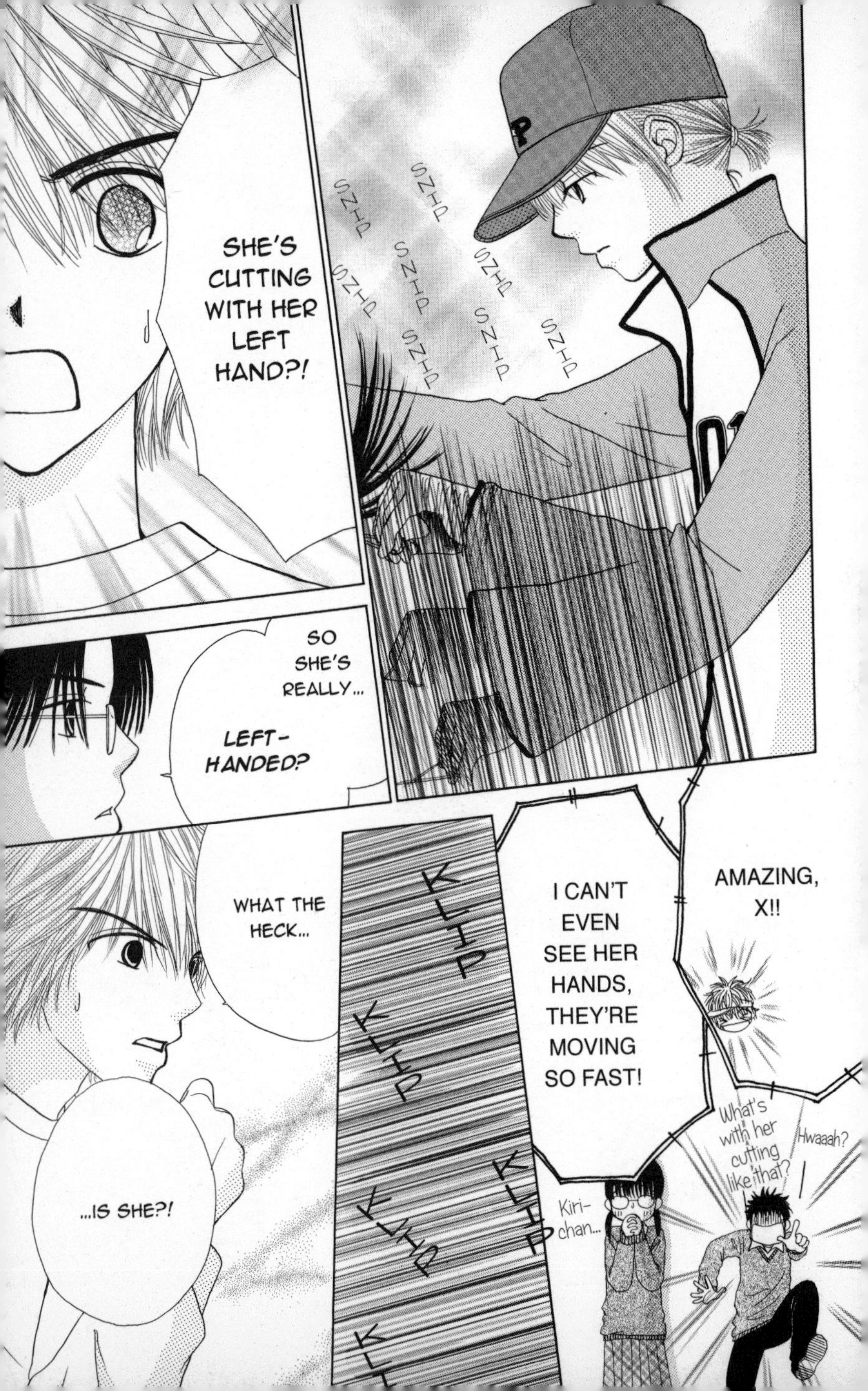
SNIP SNIP SNIP SNIP SNIP SNIP SNIP SNIP
SHE'S CUTTING WITH HER LEFT HAND?!
SO SHE'S REALLY...
LEFT-HANDED?
AMAZING, X!!
I CAN'T EVEN SEE HER HANDS, THEY'RE MOVING SO FAST!
Hwaaah?
What's with her cutting like that?
Kiri-chan...
KLIP KLIP KLIP KLIP KLIP
WHAT THE HECK...
...IS SHE?!

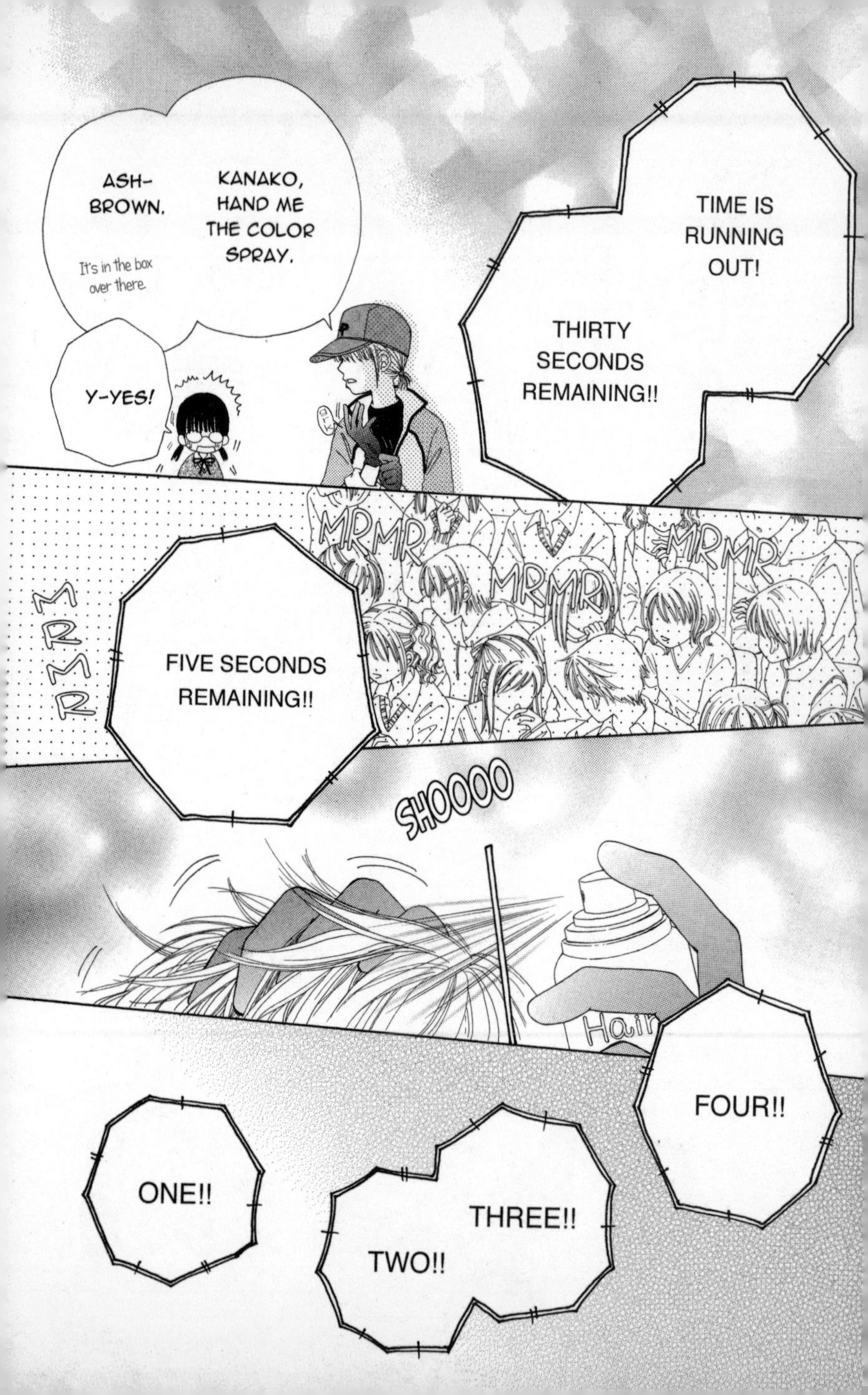
TIME IS RUNNING OUT!
THIRTY SECONDS REMAINING!!
KANAKO, HAND ME THE COLOR SPRAY.
ASH-BROWN.
It's in the box over there.
Y-YES!
MRMR
MRMR
MRMR
FIVE SECONDS REMAINING!!
MRMR
SHOOOO
Hair
FOUR!!
THREE!!
TWO!!
ONE!!

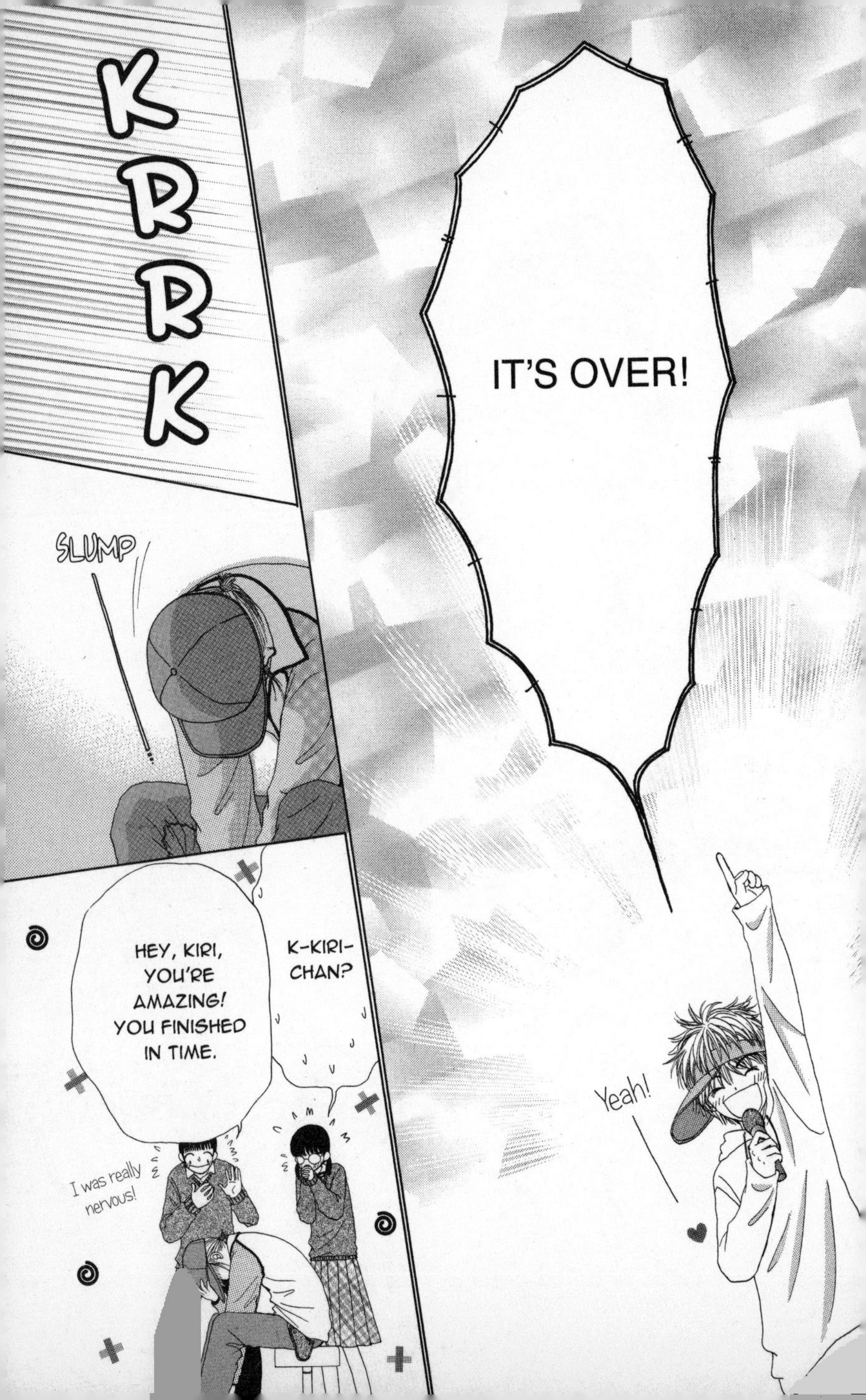
IT'S OVER!
Yeah!
KRRK
SLUMP
K-KIRI-CHAN?
HEY, KIRI, YOU'RE AMAZING! YOU FINISHED IN TIME.
I was really nervous!

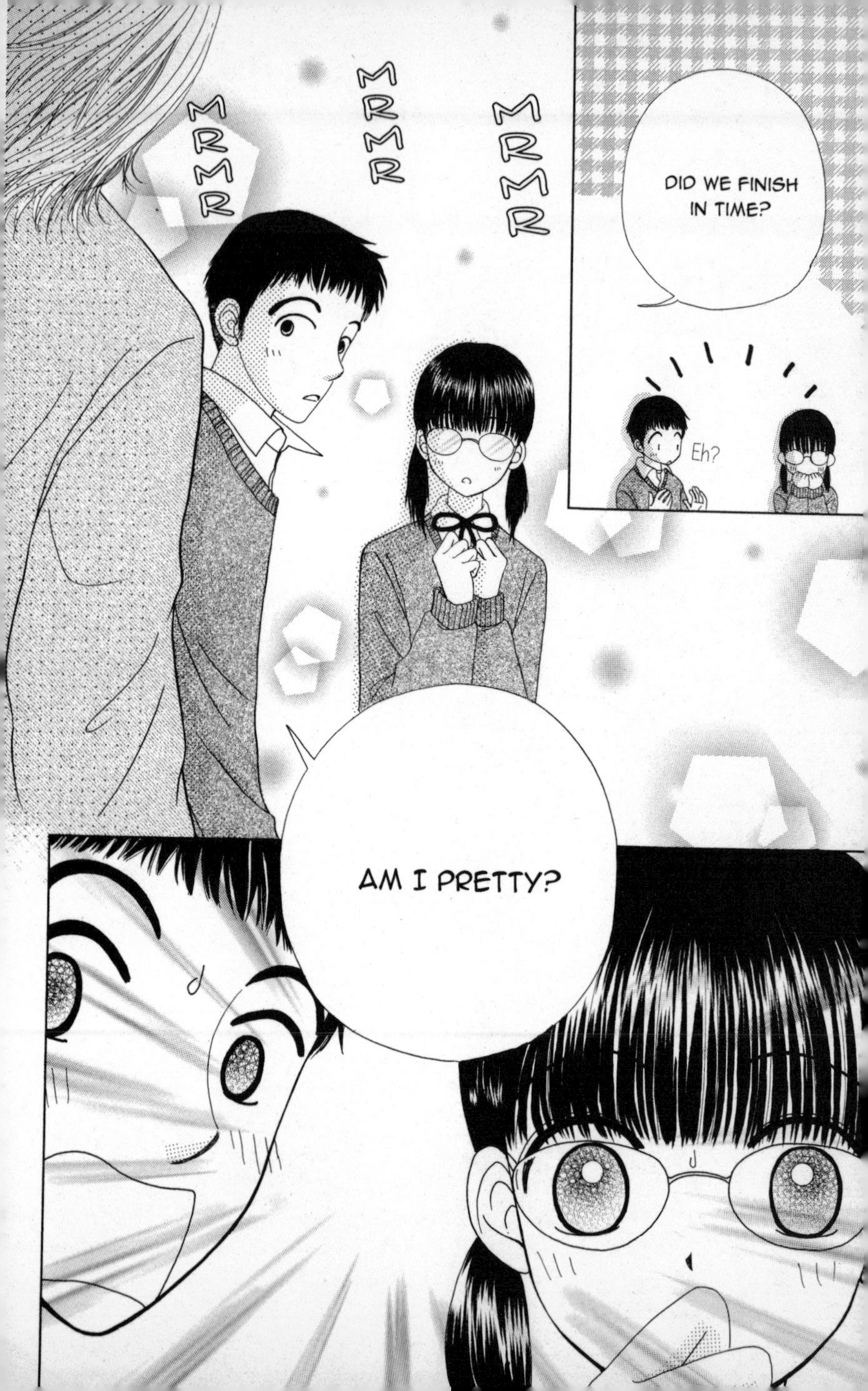
DID WE FINISH IN TIME?
Eh?
MRMR
MRMR
MRMR
AM I PRETTY?

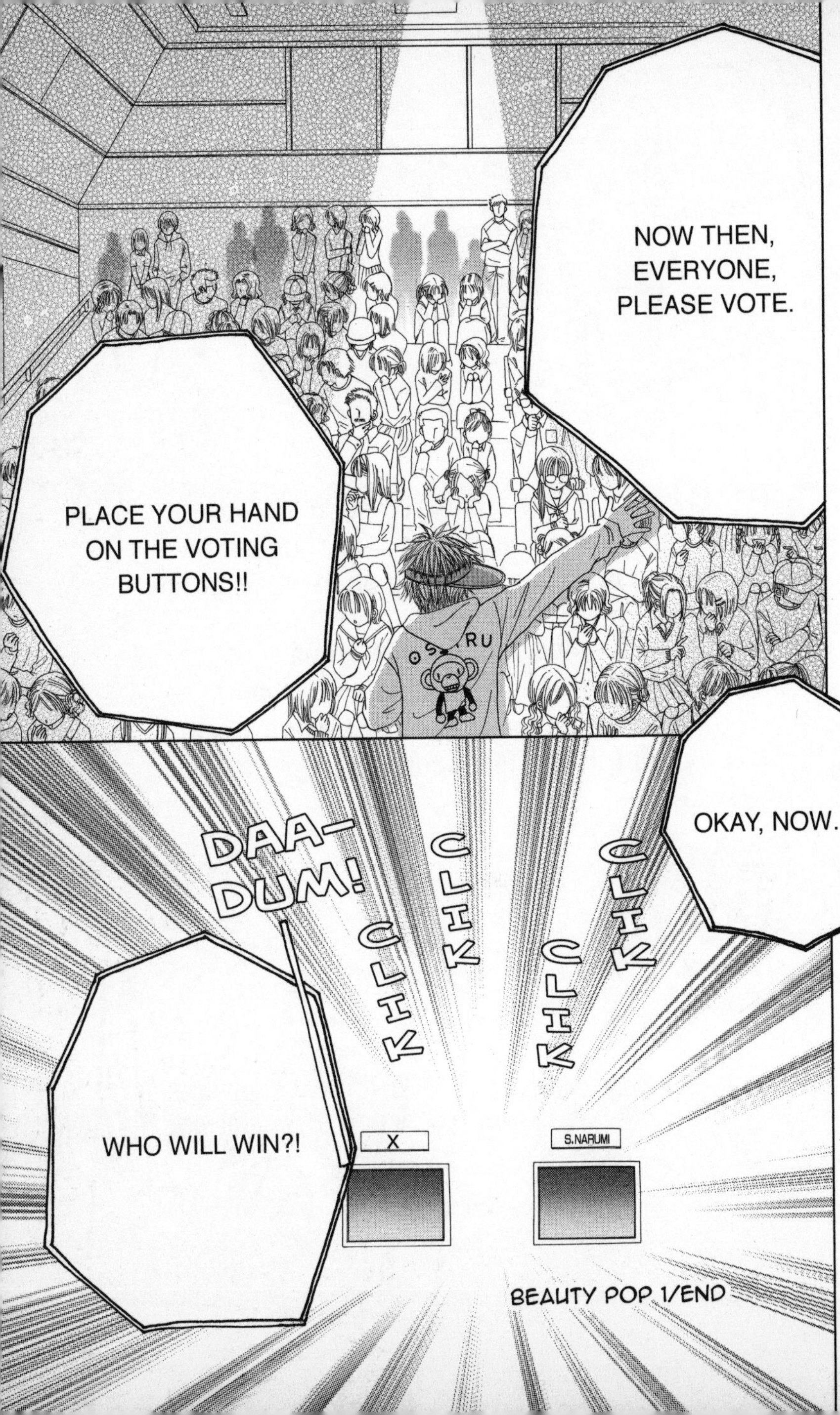
NOW THEN, EVERYONE, PLEASE VOTE.
PLACE YOUR HAND ON THE VOTING BUTTONS!!
OKAY, NOW...
CLIK
CLIK
CLIK
CLIK
DAA-DUM!
WHO WILL WIN?!
S.NARUMI
X
BEAUTY POP 1/END

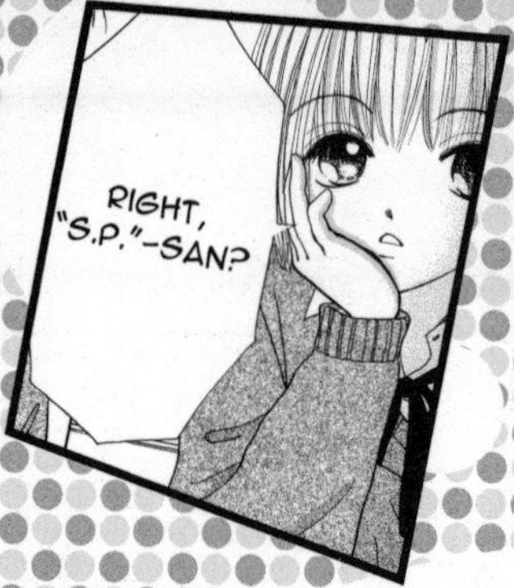
RIGHT, "S.P."-SAN?

Honorifics

In Japan, people are usually addressed by their name followed by a suffix. The suffix shows familiarity or respect, depending on the relationship.

Male (familiar): last name + kun
Female (familiar): first name + chan
Upperclassman (polite): last name + senpai
Adult (polite): last name + san

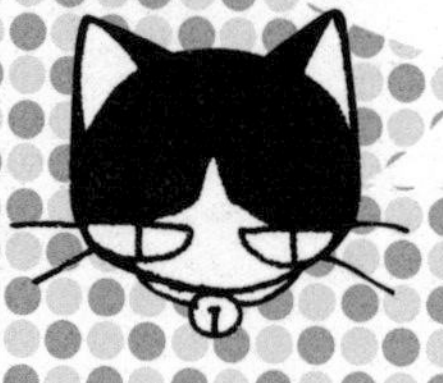

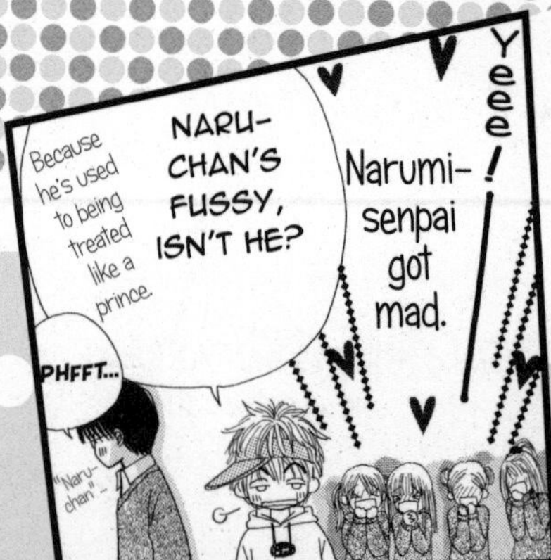
Yeee!
Narumi-senpai got mad.
NARU-CHAN'S FUSSY, ISN'T HE?
Because he's used to being treated like a prince.
PHFFT...
"Naru-chan"...

Author's Note

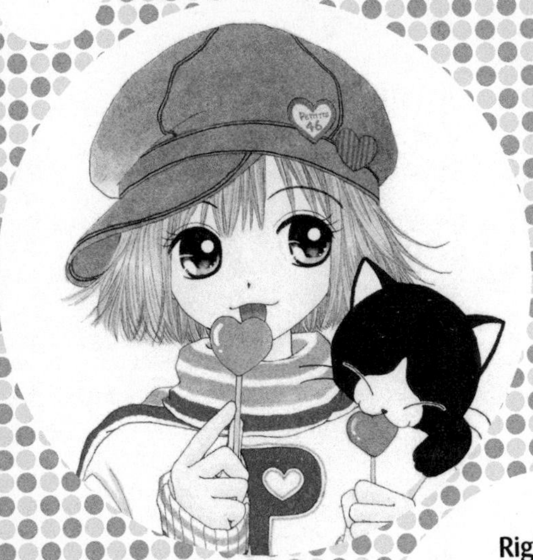

Right now, I'm really into major league baseball! During the season, I never miss a game on TV. I get so excited by all the great plays and powerful hitting. ♥ I'm gonna go to the States again this year to support the teams!!

Kiyoko Arai was born in Tokyo, and now resides in Chiba Prefecture. In 1999, she received the prestigious Shogakukan Manga Award for *Angel Lip*. The popular *Dr. Rin ni Kiitemite!* (Ask Dr. Rin!) was made into an animated TV show. *Beauty Pop* is her current series running in *Ciao* magazine.

Beauty Pop
Vol. 1
The Shojo Beat Manga Edition

STORY AND ART BY
KIYOKO ARAI

English Adaptation/Amanda Hubbard
Translation/Miho Nishida
Touch-up Art & Lettering/Elena Diaz
Design/Izumi Hirayama
Editor/Nancy Thistlethwaite

Editor in Chief, Books/Alvin Lu
Editor in Chief, Magazines/Marc Weidenbaum
VP of Publishing Licensing/Rika Inouye
VP of Sales/Gonzalo Ferreyra
Sr. VP of Marketing/Liza Coppola
Publisher/Hyoe Narita

Printed in Canada

Published by VIZ Media, LLC
P.O. Box 77010
San Francisco, CA 94107

Shojo Beat Manga Edition
10 9 8 7 6 5 4 3
First printing, September 2006
Third printing, November 2007

www.viz.com

store.viz.com

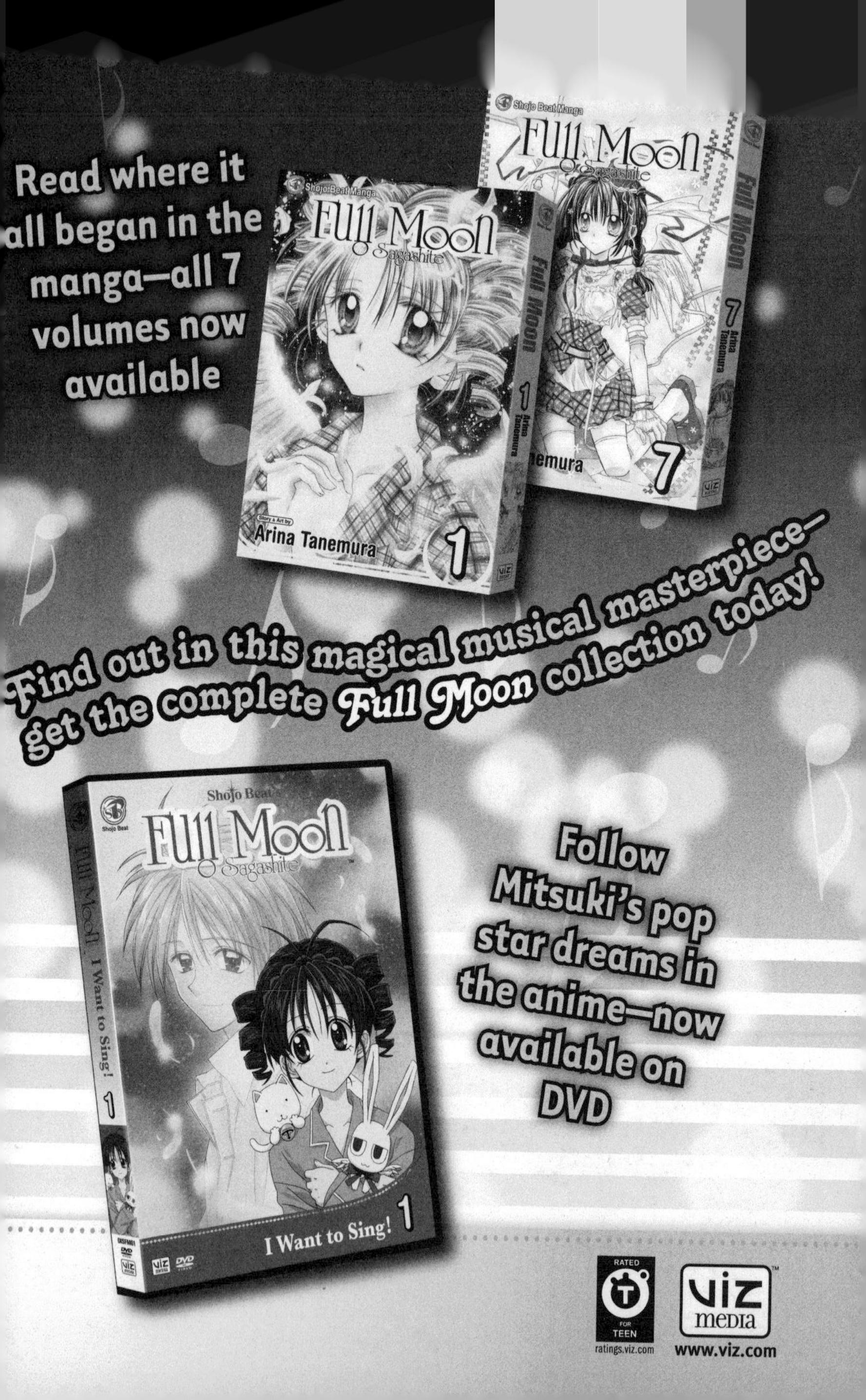
Read where it all began in the manga—all 7 volumes now available
Shojo Beat Manga
Full Moon O Sagashite
Story & Art by Arina Tanemura 1
Full Moon 7
Find out in this magical musical masterpiece—get the complete Full Moon collection today!
Shojo Beat
Full Moon O Sagashite
I Want to Sing! 1
Follow Mitsuki's pop star dreams in the anime—now available on DVD
RATED T FOR TEEN
ratings.viz.com
VIZ MEDIA
www.viz.com

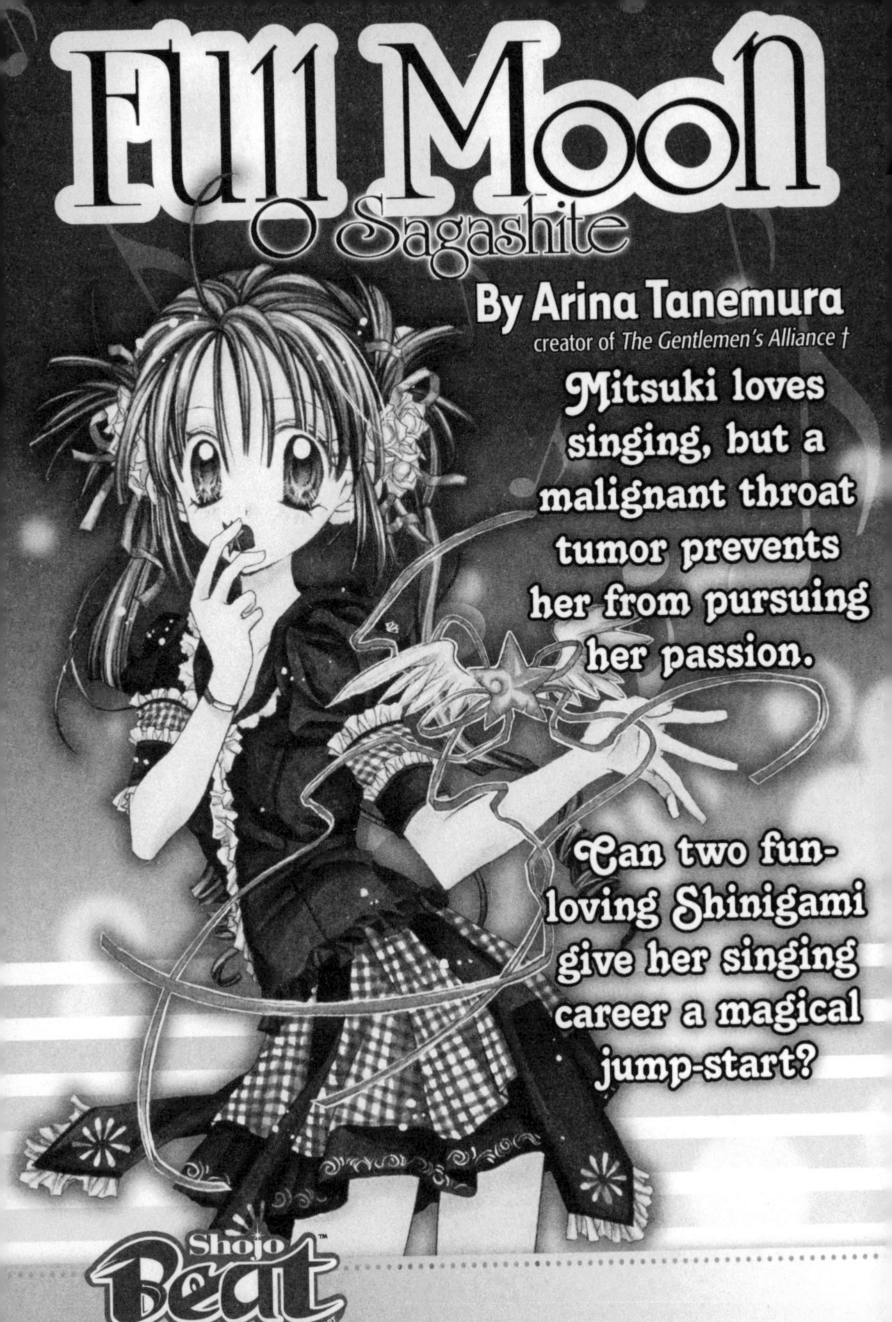
Full Moon
O Sagashite
By Arina Tanemura
creator of The Gentlemen's Alliance †
Mitsuki loves singing, but a malignant throat tumor prevents her from pursuing her passion.
Can two fun-loving Shinigami give her singing career a magical jump-start?
Shojo Beat™
MANGA from the HEART
On sale at:
www.shojobeat.com
Also available at your local bookstore and comic store.

Tell us what you think about Shojo Beat Manga!

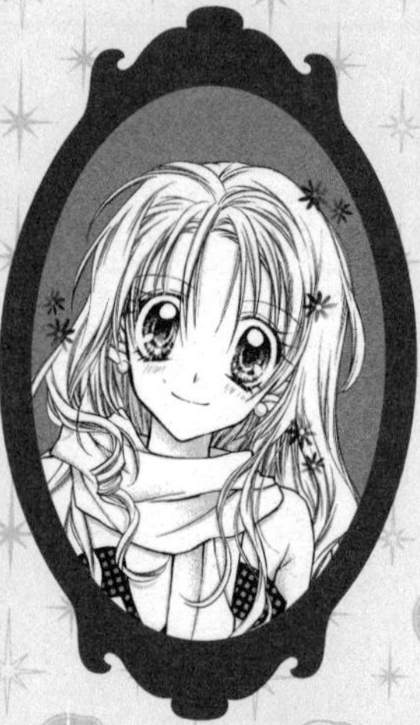

Our survey is now available online. Go to:

shojobeat.com/mangasurvey

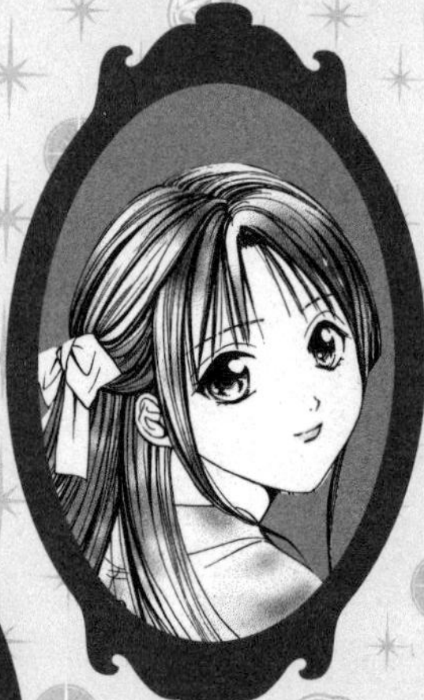

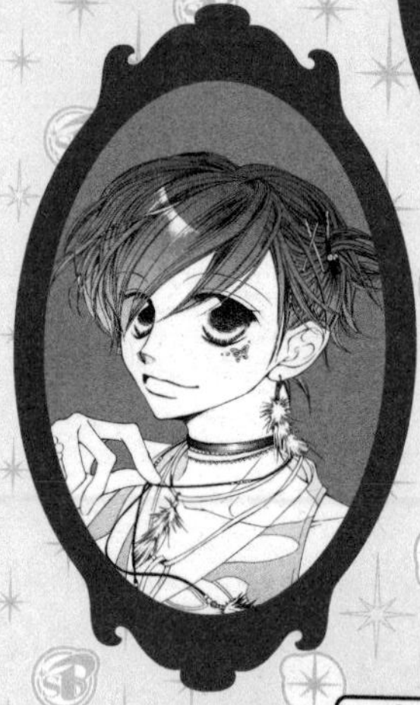

Help us make our product offerings better!

VIZ media

Shojo Beat MANGA from the HEART

THE REAL DRAMA BEGINS IN...

Save OVER 50% off the cover price!

Shojo Beat
MANGA from the HEART

The Shojo Manga Authority

This monthly magazine is injected with the most **ADDICTIVE** shojo manga stories from Japan. PLUS, unique editorial coverage on the arts, music, culture, fashion, and much more!

☑ **YES!** Please enter my one-year subscription (12 GIANT issues) to **Shojo Beat** at the LOW SUBSCRIPTION RATE of **$34.99!**

Over **300 pages** *per issue!*

NAME

ADDRESS

CITY   STATE   ZIP

E-MAIL ADDRESS   P7GNC1

☐ **MY CHECK IS ENCLOSED** (PAYABLE TO *Shojo Beat*)   ☐ **BILL ME LATER**

CREDIT CARD: ☐ **VISA**   ☐ **MASTERCARD**

ACCOUNT #   EXP. DATE

SIGNATURE

CLIP AND MAIL TO ➤   SHOJO BEAT
Subscriptions Service Dept.
P.O. Box 438
Mount Morris, IL 61054-0438

Canada price for 12 issues: $46.99 USD, including GST, HST and QST. US/CAN orders only. Allow 6-8 weeks for delivery. Must be 16 or older to redeem offer. By redeeming this offer I represent that I am 16 or older.

Vampire Knight © Matsuri Hino 2004/HAKUSENSHA, Inc. Nana Kitade © Sony Music Entertainment (Japan), Inc.
CRIMSON HERO © 2002 by Mitsuba Takanashi/SHUEISHA Inc.

RATED
T+
FOR OLDER
TEEN
ratings.viz.com